Selling t

An Inside Look
at the Cruise Industry

SECOND EDITION

Bob Dickinson, CTC
Andy Vladimir, CHE

WILEY

John Wiley & Sons, Inc.

This book is printed on acid-free paper.♾

Published by John Wiley & Sons, Inc., Hoboken, New Jersey
Published simultaneously in Canada

For general information on our other products and services or for technical support,
please contact our Customer Care Department within the United States at
(800) 762-2974, outside the United States at (317) 572-3993 or fax (317) 572-4002.

Wiley also publishes its books in a variety of electronic formats. Some content that
appears in print may not be available in electronic books. For more information about
Wiley products, visit our web site at www.wiley.com.

Library of Congress Cataloging-in-Publication Data:

Dickinson, Bob.
  Selling the sea : an inside look at the cruise industry / Bob Dickinson, Andy Vladimir. —
2nd ed.
    p. cm.
  Includes index.
  ISBN: 978-0-471-74918-9
  1. Ocean travel. 2. Cruise ships. I. Vladimir, Andrew. II. Title.
  G550.D53 2007
  387.2'430688—dc22

                                                                    2006022537

Printed in the United States of America

10 9 8 7 6 5 4 3 2 1

For Jodi and Ute,
our touchstones

CONTENTS

PREFACE

It's a typical Saturday morning in July. Americans all over the country are heading off on their one-week or two-week vacations. In New York, men and women wearing white gloves and dressed in the navy blue crew uniforms of the *Queen Mary 2* are at LaGuardia and Kennedy airports to greet passengers coming in from all over the world. There are the Ow family from Beijing, the Tatas from Bombay, the Ambersons from Liverpool, and the Alberginis from Salt Lake City. All of them, along with a couple thousand others arriving by taxis, cars, and trains, will be boarding the *Queen Mary 2* that day to cross the Atlantic to Southampton, England, in six and a half days. For many of them, perhaps one third, this will be their first voyage on any ship ever. For others, it will be their first transatlantic voyage.

In Miami, Fort Lauderdale, Port Canaveral, Tampa, and Jacksonville, the Smiths, the Gonzaleses, the Jacksons, the Finches, the you-name-them are lining up to get onto the *Carnival Destiny,* the *Voyager of the Seas,* the *Norwegian Dream,* the *Caribbean Princess,* or the *Celebrity Millennium.* They will be sailing to Puerto Rico, Jamaica, Mexico, and dozens of other ports in the Caribbean and beyond. Some will be going through the Panama Canal and disembarking in Los Angeles, where thousands of people will be standing in line for the return trip. In Honolulu, the push to get on Norwegian Cruise Line's *Pride of America* will have started, and in Lisbon, Monte Carlo, and Piraeus, passengers will be boarding one of Seabourn's luxurious vessels. In fact, with 10 million North American cruisers in 2005, we can say that all over the world, on every one of the seven continents, people will be boarding cruise ships to go somewhere—not just on Saturdays, but every day of the week. In a few short decades, what began in Miami as a small cottage business has turned into a mega-industry, pouring $32 billion into the U.S. economy in 2005 alone.

The ships themselves are no secret. They belong to the nineteen industry members of Cruise Line International Association (CLIA), an industry association composed of cruise line sellers (travel agents) and cruise lines. The two biggest players are Carnival Corporation, which by itself owns eleven brands and controls 55 percent of the market, and Royal Caribbean International, with two brands and 25 percent of the market. Norwegian Cruise Lines is a distant third, with 8 percent. Everyone else shares what's left over—which is, to be honest, not much!

So who are these 10 million people who like to take cruises? For the most part, they are married Baby Boomers who have a current passport, love to travel, and do so frequently, according to CLIA research. Other studies show that, for the most part, their average age is forty-nine. Only one in four of them is retired. Sixteen percent take children under eighteen along with them.

Then there are the travel sellers themselves—agents and agencies that make nine out of every ten sales of cabins on cruise lines. About 16,500 of them are members of CLIA, making it the largest travel association in the world.

So there it is: nineteen cruise lines, 16,000 travel agents, and 10 million cruisers. That's the cruise industry—but not all of it, of course. There are the yards that build the ships—four of them particularly: Fincartieri in Italy, Chantiers de l'Atlantique in France, Meyer Werft in Germany, and Kvaerner Masa in Finland. There are the provisioners that deliver thousands of cases of everything from lobsters to tomatoes to vodka weekly to these ships, as well as thousands of other businesses, big and small, that supply sheets and towels, tablecloths, uniforms, entertainers, and more.

So what's to get excited about? Why are the people engaged in this business, like us, so passionate about what they do? Why are the cruisers so excited about their vacations that many of them are already planning their next cruise—before this one is even over? Why does the media spend so much time reporting on the cruise industry—much more than they spend reporting happenings at land-based resorts? Why is CLIA the largest travel organization in the world?

One answer to that question comes from Terry Dale, the CEO of CLIA.

> This is a product like no other I have ever experienced, and as our research shows, so many Americans haven't experienced it yet. Only 17 or 18 percent of the U.S. population has ever cruised. Once you get them to take that initial step and board that ship, they become hooked on our product because it's phenomenal. When you look at the value of the vacation experience on board and off board. The level of staff and service that the crew provides, the quality of the food and cuisine, the entire experience from the moment you board to the moment you disembark that is truly magic. This is an experience a consumer can never have except aboard a ship.

Dale is passionate about what he does and who he represents. "The beauty of our industry is that today we have approximately 150 vessels as part of what we call 'the CLIA fleet,' and each one has its own personality, whether it's a 150-passenger sailing yacht or one of the major contemporary ships that has over 3,000 passengers. They're all very unique and provide different kinds of experiences."

In fact, the cruise industry is just another service industry. Each ship is like a factory where people come to get serviced.

A hair salon is a service factory; so is a restaurant, or a hospital. The customer comes in and is "serviced" in one way or another. Then they leave. But on cruise ships, people pay anywhere from $125 to $1,000 a day for this privilege. And when they come off, 80 percent of them say they plan to take another cruise in the next two years. That's remarkable. Hotels don't do that well. Neither do destinations.

In this book, we explore the behind-the-scenes world of the cruise industry. Who are the people who make this magic? How do they decide to build a cruise ship, which can easily cost as much as $800 million? Who designs these floating palaces? Why do people get addicted to cruising? Some have taken more than one hundred cruises with the same cruise line! How do the cruise lines make money while delivering such a high-quality product for a price that people consider a good value? Can this business continue to grow at a rapid pace, as it has done in the past, or will America be all cruised out in a few years?

We haven't got all the answers, but we'll bring you the best thinking from the people who run the ships, the people who work on them, and the travel agents who sell them. Because we are insiders, we can tell you things no other book will, or wants to.

Read on, and enjoy!

ACKNOWLEDGMENTS

This book could not possibly have been written without the help of a great many people in the cruise industry. Because this is a second edition, we need to begin by restating our thanks to all of those who helped us with the first edition. Many of their stories and insights have been retained for use in this edition as well. However, in the last two years we have interviewed many more persons, both on land and at sea. We generated and transcribed over 450 pages of interviews—enough for another whole book. We especially want to thank the managements of the three major cruise lines, Carnival, Royal Caribbean, and Norwegian Cruise Lines, for opening their doors to us and providing access to their ships and their crews. The captains and crew of the *Carnival Liberty* and the *Celebrity Constellation* deserve special mention for their hospitality and forthrightness.

That said, the following is a partial list of people we interviewed or solicited ideas and data from for this second edition:

Glenn Aprile, Christine Arnholt, Nikos Batistatos, Julie Benson, Roger Blum, Captain Apostslos Bouzakes, Shannon Cannon, Guna Chellam, Pam Conover, Mark Conroy, Brendan Corrigan, Jennifer de la Cruz, Terry Dale, Frank Del Rio, SanJay Dhall, Tatina Dianderas, Georgios Dimitriou, Captain Jim Drager, Josko Duric, Captain Agostino Fazio, Zuzana Fiantohora, Howard Frank, Vicki Freed, Tim Gallagher, Adam Goldstein, Dan Hanrahan, Derrick Hubbard, Roberta Jacoby, Elizabeth Jakeway, Stein Kruse, Carol Marlow, Lynn Martenstein, Jackie Mathews, Tom McAlpin, Rod McLeod, Rick Meadows, Gregg Michael, Rajesh Kumar Motee, Valentina Munteam, Deborah Natansohn, Michele Parker, Ashlea Pearson, Albert Peter, Danny Petrenko, Susan Robison, Rick Sasso, Jan Schwartz, Christopher Scott, Harjinder Singh, Andy Stewart, Captain Tom Thomason, Lynn Torrent, Colin Veitch, Deitmar Wertanzl, and Brenda Yester.

It takes a good publisher to publish a good book, and we have one with John Wiley & Sons. Every author should be so lucky! Thanks especially to JoAnna Turtletaub, Melissa Oliver, and Julie Kerr.

Finally, it takes a marvelous executive assistant to keep us organized, dig up stuff we couldn't find or didn't know, and generally move things along for the twenty months it took to write this volume. Bob Dickinson has one—Janet Simpkins—and without her there might not have been a book. We are both in her debt.

Bob Dickinson and Andy Vladimir

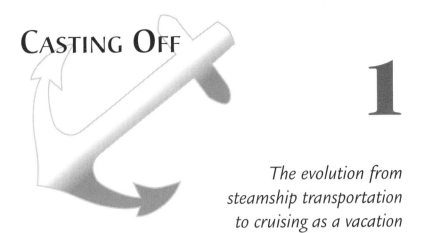

Casting Off

1

*The evolution from
steamship transportation
to cruising as a vacation*

Talk about extraordinary shipbuilders! First there was Noah. Noah built the ark because he had been told by God to get all of the animals out of harm's way. Next there was Samuel Cunard. He had been told by the British Post Office that they needed a safe, reliable, regularly scheduled liner to carry mail across the Atlantic. So in 1840 Cunard inaugurated regular mail and passenger service when he formed the British and North American Royal Mail Steam Packet Company, which later took its founder's name and became the Cunard Line. Cunard was mainly interested in building ships that were safe, fast, and reliable. Comfort was important, but only after the first three conditions had been satisfied. Sailing ships that crossed the Atlantic and even the new steam-assisted ships did not meet these conditions. Cunard wanted to offer something new: ships that left and arrived at scheduled times. He did not want ships that were subject to the vagaries of wind and weather, or ships that would run aground. In 1840 and 1841, Cunard commissioned four small steamers, all of which were designed to carry the Royal Mail—and, of course, 115 passengers, for revenue purposes. *Speed* and *safety* were the company's two watchwords. But the company did its best to take care of its passengers as well, although it did not always succeed. The novelist Charles Dickens had been invited to give lectures in America and was a passenger, one of eighty-six, on the first of those ships, the *Britannia,* which sailed on 3 January 1842 from Liverpool for Halifax. Dickens wrote about his experience in *American Notes.* For the most part, he was disappointed. First of all, he hated his cabin, which was nowhere near like the painting he had been shown in the ticket agent's office. In fact, at first he believed the cabin being shown to him was a joke and that his real cabin would be presented to him later by the Captain. It was no joke, as Dickens described the stateroom allotted to him and his wife: "[N]othing smaller for sleeping in was ever made except coffins," he wrote. Nor was the food what a modern Cunard passenger might expect:

> At one a bell rings, and the stewardess comes down with a steaming dish of baked potatoes and another of roasted apples, and plates of pig's face, cold ham, salt beef; or perhaps a smoking mess of rare hot collops. We fall-to upon these dainties; eat as much as we can (we have great appetites now); and are as long as possible about it. If the fire will burn (it *will* sometimes) we are pretty cheerful. If it won't, we all remark to each other that it's very cold, rub our hands, cover ourselves with coats and cloaks, and lie down again to doze, talk and read (provided as aforesaid), until dinner time.
>
> At five another bell rings, and the stewardess reappears with another dish of potatoes—broiled this time—and a store of hot meat of various kinds; not forgetting the roast pig, to be taken medicinally. We sit down at the table again (rather more cheerfully than before); prolong the meal with a rather mouldy dessert of apples and grapes and oranges, and drink our wine and brandy-and-water.[1]

We should remember that Dickens's trip in 1842 was not really a cruise at all; it was a destination voyage to get from one place to another. The ship was only a means of transportation; in fact, it was the best and *only* means of transportation available at that time. Cruises, which are taken for pleasure, are a different thing altogether.

The First Cruise

It isn't easy to state authoritatively when the first real cruise set sail, or, for that matter, where it went. While almost everyone agrees that the first travel agent was Thomas Cook, who organized his first Grand Tour of Europe in 1856, historians disagree as to who organized the first cruise. There's little doubt, however, that it happened in the mid-nineteenth century, when traveling to distant places was becoming safer and more fashionable.

We support Peninsula and Oriental Steam Navigation Company's claim that it invented cruising. The line, popularly known as P&O, ran ships from Britain to Spain and Portugal on the Iberian Peninsula and to Malay and China in the early 1800s.

---

[1]Charles Dickens, *American Notes* (London: Chapman and Hall, 1896).

William Makepeace Thackeray traveled to Malta, Greece, Constantinople, the Holy Land, and Egypt in 1844, utilizing a series of P&O ship connections. He told of his "delightful Mediterranean cruise" in an elegantly written book titled *Diary of a Voyage from Cornhill to Grand Cairo,* which he published under the nom de plume Michael Angelo Titmarah.

Clearly, Thackeray (not unlike most travel writers today) wanted to reward his host's hospitality, but it was not easy to do considering that everyone aboard got seasick crossing the Bay of Biscay, and again going from Gibraltar to Malta. However,

> at last the indescribable moans and noises which had been issuing from behind the fine painted doors on each side of the cabin happily ceased. Long before sunrise I had the good fortune to discover that it was no longer necessary to maintain the horizontal posture, and, the very instant this truth was apparent, came on deck, at two o'clock in the morning, to see a noble full moon sinking westward, and millions of the most brilliant stars shining overhead. The ship went rolling over a heavy, sweltering, calm sea. The breeze was a warm and soft one; quite different to the rigid air we had left behind us, off the Isle of Wight.

That was the good part. Thackeray was a bit of a snob, and while he liked the cruise, he didn't enjoy many of the sights on shore. In Athens, he complained about the prices, the bugs, and the lack of pretty women. In Constantinople, he complained that he didn't get to see the dancing dervishes or Saint Sofia or the harem or any of the royal palaces or mosques because it was the month of Ramadan and everything was closed. And in Egypt, he climbed a pyramid but condemned "the swarms of howling beggars, who jostle you about the actual place. And scream in your ears incessantly, and hang on your skirts, and bawl for money." At the end, however, he granted that he had a good time. "So easy, so charming, and I think profitable—it leaves such a store of pleasant recollections—that I can't think but recommend all persons who have the time and means to make a similar journey." P&O stopped cruising during the Crimean War but by the 1880s, after the *British Medical Journal* recommended sea voyages as curatives, resumed them and in fact converted one of their ships, the SS *Ceylon,* to a cruising yacht that sailed around the world.[2]

---

[2]For more about the history of P&O and her role in steamship travel, we recommend David Howarth and Stephen Howarth, *The Story of P&O* (London: Wiedenfield and Nicolson, 1986).

The first American-originated cruise was probably the 1867 voyage of the paddle-wheel steamer *Quaker City* from New York. Its organizer, an entrepreneur named Charles C. Duncan, advertised this cruise as an "Excursion to the Holy Land, Egypt, the Crimea, Greece, and Intermediate Points of Interest." We know a good deal about this cruise because the advertisement caught the attention of Mark Twain, who promptly sent in his application, references, and a deposit of 10 percent to join the trip along with 150 "select companions" who would sail from New York and return six months later. The idea that one could visit a number of places in relative ease and safety appealed to Twain, as did the fact that 1867 was the year of the Paris Exposition. He anticipated that this cruise would be a "picnic on a gigantic scale," and wrote:

> They were to sail for months over the breezy Atlantic and sunny Mediterranean; they were to scamper about the decks by day, filling the ship with shouts and laughter—or read novels and poetry in the shade of the smoke-stacks, or watch for the jelly-fish and the nautilus over the side, and the shark, the whale, and other strange monsters of the deep; and at night they were to dance in the open air, on the upper deck, in the midst of a ball-room that stretched from horizon to horizon, and was domed by the bending heavens and lighted by no meaner lamps than the stars and the magnificent moon— dance and promenade, and smoke, and sing, and make love, and search the skies for constellations that never associate with the Big Dipper they were so tired of; and they were to see the ships of twenty navies—the customs and costumes of twenty curious peoples—hold friendly converse with kings and princes, Grand Moguls, and the anointed lords of mighty empires.[3]

The trip did not turn out as advertised. The *Quaker City* had no sooner cast off and sailed when it encountered a storm which forced it to anchor for two nights in the foot of New York harbor! Twain was proud that he did not get immediately seasick in the heavy weather. "We all like to see people seasick, when we are not, ourselves," he observed. After the *Quaker City* finally left the harbor, the seas eventually calmed and a more normal pattern of activities emerged. Every evening after dinner, for example, guests would promenade the deck, sing hymns, say prayers, and listen to organ music in the grand saloon or read and write in their

---

[3]Samuel Clemens, *Innocents Abroad* (New York: Harper and Row, 1869).

journals (low-cost entertainment by today's standards). Sometimes they did hold dances on the upper deck to the music of a melodeon, a clarinet, and an accordion, which Twain did not particularly like. "However," he wrote, "the dancing was infinitely worse than the music. When the ship rolled to starboard the whole platoon of dancers came charging down to starboard with it, and brought up in mass at the rail; and when it rolled to port, they went floundering down to port with the same unanimity of sentiment. The Virginia reel as performed on board the *Quaker City* had more genuine reel about it than any reel I ever saw before." Other forms of entertainment consisted of a mock trial where the purser was accused of stealing an overcoat from a passenger's stateroom and other passengers were appointed to serve as judges, lawyers, witnesses, and the jury. The group visited, among other countries, Morocco, France, Italy, the Greek Islands, and Turkey, where they took a shore excursion to Ephesus and had their pictures taken there, just as modern tourists do today. Then they continued to Jerusalem and Egypt, finally returning to New York six months later.

Twain had mixed feelings about the cruise upon his return. He found the passengers too somber and too old for his taste, with three-fourths of them being between forty and seventy years old, and no young girls, which at that stage of his life was a distinct disappointment. Twain described this historic voyage in his book *Innocents Abroad*, written a year later from his home in San Francisco. His view had become somewhat more positive. "If the *Quaker City* were weighing her anchor to sail away on the very same cruise again, nothing could gratify me more than to be a passenger," he remarked. He particularly liked that he did not have to pack and unpack at every new city and that he could choose friends he had made on board to accompany him on excursions and not be dependent on strangers for companionship. Clearly, while cruises have become a good deal more comfortable and entertaining since those early days, some of the main attractions they offer have stayed the same.

The current popularity of cruise travel can probably still be traced to those original ideas articulated by Twain—that cruise travel is relatively hassle-free because you pack and unpack once, it's safe, and you can make new friends. Twain's notion of cruising as a grand picnic suggests the nonstop diverse festivities—dining, dancing, activities, entertainment, etc.—that characterize today's cruises.

But it would take another century and a whole new technology for that picture to take hold. In 1977, when the *Love Boat* television series was launched and broadcast all over the world, there is little doubt that it increased public awareness of cruising as a romantic and relaxing vacation. The thought of chucking it all and escaping the work-a-day world by going to sea is a fantasy that most of us have entertained at one time or another. Thus, it's no surprise that one of Carnival's most popular ships is called the *Carnival Legend,* while Royal Caribbean invokes these deep-seated stirrings with the *Freedom of the Seas.* Noel Coward's song "Sail Away" expresses an almost universal sentiment:

> When the storm clouds are reigning in the winter sky, sail away.
> When the love light is fading in your sweetheart's eyes, sail away.
> When you feel your song is orchestrated wrong, why should you prolong your stay? Sail away.[4]

Of course, there were and still are other reasons for sailing away. In August 1896, the Boston *Evening News* included this article, which we copied from a display of marine history on the *Queen Mary 2:*

> A few days ago the wife of a well-to-do publican named Beldham, eloped with a cattle salesman named John Archer. . . . Mrs. Beldham appropriated a considerable amount of money belonging to her husband, and also took away the whole of her wardrobe.

⚓ The Growth of Transatlantic Travel

From the time of the *Quaker City* until the late 1950s, far more people crossed the Atlantic because they had to rather than for pleasure. Late nineteenth- and early twentieth-century ocean traffic was dominated by immigrant traffic between Europe and America and Great Britain, Australia, and New Zealand. But this era of immigration contributed nothing to the romance of the sea. Immigrants were not tourists, shipboard conditions were miserable for them, and a long ocean voyage with no intermediate ports of call was something to be endured, not enjoyed. People regarded the ship purely as a means of transportation, carrying them away from political, economic, or social repression to new lands of opportunity.

As commerce between Europe and North America developed in the 1900s, increasing numbers of people took transatlantic voyages. While the elite traveled in the grand style in first-class accommodations on luxurious ocean liners, others did not. Their second- and third-class accommodations were spartan at best: four berths, six berths, and dormitory-style accommodations with crowded public toilet and bath facilities. The rough seas of the North Atlantic, particularly in the winter, combined

---

[4]Noel Coward, "Sail Away," Bonard Productions, 1962.

with top-heavy vessels subject to pitching and rolling, caused many to fear or experience severe seasickness. (Remember, this was before modern hull designs and stabilizers.) For those travelers, the voyage lived up to their worst fears, and they hated every minute of it. The stories of both groups contribute to the legend of ocean travel today. On one hand, we have the reality that a modern cruise embraces food, service, activities, entertainment, and ambience on a grand scale, and on the other, the false perception that ocean travel is by definition an uncomfortable experience (the old reality of steamship transportation).

Even the earliest promoters realized that a major factor in popularizing ocean travel was the ocean itself. Because of their fears of the unknown, many people were happy to forget that they were at sea. Ships were therefore designed to nurture the illusion that one was *not* at sea and to shield passengers as much as possible from even being aware of the extremes in weather they might encounter. English architect Arthur Davis, who started designing the great Cunard liners in 1907, put it this way:

> The people who use these ships are not pirates, they do not dance hornpipes; they are mostly seasick American ladies, and the one thing they want to forget when they are on the vessel is that they are on a ship at all. . . . If we could get ships to look inside like ships, and get people to enjoy the sea it would be a very good thing; but all we can do as things are is to give them gigantic floating hotels.[5]

This illusion of being in a gigantic floating hotel was, of course, created only for those who were able to afford it, and so it was the glamorous experience of first-class steamship travel that was responsible for the legend of cruising as one of the most luxurious of all vacation experiences.

But look at how modern tastes and new technology have changed things. Today, everyone wants to be as close to the ocean as possible. Thus, modern ships are built with as many balcony cabins and ocean-view cabins as possible, as well as large window areas (to the sea) in public rooms.

The Race for Market Share

By 1897, the German empire was looking with an envious eye at British outposts worldwide. The Germans pursued an expansionist strategy, launching a maritime fleet that would beat the British on all fronts. From

---

[5]John Maxtone-Graham, *The Only Way To Cross* (New York: Collier, 1972), 112–113.

1897 to 1907, they were on a roll. By 1903, Germany had the four fastest ships on the Atlantic. The new German ships were small by today's standards—they averaged only 15,000 to 20,000 gross tons—compared to today's 100,000 plus tons but they could achieve a speed of 23 knots. Typically, they held around 2,000 passengers, of whom 700 were traveling first class. Despite the best efforts of their designers, however, these vessels were not comfortable. Hamburg-Amerika's *Deutschland* and *Crown Prince William* rolled a good deal because they were built to ride high out of water. As a result, all of the furniture had to be bolted down to keep it in place during inclement weather. But speed was what counted, and in 1900 the *Deutschland* won the Blue Ribband, a prestigious award recognizing its accomplishment as the fastest ship to cross the Atlantic. Not surprisingly, it took a good deal of machinery to propel this vessel at 23 knots. Much of the interior space was taken up by engines and coal bunkers. In fact, only three decks were completely open to the public, and there were just eight cabins with private baths. (*Deutschland* did offer dining tables for two, which was a break from the English tradition of putting everyone at rows of long communal tables.) Moreover, the ship's design, with three large funnels rising from the engine room to the top, made it impossible to incorporate any grand salons except between the funnels, which limited their size.

The Excursion Voyage: The Precursor to Cruising

While most steamship lines of the time were focusing on the highly competitive North Atlantic run, some took their older ships, which were no longer suitable for this service, refurbished them, and sent them on one-of-a-kind excursions. North German Lloyd, Hamburg-Amerika, and Royal Mail were the first lines to initiate this practice toward the end of the nineteenth century. These excursions were clearly a forerunner of modern-day cruising. While still simultaneously going from point A to point B (like their North Atlantic brethren), rather than offering the convenience of round trip, the customer appeal was a touring vacation experience rather than just transportation. Other early forays into cruising included Hamburg-Amerika's initiative of temporarily converting two three-class liners to a one-class cruise service. These ships, the *Cleveland* and the *Cincinnati,* would do extended cruises each winter, including one 125-day world cruise each year. The world cruises were so successful that in 1914 the company began advertising two simultaneous world cruises from New York, one leaving 16 January and the other leaving 31 January 1915. Because of the subsequent outbreak of World War I, however, German passenger ships were banned from the seas, so the cruises never got off the ground. Cunard, Canadian Pacific, and Red Star Line also offered world cruises each winter in response to a fall-off in seasonal demand.

Until now, the only cruise or excursion activities available were offered by old ships or during the winter season by transatlantic liners. Those on older ships represented attempts to develop some meager revenue for outdated vessels. These were secondary revenue sources for the lines involved—in theory, it was a better alternative than laying up the vessels. One of the first significant, year-round business commitments to the cruising concept was the conversion of the *Deutschland* to the *Victoria Louise* in 1912. The Hamburg-Amerika Line invested significant sums to remove half its engines, install much more spacious public rooms, and paint the hull white—a first in those days. White was chosen because it better reflects the heat (keeping the ship cooler), as it was destined now to sail in the sunny Caribbean rather than the colder climates of the North Atlantic. White vessels are still favored today because of white's superior heat-reflecting qualities and its fundamental attractiveness. After all, what is more alluring than a sparkling white ship on an azure sea?

The Pacific Gets Into the Act

On the other side of the world, liner operations in the Pacific also contributed to the excursion/early cruise phenomenon. Canadian Pacific had three express liners, the *Empresses of Japan, China,* and *India,* constructed in Britain to sail between Vancouver and China. Because it had to position the ships in the Pacific Ocean, the line organized round-the-world excursions in connection with each ship delivery. These excursions began in Britain, transited the Suez Canal to India and China, and then finally went on to Vancouver. There, the passengers disembarked and boarded a Canadian Pacific train across Canada to Montreal, where they embarked on yet another Canadian Pacific vessel for the return leg home. These voyages were offered to provide a revenue stream to offset the positioning cost. Positioning cruises continue to be a common practice today; they are rarely profitable to the lines but still help defray costs. They generally offer terrific consumer value, as the lines price these one-of-a-kind cruises very attractively, as they don't wish to spend significant marketing dollars on them.

Moreover, the Pacific operation of the P&O Line, because its unique weather and seasonal demand pattern, created the need for seasonal cruise and excursion activities to utilize ships during periods of slow demand.

⚓ Meanwhile...

Back in the North Atlantic, the British were not about to lose their superiority to the Germans. To regain it, they commissioned two new ships, the *Lusitania* and the *Mauretania* (at the time, Cunard liked to name its ships after Roman provinces). These were to be a new generation of express liners. Because each was to be over 30,000 tons, there was space to do something with the interiors besides house machinery to propel the ship. More space meant more elegance. It also meant more money. But British maritime pride was suffering, and the country was militarily vulnerable. Given the times and rising German militarism, the British government saw the need for armed merchant cruisers and troop ships in the event of war. Cunard offered to build these two new steamers to Royal Navy specifications, incorporating a speed of 24½ knots, a double hull, and strong decks on which to mount guns if needed. An important innovation on the *Mauretania* was a propulsion system that had been used experimentally on a few smaller ships, including one Cunard ship, the *Carmania*. This was a steam turbine invented by Charles Parsons. The Parsons steam turbine was not only much more efficient than the conventional steam engine but also had much less vibration and was quieter as well. When launched in 1906 into the Tyne River, the *Mauretania* showed an amazing maximum speed of 26 knots. Britain was now able to regain her lost crown, and the *Mauretania* held the Blue Ribband for the Atlantic speed record for twenty-two years, until 1929. The exterior design of four evenly spaced funnels in a row was unique as well—the Germans used two pairs side by side. The new design gave the British ships a more streamlined look. An interesting side note: There was a perception among both passengers and observers that the more funnels the better. Funnels were equaled with power and speed, and they looked good! In later years, when only three funnels were needed to vent more efficient power plants, some ships continued to use a fourth as a dummy because designers felt it added to the vessel's overall favorable impression.

The *Mauretania* also had another important design innovation whose effect on cruise ships continues today. Up until the *Mauretania,* the stern or rear of the vessel had been considered the premium space for all living accommodations. But given her four propellers and giant steam turbine engines, *Mauretania*'s midship area was quieter and had less vibration than the stern. Thus, the best cabins as well as the major public rooms were moved to the middle of the ship. Even with this spacious layout, however, Cunard did not forget the basic principle that had guided it since Samuel Cunard started a speedy transatlantic mail service: Speed always took precedence over comfort. Indeed, speed sold more tickets than comfort back then, as people didn't want to be at sea any longer than they could help it. So, while luxury had been given a higher priority, passengers were still forced to share tables and public space was sparse. Moreover, the four funnels spaced along the length of the ship and running from top to bottom meant there could be no large, grandiose public rooms. Clearly there was still room for improvement, and that opened the door for Cunard's biggest British competitor, the White Star Line.

White Star's strategy was to build even bigger and safer ships that offered a quieter and more stable ride than ever before possible but were somewhat slower than the *Mauretania* and two other new Cunard liners, the *Lusitania* and the *Aquitania*. The new White Star vessels would not shake you up or roll in normal seas, and passengers could truly forget (except in times of nasty weather) that they were at sea instead of at their country home in Oxford or Bath. White Star decided to build three new ships—over 40,000 tons each—quieter, more stable, and more luxurious than anything that had ever sailed the transatlantic route before. It was a bold scheme and an expensive one, as no facilities to build a ship that size existed, nor were there any piers on either side of the Atlantic big enough to hold them. The ships were to be named the *Olympic,* the *Titanic,* and the *Britannic.* These ships were to be veritable floating palaces with a noble and majestic profile and a good deal of open deck space (the nautical equivalent of palatial gardens). Both requirements were feasible only because safety regulations at the time called for only enough lifeboats to carry half the number of people aboard. More than that might have caused unsightly lines or occupied valuable deck space much more suitable for strolling around on a pleasant day to take in the sea air.

Although these ships were less than 100 feet longer and 4 feet wider than the *Mauretania,* they appeared to be much larger. This was accomplished by purposely designing a ship that would not break speed records. The company thereby freed itself of all kinds of constraints, such as weight and power. Public space and cabin size could be expanded dramatically. If you were one of the lucky 700 first-class passengers, there was always room for everything—whether a private corner to share a brandy or an intimate table for two in the opulent dining room or Ritz restaurant. Indeed, a table for two was an innovative and prized amenity. These dining rooms were the largest afloat and the first to offer small private dining alcoves. The ships also boasted the largest athletic facilities afloat—electric bodybuilding equipment, a squash court with a spectators' gallery, and an indoor pool and sauna. The maiden voyage in 1911 of the first ship of the trio, the *Olympic,* was a roaring success. She was hailed as an unprecedented event in maritime history. The dawn of a new era of sea travel had emerged.

By the time *Olympia's* sister ship, the *Titanic,* was ready to sail on her maiden voyage the following year, the word was out and the rich and famous were lining up to be part of the inaugural celebration. Benjamin Guggenheim was aboard, as was John Jacob Astor. They were accompanied by Bruce Ismay, White Star's managing director. One writer called the event "the millionaire's special." The *Titanic* sailed from Southampton on 10 April 1912 with 2,228 passengers and crew. Only 705 passengers survived the voyage after the ship struck an iceberg the night of 15 April and sank—the saddest day in the history of passenger shipping. At the White Star offices on Canute Road, London, a sign was posted that said it all: "*Titanic* foundered about 2:30 AM April 15th." A woman who survived the tragedy later wrote about that Sunday evening in her diary:

> We dined the last night in the Ritz Restaurant. It was the last word in luxury. The tables were gay with pink roses and white daisies, the women in their beautiful shimmering gowns of satin and silk, the men immaculate and well groomed, the stringed orchestra playing music from Puccini and Tchaikovsky. The food was superb—caviar, lobster, quail from Egypt, plover's eggs, and hothouse grapes and fresh peaches. The night was cold and clear, the sea like glass. But in a few short hours every man in the room was dead except J. Bruce Ismay, Gordon Duff, and a Mr. Carter.

The unthinkable had happened. The unsinkable *Titanic* had sunk; the public and the media looked for a scapegoat. They found one in Ismay, who did not go down with his own ship—unlike Captain Edward Smith, who worked for him. Writing in the Chicago *Record-Herald,* Ben Hecht composed these lines:

> To hold your place in the ghastly face
> Of death on the sea of night
> Is a seaman's job, but to flee with the mob
> Is an owner's noble right.[6]

In retrospect, the *Titanic* accident should not have happened, and if anyone was to blame it was Captain Smith. In the true Cunard sprit of running on schedule like their early mail boats, Smith decided not to slow down even when he was advised that icebergs were in the area. This

---

[6]Ibid., 76.

breach of good seamanship and common sense caused the loss of more than 1,500 lives—most of them second-class passengers and immigrants who were kept below, while the first-class women and children filled most of the seats on the few lifeboats provided. After the *Titanic* disaster, a number of changes affecting passenger safety were instituted, including the shifting of the transatlantic routes to a more southerly course, the raising of watertight bulkhead levels, and the addition of more lifeboats.

Meanwhile, in Potsdam, Kaiser Wilhelm II, a grandson of Queen Victoria, was not at all pleased with the idea of Germany losing the superiority of the seas it had won with the *Deutchland* in 1903. He understood that having the fastest or largest navy was not enough. Passenger ships were an important part of the equation that gave the British their sea power and prestige. Hamburg-Amerika's management, as frustrated as their emperor, realized that to compete, Germany needed passenger ships that were bigger, more luxurious, and, in view of the *Titanic* disaster, safer than anything the British had afloat. It seemed logical to engage the services of a top British hotel architect, and they found him in the person of Charles Mewes. Working with famed hotelier César Ritz, Mewes had designed the famous Paris Ritz Hotel on the Place Vendôme and then the Ritz in London. He had also collaborated with Ritz on an earlier German ship, the *Amerika*. If people crossing the Atlantic wanted to travel on a world-class floating luxurious hotel, Hamburg-Amerika, with the backing of Kaiser Wilhelm, would give it to them, and recapture the prestige of the seas for Germany.

The first of these new ships, *Imperator,* was completed in late 1912. Because of the *Titanic* disaster, the builders had implemented additional safety regulations, including more secure watertight measures and more lifeboats. Another piece of new technology, a stabilizing system using water ballast tanks, was also installed to make the ship less susceptible to rolling. This huge ship, the largest yet built, carried a maximum of 4,000 passengers and an 1,100-member crew. Mounted on her prow was a grotesque bronze eagle clutching a globe with its claws and the inscription "Mein Feld ist die Welt" ("My Field is the World"). At a time when the proliferation of Prussian imperialism was already a concern, many felt there was more than a little political significance to this figurehead, which in fact looked out of place because the architect who designed the *Imperator* had made no provision for it. Inside the ship, the decoration was eighteenth-century French palatial with a Teutonic flavor. Because there were three funnels instead of four, there was room for a huge social hall with a 30-foot ceiling where all 700 first-class passengers could gather for tea or conversation. From the grand lounge, diners ascended a wide staircase to enter the Ritz-Carlton restaurant in grand style. Formal entertainment, however, was not a prominent feature on these ships. Listening to music, dancing, reading, watching people, conversation, and playing shuffleboard were the main forms of recreation.

In the following year, 1913, the Germans launched the second ship in the trio, the *Vaterland* ("Fatherland"). In 1914, with the breakout of war, passenger shipping was disrupted. The *Vaterland* was in New York, where she was seized and converted to an American troop ship. Some British ships were converted to armed merchant cruisers, including the *Mauretania* and the *Britannic;* others continued to carry passengers. One of these, Cunard's *Lusitania,* was torpedoed by the Germans. Her sinking occasioned a national holiday in Germany.

The *Imperator* was in port in Hamburg when the war broke out. The third ship in the series, the *Bismarck,* was still under construction, and so all work was stopped. At the end of the war, the British received the *Imperator* and the *Bismarck* as reparations, while the United States kept the *Vaterland,* which was renamed the *Leviathan.*

Michael A. Musmanno, a lawyer from Philadelphia, traveled home from England aboard the *Leviathan* in 1958 and gives us an account of the ship's cuisine in those days:

> In all the history of good eating, not even King Henry VIII feasted more felicitously than I did during that five-day journey between Southampton and New York. At seven-thirty each morning fruit juice and black coffee appeared like magic in my stateroom. At eight-thirty, in the ship's dining room, I attacked a matinal repast of cereal, eggs, bacon, potatoes, and hot cakes. At noon the table glowed, smiled, and chuckled with soup, steak, vegetables, salad, dessert, and coffee. At four o'clock tea, little sandwiches and cakes refreshed the oceanic afternoon, and at seven each evening a royal banquet unfolded in the large dining hall where one's eyes dilated as his belt yielded to appetizers, smoked oysters, celery soup, roast fowl, vegetables, salad, nuts, fruit pie, ice cream, and demitasse. At ten o'clock—I skipped the chaffing-dish supper available to those trenchermen who had the capacity for it.
>
> Musmanno added, "The voyage added nine pounds to my sparse frame."[7]

After the war, transatlantic traffic resumed on ships that had been refurbished for peacetime use. In the 1920s, the United States curtailed its

---

[7]Michael A. Musmanno, *Verdict! The Adventures of the Young Lawyer in the Brown Suit,* quoted in *All in the Same Boat,* ed. Robert Wechler (Highland Park, N.J.: Catbird, 1988), 186.

open-door immigration policy. Everyone who was tired and poor was no longer welcome and thus could not be a customer of steamship companies. Even though first-class passage produced pages of news, the major lines earned most of their money from immigrants. When that business dried up, they needed to find new sources of passengers to fill ships. This marketing problem was aggravated by a postwar overbuilding of fleets. Cunard and other lines replaced war losses with more and larger ships in anticipation of an immigration business that never materialized. Thus there was a major change in the kind of passengers these vessels carried. Fortunately, the Great War had spurred a major interest in visiting Europe. With a strong marketing thrust, immigrants were replaced by teachers, students, and tourists who wanted to visit the sites of famous battles or gaze upon Paris, Berlin, and London, which they had viewed for the first time in war newsreels. There was another incentive for transatlantic travel: Prohibition had dried up the United States in 1919. For those who craved a martini, a scotch, or glass of champagne, a transatlantic voyage was a trip to nirvana!

To take advantage of all of these trends, changes in design were necessary. What had been immigrant quarters were turned into third-cabin or tourist-class accommodations. Additional bars and cocktail lounges were added to the vessels, and brochures prominently featured the availability of all kinds of alcoholic beverages on board.

The large luxurious ships were still the most prestigious—patronized by the rich and famous. Newspaper society columns published travel plans of celebrities. It was not uncommon for social climbers to book passage, hoping for the opportunity to reserve a deck chair or a dining room table next to a famous personality. With luck, ambitious parents might even light the spark for a suitable marriage. If one could not meet the right targets by sitting or dining next to them, there were other opportunities as well: Passengers organized games of deck tennis, billiards, potato sack races, and a host of other silly pastimes in which anyone who was willing could participate. Masquerade balls were particularly popular (and still are on some ships), and some guests spent long hours designing and making elaborate costumes with materials brought on board specifically for this event or supplied by the ship's crew.

Although there were no casinos on board, waging bets on everything from the outcome of games to the ship's daily mileage was a common and widespread pastime. Professional gamblers soon discovered that a five-day voyage with people of means was an easy way to make a living. Lines warned their guests not to play poker with strangers. Nevertheless, these suave, sophisticated adventurers added a certain aura of excitement to the voyages and helped build the image that a large ocean liner was an exciting place to be. In short, spending a week at sea was no longer something to be avoided but, in fact, *the* fashionable thing to do. This newfound cachet of the ocean voyage, promulgated by the widespread press coverage of the lavish (and expensive) first-class lifestyle—where one could eat sumptuously, drink, and party into the late hours and form significant relationships with desirable companions—shaped the perception that ocean voyages were costly, elitist vacations. Imagine extravagant dining around the clock, drinking and partying into the wee hours, and hobnobbing with the rich and famous! Transatlantic voyages during this era attracted the hoity-toity, the crème-de-la-crème, the rich, powerful, and famous from all over the world. What a phenomenal transformation! In a few short years, the ocean voyage went from a dreaded, uncomfortable, and life-threatening experience to the grandest of trips, and the clientele went from the downtrodden to high society.

Sadly however, the pendulum swung too far. Because all the press and public interest centered on the first-class voyage experience, the broadest-held perception was that this type of travel was for a very few. Moreover, those few, to the common man, were stuffy swells, intimidating to be with—or boring—or both.

More Cruises Are Offered

The Great Depression, which began in 1929, prompted many companies, such as Holland America and the Italian Line, to minimize their losses by sending ships cruising, thereby reducing unneeded transatlantic capacity. Given the state of the economy and Prohibition, the market was ripe for short booze cruises to Nova Scotia, Nassau, and Bermuda—cheap respites. The ships that offered these cruises were not, of course, really suited for cruising. They were obsolete and could no longer compete with the newer ocean liners. They lacked the necessary air conditioning for cruising in warm waters, and their dark, enclosed design discouraged sunbathing, swimming, and other resort-type activities.

By the end of the 1930s, these short, inexpensive cruises were but one segment of a larger cruise market. Fancier and more modern ships were redeployed into cruising, and longer, more expensive, and more lavish itineraries were fashioned. Unfortunately, these elaborate cruises reinforced the elitist image that had emerged from the first-class transatlantic voyages of the 1920s. One can just imagine the passenger composition when the French liner *Normandie* sailed in 1939 from New York to Rio de Janeiro on a monthlong cruise chartered by American Express.

Regarded by many as the most beautiful ship of all time, the *Normandie* was the quintessential ocean liner. Built in 1935 at an extravagant cost, she featured the grandest staircase at sea. This grand sweep ended in an air-conditioned dining room 400 feet long! Original art commissioned by the French Line for the *Normandie* was the most expensive collection afloat. Every stateroom was uniquely decorated—one was even done in sparkling stainless steel. The suites featured grand pianos and, of course, more original works of art. After the fall of France in 1939, the *Normandie* took refuge in New York Harbor. While undergoing conversion to a troop ship, to be renamed the *Lafayette,* she caught fire, capsized, and was lost.

We give credit for glamorizing warm-weather cruising to the Italians. The Italian Line built two large ships, the *Rex* and the *Conte di Savola,* which began operations with transatlantic cruises from New York to Italy. These itineraries necessarily entailed several days of warm-weather cruising in the Mediterranean. The ships were lighter toned, more open, and thus more resort-like. With unusual marketing savvy for the time, Italian Line posters portrayed visuals of gaily dressed passengers pursuing vacation activities, while the Germans lines showed serious-looking businessmen and their well-dressed spouses strolling the decks.

Even though the focus was beginning to shift from crossing the Atlantic to cruising and despite the fact that the passengers were mostly Americans, the steamship business was still dominated by European interests. American companies were generally not trendsetters, as they never really competed for the transatlantic market.

There were, however, several niches that American-owned steamship companies filled nicely. The Matson Line offered service from San Francisco to Hawaii and the South Pacific. The Grace Line sailed to the Caribbean and South America. Moore McCormick also sailed to South America. American Export Lines did manage to offer transatlantic voyages as well as extended cruises to the Mediterranean.

On the other side of the Atlantic, the cruise business was also being developed for the same reasons as in America—too many ships and not enough passengers and immigrants to fill them. Seasonally, cruises went from England, France, Italy, and Germany to Scandinavia and the Mediterranean. Had World War II not intervened, cruising in Europe might have become far more developed than it is today.

Annual world cruises were offered by Cunard, Canadian Pacific, and the Red Star Line, a subsidiary of the same group that owned White Star. A look at the brochures for these cruises shows that they stressed the ports that would be visited rather than the experience of being aboard the ship. In 1935, Cole Porter and Moss Hart went around the world on Cunard's *Franconia,* which was one of the ships built to replace war losses. One pivotal ship during this period was the 40,000-ton *Empress of Britain.* Built by Canadian Pacific, she was the first major liner built for a dual purpose. In the winter, she would take a world cruise carrying only 400 passengers, while in the summer she operated express service from Southampton to Quebec with a passenger load of 1,100—many, of course, traveling second and third class. The *Empress* was a truly elegant ship that was influenced by the same design characteristic of Canadian Pacific's grand hotels built during the same period. Her amenities included a full-sized tennis court. Unfortunately, her funnels were not tall enough and often scattered soot over the passengers. Canadian Pacific also used the *Empress of Australia* for world cruises; she was one of the ships taken from Germany as part of war reparations. Britain's largest passenger shipping company in those years was the venerable Cunard Line. While Cunard's transatlantic fleet was extensive, its two largest and most notable liners were the *Queen Mary* and the *Queen Elizabeth.* The *Queen Mary,* built in 1934, had the ambience and glamour of a stately London hotel. Today she is a tourist attraction berthed in Long Beach, California. While somewhat modified, a tour of her today at the dock can still provide the flavor of crossing the Atlantic in those days. She is the only surviving liner from this era.

Her sister, the *Queen Elizabeth,* was, when launched in 1940, the largest passenger ship ever built—a vessel of 80,000 tons. Her size has been significantly eclipsed, however, with well over a dozen ships in excess of 100,000 gross registered tons, including the *Queen Mary 2,* at 150,000 tons, and the *Freedom of the Seas,* at 158,000 tons.

With the outbreak of World War II, all of the major steamship lines converted their ships to troop carriers or stayed in port, except the Swedish Line, whose country was neutral. Eventually, however, everything afloat was taken over for troop transfer. Even the *Gripsholm* was sold to the United States for that purpose. Crossing and cruising closed down for the duration of the war and would never be the same again.

After the war came the postwar boom. The rebuilding of Europe spurred a growing demand for transportation to Europe for both tourists and business travelers. There were also many refugees to be resettled in the United States and Canada. The steamship business became enormously profitable. But all the profits were going to Cunard, the French Line, and other European lines. Why was the United States left out of this picture? The answer is simple: The European lines were operating ships whose construction had been heavily subsidized by their governments. The United States, on the other hand, had no significant passenger fleet because government shipbuilding subsidies strictly applied to the U.S. Navy only. The war, however, had clearly demonstrated the need for ships that could be quickly converted to troop carriers. Something had to be done.

The United States realized it might need additional troop ships and thus subsidized the building and operation of some new vessels.

American Export Lines built two ships in 1951: the *Independence* and the *Constitution* at Bethlehem Steel's Ford River Shipyard in Quincy, Massachusetts. These were 30,000-ton vessels. Specifications for both required that they be able to sail at 25 knots from Norfolk, Virginia, to Capetown, South Africa, without refueling. American Export quickly established itself as a luxury American ship line. While the *Independence* crossed the North Atlantic and cruised the world, the *Constitution* cruised from New York to Italy, visiting the ports of Gibraltar and Cannes en route. In 1956, when actress Grace Kelly became the Princess of Monaco, she sailed on the *Constitution* with her wedding party. Eventually, these two ships were retired from service in 1967, when American Export discontinued its passenger service.

Subsequently, Congress appropriated the funds to subsidize the building of a state-of-the art transatlantic liner, the *United States*. This ship was designed with two purposes in mind. The first was to provide fast troop ship capability after quick conversion. The second was to display (albeit late to the party) superior American ingenuity and technology to the world. This was one of the country's more significant ego trips. Many of her design and performance details were kept confidential to ensure that other governments would not try to steal her thunder. Because she was designed and built to be faster than any other passenger ship afloat, concessions had to be made. Consequently, despite the owners' desire to make her a luxury liner, the *United States* was, in fact, quite austere. She offered little open deck space (which obviously would be of little use as a troop carrier), and her watertight doors were not disguised or concealed. All of these elements contributed to her spartan look. But she could do 40 knots, and on her first crossing in the summer of 1952 she beat the *Queen Mary*'s record by a full ten hours, completing her eastbound voyage in 3 days, 10 hours, and 40 minutes. As a result, she finally secured the Blue Ribband for the United States—which held for fifty years because of that singular performance! Since 1998, the Blue Ribband has been held by a Dutch catamaran ferry, CAT-LINK V, which crossed the Atlantic in just 2 days, 20 hours, and 9 minutes!

By the 1950s, the future of the steamship business seemed clearly established. Companies like Swedish American built new ships with spacious cabins and marketed them heavily to the tourist trade. Another American line, Moore McCormack, launched the *Argentina* and *Brazil*, both in 1957. These ships operated liner and cruise routes to South America, as did Grace Line, whose passenger-cargo ships all carried the "Santa M" nomenclature (*Santa Maria, Santa Mercedes*, etc.). The *Argentina* and *Brazil* later operated as the *Veendam* and *Volendam* for Holland American; the *Monarch Sun* and *Monarch Star* of Monarch Cruise Lines (now defunct), and the *Enchanted Isle* and *Enchanted Seas* of Commodore Cruise Lines (also defunct).

The transatlantic passenger boardings built steadily after World War II, reaching their peak in 1957. In 1958, however, Pan American offered the first nonstop transatlantic crossing with a Boeing 707 jet. The plane left New York's Idlewild airport in the evening and touched down early the next morning. This seminal event effectively sounded the death knell of the transatlantic steamship business. While a few ships built after 1958 were aimed at the transatlantic market (most notably the *Empress of Canada* in 1960, the S.S. *France* in 1962, the *Queen Elizabeth* in 1967, and the *Mikhail Lermentov* in 1973), the majority of new ship construction was built with cruising in mind. Examples include Holland America's *Rotterdam* (1959; 38,645 tons) and Norwegian American's *Sagafjord* (1965; 25,147 tons) and *Vistafjord* (1973; 24,492 tons). Other cruise-specific vessels included Incres's *Victoria* and Chandris's *Amerikanis*.

As the transatlantic boardings declined in the 1960s, the companies that did not redeploy their fleets began to take on water. The list of fatalities include Canadian Pacific, Furness Bermuda, United States Lines, Hamburg American Line, and Swedish American Line.

⚓ The Advent of Modern Cruising

In 1966, Ted Arison, a young Israeli from Tel Aviv who had fought in Israel's War of Independence as a colonel in the Israeli army and subsequently retired after starting and then losing two air cargo businesses, was calling on friends in the shipping business who owned two car ferries that were under charter as cruise ships in Miami—the *Bilu* and the *Nili*. The charterer was a Miami cruise pioneer, Leslie Frazer. While Arison was in their office they received a telex from Frazer advising them that his business was not doing well and facing serious financial problems. Arison volunteered that this was clearly a negotiating tactic by Frazer to secure a lower charter fee and suggested that as he knew the charter business, he would be glad to go to Miami take over their ships and run them. "He was basically bluffing," recalls his son Micky, now CEO of Carnival Corporation, "because he in fact knew nothing about the passenger cruise business." Sure enough, a day later Frazer sent another telex asking for a lower fee, and rather than accept this, Frazer's charter was canceled and Arison flew to Miami to manage the ships.

As in Arison's other ventures, Lady Luck was not with him, and his Israeli partners went bankrupt as a result of other business interests they had in Europe. The Israeli government, which held a first mortgage on the ships, foreclosed and ordered the ships back to Israeli waters, where they would be available in case of a military emergency. This move left Arison with a cruise line consisting of a sales and marketing organization but no ships. While perusing a stack of trade publications—the remnants of his now defunct shipping business—he saw a picture in *Travel Weekly* of a brand-new ship, the *Sunward,* which had been purpose-built by a Norwegian, Knut Kloster, to sail to Gibraltar. However, Gibraltar was having political difficulties, and the ship was unable to operate. Arison called Kloster and explained that Kloster's ship was very much like the *Nili,* which he had just lost, and that he had future passenger bookings but no vessel to carry them. He suggested that if Kloster would send the *Sunward* to Miami, they could both make some money. Kloster agreed, but only on the condition that Arison guarantee him a half-million dollars a year in profit; Arison agreed. Of course, he didn't have the money, but Kloster didn't know that, and the *Sunward* moved to Florida. It entered service on 19 December 1966, offering three- and four-day cruises. This arrangement between Arison and Kloster was really a partnership between Arison Shipping Company, Arison's management company, which was a general sales agency, and Kloster Rederi, Knut Kloster's Norwegian firm, which owned the *Sunward.* While they did business under the name Norwegian Caribbean Lines (NCL), in reality there was no such company.

By 1968, business was good enough that a second ship, the *Starward,* was added to the fleet. It had two decks of ferry space, so passenger cabins were located on the outer hull of the ship, where the portholes were, while the inner spaces were utilized for a roll-on, roll-off cargo service between Florida and Jamaica. Business continued to expand, and two more ships were soon added: the *Skyward* in 1969 and the *Southward* in 1971. With her fleet of four modern cruise ships operating regularly from Miami on a year-round basis, Norwegian Caribbean's enterprise represented the beginning of the contemporary cruise business as we know it today.

From the start, Arison and Kloster realized that a national marketing campaign would be key to their success. There were simply not enough prospects living in Florida to fill their cabins every week. The large (at the time) weekly capacity of 3,000-plus berths forced NCL to reach out for prospects in other parts of the country, thereby transforming South Florida contemporary cruising from a regionally marketed hodgepodge of very old ships built originally to weather the North Atlantic waters to a nationally marketed contemporary vacation product featuring brand-new vessels designed for Caribbean cruising.

Like any successful new concept, this fast-growing new market quickly attracted competition. Sandy Chobol, a Miami real estate developer and hotelier, recognized the potential for converting hotel landlubbers to sailors and founded Commodore Cruise Lines. He brought in a brand-new combination ferry-cruiser, the *Bohême* in 1968 on year-round seven-day cruises. The *Bohême* was built in Finland and owned by a man named Olaf Wallenis who liked opera names. At the time she was named the *Aïda.* Chobol and his general manger, Ed Stephan, did not like the name, so it was agreed to change it to the *Bohême,* which was also an opera—but suggested a carefree, Bohemian way of life. The ship was an overnight success.

After leaving Commodore Cruise Lines, Ed Stephan decided to pursue his dream of starting his own line. Stephan, originally from Madison, Wisconsin, had started in the hotel business as a bell captain at the Casablanca Hotel on Miami Beach and worked his way up to general manager of the Biscayne Terrace Hotel while teaching hotel management at Lindsey Hopkins Vocational School. In time, he was offered the job of general manager for Yarmouth Cruise Lines by Jules Sokoloff, a Canadian living in Jamaica. Yarmouth had two ships, the *Yarmouth* and the *Yarmouth Castle.*

History buffs may recall that on 13 November 1962, the *Yarmouth Castle* burned and sank, killing eighty-nine people. While the cause of the fire was never pinpointed, several officials felt it was the work of an arsonist. This deduction was based on cross-referencing employment records; it was found that one crew member on board the *Yarmouth Castle* had previously worked on other cruise ships that had experienced unexplained fires. Fortunately, this was the last major catastrophe involving cruise ship passengers in North American waters. The ship was old, built in 1929, and of largely wooden construction. It would not have been allowed to sail, let alone carry passengers, under today's much tougher safety standards.

During this period between jobs, Stephan produced some designs and plans for a new cruise line. In 1967, at the suggestion of a shipbroker employed by Fearnley and Egar, Stephan took these plans to Oslo, Norway, where they impressed two prominent Norwegian shipping executives, Sigor Skaugen and Anders Wilhelmsen. They decided to invest in Stephan's concept, which was the beginning of another industry giant, Royal Caribbean Cruise Lines (RCCL). Later, Gotaas Larsen, a subsidiary of International Utilities in Canada, bought in for a one-third share. Harry Larsen, the chairman, had to pay one-third of all expenses since the beginning of the company to consummate the deal, we were told.

The company quickly launched a modern fleet of three vessels destined for year-round Caribbean sailings from Miami. These vessels incorporated Ed Stephan's design innovations, including a sleek, yacht-like profile and an observation lounge located in the ship's funnel, high above the superstructure—inspired by Seattle's Space Needle. The first, *Song of Norway,* entered weekly service in 1970. She was followed by the *Nordic Prince* and the *Sun Viking* in 1971 and 1972. These latter ships were originally deployed to offer fourteen-day cruises departing from Miami on alternate Saturdays. From an operation and marketing standpoint, the plan was simplicity itself: Every Saturday would see two RCCL ships debarking and embarking passengers in Miami. Travel agents and customers alike quickly understood that each and every week you could take a one- or two-week Royal Caribbean cruise. The marketing was further simplified by several other innovative ideas. First, unlike previous entrants to the marketplace, Royal Caribbean started promoting her ships a full year before the first one went into service. This provided enough time to fill the ships well before they operated. In contrast, the *Sunward* had had only a few weeks of advance marketing.

Next, rather than scattering their promotional efforts over a large area, Royal Caribbean concentrated on two major markets. This allowed for maximized efficiency of sales and promotional efforts and reduced costs by chartering and filling back-to-back wide-bodied aircraft departing weekly from Los Angeles and San Francisco. Royal Caribbean passed on these savings to their guests, creating what was a terrific travel bargain at the time.

While RCCL was building ships for cruising in the Caribbean, another group of Norwegian investors, headed by Bergen Line, decided to launch a new cruise line of ships built especially for world cruising. They recruited Warren Titus, the first president of P&O Lines in North America, to found their company, which was to be called Royal Viking Line. Their concept was to operate worldwide cruises that were expensive but luxurious. Royal Viking soon had a fleet of three ships: the *Royal Viking Star,* brought into service in 1972, and the *Royal Viking Sky* and *Royal Viking Sea,* in 1973. Unlike the other lines operating at the time, says Titus, "Our marketing approach was based not only on tapping existing markets, but going after and rewarding those people who cruised with us repeatedly." Their method was to introduce the Skald Club at the outset, which recognized and offered special programs for repeat passengers. (Remember, this was ten years before the first airline frequent flyer program.) Titus recalls that by the time he left the company in 1987 to found Seabourn Cruise Lines, their repeat factor was well over 50 percent per average cruise and 65 to 70 percent on their longer cruises.

An incredibly complex web of relationships spawned the rapid growth of the cruise line industry. Going back to Yarmouth Cruise Lines, it is important to note that the *Yarmouth* had been acquired from a Canadian-born Seattle businessman, Stanley B. McDonald, who ran package tours combining the cruise with land options—California to Oregon, British Columbia, and the Seattle World's Fair. McDonald's venture had been so successful that it inspired him to try winter cruises to Mexico. In 1965 he chartered another ship, Canadian Pacific's 6,000-ton *Princess Patricia,* and named his company Princess Cruises. During the winters of 1965 and 1966, the *Princess Pat* pioneered cruising to Mexico's West Coast and became an overnight success. After two highly successful seasons and demand far exceeding the capacity of the small vessel, Princess Cruises chartered the newly completed Italian ship M/S *Italia* and renamed her the *Princess Italia*.

By 1972, Princess had added two more ships to their fleet, the *Princess Carla* and the *Island Princess* (formerly the *Island Venture* of Incres Line). But then came the recession and the Arab oil embargo. The cash-strapped company was saved by a takeover bid from the London-based Peninsular and Oriental Steam Navigation Company, the same P&O that in 1844 had pioneered the business by offering the world's first cruise. P&O decided to keep the newer *Island Princess* but replace the older ships with two newer ones—the *Sun Princess* and the *Pacific Princess* (the sister to the *Island Princess*, the former *Sea Venture*).

In 1977, an event occurred that would catapult Princess into becoming the best-known cruise line in North America at the time and popularize the idea of cruising as a mass-market vacation to the extent that virtually every cruise ship afloat at the time benefited. A television producer, Aaron Spelling, suggested that a luxury cruise ship would be an ideal setting for a TV series. He had successfully produced *Love, American Style* and saw this new show as a logical iteration. They approached Princess, as they were located on the West Coast near Hollywood. Princess agreed to make their two ships, the *Island Princess* and the *Pacific Princess,* available. Veteran actor Gavin MacLeod (known for his portrayal of Murray on the *Mary Tyler Moore Show*) was cast as Captain Merril Stubing after two previous TV pilots with other actors in the role failed to be sold. The name *Stubing* was picked by a writer who was a baseball fan and remembered a great ballplayer with the same name. "Thank God, I hit a home run," MacLeod says. The show's producer, Douglas Cramer, told MacLeod that every episode would consist of three stories—a sophisticated one, a farce, and a poignant one. MacLeod liked the idea but insisted that every story in every show have a happy ending. As the captain, he wanted to play the paternal figure that at the end would make everyone feel good. He felt then, as he does today, that television should offer programs that help people who are trapped at home in dull jobs to escape, to travel and become vicarious adventurers. "Today there's nothing on TV that makes me cheer," he says wistfully. When filming began, MacLeod, who had never set foot on a cruise ship, recalls that they far exceeded his expectations. He was absolutely astounded that the ships had real elevators. The *Love Boat* series attracted a worldwide audience and a public relations bonanza for Princess and the fledgling cruise industry. "It made you feel good," says MacLeod, "and that's very important." The series continued in production for ten years and six months and is still in syndication today.

Another important pioneer that revolutionized the cruise business in those early days was a company that traces its roots to 1860, to an Italian olive oil producer named Giacomo Costa. The Costa family's business prospered so much that by 1924 they had bought their first freighter to ship their olive oil. In 1948, they entered the passenger business with the *Anna C.,* the first postwar Italian luxury liner. In 1959, the company moved into the U.S. market with the *Franca C.,* offering thirteen-day cruises from Miami. By 1968, Costa was firmly established in the U.S. market and decided to reposition the *Franca C.* to San Juan, Puerto Rico, and offer lower Caribbean cruises from there. There was only one problem to solve—how to induce people from the Northeast to go to San Juan to embark on a cruise. The answer was logical and earthshaking in its ultimate impact: Sell the cruise together with the airplane trip as an air/sea packaged vacation. Costa did just that by teaming up with Simmons Group Journeys of New York and pioneering weekly air/sea programs from Puerto Rico. Air/sea programs were without doubt a key component in the success of today's cruise industry. They are now offered by all cruise lines in one form or another. Basically, the cruise is packaged with a round-trip airfare between the passenger's home city and the port of embarkation. A hotel room is also included if necessary because of flight scheduling, as well as ground transfers between the airport and the seaport. However, new technology is clouding the future of air/sea packages. The culprit is the Internet. With websites like Travelocity, Expedia, and Orbitz, consumers have enough information to purchase their own air tickets and frequently save money doing just that.

While the year-round cruising business was building a steady stream of regular customers from the East Coast, in the western part of the country a young tour operator named Chuck West was building a seasonal cruise operation along Alaska's Inside Passage. A former bush pilot for Wein Airlines, West had originally founded a travel agency to promote Alaska tour packages. He soon realized that the best way to see Alaska was by sea, and so he first chartered and then bought a fleet of ships under the banner of Alaska Cruise Lines. These ships departed from Vancouver, British Columbia, and visited Glacier Bay and other ports in combination with a railway trip through the mountains. West's cruise line was part of his overall tour operation, which was called Westours. West was popularly referred to as "Mr. Alaska," served as president of the American Society of Travel Agents, and owned four small cruise ships, a motorcoach company, and several hotels in Alaska. He opened up Alaska not only to mass tourism but also to the cruise industry, as visitors returned with stories of seeing glaciers calving, bald eagles nesting, and herds of moose grazing contentedly—up front and personal from their vantage points on cruise ships.

Unfortunately, by expanding so rapidly, West overextended himself, and by 1970 he was over his head financially. His controller, Kirk

Lanterman, was forced to chop personnel by one-third and institute other cost-saving measures, but they were not enough. West had a $1 million payment due on his newest ship, the *West Star,* and no funds to make it with. The 1970 World Congress of the American Society of Travel Agents (ASTA), over which West presided, was held in Amsterdam. During a social event he met Nico Van der Vorm, of the venerable Holland America Line, who expressed an interest in buying Westours. "The Dutch possessed the one cruise-tour component that was vital to the future of Westours and which I had not been able to supply," said West. "Large efficient ships. They knew how to manage those ships economically and profitably." West sold his company to Holland America that same fall. He left the company shortly after the sale but remained in the cruise tour business in Alaska for many years. He started a new company called Alaska Sightseeing/Cruise West, now headed by his son Richard. Chuck West died in 2005.

In the summer of 1971, a schism formed between Knut Kloster and Ted Arison. Kloster served notice that they intended to cancel Arison's ten-year contract at the end of the year. The contract was set up in such a way that if Kloster didn't make $1.5 million two years in a row, they had the option to cancel the deal. Meanwhile, a jealousy had been slowly forming in Miami between Kloster's Norwegian employees and Arison's Americans. According to Micky Arison, even though the Norwegian company was profitable, the Norwegians felt their American partners were making too much money. A simple plan was devised for getting rid of Arison. It was alleged that the Norwegians, aware of the contract provision, decided to sabotage Arison's profits by purchasing equipment such as deck chairs and engine parts and then throwing them overboard. This ensured that the inventory would not exist on the ship, throwing a shadow on Arison's integrity and guaranteeing that he would not be able to deliver the agreed-on profit goals, as the nonexistent inventory would not show up on the balance sheet. (These facts later came out in the discovery process of a lawsuit between the two parties.) As a result of these actions, Arison did not meet his profit commitment, and Kloster, as predicted, canceled the contract. Because Arison Shipping Company's cash flow stemmed from NCL's advance ticket sales, the company quickly moved to protect itself by seizing all advance moneys on hand at NCL sales offices around the country. Arison believed the cancellation of his contract was invalid and that he was entitled to his commission, which amounted to 18 percent of the gross revenue. The lawsuit was eventually settled out of court, with Arison agreeing to return half of the funds he had seized, the rest legitimately belonging to him as a result of the Norwegian's actions.

As 1971 was drawing to a close, Arison once again found himself with a cruise line but no ships. With the funds he had withdrawn from NCL bank accounts, he immediately set off for Europe, where he had learned that two older Cunard ships, the *Carmania* and the *Franconia,* had been retired from service and were laid up in England. Wasting no time, he prepared ads for his new "golden fleet" of two ships. He asked his employees to stick with him, have faith, and he said he would soon start a new company. Most didn't believe him. Micky Arison remembers standing with his father on the last day of business as former employees and friends filed out of the building. Only a handful took Arison at his word; the others knew Kloster had the ships, and they wanted to get paid at the end of the week. But a few loyal employees, including Mike Zonis, Carnival's former long-time senior vice president of operations, decided to abandon the security of Kloster-NCL for the uncharted waters of a nameless, shipless company.

However, Arison was unable to work out a deal with Cunard, and his plan had to be abandoned. Depressed, Arison talked to his friend Jacob Victor, of Technical Marine Planning, a firm of naval architects. Victor suggested he look at another laid-up vessel, the ex-Canadian Pacific liner *Empress of Canada.* Lacking the capital to buy it, Arison turned to his old schoolmate and pal from Israel, Meshulam Riklis, an ultrasuccessful entrepreneur at the time, who assembled and chaired a multibillion-dollar conglomerate, Rapid American Corporation. Riklis was also the principal shareholder in a Boston-based travel operation called American International Travel Service. This latter company operated group and individual tours to Hawaii, South America, Europe, and other destinations using the name Carnival. For example, they had a Hawaiian Carnival program, a Rio Carnival program, and others. Arison convinced Riklis to set up an American International Travel Service (AITS) subsidiary, Carnival Cruise Lines, to own and operate the *Empress of Canada,* which would be financed by the $1 million he had seized from NCL. They renamed the ship the *Mardi Gras,* consistent with the Carnival name. Arison's sales and marketing team, remnants of the NCL management, positioned the *Mardi Gras* as "the Flagship of the Golden Fleet," based on their expectation of obtaining the two Cunard ships. These were painted yellow, and two of them could be considered a fleet. Unfortunately, the *Empress of Canada* wasn't golden, she was white, and of course there was no longer a fleet. But it was too late to change anything.

When the *Mardi Gras* entered service on 7 March 1972, she ran aground on her maiden voyage in Government Cut, at the tip of Miami Beach. She sat there ignominiously for twenty-four hours in plain view of thousands of vacationers who crowded the beach to gawk at her before she was refloated. On her maiden cruise, because of nonexistent cash flow, Ted Arison didn't have the funds to refuel the ship in San Juan for her voyage home. After unsuccessfully wining and dining his Puerto

Rican suppliers, hoping to obtain credit, he literally collected money from the bar cash registers on board and had the advance deposits for future cruises wired to him from Miami to purchase the fuel he needed to return the *Mardi Gras* to Miami.

For the first year and a half, two of the four decks of passenger cabins were being converted from two-class transatlantic service to one-class cruising. This entailed sailing with a work crew of several hundred plumbers and carpenters installing compact showers and toilets in the cabins. During this period, the company lost millions of dollars as the *Mardi Gras* sailed on a sea of red ink. In the late fall of 1973, the Golden Fleet positioning was scrapped as inappropriate shortly after Bob Dickinson arrived at the company. The question was: What slogan or positioning to replace it with? Dickinson gathered all the available cruise brochures then on the market and noticed that one stood out: Commodore's "Happy Ship," the *Bohême.* This appealed to Dickinson; the cruise slogan applied to a specific ship and not the company—after all, people buy ships and not companies. "Happy" was already taken, and it sounded a bit weak anyhow. What is the one universal need—the one ingredient everyone wants in their vacation? FUN! And, fortunately, the product at the time backed up the slogan. The *Mardi Gras,* being 50 percent larger than her competition, had the space to provide activities and entertainment choices to provide fun for everyone. With the "Fun Ship" position, the ship itself became the destination and the ports of call became green stamps—a total reversal of previous cruise marketing. Cruise marketing up to that time had been destination driven. But in the early 1970s, less than 1 percent of the public had been on a cruise; the vast majority of the population was leery of this unknown concept. By focusing on the ship rather than the ports of call, Carnival was forced to communicate to the public what the experience of the ship and cruising on her was all about. Therefore the story of what a vacationer could expect on board was a salable one. Moreover, Arison recalls that because the *Mardi Gras* was an old ship, Carnival was forced to price her low. The low prices attracted a younger crowd that had previously not been able to afford cruising. They were drawn to the enjoyment Carnival promised, which was viewed as a departure from the typical impression of stodgy cruise ships whose average passenger age was deceased! The "fun" concept became a self-fulfilling prophecy. The repositioning worked, and Carnival turned its first profit in 1975.

Like a man on a roll at a craps table, Arison took the profit and immediately bought the *Mardi Gras*'s sister ship, the *Empress of Britain,* and put her into service on 7 February 1976 as the *Carnivale.* To make room for her at the port of Miami, Carnival shifted the *Mardi Gras* to Sunday sailings. Within the industry, this was a controversial move at the time because no one had offered Sunday departures before. The conventional wisdom said there would be little demand. Today, almost half of the seven-day cruises sailing from North American ports depart on Sunday.

Incredibly, the *Carnivale* made money in her first year of operation, so Arison, ever the optimist, began scouring the world for a third ship. He found the S.A. *Vaal*, a South African passenger/cargo ship. Without even seeing her, he bought her and negotiated with the Japanese to have her rebuilt in Kobe. This was the first time the Japanese had built or rebuilt a deep-water cruise ship. Taking advantage of their eagerness to get into the business, Arison negotiated an extremely favorable price of $16–18 million, to be paid in Japanese yen. By the time he took delivery the cost was $30 million. "We learned our lesson on currency fluctuation," Micky Arison recalls. "We lost money tremendously because we didn't hedge the yen, and I'm sure they did too." At the same time, Carnival was negotiating with the yard on a new building project for about $40 million. But because of the movement on the yen, by the time the project was finalized the cost was more like $80–90 million. This was simply too expensive. Carnival was forced to turn to Europe for its shipbuilding needs. Since then, Carnival has spent billions in European shipbuilding contracts, and the Japanese yards have only built a handful of ships for the North American market.

At about the same time Carnival Cruise Lines was being formed, John Bland was charged with the unenviable task of establishing a new North American cruise brand, Sitmar, with two large ex-Cunard vessels that were refurbished and renamed the *Fairwind* and the *Fairsea*. As president of this fledgling operation, he had little time or money to accomplish the task. As a result, early voyages of these 900-plus passenger vessels sailed with few guests. He needed a marketing gimmick, and he devised a great one. He priced his one-week cruises with unusually low air supplements. Sitmar's air add-on prices were so much lower than the cost of the airline ticket that prospective vacationers could easily grasp the value. For example, Sitmar's air add-ons from New York to Fort Lauderdale were $20 per person, about 10 percent of the ticket price. The ships filled almost overnight, and the Sitmar brand gained recognition because of this pricing deal. Once onboard the two Sitmar vessels, passengers quickly appreciated the Italian food and service. Successfully launched, Bland was able, over time, to ratchet up his rates and make a profit. Through pricing actions and a great product, Sitmar was transformed from a bottom feeder priced below the Miami-based cruse lines (the contemporary or mass-market segment of the business) to a higher-priced, premium line.

Cunard, of transatlantic fame, decided to get into the cruise business on a year-round basis by building two 600-passenger vessels, the *Ambassador* and the *Adventurer,* in 1970 and 1971. These operated one-week contemporary cruises from Fort Lauderdale and San Juan, competing with NCL, Royal Caribbean, and, later, Carnival. Recognizing that the ships were too small to be particularly profitable, Cunard replaced them with new 800-passenger sister vessels, the *Cunard Countess* and the *Cunard Princess*. Cunard had a difficult marketing challenge, as these ships carried the same brand name as the only other ship in their fleet at the time, the *Queen Elizabeth 2*. The hardware was decidedly different and, because of the lower price point, so was the software (food quality, service levels, entertainment, and other amenities).

From 1966 onward, New York was slowly and inexorably losing its grip as the number-one passenger port in the United States. Miami garnered this honor in 1974 and has held it ever since. A good object lesson in the demise of the port of New York is Home Lines. Home Lines first operated the *Homeric* on cruises to Bermuda. In their heyday in the 1960s and 1970s they offered seven-day Bermuda cruises from May to November (some including Nassau as an extra destination) as well as longer cruises to the Caribbean during the fall and winter. But Home Lines identified itself as a Manhattan-based cruise line; not only was its headquarters there but so were the departures of all of its ships. As the market shifted to Miami (which was much closer to the popular Caribbean destinations), Home Lines was slow to reposition its vessels southward.

Perhaps more important, during the late 1970s and into the 1980s, Home Lines focused its marketing and sales efforts in their traditional area, the Northeast—and, critically, to their past passengers. Over time, their market died—literally!

The Miami-based lines had the huge geographical advantage of being two to three days steaming time closer to warm weather. Moreover, they didn't have to traverse the rough seas of the North Atlantic on their way south. Sailing from Miami, ships are in the lee of the Bahamian islands, which protect them from the swells of the open ocean. On the other hand, folks from the Northeast had to fly to Miami. This was not what New York–area cruisers were used to; they expect to drive to their ships. Also, their travel agents typically didn't view them as willing to fly. Consequently, the Miami-based cruise industry had a difficult time penetrating the New York cruise market. The breakthrough came when the Miami lines stopped targeting the traditional New York cruisers and went after the fly/land vacationers.

Until 2004, New York continued to be the seasonal home for Bermuda- and Caribbean-bound cruises, as well as a few seasonally to New England and the Canadian Maritime Provinces. In that year, NCL repioneered year-round cruising from New York. This meant occasionally sailing with a few inches of snow on the deck at departure in the winter! New York's days as the hub for transatlantic travel and the cruise capital of the world are long gone, but a renaissance is in the works. Cunard has built a terminal for the *Queen Mary 2* in Brooklyn, and Royal Caribbean has invested in terminal facilities in New Jersey. With faster ships, it is now possible to get to the Caribbean and back in eight days. Some have theorized that the cruise industry benefited from the tragedy of 9/11, as many New Yorkers became leery of flying. Cruising from New York was convenient, hassle-free, and generally less costly than air vacations.

Florida remains the cruise capital of the world and will continue that way well into the foreseeable future. But nothing is forever, and cruise ships, unlike hotels, can be moved as new ports develop, ships are redeployed, and the infrastructure of new home ports evolves. Indeed, since the 2001 bombing of the World Trade Center, cruise lines have accelerated the use of more embarkation ports in the United States to meet a demand for more ports within driving distance of home. In the meanwhile, many of the preemptive strikes in the battle for a larger share of the vacation dollar will be launched by the cruise industry from the port of Miami and its sister Florida ports in Fort Lauderdale, Cape Canaveral, Tampa, and Jacksonville.

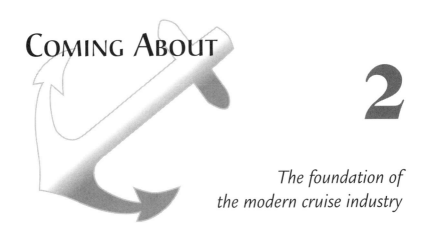

COMING ABOUT

2

*The foundation of
the modern cruise industry*

Somehow, without too many people noticing, cruising has grown phenome-nally in the last thirty-six years—from a mere half-million people a year in 1970 to over 10 million in 2006. During this time span, cruising has been far and away the fastest-growing segment of the entire travel and tourism in-dustry in the United States, outpacing hotels, restaurants, and theme parks.

Thousands of people who hadn't the foggiest idea of what a cruise ship is, or what happens aboard one, who may have never seen an ocean be-fore, and who had never left Fargo, North Dakota, or other urban or ru-ral communities, are finding themselves literally at sea!

In the early 1970s, what few cruise passengers there were came from large cities—typically coastal cities. If you lived in New York or San Francisco, because of your proximity to the ocean, you might have been able to imagine what a trip across that limitless horizon might be like—and even have some familiarity with deep-water vessels, even if they were only the ferries to Staten Island or Sausalito.

These early passengers were something like pioneers, the first on their block to try out this newfangled product. Their primary motivation was to see places they had only read about or seen pictures of in *Life, Look,* and *National Geographic.* They sought the fabled pink sand beaches of Bermuda, the great sugar plantations of Jamaica, and the old Spanish forts and rain forests of Puerto Rico. There were bargain prices to be had on perfumes, cognac, and champagne from France, watches from Switzerland, and, of course, rum distilled on the islands (some things never change; the Bacardi distillery is still one of the most popular tours in Puerto Rico).

Cruising in those days was viewed primarily as a novel way to travel to interesting places, conferring at the same time a certain status on the travelers—who were often the same people to acquire the first color television set in their circle of acquaintances. The ships themselves, however, were merely by-products of what was basically a sightseeing vacation. Although early slogans promised that getting there was half the fun, in truth, this was largely wishful thinking. Getting there often was rough if the weather was inclement, crowded as the ships were small, and even boring if there were not enough activities on board. Cruise lines hawked their wares by touting the ports of call—Port au Prince, where you could shop for handicrafts in the Iron Market; banana and coconut plantations in Montego Bay; and even an active volcano in St. Lucia. Little was said about the cruise itself.

Changing Lifestyles, Changing Passengers, Changing Cruises

Veterans of this business, when asked, tend to observe that while everything about early cruises was different from the way it is today, everything in many ways remains the same. "We do today essentially what we did then," says Rod McLeod, Royal Caribbean's former long-time executive vice president of marketing, sales, and passenger services. "The only things that have changed are the type of people we do it for and the way that we do it." He adds, "We have to do it differently because the people have changed. One example is how we handle smokers. There was no issue then, for instance, about smoking in the dining room."

McLeod's reference to smoking is a single but dramatic example in the changing lifestyle of the American consumers in the last thirty-five years and its impact on all segments of the hospitality business. Thirty-five years ago, over half the adult population smoked; today about 20 percent do.

This change has been gradual, and the cruise industry response has been equally measured. About twenty-five years ago, the first "no smoking" signs appeared in designated sections of some public rooms on a few ships, most notably in the dining rooms and main lounges. At first, these first designated areas were quite small, but as demand grew, the number of seats for nonsmokers grew proportionately. Finally, in the early 1990s, smoke-free cabins and dining rooms appeared. At Carnival, the decision to introduce smoke-free dining rooms on all their vessels was made with a certain amount of internal controversy and anguish. Some executives were concerned about passionate backlash on behalf of the remaining smokers. A typical comment was, "Ours is a business whose trademark is hospitality. Inviting people on board and then telling them that they can't smoke hardly seems hospitable."

Carnival's managers felt it might not be unreasonable for many avid smokers to respond by canceling their reservations, refusing to sail with Carnival again (or for the first time), and even demanding their money back on the grounds that they were not aware that their smoking on board would be restricted. With the exception of those who complain vocally (and many don't; they just don't come back), in the cruise, hotel, and restaurant businesses, you can't easily measure how many guests would have returned and didn't.

This is one of the reasons, we think, why many cruise and hotel executives fail to act to define or delimit their product offerings: They are afraid to make choices. Michael Porter of the Harvard Business School, whose specialty is competitive strategy, has written extensively on the subject of how to obtain a competitive advantage. Porter believes that every successful business strategy focuses on particular market segments and then creates value for customers by delivering added-value services the customers in those specific segments consider important. Because it is impossible to create a product or service that appeals to everyone, Porter points out, successful strategies involve choosing which market segments you are going to pursue and then making trade-offs (i.e., recognizing that you are going to inevitably lose some customers—who are, by definition, in the least desirable segments). Thus, you risk losing some customers in the hopes that they will be replaced in spades by the ones you really want to attract.[1]

While it is true that you can't know how many people would have bought and didn't, you do have the ability to measure cancellations and read the mail. When Carnival took the no-smoking decision, they monitored both activities closely. Everyone in a guest contact situation, both on ship and ashore, was coached to watch for any negative reactions. One three- and four-day vessel and one seven-day vessel were selected for the test. Less than thirty days' notice was given to travel agents, so they didn't have time to worry about how their clients would react and thus negatively influence their buying decisions. During the test period, there were fewer than a dozen cancellations on a base of tens of thousands of passengers. There were indeed several irate guests who wrote blistering letters or beat up on the hotel directors of the two ships involved. If Carnival had responded in kind to the degree of emotion expressed by these individuals, the no-smoking decision would have been quickly and quietly rescinded. But the majority of passengers responded positively, so the fact remained that the few passionate dissenters represented a very small market segment that Carnival and other lines could not serve without disturbing the vast majority who, it turned out, were appreciative. In practice, a few smokers were observed *in flagrante delicto* in the dining room. They were discreetly approached by the ship's staff, and, when asked, were more than willing to suffer the slight inconvenience to leave

[1]"Michael Porter on Competitive Strategy," Harvard Business School Video Series, 1988, President and Fellows of Harvard College, A Nathan/Tyler Production.

the dining room to smoke, realizing how much more comfortable it made their fellow passengers.

It's amazing the extent that all of us respond to peer pressure! While it is true that McDonald's has long since banned all smoking in their restaurants, it would be difficult for any cruise line to market a smoke-free ship. After all, McDonald's customers are not, for the most part, on vacation, they aren't planning to spend more than few dollars, they typically spend fewer then thirty minutes in the building, and of course they can take their meal out and smoke up a chimney while eating it! So what happened over time? Cruise lines went from smoking everywhere on a ship, to no-smoking sections of dining rooms and some lounges, to smoke-free dining rooms and lido restaurants and selected (typically about half) no-smoking public areas. Further, cigar smoking was usually limited to on deck and one public room.

A few years later, in 1998, Carnival introduced the first smoke-free cruise ship, *Paradise*. Smoking was not allowed anywhere on the vessel, including even the open decks and crew area. In fact, the ship workers were not allowed to smoke when they constructed the ship!

Carnival was so serious about this that they charged guests $250 damages and threw them off the ship if they even brought smoking material on board! (After all, how many of us have checked into a so-called non-smoking hotel room only to get the impression that Fidel Castro had just stayed there while enjoying a Cohiba or two?)

Unfortunately, after an eight-year run, Carnival gave up on the non-smoking *Paradise,* which had been operating alternate seven-day eastern and western Caribbean itineraries from Miami. She was repositioned to Long Beach, California, on three- and four-day cruises—without her smoke-free designation. Despite the fact that 80 percent of the adult population didn't smoke, the consumer demand for the ship wasn't as strong as for other Carnival ships on comparable itineraries.

Group business, for example, was running in the 10–15 percent range, or about half of Carnival's normal group mix. Remember, it takes just one adamant smoker to say "no," and the group goes elsewhere. With only one smoke-free vessel out of over a hundred to sell, travel agents rarely focused on it. There simply wasn't critical mass for this type of vacation experience.

Carnival's marketing folks reckoned that the lower demand cost the company up to $10 a day in guest ticket revenue and close to another $10 a day in net on-board revenue. (Nonsmokers drank and gambled far less than their smoking counterparts.) The estimated lost profit opportunity amounted to as much as $16 million per year by the time the *Paradise* was converted to a traditional smoking cruise ship.

Public and Private Spaces

Another difference between early cruise ships and those of today is in public space; the early ships offered relatively little public space compared with modern ships that carry many more passengers. One of NCL's original ships, the *Skyward,* was only 16,000 gross registered tons (GRT) and carried 724 (basis two to a cabin) people for a space ratio of 22 tons per passenger. We might note here that gross tonnage in the cruise ship business has nothing at all to do with weight—it is the amount of usable space per passenger on a ship. By definition, 1 gross registered ton is 100 cubic feet of volume. Travel writers in guidebooks often refer to the space ratio of a ship, which is simply the number of tons divided by the double occupancy passenger capacity. Because there are normally two passengers in each cabin, a ship containing 1,000 cabins is 100 percent occupied when it has 2,000 passengers on board. In other words, in the cruise industry, unlike the hotel business, capacity is not expressed in rooms or cabins but in double occupancy passenger capacity. In our hypothetical example, if this 2,000-passenger ship (basis two to a room) was carrying an additional 100 children in the third or fourth berths of their parents' cabins, the ship would be 105 percent occupied. When we use the term *total occupancy,* we are including the usage of third and fourth berths up to the lifeboat carrying capacity of the vessel. This explains how Carnival has been able to state in its promotion that its vessels have sailed in excess of 100 percent paying occupancy for over thirty years.

In sharp contrast to the ships of thirty years ago, today's ships are dramatically larger and more spacious. The *Caribbean Princess* is 113,000 tons and carries 3,100 passengers (basis two to a room). This results in a space ratio of 36. The *Carnival Spirit* is 88,500 tons and carries 2,124 passengers for a space ratio of 42. Royal Caribbean's *Freedom of the Seas* is 158,000 tons and carries 3,600 passengers for a space ratio of 44.

On the other hand, when you move up significantly in the price of a cruise, you move up proportionately in space expectations. In the ultraluxury segment, for example, the Seabourn *Pride, Spirit,* and *Legend* are 10,000 tons each and carry 200 passengers—for a whopping 50 tons per passenger space ratio. Note that this is not apparent from the size of the vessel alone. The Seabourn vessels are small, intimate, and yacht-like—less than 10 percent of the size of the 100,000-plus tonners, yet more spacious on a per-passenger basis. The majority of this additional space is found in the staterooms. All Seabourn staterooms are suites—277 square feet is the smallest—compared with 132 feet on *Sovereign of the Seas* and 190 feet on any of the eight Carnival Fantasy-class vessels.

Cabin Fever

Cabins were not very comfortable on early cruise liners. D. Keith Mano, writing in the *National Review* in 1979, had this description from his mother of a Cunard cruise ship cabin she occupied:

> Deluxe this was. Each with an iron rail six inches high around, like we were in intensive care. You know my condition, I have to get up three or four times a night—what was I to do, pole-vault out in pitch blackness? So I call the steward and he asks, "Are you in an upper bunk?" That's deluxe, with undeluxe you also have to vault six feet to the floor. Not one place to sit, it was either on the intensive care rail or on the toilet. Worse, the air conditioning was so glacial your body would keep until the boat got back to Puerto Rico. No adjustment knob except, just where it was handiest, in the middle of the ceiling. Your poor sister had to make a staircase out of the bureau drawers and climb up to move it from COMFORT for Popsicles—to OFF. Which should have read DEATH, because in five minutes the room was a floating can of Sterno.[2]

RCCL cabins in those days were decorated in what Peter Whelpton, the former executive vice president of Royal Caribbean Cruises, describes as "a plethora of bright warm Caribbean colors—vibrant orange, vivid yellow, and a green that would jump right off the wall at you." There were no pastels or other muted colors. Nor were there any television sets. Many cabins did, however, have radios on which the world news was broadcast twice a day—usually at nine in the morning and again at six in the evening. One hot amenity of modern ships—cabins with balconies—were entirely absent in early mass-market ship designs.

Bruce Nierenberg, founder and former president of Premier Cruise Lines, former executive vice president of sales and marketing of NCL, and current president of Delta Queen Steamboat Company, recalls the story of a thin elderly lady passenger who was missing one day on NCL's *Skyward.* Her traveling companion couldn't locate her and after some hours became concerned and notified the ship's staff. They put out a ship's version of an all points bulletin and searched thoroughly from bow to stern, to no avail. Later that afternoon she was discovered by the cabin

---

[2]D. Keith Mano, "My Mother Doesn't Go To Haiti," quoted in *All in the Same Boat: The Humorists' Guide to the Ocean Cruise,"* ed. Robert Wechler (Highland Park, N.J.: Catbird, 1988), 196. Reprinted with permission of National Review, Inc., 150 East 35th St., New York, NY 10016. Copyright 1979.

steward rolled up in a convertible sofa bed. Apparently the pull-down sofa back that formed the bed somehow released, flipping her back behind the sofa bolster and putting her out of sight. Because of the mattress, she was out of earshot as well. She was quite pleased to be found!

There are anecdotes about early cabin stewards as well. Because the cruise industry was just a fledgling, shipboard personnel on the whole were not as well trained as they are today. For them, the experience of being on a cruise ship was as new as it was for their guests! There is a story of a Haitian cabin steward who, while cleaning a passenger's cabin one day, shook out a pillow so vigorously that it burst open, and the feathers it was stuffed with went flying around the room. This particular steward believed chicken feathers were an evil voodoo charm, and the very sight of them sent him fleeing from the cabin and right off the side of the ship. He was never heard from or seen again!

As the industry evolved, so did the recruitment and training of on-board personnel. Today, all of the major lines have elaborate training facilities and schools to orient their hotel staff, most of whom have never been to sea before and may not have had training either in the practical or social skills required to serve passengers. Holland America has a school in Indonesia, and Princess has one in the Philippines. Carnival operates its own Carnival Colleges at sea and ashore that stress hospitality training, team building, and motivational techniques at all levels (officers, staff, and crew). All cruise lines have similar programs in place.

An important aspect of recruiting and training is making certain that all employees speak fluent English. On the whole, it is a requirement on North American ships, but the different lines have had varying degrees of success in achieving this. Even though they are supposed to be screened on shore, Princess, for example, requires that all new shipboard personnel from the captain to the lowliest deck hand or dishwasher receive a recorded test in English administered by a third party. They are required to answer questions like "What is the appropriate fire extinguisher for this fire, and where is it located?" as well as "Where can I find the purser's office?" These tapes are sent to Princess's headquarters in Los Angeles, where they are evaluated. Crew members who do not pass are supplied with tape recorders and recorded English lessons to listen to in their spare time.

The crewing situation changed dramatically with the fall of the Iron Curtain in 1989. Bright, well-educated English speakers from countries such as Croatia, Slovakia, the Czech Republic, Romania, and Russia quickly gravitated to the cruise industry, which afforded them far greater economic opportunity than could be found in their native countries.

In deciding how many cabins to put on a modern vessel and what their size should be, cruise lines take several factors into consideration. These factors are weighted differently as a result of different product philosophies. Some lines have pursued a strategy of smaller cabins and therefore higher-density vessels—that is, more cabins for a given size ship than lines that opt for fewer but larger cabins. Their rationale is that as long as the cabin is functional, size isn't that important because so little time is spent in the cabin. Proponents of this strategy for many years included Royal Caribbean and Norwegian Cruise Line. On the other hand, Disney Cruise Line has made a point of promoting what they claim to be the biggest staterooms in the mass-market segment of the industry. One reason, of course, is that they have a focused strategy of pursuing the family market. Thus, most cabins must be big enough to accommodate three, four, or even five persons. Disney offers significant numbers of connecting rooms to provide for even larger families.

Jon Rusten, a naval architect who designed ships for NCL, including the *Dreamward* and the *Windward,* and later for Disney Cruise Line, suggests that a cabin smaller than 150 feet is perceived by consumers as small today no matter whose ship it's on or how it is decorated. It may be that this is a leftover perception from the *Love Boat* television series, where cabins were actually Hollywood sets and at least double the size of actual ones. Even today, photographers use wide-angle lenses in shooting photos for brochures and commercials to make cabins appear as large as possible.

The fact is it makes more sense from an economic point of view to make the cabins as small as possible. Early pioneers of mass-market cruising all followed this formula. The situation changed, however, when Carnival introduced the *Tropicale* in 1982. That ship set a new mass-market standard (which was ignored for ten years) with inside cabins at 165 square feet and outside cabins at 180 square feet. Previously, the standard was between 125 and 135 square feet. Royal Caribbean and NCL continued to build ships through the early 1990s with smaller cabins, adhering to their philosophy that the size of the cabin was relatively unimportant. Carnival, on the other hand, stayed with their philosophy of large staterooms.

Today, however, RCCL's ships built from the mid-1990s onward as well as Princess's new mega-ships all feature larger cabins, comparable in size to those of the Carnival fleet. Had Carnival decided to build ships with small cabins, thus conforming to the industry norm, undoubtedly all today's new mass-market ships would have small cabins. Carnival gambled that their high-cost, low-density approach would eventually pay off, and it did. One can easily imagine that the same thing would happen in the airline industry today if a major carrier decided to focus on consumer demand and increase the size of all seats and spacing on every flight in coach class. In the airline scenario, however, enormous cost pressures preclude accommodating the consumer to that extent. Moreover, if a major carrier did make the move to larger, more comfortable seating in coach class, its competitors would be forced to match the product upgrade to negate the competitive advantage. At the end of the day, the airlines would have a higher cost operation for which they could *not* increase price to recover the cost. Why? Because the domestic airline industry offers a commodity product with relatively low-capacity utilization—in the 70–80 percent range. Therefore, suppliers cannot increase their prices to recover the cost of product enhancements that offer no competitive advantage. In fact, today's airline industry has been methodically reducing costs even to the point of reducing consumer benefits, such as eliminating meals and pillows and lowering the number of flight attendants in an attempt to keep prices down to encourage more purchase. (Yes, Virginia, the law of price elasticity of demand does, in fact, apply in the real world!)

Eating and Drinking

Food aboard modern cruise ships as well as their ocean liner ancestors has always been considered an important component of the product as well as a necessary one. Some historians believe that one of the reasons the Pilgrims landed at Plymouth Rock instead of continuing on to Virginia, where they were originally headed, was that they were running out of food, especially beer.[3] On today's cruise it may have something to do with the sea air, the companionship and sociability fostered by a meal together, and the feeling of being taken care of by being offered three full meals a day, served in style and featuring a wide choice of dishes that one would have difficulty finding at home or even in the average restaurant.

But in the early days of cruising, because of limited galley facilities, menus were also limited. In the 1970s out of Miami, a typical dinner menu might consist of a fruit or shrimp cocktail, consommé, a choice of filet of sole or beef Wellington, and Black Forest chocolate cake or a tray of cheese and crackers and a fruit basket. On the whole, cruise passengers back then favored large portions of hearty, plain American food—beef and mashed potatoes were favorites, along with lobster. Ships did not have dieticians—they would have been run off the ship by the chefs had they even appeared! Before dinner, passengers would meet in the main lounge for cocktails; scotch and soda, seven-and-sevens, Manhattans, and martinis were consumed in large quantities. Dark whiskies were a much more important part of beverage sales thirty years ago. Umbrella drinks

---

[3]Marcel R. Escoffier, "Food Service Operations in the Cruise Industry," *FIU Hospitality Review* (Spring 1995).

(as today's piña coladas and rum punches are called in the trade) were not much in evidence and served mainly to the few people who didn't drink regularly. The conventional wisdom was that if you didn't eat and drink until you practically passed out (hopefully in the company of an attractive companion), you didn't have a successful cruise.

Industry food and beverage veterans point out that wine lists on early ships were quite narrow by today's standards. California wine was unheard of. Early cruisers demanded European wines and champagnes. Choices ran a rather limited gamut from *rouge ordinaire* to Moët et Chandon White Star non-vintage champagne and Dom Perignon. Lancers, Mateus rosé, and Blue Nun Liebfraumilch were popular favorites of the time. Today's wine lists are significantly more extensive and include the notable addition of Californian, Australian, and Italian selections. A theme that will be repeated frequently is that the cruise industry changes its product offerings to keep pace with lifestyle changes with the vacationing public. Today's winelists on Carnival, for example, are far more extensive than those of the luxury and premium lines of even ten years ago. As Americans became more wine savvy, they expected broader, more sophisticated wine lists.

All of this meant that a good deal of provisions and water had to be brought aboard, as cruises were typically seven days or longer and there were no reliable provisioners in the Caribbean ports of call. Storage rooms and freezers were stuffed to the gills (as were the passengers). Sometimes the lack of storage space proved an embarrassment. Take the case of death at sea. Today's ships have morgues because passengers who suffer fatal heart attacks, for example, can hardly be off-loaded at the next port. But these facilities are relatively new; the custom in the 1970s was to wrap dead bodies and store them in the freezer. There was one story (true) about a butcher who removed a package of what he believed to be beef from the freezer. When he began to unwrap it, a human foot appeared and the poor man went running and screaming from the galley. He was so upset that the doctor finally had to sedate him.

Today's foodservice is different. To begin with, marine architects now work with chefs and marketing executives to determine how to best satisfy the needs of the target market for a new ship. This results in menus specifically designed to please those market segments the ship intends to attract. Once the caliber of food is selected, the galley size and the equipment that will be needed to produce that style of foodservice and the specific menu selections are designed—not before. For instance, when Seabourn commissioned its ships, its research showed that luxury travelers regarded the perceived quality of a line's cuisine as the single most important factor in determining the success or failure of the entire cruise. They recognized that all meals on this luxurious vessel would need to be true haute cuisine—or, as they decided to dub it, "nouvelle classic." This style of food would be cooked to order—à la minute. Also, the galley had to be able to offer many special orders that were not even on the menus. There were two more considerations at this point in the planning process: the amount of space that had been set aside for the galley and the number of crew available. With this information factored in, a menu plan was established. Each dinner menu would contain four appetizers (two hot, two cold), three soups (two hot, one cold), two salads, five entrées (one fish, one seafood, one roast, one grill, and one sauté), a cold seafood plate, and four desserts. Similar decisions were made for breakfast service (in-suite, restaurant, and verandah buffet), luncheon, twenty-four-hour suite service, tea service, and the cocktail hour. Sample menus were then developed for each of these. Furthermore, it was recognized that for proper restaurant service the food would have to be plated in the kitchen to ensure an attractive presentation.

Once Seabourn executives knew what the galley had to produce, they were in a position to design it. There were some immediate problems to overcome. One was the shape of the space that had been allocated for the galley; this was broken into a U shape because of a large spiral staircase that descends through the center of the ship. Then there was placement of equipment. For example, the hot galley (where the hot dishes are cooked) had to be placed as close as possible to the exit into the dining room so passengers would receive their hot food hot. Plating the food in the kitchen also required special storage space for the silver cloches that cover each plate while en route to the table. And, of course, all designs and equipment had to conform to the sanitation standards of the U.S. Public Health Service.[4]

Another design consideration is the kitchen organization, which on a ship may be very different than in traditional land-based resorts. Dedrick Van Regemorter, a Holland America hotel director and formerly with Marriott's Marco Island Resort, points out that in a typical land-based resort one might find a hot preparation area, a cold preparation area, a banquet kitchen, and an à la minute section. But the *Star Princess* galley, for example, is more traditional, with a sauce station, a soup station, a vegetable station, and fry and grill stations.

The point here is that because people are different, menus are different, and because menus are different, ships themselves must be designed differently. One of the mass-market cruise lines, in an effort to improve foodservice, invited culinary consultants on board for a month to make recommendations for improvement of the product. One of the

---

[4]We wish to acknowledge the assistance of Larry Rapp, Vice President, Hotel Operations, Seabourn, in developing this material.

recommendations seemed simple enough: Plate the entrées in the kitchen so they could be decorated for that "nouvelle cuisine" look—for example, make the carrots look like butterflies and the tomatoes look like flowers and add a few swirls of colorful sauces. However, to implement this simple solution would require more chefs in the galley. The crew quarters had been designed carefully with room for only a fixed number of food and beverage personnel. That number could not be increased without reducing the number of cabin stewards, social staff, or other equally important personnel. As a result of this physical constraint, the program was not implemented on that cruise line.

Storage space for provisions is another constraint. The *Queen Mary 2* carries 1,433 items in its food inventory on an average sailing—about three times as much as many full-service hotels require to operate. A Carnival ship's provision list is 950–980 food items. Remember, if you run out of bananas at sea (which American Family Cruises—no longer in business—did on her inaugural voyage), you can't call up a vendor to send for more. The amount of space needed for provisions is a subtle calculus involving the complexity of the inventory, the number of days between provisionings, and the food and beverage management's focus on efficiency. Obviously, the more frequently a ship can provision, the less storage room is needed. The ability to minimize waste and to watch for slow-moving items (by adjusting par stocks) assures no unnecessary storage. This becomes critical as the vessel ages. Why? Because the provision stores were planned and designed years earlier. In the case of the *Carnival Liberty,* her provision stores design dates back to 2000, but food choices have been greatly expanded over those intervening years and will inevitably continue to expand, requiring better storage utilization to compensate for the inability to add space.

Provisioning a ship poses a series of unique problems. First of all, there is the matter of vendors. Cruise ships have a very short turnaround cycle—in the port of Miami, a ship arrives at 7 A.M., the waste is off-loaded, and new provisions for the next cruise have to be on board by 4 P.M., when the ship is ready to sail. That means suppliers have just a few hours to load provisions. Because storage space is at a premium, virtually the whole ship must be restocked—even down to the ketchup and mustard used on the hamburgers and hot dogs. While just-in-time inventory control is now the standard in retail and manufacturing, it has been a linchpin of the cruise industry for over thirty years. Not only must provisions be delivered on time but also there is no room for quality errors. There is no time to replace a crate of spoiled tomatoes. If they are discovered at sea, it is too late. For quality reasons, ships generally cannot be provisioned at ports of call (notable exceptions are local seafood and produce). Even when cruising the Mediterranean, lines regularly fly in beef and other foodstuffs from the United States. The cuts and quality of beef available in Europe are generally different from those that satisfy the tastes of American passengers. To supply the voracious appetite of cruise lines, many vendors have set up separate operations. City Sea Food, a Los Angeles–based food wholesaler, has an office and cold storage plant in Miami that employs fifty people and supplies Carnival, NCL, and Princess ships. Vendors have even formed their own trade group, the Marine Hotel Catering and Duty Free Association, based in Sausalito, California. Estimated annual purchases of food and beverages by the cruise lines top more than $1.3 billion!

Today's cruise menus are much more varied than ever before—and a good deal healthier. The change, just as with smoking, has to do with the changing American lifestyle, which calls for an increased emphasis on fitness and healthy diet. Restaurants were quick to respond to new consumer demands for lighter and healthier foods. McDonald's introduced salads; pasta started appearing on more menus, along with a larger selection of seafood and poultry dishes than in prior years. The cruise lines were at first hesitant to follow their lead. In the minds of many passengers, quality equaled quantity, and the kind of quantity people wanted was lots of prime roasts, 16-ounce New York strip steaks, and mounds of ice cream topping their enormous slices of fresh baked apple pie. But as post-cruise comment cards reflected a real demand for lighter fare, lines started experimenting with adding healthier dishes and smaller portions. Curiously enough, it didn't come easily. Restaurants were universally applauded for responding to dietary concerns; indeed, some writers suggested it was unethical not to offer a wide variety of healthy dishes because traditional menus forced people to eat foods with too many calories, too much fat, or an overload of sodium.

On the other hand, some travel agents (especially the more corpulent freeloaders) immediately complained that the cruise lines were trying to cut costs by serving lighter foods and smaller portions! *ASTA Agency Management* actually ran an article in February 1992 titled "Cruise Cuisine: Cutting Costs or Cutting Calories?" In fact, healthier food is often more difficult and more expensive to prepare. Lendal Kotschevar and Marcel Escoffier, in their well-known text *Management by Menu,* third edition (John Wiley and Sons, Inc.) point out that food costs increase when the variety of menu selections is expanded, which results in increased spoilage.

To ignore passengers' dietary concerns is not only insensitive but bad business. Enough variety must be offered to satisfy every taste and health concern. All of the North American–based cruise lines recognize this. Today, Holland America, for instance, offers seven regular dinner entrées each evening, including a vegetarian entrée such as vegetable kebab, and a "light and healthy entrée" prepared in accordance with the American Heart Association and low in cholesterol and sodium. Even most of the regular entrées are available without sauce on request. Carnival labels certain appetizers, salads, entrées, and even desserts as either "low-carb selection" or "Spa Carnival," which indicates items that are low in sodium, cholesterol, and fat. Salads are prepared with diet dressing, and desserts are made with NutraSweet instead of sugar. Royal Caribbean has a similar system on their dinner menus; they call it their "Shipshape" program. Princess also identifies dishes that are low in calories and can be served plain with no sauce. All of these lines also invite passengers with special dietary needs to contact the maître d'.

Cruise lines today have become more sophisticated in their menu planning. Both Princess and Holland America told us about changes they made every year when they repositioned ships from Alaska to the Caribbean. Princess is sensitive to taste buds. Their experience is that Alaska passengers prefer food of a higher caloric content that is not highly spiced. It has to do with the climate. They have found that the closer their ships come to the equator, the spicier and lighter the food has to be to entice their passengers. Holland America noted that in the Caribbean their passengers were younger than on their Alaska cruises, which is not surprising, considering that the airfare to Miami from most places is considerably less than the airfare to Vancouver or Anchorage. At any rate, younger passengers have larger appetites. When on one cruise a table of eight guests ordered fifteen entrées, the company realized they needed to increase their portion size!

Nevertheless, not all has changed. Even celebrity chefs are still used. César Ritz is gone, but his nautical dining tradition lingers. Celebrity Cruise Lines uses famed Michelin three-star chef Michel Roux as a "cuisine consultant." Roux develops recipes and sails aboard Celebrity ships several times annually to assess the quality, preparation, and presentation of the food. He is also closely involved in wine selection. Windstar uses Joachim Splichel, the *Queen Mary 2* uses Todd English, and Carnival uses Georges Blanc, a twenty-five-year, three-star Michelin chef from Vonnas, France. But the truth is, while all lines strive for a high quality of shipboard cuisine, there is and will always be a limiting factor. True gourmet cuisine must be cooked à la minute, and when you are feeding 1,000 people at a time, that is a virtual impossibility. However, the cruise industry has, in fact, developed a widely held reputation for outstanding food and foodservice. When you consider that a cruise ship can serve 1,000 or more meals at a single sitting—at top restaurant quality—it's no wonder that food is one of the significant factors that has helped cruise lines achieve the high satisfaction rates they enjoy. After all, reflect on what your dining experience was like when you last ate at a hotel with 1,000 fellow diners! Let's face it: Convention fare, while improved over the years, is pretty uninspiring.

Research supports these satisfaction ratings. In one independent study of travel agents, more than a dozen cruise lines, including all of those mentioned here, received a score of nine or ten (ten being the highest possible) for providing high-quality gourmet food. This contrasts sharply to the hotel industry. With hotels, because 70 percent of the revenue and a larger percentage of the profits come from the rooms division, foodservice is often regarded as a necessary evil—a convenience for the guest that must be provided. Few hotels have set out to offer food beyond the commonplace. (Las Vegas hotels are, of course, noted exceptions.) Moreover, because the typical hotel cannot count on a stable, predictable, controlled utilization of restaurant facilities, food quality and service suffer. Importantly, on a ship, dining room utilization and consumer demand is predictable and controlled even to the point of knowing exactly what percentage of the guests will opt for veal milanaise at the captain's dinner or escargot on French night. As a result, at any comparable price point, cruise ships deliver a superior food product than their land-based competitors because there is practically no spoilage.

But the story is even better than that! Because of the precise predictability, high utilization of food, and fresh foodstuffs, almost any cruise ship can offer a better dining experience at a much lower cost—thus contributing meaningfully to the value advantage cruising has long been able to offer compared with a land vacation.

The cruise industry looks at food costs on a per diem or per passenger day basis. In the ultra-luxury end of the market, it is not uncommon to spend $25 to $30 a day for the raw food (exclusive of labor and overhead). In the premium segment, the cost is typically in the neighborhood of $10 to $16. For contemporary ships, food costs run $9 to $13 a day. Bear in mind that these costs include the food consumed throughout a twenty-four-hour day. A passenger can have (and some do) breakfast in the cabin, another one on deck, and a third in the dining room. That's not all. They can eat lunch twice—on deck and in the dining room—and then tackle an eight-course dinner! Of course, there are also midmorning and midafternoon snacks to tide you over, as well as one or two late-night buffets. If that's not enough—if you're still hungry—most ships offer twenty-four-hour room service. Many have pizza and ice cream bars open much of the day. All of these dining opportunities are included in the price.

In contrast, the rule of thumb in the restaurant business is that food costs ought to run between 25 and 30 percent of the selling price. Compared to a mass-market cruise line with a food cost of $10 per day, any restaurant or hotel would have to charge $33 to $40 per person for a comparable array of food offered throughout the day to be competitive. It's unlikely that any land-based foodservice operation could survive on such pricing! In addition to predictability of usage, the cruise industry benefits from enormous economies of scale, which further drive costs down. Carnival Cruise Lines, for example, uses 67,300 dozen eggs every single week throughout the year. In addition, their passengers consume 39,460 pounds of tenderloin; 47,300 pounds of prime rib; 109,700 pounds of chicken; and 2,750 cases of wine and champagne each week. On the *Carnival Liberty* alone, during an average *week* guests consume 2,200 pounds of prime rib; 4,500 pounds of chicken; 2,500 steaks; 15,000 pounds of shrimp; 1,000 pounds of lobster tail; 400 pounds of veal; 4,800 hamburgers; 2,200 hot dogs; 1,300 pounds of baby back ribs; 600 pounds of ham; 900 pounds of salmon; 1,000 pounds of pasta; 7,000 pizzas; 3,000 pounds of tomatoes; 6,700 pounds of potatoes; 5,300 heads of lettuce; 4,320 bananas; 2,500 apples; 1,003 melons; 1,100 pineapples; 6,200 pounds of flour; 22,000 eggs; 36,000 slices of bacon; 12,900 slices of white bread; 20,000 Danish pastries; 900 gallons of milk; 1,000 pounds of coffee; and 620 gallons of fruit juice. Obviously, with these huge quantities, purveyors sharpen their pencils to offer terrific prices. Part of the cost savings results from inexpensive distribution. Only twenty-one ships account for this usage. Even when a large hotel chain negotiates a blanket food contract, the cost of distributing small amounts to hundreds of hotels around the country negates much of the savings.

Remember, too, that these economies are achieved by serving identical menus on all ships in a given brand's fleet, a strategy utilized by all of the cruise lines. This is one reason why the major lines tend to build ships that have similar configuration and size, although their interior décor may vary significantly. Ships are often built simultaneously and side by side. Similar layouts and size translate into similar menus, which allows for the economies that result in increased value for customers. Carnival's eight Fantasy-class ships are examples of this. All Fantasy-class ships have the same size storerooms, kitchens, and dining rooms, and, of course, identical menus on the same itineraries! Royal Caribbean's quintet of Voyager-class vessels is equally successful through comparable, uniform designs.

⚓ The Lido

Twenty-five years ago on a Carnival ship, a lido lunch consisted of hamburgers and hot dogs with tomatoes, lettuce, and cheese to accompany, and french fries or potato chips. This was offered as a convenience for the sun worshipers who chose not to change out of their bathing suits for lunch in the dining room. (Back then, the majority of the cruisers ate all their meals in the dining room.)

Today at lunch, the lido restaurants on Carnival ships feature New York–style deli fare, Chinese food, eight different pizzas, elaborate salad bars, a carving station, four or five hot entrées, soup, a wide variety of side dishes, and desserts. Lidos on the post-2000 Carnival ships feature "Taste of the Nations"—a different international (French, Indian, Italian, etc.) cuisine each day, as well as a fish and chips seafood restaurant. Clearly, one of the advantages of today's larger ships is the space available to provide such an extensive variety of food choices.

Alternative Dining

Another new phenomenon of recent years is the availability of one or more extra-cost dining options. Royal Caribbean offers Chops Grille at $20 per guest and Johnny Rockets at $3.95. NCL offers Cagney's Steakhouse at a price of $20 per cover. Princess offers Bayou Café casual fare at $15 per cover, as well as an upscale Italian restaurant, Sabatini's, at $20 per cover. Celebrity offers a specialty restaurant on their newer ships named after famous ocean liners; the price is $30 per guest. Disney offers Palo at $10 per guest. Beginning with the Spirit Class vessels in 2001, all new Carnival ships feature a supper club with live music and dancing as a dining alternative at $30 per cover. Holland America features the Pinnacle Grille at $20 per guest.

Games People Play

Activities on earlier ships were constrained by space because there were only a few inside public rooms. The largest of these, besides the dining room, was the grand saloon or main show lounge, which was used for entertainment and dancing and a movie theater showing as many as three different movies a day. Because there was little awareness of physical fitness concerns in the 1970s, most activities were not designed to keep you healthy—just happy.

In good weather, as many things as possible were scheduled on deck—table tennis, shuffleboard, and calisthenics were particularly popular, as were other kinds of fun and games. Humorist Richard Gordon tells of a cruise he took in 1967:

> The passengers on a cruise thus face the same situation as so inconvenienced the *Bounty* mutineers on Pitcairn Island. Any females available must be fought for, and the nicer they are the nastier the scrap. Blatant rough-and-tumbles on the boat deck being frowned on by authorities, the aggression becomes restricted to the ship's games. I once watched a pair of Tarzans

playing the finals of a deck tennis competition, under a blazing sun and the eyes of the sexiest girl aboard, with a ferocity that ended the contest by putting one in the ship's hospital with a suspected fractured ankle, and the other with a suspected coronary occlusion. Table-tennis, the rowing machine, the gymnasium, fixed bicycle, pillow fighting on the greasy pole, even bouncing on the trampoline are similarly abused as primeval exhibitions of masculine vigor. Even *Walking* is a perilous activity at sea. The knowledge that five times around the promenade equals a mile seems to obsess overweight males who ashore wouldn't stroll out to post a letter.[5]

In the evening, entertainment consisted mostly of a vaudeville variety show and events in which the passengers participated, such as dancing. Dancing was, in fact, very popular, and most ships had an orchestra to replicate the sounds of Tommy Dorsey, Benny Goodman, and the like.

Joseph Meltzer of Fort Lauderdale, Florida, showed us his dance card and program for Ladies Night aboard Norwegian American Line's *Sagafjord* in the 1970s. This kind of entertainment, often called Sadie Hawkins Night, was universally popular in those early days.

Here are the rules for the evening's entertainment printed on the *Sagafjord*'s card:

1. Only ladies are allowed to ask gentlemen for dances.
2. Ladies must not leave their dancing partners stranded on the dance floor, but must escort them back to their seats.
3. Ladies may buy gentlemen drinks, but no propositions are allowed.
4. Ladies must light gentlemen's cigarettes or cigars.
5. Ladies must use discretion and not try to dance with the same partner twice.
6. Ladies are cautioned against pinching gentlemen.
7. Ladies are requested not to use cheek-to-cheek tactics while dancing and should face their partners at all times.
8. Ladies are not permitted to tempt men with offers of vicuña coats and Cadillacs.

---

[5]Richard Gordon, "Salt Water Hikers, Etc.," quoted in *All in the Same Boat: The Humorists' Guide to the Ocean Cruise*," ed. Robert Wechler (Highland Park, N.J.: Catbird, 1988), 62. Copyright 1967 Richard Gordon, by permission of Curtis Brown.

9. Single girls are at liberty to ask bachelors for their hands.
10. Ladies should select gentlemen other than their own husbands.

There were spaces on the card for twelve dances, including a Viennese waltz, a foxtrot, a quickstep, jive, a rhumba, and a blank line next to each to fill in the name of the gentleman scheduled to dance with.

Other popular forms of entertainment included 1950s and 1960s Night and Amateur Night. Passengers who wished to sing, perform magic tricks, or even recite poetry could do so. For others who wished to participate but had no special talents, the cruise director would devise a skit, which any couple could perform. One favorite was "Nothing to declare," in which the husband was given a uniform and asked to play the role of a customs inspector. His wife was given a heavy wool coat. The dialog went something like this:

Inspector: What did you buy on this cruise?
Woman: I have nothing to declare.
Inspector: You mean you didn't buy anything?
Woman: I have nothing to declare.
Inspector: Why are you wearing that heavy coat?
Woman: I have to carry it off the ship.
Inspector: Would you take it off please?
Woman: (*Holding it tightly*) I'm too cold.
Inspector then reaches for coat and opens it over woman's protests, revealing linings on both sides with knives, forks, watches, etc., sewed on.

Passengers also participated in a cruise version of the then-popular TV show *The Newlywed Game.* The idea was to see how many intimate details spouses knew about each other. There were prizes not only for the newlyweds on the ship but also for those who had been married a long time. While one spouse was off stage, the other would be asked questions such as "What is the name of the girl who gave your husband his first kiss?" and "What size bra does your wife wear?" Spouses were then brought back on stage, and the ones with the most correct answers won.

For the masquerade party, those passengers who had not brought costumes from home were given basic materials like poster board in various colors, pieces of fabric, safety pins, and crayons so they could make their own outfits (with the help of a cruise staff member). On one Princess Cruise in the Caribbean, the winner was a woman with an oversized behind who pinned clumps of navy blue fabric all over her rear and sang, "I found my thrill on Blueberry Hill."

Show Business at Sea

Of course, there was some professional entertainment as well. Former Royal Caribbean Cruise executive Pete Whelpton remembers, "We provided a three-act, hour-and-a-half variety show in those days, two days a week on our seven-day cruises. Usually they were on the evenings when we held the Captain's Welcome Aboard Dinner and the Captain's Farewell Dinner, which were also our formal nights. The show opened with a vocalist. Then there was a stand-up comedian, and finally there was always what we called a sight or specialty act—a juggler, single-wheeled cyclist, magician, or even a harmonica player." Joe Villa was a popular comedian on early Royal Caribbean cruises who often did the opening act for Frank Sinatra. Villa would come on stage dressed in his tux and singing "I'm gonna live till I die." People thought he was a crooner, but forty-five seconds into his act he'd convulse, jump into the air, and fall down flat on the stage. He would then pick himself up and go into his comedy routine.

On some cruise lines, the stand-up comedian recruited from the Borscht Belt also doubled as the cruise director and acted as master of ceremonies during the show-and-tell jokes, such as these two that were told to us by the *Star Princess*'s cruise director, Mark Iannazzo:

> Just before sailing, a new bride told her husband that she had left her birth control pills home and was worried about getting seasick. He told her not to worry—there was still time for him to get off the ship and go to a drugstore. When he got there, he told the druggist, "I need some birth control pills and some Dramamine." The druggist looked at him and said, "Pardon me, but if it makes you sick, why do you do it?"
>
> Then there's the story of the passenger who was locked in her cabin all day and finally calls the purser's desk and said, "I can't get out of my cabin, there's no door." "Of course there is, Madam," said the purser. "As a matter of fact, there are two doors in your cabin." "I know," she said, "but one goes into the bathroom and the other one has a sign on it that says "Do not disturb."
>
> Brian Price, the cruise director on the *Queen Mary 2*, has been a cruise director since 1969. Recalling the 1970s, he says, "The cruise director in those days would stand at the gangway and welcome the passengers onboard and be on the gangway at every port of call. He would wave good-bye to the passengers as they went off on shore excursions.
>
> "In those days we'd make our own shows and bunch shows together, and we'd use the cruise staff and anybody else we

could get our hands on. We could even put a French night together. I remember in the days of the *QE2*, before the days of proper production shows, I put a show together called an around-the-world show. We did it basically with just cruise staff and the musicians. The bandleader wrote the music. It was bits of comedy. We had a plywood cutout of the *QE2* that went across the stage. There were things that happened on the ship and things that happened off the ship, and that was what the show was. We put that show together ourselves, and it was very, very popular. You wouldn't survive in the industry now if you were doing those things."

Today, given the competition for vacationers, entertainment quality has become a major strategic weapon and one in which the major players spare no expense. Comedians who have been featured on *Saturday Night Live* and the Comedy Channel are commonplace.

But more than anything, a trademark of the big contemporary and premium ships is the lavish Las Vegas–style production show, produced twice nightly. These are huge productions with casts of as many as thirty performers accompanied by a full orchestra in a show lounge typically seating 1,000 or more guests and using state-of-the-art equipment. John Maxtone-Graham recalls watching in awe a huge video wall, the only one afloat at that time, being installed in the Sound of Music Show Lounge at the Chantiers de l'Atlantique shipyard in France, which was building the *Monarch of the Seas* for Royal Caribbean Cruises. The screen can be suspended in alternative flexible modes—either as two separate sections, each five screens by five screens square, or joined into one broad façade. Thus, the video wall can hang to either side of the stage or be united to form a fifty-screen mega-show effect as a backdrop during production shows.

These theaters are among the most complicated parts of a ship to put together because they depend so much on special effects and computers. To begin with, there is the question of where to put them. They are huge—often three or more decks high for seating and space on an additional deck for the sets to be raised and lowered. Theaters are noisy—on Carnival ships, for example, staff cabins rather than guest cabins are located above and below show lounges. They must be well insulated, as these people have rotating shifts and are often trying to sleep while the shows are on. Show rooms require complicated audio and lighting equipment built especially for use at sea, as standard theater equipment is not designed to function in the rigors of a seagoing environment. Land equipment is not designed to withstand the vibrations from machines and propellers. Moreover, because the equipment is placed on a ship, the weight must be evenly distributed. You can't necessarily just put lights and speakers where they logically ought to go; if you do, it may affect the stability of the ship. Regulations, installation materials and methods, ceiling heights, electrical systems—everything is different from working on land. Power consumption, a factor hardly ever considered in designing land-based theaters, is crucial; more power means more cables, which can easily add a couple of tons to the ship's weight and thus reduce her speed.

Nevertheless, being able to mount a top-quality show is crucial, and that depends, to a large extent, on the technical facilities. The Carnival Destiny- and Conquest-class vessels feature a traditional-style orchestra pit that can be raised and lowered in front of a 58-foot-wide stage housing a 26-foot turntable, smoke ejectors, and substantial laser pyrotechnic and scene projection equipment.

The *Grand Princess,* which debuted in 1997, was the first ship to feature a motion-based virtual reality theater and a blue-screen room that gives passengers who yearn to be in show business the chance to star in their own video production. The *Sun Princess,* introduced in December 1995, features two main show lounges, both theater and cabaret style. Celebrity's 1,740-passenger *Millennium* boasts a show room designed to replicate an outdoor amphitheater. Designed for Broadway-scale productions, it includes fly towers, a telescoping wall, a revolving stage, a hydraulic orchestra pit, interactive equipment, and sophisticated sound, lighting, and special effects.

Once you have the equipment, you still need the shows. These are often provided by theatrical production firms that specialize in cruise line entertainment. One such company is Jean Anne Ryan Productions in Fort Lauderdale, Florida, which provides the entertainment for Norwegian Cruise Line ships; another is Stilesto Entertainment, with offices in Los Angeles and London, which produces the Holland America shows. An exception is Carnival; as Brent Mitchell, cruise director on *Carnival Liberty,* points out, "We're very proud of the fact that, at Carnival, all the show production is done in house. We probably are the largest show production company in the country." Roger Blum, Carnival's vice president of cruise programming, notes, "We're in the vacation business—people want great vacation experiences. On the entertainment end, we want to be able to offer equal or better to what they would find in Las Vegas, New York, London, or Paris. By bringing the production in house, we felt we had better control over the product. At least, for better or worse, it is on our shoulders. We felt we would have much better control over the product from beginning to end."

In the old days, with small ships, scenery was controlled by an up-and-down button that lifted and lowered the sets. Today, on the larger ships (typically 70,000-plus GRT) there are so many sets, turntable sets, and lifts that automation is the only way to animate. There are so many computers for video, special effects, scenery, turntables, and so on that there's actually a computer called "show control" that coordinates all the other computers! Again, there are differences asea that require special consideration. Costumes must be lighter than in the theater. Dance routines must be choreographed so they can be performed easily even if there is some motion aboard the ship. And because different itineraries attract audiences of different age groups and cultural backgrounds, music must be adapted to the tastes of the audience.

While the cast of the production shows stay on the ship (typically under a six-month contract) many larger lines use so-called fly act performers. These may be comedians, vocalists, magicians, or jugglers who move around ships of the fleet. It's possible that a comedian may perform on three ships in a given week. In this way, the audience on each ship sees these performers only once each but sees much more variety in the entertainment. The same crew cabin that housed the vocalist will be used for the comedian and then the magician over the course of a week. While it obviously costs to fly these people around, it's worth it to keep the entertainment fresh and varied.

This is another huge advantage for cruising versus hotels and resorts, which typically contract entertainers for months at a time and simply don't have the size or scale to offer the breadth of entertainment cruising provides. While destinations such as Las Vegas and New York do offer this, the onus is on the customer to secure tickets and transportation between hotels and theaters to take advantage of this variety. On a cruise ship, guests merely stroll from their cabin and enjoy a wide variety of great entertainment without tickets, cover charges, drink minimums, or transportation. Talk about convenience!

Everything, of course, is not better than it used to be. Some niceties have disappeared—some because of the large number of passengers on today's ships, and some because of our contemporary lifestyle. For instance, all of the old Home Line ships used to feature reserved teak deck chairs. When one boarded the ship, usually before or immediately after sailing, passengers could go to the sun deck and pick a teak deck chair. Staff would insert their name in a holder, and thus that chair was reserved for them exclusively for the duration of the cruise. Home Lines also published a passenger list by the third day out so people could check off the names of people they met and remember them. Today, people value their privacy more and probably wouldn't want a passenger list published (although luxury lines like Seabourn and Silverseas still provide them). As for reserved deck chairs, the informal lifestyle of a ship today makes that an anachronism.

Ships like those of Royal Caribbean's Freedom class feature ice-skating rinks, rock-climbing walls, a wave machine where folks can surf, and a five-story indoor mall-like promenade with myriad shops and bars. The Carnival Conquest-class vessels feature twenty-two bars and lounges as well as the multistory Carnival signature waterslide. Some Princess and Carnival ships have huge outdoor TV screens offering news in the morning, movies, concerts, games for children, and music videos. Some Celebrity ships offer Cirque de Soleil entertainers. Crystal, Princess, and Holland America offer interactive cooking demonstrations in state-of-the-art kitchen theaters. Clearly, the cruise industry is listening to the vacationing public and responding with a wide variety of entertainment and activity options. Consider these two daily activity sheets for a typical day at sea:

Carnival Capers

80s Retro Dance Party	Dance and Party Music	Piano Bar Music
Basketball and Volleyball	Dance Music	Ping Pong
Big Screen Movie	Famous Faces Trivia	Rockin' Party Music
Blackjack Tournament	Fitness Fantasia	Secrets to a Flat Stomach
BODYStep Aerobics Class	Funship Airbrushed Tatoos	Shuffleboard
BODYSymmetry Stretch	Island Music on Deck	Skincare Secrets
and Relax Class	Jazz Trio Music	Soft Dance Music
Camp Carnival	Karaoke Kraziness	Sunset Yoga
Classical Music	Mocktail Party	Teen Disco
Club O2	Perfect Abs	Wacky Trivia Quiz
Cocktail Music		

Celebrity Today

Wake-Up Stretch	Table Tennis	Art Lecture
Step Aerobics	Jenga	Computer Class
Virtual Cycling	Paddle Tennis	Celebrity Discoveries
Virtual Gold Simulator	Tri-Bond Trivia Quiz	Enrichment Series
and Lessons	Golf Putting Contest	Doubles Paddle Tennis
Movie Time	Pictionary	Fragrance and Cosmetics
Walk-a-Thon	Volleyball Play	Seminar
Sit and Be Fit Class	Matchword Game	Dewars Scotch Seminar
Daily Quiz and	Barbados Folkloric	Happy Hour
Crossword	Show	Catholic Mass
Shuffleboard	Basketball Free Throw	Serenada Quartet
Morning Chat	Competition	Unison Duo
Morning Trivia	Champagne Tasting	Piano Bar
Bridge Play	Island Music	Cigars Under the Stars
Acupuncture at Sea	Battle of the Sexes Trivia	Lightning Bingo

Now we all know that folks can't possibly do everything that's offered. But that's not the point. They have the option, the choice, to be as active or passive as they wish. We believe the ability to have such a wide spectrum to choose from, on a daily or even hourly basis, is very much appreciated by vacationers today and almost unique to cruising.

There's No Business Like Fat Business

Picture the gymnasium of a cruise ship sailing out of the port of Miami in the early 1970s. The room was 20 feet square. One wall was mirrored from floor to ceiling, with a dance barre bisecting it. Typically, the room was located in the bowels of the vessel in a hard-to-find, out-of-the-way spot. Presumably, the conventional wisdom of the time was that those few people who wished to exercise would be sufficiently motivated to find the place!

The equipment consisted of a vinyl-jacketed exercise mat, a manual cast-iron and wood rowing machine, and the watchamacallit—that funny-looking machine with the big strap that went around your fanny. When you flipped on the toggle switch, the strap would simultaneously undulate and vibrate. As you stood up and leaned back, theoretically, your caboose would get loose and the pounds would melt away. No respectable cruise ship of that day would be without this gizmo.

As you can imagine, the fat-consuming, cholesterol-unconscious passenger complement had little interest in shedding their recently garnered tonnage. Today—my, how times have changed!

Today's passengers expect cruise ships to have thousands of square feet of exercise and spa area. Electronic rowers with computerized graphics, Stairmasters, treadmills, elliptical machines, and exercise bicycles have replaced the manual rowing machine. But that's not all: There are free weights, progressive-resistance exercise stations, steam baths, saunas, massage rooms, herbal wrap rooms, mud baths, and more. The small gym of twenty-five years ago may have cost $1,000 or so to equip. Today, cruise ships spend four to six times that amount on just one machine! A well-equipped spa today occupies more than 8,000 square feet, has a staff of roughly twenty professional trainers, aerobic instructors, masseuses, and spa technicians, and can cost in excess of $3 million. In fact, cruise facilities put most resort and hotel spas to shame!

The spa services themselves have evolved from the simple massage and facial to aromatherapies, hot stone massage, couples massage, thalasso therapy pools, rasul rooms, and pilates and yoga lessons. Med-spa services include teeth whitening, botox, collagen, and hyaluronic acid treatments. The spa industry has more than doubled between 1999 and

2004. As Glenn Fusfield, CEO of Steiner Leisure Ltd., the largest spa provider in the world, relates:

> The spa industry of the future knows no boundaries. It seeps into every facet of life because the spa lifestyle is as much about a way of thinking as it is an activity. At one time, a show in the morning was a luxury. And so it is with the spa experience today. For some it is a luxury, but soon it will have a permanent thread in the social fabric of our lives.

Start 'Em Young

Back in the early 1970s, children were seen aboard cruise ships over the holidays and during the summer only. Pundits said cruising was for old people—and their parents.

At Carnival, the marketing folks reasoned that it took roughly the same amount of effort to appeal to a family with children as it did to the senior market. The bonus, of course, was obvious: If you could get a young couple with children to try cruising, they had the opportunity to purchase cruises for many more years than a senior. Acclimating a child to cruising was the equivalent of a seventy-year annuity!

The company started Camp Carnival, a program of planned and organized activities for kids from the age of two. The program was first offered during times when children were not in school (the summer and holiday season) but it quickly, by positive word of mouth, became a year-round program. To give you an idea of its growth, in 2005 Carnival carried over 550,000 children, more than any other line and more than the *total* number of guests it carried sixteen years before.

Other contemporary lines offered similar children's programs but were limited to some degree in attracting families by the small size of their cabins. In the mid- to late 1990s, even the premium lines were retooling their products to offer child and teen areas and activities.

Teenagers were a particular challenge to cruise lines in the 1970s and 1980s. As they were too old for children's programming, they preferred to roam about the ship, much like hanging out at shopping malls. In recent years, the cruise lines figured out that what teens wanted was their own space, separate from the younger kids and the adults. A dedicated, teen-oriented cruise staff member provides the focus for activities and entertainment. At Royal Caribbean, the teen program is called Navigator, at Princess it's Off Limits, at NCL it's Teens Crew, at Celebrity it's Celebrity X Club, at Carnival it's Club O2, and at Costa it's TeenZone.

This recent focus on children created the opportunity for the cruise industry to capitalize on the multigenerational vacation market. Three or four generations could travel together in ease and comfort, knowing that everyone would be entertained and catered to in grand fashion. Importantly, the adults don't feel compelled to spend their vacation entertaining the youngsters. Few places shoreside offer programs even remotely comparable to those on cruise ships today. And of course, on a cruise, no one has to cook or clean up.

Ports of Call

Ports of call in the Caribbean were the same ones that are still popular today, but they often lacked the infrastructure to handle the number of passengers that even a small ship brought in at one time. Few buses were available, so tours were most often sightseeing rather than experience oriented. Given their age, cruisers in the 1970s generally weren't interested in participative sports such as snorkeling, golf, or horseback riding on the beach. You'd climb in a taxi that would show you the governor's home, a sugar or banana plantation, the marketplace, and the rain forest. Then you'd return to the ship. The most popular Caribbean tours by far were the nightclub shows in San Juan and Nassau. Few cruisers had ever seen a flesh-and-feathers production show unless they had visited Las Vegas or Paris. The ones in San Juan featured name entertainers like Sophie Tucker, Sammy Davis Jr., and even Jack Benny (who owned a piece of the Condado Beach Hotel and played there every year). There were casinos in the Puerto Rican hotels but none on the cruise ships (except for slot machines). Casinos were introduced slowly into cruising because operators were fearful of getting involved with organized crime. Carnival began operating full casinos in 1975. Royal Caribbean didn't have them until the late 1970s because their Norwegian owners were opposed to them.

The number of ports of call in the Caribbean has grown to match both the growth of the cruise industry and the appetites of experienced cruisers to try new and different locales. The tables on the following page show the year-round Caribbean ports of call utilized in 1970 as well as the extended list thirty-five years later, in 2005. Note the 75 percent increase in ports of call. Clearly, necessity is the mother of invention.

The cruise industry has grown twenty-fold between 1970 and 2006. In the early years, with smaller number of passengers, fewer and smaller ships, the passengers were older, typically empty nesters, with relatively simple tastes. Today's cruise vacationer is everyman—and, consequently, the ship's product delivery, whether food, entertainment, or ports of call, of necessity is more diverse and complex, complementing more diverse vacationers.

While there has been an impressive growth in the number of ports offered in the Caribbean, growth has barely kept pace with the demand. Some ports are woefully congested on peak days. They simply have not

Caribbean Ports of Call: 1970s Versus 2005

Region	1970s	2005	Change
Bahamas	2	2	+0.0%
Florida	1	3	+200.0%
Eastern Caribbean	6	8	+33.3%
Southern Caribbean	11	9	−18.2%
Western Caribbean	4	13	+225.0%
Private Islands	0	7	New
Total	**24**	**42**	**75.0%**

Southern Caribbean		Eastern Caribbean	
1970s	*2005*	*1970s*	*2005*
Antigua	Antigua	Cap Haitien	—
Aruba	Aruba	—	Grand Turk
Barbados	Barbados	—	La Romana, DM
Cartegena	—	San Juan, PR	San Juan, PR
Curaçao	Curaçao	Santo Domingo	—
—	Dominica	St. Croix	—
Grenada	Grenada	—	St. Kitts
Guadaloupe	—	St. Maarten	St. Maarten
La Guaira	—	St. Thomas	St. Thomas
—	Margarita Island	—	St. Bart's
Martinique	Martinique	—	Tortola
St. Lucia	St. Lucia		
Trinidad	—		

Western Caribbean		Bahamas	
1970s	*2005*	*1970s*	*2005*
—	Belize City, Belize	Nassau	Nassau
—	Calica, MX	Freeport	Freeport
Colon, Panama	Colon, Panama		

Private Islands	
1970s	*2005*

Western Caribbean		Private Islands	
—	Costa Maya, MX	—	Coco Cay
—	Cozumel, MX	—	Princess Cays
—	Grand Cayman	—	Half Moon Cay
Kingston	—	—	Labadee, Haiti
Montego Bay	Montego Bay	—	Catalina Island
—	Ocho Rios	—	Great Stirrup Cay
—	Playa del Carmen, MX	—	Castaway Cay
Port Antonio	Port Antonio		
—	Progresso, MX		

Florida	
1970s	*2005*

Western Caribbean		Florida	
—	Puerto Limon, Costa Rica	Key West	Key West
—	Roatan, Honduras	—	Pt. Canaveral
		—	Miami

Note: Cruise lines include CCL, RCI, NCL, Costa, and Disney.

kept pace with sufficient investment in infrastructure to accommodate the growth. The cruise industry is an important economic driver in these countries, and investment in piers, terminals, roadways, etc., would surely pay off quickly as a result of the increased revenue from the cruise lines and their passengers. The cruise industry has long maintained that it's spending hundreds of millions in marketing and advertising to generate cruise demand. This demand, in turn, brings hundreds of thousands of vacationers to these countries. A typical cruise itinerary is a sampler of ports of call to vacationers who've had no prior experience with them. Those ports that put their best foot forward with a congestion-free, hassle-free experience stand to gain the largest numbers of folks who will want to return with a land stay.

Therefore, the entire vacation industry in each of these ports should press to encourage the governments to make sure the infrastructure is adequate for today—and tomorrow! Because of high customer satisfaction, repeat cruisers average 60–65 percent of all cruisers each year. And while it's true that some experienced cruisers rarely get off the ship, the majority are always keen on exploring new destinations. Cruise lines know that strong itineraries are important, especially in the highly competitive Caribbean market. An itinerary edge translates into higher demand and higher ticket revenue. As we discuss later on, higher ticket revenue means higher on-board revenue. Talk about good karma!

LIFE ON THE OCEAN WAVE

3

Living and working
aboard modern cruise ships

 ## Whose Country Are We in Anyway?

Every commercial ship is registered to a flag state (country) under whose rules and authority the ship wishes to operate. The choice of country depends on many factors including, perhaps, the financing of the vessel, the cost of operation, and the routes the vessel may elect to operate. Many countries, including the United States, Italy, and Britain, have strict regulations, including unionized labor, that severely constrain the ability of a ship to staff with an optimal crew mix. This invariably results in a higher labor cost than in a free market environment. Other countries, so-called flag of convenience countries, do not have these constraints. Panama and Liberia, which together account for 30 percent of the world shipping tonnage, are the most popular of these. Other popular countries for registering ships include Monrovia, Bermuda, the Bahamas, and the Netherlands Antilles. The flag of convenience tradition dates back to the early days of naval warfare, when merchant ships, in order to avoid being attacked, would carry the flag of a neutral nation so as to protect their passengers and cargo from the ravages of war.

Today, cruise liners as well as cargo ships continue to use flags of these and other nations rather than of their own country because of convenience. Ships roam all over the world. It is not only convenient but practical for them to hire crew wherever they like, without concern for nationality. If a chief engineer gets ill in Istanbul, it makes sense to recruit a new engineer in Turkey, if one is available, because that is where the ship is located. A U.S.–flagged vessel, for example, would not have that option. Great Britain, Italy, Norway, and Greece are all renowned for their nautical skills, rigorous training, and strict licensing standards, and just about every major cruise line recruits its captains from one or more of these four countries. On the other hand, the French, Germans, and Austrians often manage the world's finest dining rooms and kitchens. In other words, on a ship, an international crew is often the most desirable as well as the most practical to staff. The problem is that most countries have labor unions and regulations that severely restrict the ability of a ship to staff itself with what may clearly be the optimal crew mix. These laws are designed to protect the jobs of each country's citizens, but they are not only sometimes impractical but always costly. For example, all ships registered in the United States may use only licensed American officers, and three-quarters of the unlicensed crew must be U.S. citizens. Other countries have similarly restrictive regulations.

When a ship carrying an international crew is registered in Liberia or Panama, it is not subject to unions and other restrictive crewing policies. This means that owners are in a better position to negotiate fair and equitable compensation packages in a global free-market environment. Of course, it is true that ships registered in these flag-of-convenience nations pay lower wages and taxes on an aggregate basis than those registered in the United States (or Norway or Italy, for that matter). But that makes it possible for them to offer cruises (or cargo transport) at a much lower cost than if their ships were registered in non-flag-of-convenience countries. That's one reason why American-headquartered cruise lines such as Royal Caribbean and Carnival choose not to operate under the U.S. flag. Another reason is that, frankly, it is much more difficult to find Americans who have a flair for service hospitality. The egalitarian nature and heritage of Americans tend to work against their ability to be subservient to others. Moreover, citizens of highly developed countries like the United States who work on ships generally make about the same as they would make at home. Citizens of less developed countries, like Costa Rica, Croatia, and the Philippines, on the other hand, make considerably more on board a ship than they could make at home—if they could find a job at all, given that unemployment may be as high as 30 percent! The plain fact is that many Americans aren't eager to get a job at sea because there are so many comparably compensated positions shoreside. (Remember, the U.S. unemployment rate generally hovers between 5 and 8 percent.) When Americans do work at sea, they're typically not as motivated to excel. Third World citizens hold these jobs in high esteem because they can become both employed (which is not a given at home) and wealthy by the standards of their own economy. From the standpoint of a global economy, flag-of-convenience cruise ships, operating in a free market, provide more value to the worldwide labor pool with significantly less cost to their operators and therefore lower prices to their consumers.

Despite these factors, members of the U.S. Congress have attempted over the years to gain more control over foreign-flagged tonnage and thus gain a foothold for U.S. labor and shipping interests. For example, Representative William Clay, a Democrat from Missouri, proposed a series of bills (none of which passed) to extend U.S. labor laws to foreign-flagged vessels even though the U.S. State Department has insisted for years that any such legislation would violate longstanding international law and comity. Kirk Lanterman, former president of Holland America, points out some of the problems of this type of legislation. "It could create a situation where when we leave Miami we are under U.S. labor laws, but when we dock in the Bahamas, we'll be subject to a different set of local laws. It would be so onerous as to push cruise lines offshore." Imagine what would happen if cruise ships no longer sailed from Miami or Los Angeles but rather Nassau or Encinada.

It's amusing to us to watch congressional attempts to legislate the free world marketplace. Isn't it ironic that a country built on the principle of open market competition has created a situation where its maritime industry is puny by global standards and its cruise industry practically non-existent? Longstanding U.S. cabotage laws have, in the case of the cruise industry, cost the nation billions of dollars and tens of thousands of jobs. If the United States truly wanted to capture a fair share of cruise line jobs and other economic benefits, we believe it needs to exempt the cruise industry from the Passenger Shipping Act of 1896. This act precludes foreign-flagged vessels from operating between U.S. ports when there is no U.S.-flagged competitor. Presently, virtually all of the lucrative Alaska cruise business is home ported in Vancouver, British Columbia, because of this cabotage law. Well over $1 billion annually is lost to the Seattle, Washington, economy and reaped by its neighbor to the north. Seattle would be the natural home port for Alaskan cruises because of its superior airline infrastructure. Indeed, all lines offering cruises to Alaska fly a significant number of their passengers to Seattle and then bus them 150 miles to the port of Vancouver. However, as no deep-water port or U.S.-flagged cruise ships operate to Alaska, there is simply no U.S.-flagged cruise business to protect!

There were only two deep-water U.S.-flagged cruise ships—the *Independence* and the *Constitution,* built in 1950 as transatlantic liners and converted to cruising. They operated a seven-day inter-island service in Hawaii. Foreign-flagged ships operated occasionally in Hawaii, usually as positioning cruises before and after the Alaska season. A typical cruise might originate in Mexico (such as Acapulco or Encinada) and terminate in the Hawaiian Islands. The next cruise would begin in Hawaii and end in Vancouver, for a series of Alaska cruises. At the end of the season, the pattern would reverse, with two more Hawaii cruises to position the ship south. Clearly, the U.S.-flagged ships had a huge advantage as they could operate inter-island, picking up and discharging passengers at any port if they chose, without having to go "far foreign," as the terminology of the cabotage law calls for.

NCL created inter-island itineraries that went far foreign, first at Christmas Island in the Republic of Kiribati and then at Fanning Island. NCL's parent, Star Cruises, gave NCL the *Superstar Leo,* which had a speed capacity of 25 knots. This allowed the ship, renamed *Norwegian Spirit,* to operate inter-island seven-day itineraries each week from Honolulu. Advance sales were great, but new legislation forced NCL to operate the itinerary with the *Norwegian Star,* an even newer, larger vessel that had been earmarked for Star's Singapore trade. This service began in December 2001. NCL had the Hawaii market to itself by then, as American Hawaii and its parent, Delta Queen, went bankrupt in the weeks after 9/11. They were clever enough to arrange an exclusive deal with Fanning Island so competitors couldn't duplicate the seven-day itinerary.

Not content, NCL took the out-of-the-box decision to start up a U.S.-flagged carrier by obtaining legislative dispensation that allowed them to complete, in Europe, a half-built ship that had been ordered by the now-defunct American Hawaii. They were also able to duck the requirement that the ship ultimately be owned by a U.S. company. Foreign-owned NCL/Star formed NCL America, which is a U.S. subsidiary that owns the ship, has a U.S. chairman and U.S. officers, and is based in the United States. As a result, NCL has a clear monopoly in the Hawaiian inter-island trade, and the United States has some U.S.-flagged vessels.

There is only one U.S.-flagged deep-water cruise line as the result of other forms of longstanding protectionist policy. U.S. flagging required (with the notable NCL exception) that the ship be built in the United States as well as operated by a predominantly U.S. crew. The U.S. shipbuilding industry has for years been entirely focused on lucrative, cost-plus U.S. Navy contracts. Because of their cost-plus nature, they are inherently highly subsidized. If there is a cost overrun (remember the stories of the $1,350 hammer?), it is added to the bill plus the normal shipyard markup. For the record, no self-respecting cruise line would ever sign a shipbuilding contract without a firm price guarantee. The U.S. Navy, however, apparently can operate in a more cavalier manner. Stockholders are always harder to please than taxpayers!

⚓ The Captain and the Crew

In chapter 2, we described what is generally called the front of the house in most hospitality enterprises. The term has its roots in the theater, where the front of the house is what the audience sees—the lobby, the theater itself, with its ornate boxes, chandeliers, and seats, and, of course, the stage. Framed by the proscenium and behind the curtain is the set on which the action takes place. This front stage is where the illusion occurs that turns actors into characters and flats of painted canvas supported by unseen wooden two-by-fours into city streets, country gardens, and the like. Backstage, or behind the scenes and out of view of the audience, are the stage hands, the wardrobe and makeup artists, the lighting and set designers, and, of course, the producer, director, and choreographer. Cruise ships, like hotels and restaurants, also have a front of the house and a back of the house. One reason the term is appropriate in all of these enterprises is that many service businesses recognize that part of their service consists of a performance in which the customers are the audience and the staff are, in a sense, actors playing roles. The Disney organization calls all of the employees in their parks and cruise ships "cast members." Whether they are sweeping Main Street or boarding guests onto the Space Mountain roller coaster, they play the parts they have been assigned when they are "on stage," which is anywhere they can be seen by guests.

Hotels have always called their lobbies the front of the house and their kitchens and laundries the back of the house. So it is with cruise ships. A cruise ship such as the *Freedom of the Seas* carries 3,600 (basis two) passengers and a crew of 1,360. Holland America's Vista-class ships carry 1,848 passengers and a crew of 800. The *Seabourn Spirit* carries 202 passengers along with a crew of 140. Many of these people, such as waiters and pursers, are seen by the ship's guests regularly when they are in the front of the house. Others, such as engineers, may never be seen. All of them live their personal lives aboard the ship in the back of the house and are under the command of the ship's captain.

Four senior officers report directly to the captain: the staff captain, the chief engineer, the doctor, and the hotel manager (or chief purser, as he or she is called aboard British ships). Everyone else on the ship reports to a department under the supervision of one of these four officers. Passengers are frequently curious as to what the captain actually does all day. Simply put, the captain is the ultimate authority on board, charged with carrying out company policies and rules and complying with all applicable national and international laws and regulations. The captain has legal authority to enforce these laws—it is granted to him by the government of the flag state. In truth, most flag-of-convenience countries have relatively few laws governing ship operations, which allows the ships to operate under their own company policies and procedures. Some cruise lines operate ships under more then one flag, and their captains must be familiar with all of the laws of their various flag states.

In addition, vessels must comply with local laws of the ports they sail from and visit. For example, the U.S. Coast Guard inspects all ships sailing from the United States four times a year. Three of these are quarterly inspections; the fourth is an annual inspection. During the quarterly inspection, the Coast Guard observes the crew performing a full-fledged fire drill and an abandon ship drill. Crew members climb into lifeboats, which are then lowered. In the annual inspection, the focus is not simply on the crew's ability to perform tasks but also on inspecting all of the safety equipment used on board. The Coast Guard checks that everything is where it is supposed to be and that all escape routes are clear and haven't been turned into storage space, for example. They then issue a certificate showing that the ship has passed inspection. Most lines don't wait for the Coast Guard to appear but routinely perform these same inspections and drills weekly for their own training and inspection purposes.

The U.S. Public Health Service Centers for Disease Control and Prevention (CDC) inspects galleys and other food-handling and storage areas and awards scores to ships for their sanitation (more about this later).[1] Ships carry a good many insurance policies as well, covering such equipment as the hull and machinery—as well as liability insurance. All of these policies have attached conditions that the captain is responsible for enforcing. The insuring organization, such as U.S. Bureau of Shipping, Lloyds, or Den Norske Veritas, inspects each vessel to make sure it is "in class." If a ship isn't, it cannot operate, as it is deemed uninsurable until the problem is solved!

Everything else aside, the captain's primary responsibility is to ensure the care and safety of everyone on board and, with that in mind, to make sure the ship is seaworthy and that proper and safe navigation and operating procedures are carried out. He is responsible for the navigation of the vessel: its speed, direction, bearings (location), maneuvering into and out of port, and the ability to maintain its itinerary and schedule. Captains are on duty all of the time, and when safety problems of any sort are spotted, the captain must be called. One veteran captain recalls that he was summoned one evening when a fire alarm in one of the cabins went off. The captain personally responded to the alarm, only to discover that a honeymoon couple had decided to have a candlelight dinner in the cabin. The heat from the candle had set off the alarm!

Norwegian Cruise Line's job description for their captains includes these tasks, among others:

1. Ensuring the ship's officers, staff, and crew carry out their assigned duties in a seamanship manner at all times.

---

[1]Copies of these scores are issued monthly, and interested consumers may receive copies by writing Chief Vessel Sanitation Program, National Center for Environmental Health, 1015 N. America Way, Room 107, Miami, FL 33132. Results are also published in *Consumer Reports Travel Letter.*

2. Maintaining a high standard of discipline on board using any lawful methods deemed necessary as the situation demands and ensuring the department heads instruct the crew members in all applicable rules, regulations, and company policies. (He is ultimately responsible for the discipline of the crew, using the staff captain and other department heads to carry out this responsibility.)

3. Promoting the welfare and well-being of the crew, being attentive to their environment, and ensuring each enjoys the privileges to which they are entitled. He shall use periodic inspection rounds as an opportunity to strengthen the personal contact between himself and the crew.

4. To maintain a world-class standard of service to the passengers.

5. To take actions as necessary to prevent or mitigate circumstances that place the ship, passengers, or crew in danger.

6. The captain shall have a thorough knowledge of the ship, including the construction, safety equipment, stability characteristics, ship handling procedures, and emergency procedures. He shall ensure his officers have the same knowledge in their areas of responsibility. He shall ensure the ship's maintenance program meets or exceeds that required by the company and the authorities.

7. The Captain shall determine the extent of participation by the officers and staff in social activity with passengers and the applicable dress code, ensuring the regulations of the company are observed.

It is worth noting here the emphasis and use of words in this job description (which is typical for all of the cruise lines) such as "assigned duties," "seamanship manner," "standard of discipline," "privileges," "prevent or mitigate circumstances" and "regulations of the company." A ship is a paramilitary organization. Officers wear uniforms. Regulations, laws, rank, and discipline play a prominent role in the way things get done. This is both an advantage and a disadvantage in a service industry whose success depends heavily on customer satisfaction. It can be a disadvantage because motivation is somewhat inhibited by the nature of the organization. Everyone has an assigned rank and narrowly specified duties. One cannot overstep established boundaries. If duties are not performed in a prescribed manner, the crew member is subject to discipline. Sound service management theory, which emphasizes empowerment and shared responsibility, can have a somewhat limited role on board a vessel run in a paramilitary manner. This is a business where you earn your stripes by obeying orders and regulations and through demonstrating your mastery of them as you advance your career.

Captains often begin their careers as deck hands when they first go to sea, then attend navigation school to receive a master's license. From there, they usually move up the ladder from cadet to third officer, second officer, first officer, staff captain, and, finally, captain. Most navigating officers on cruise ships hold a captain's license. On the *Queen Mary 2,* nine officers hold Master Mariner's certificates—that is, they are qualified to command any British oceangoing ship. In the case of Carnival, *all* first officers (and higher ranks, of course) and many second officers have master's licenses.

The captain is the ship's chief executive officer and in that capacity organizes and maintains a staff of officers to carry out all of the duties necessary to operate the vessel. He does have an office (usually in the living room of his suite) but also works from the navigational bridge. He is the ship's ultimate disciplinarian and, while at sea, he acts as both judge and jury in any dispute that cannot be resolved at a lower level. On a day-to-day basis, however, the staff captain handles routine disciplinarian issues. Guidelines as to what kind of actions can be subject to discipline are usually found in the "Masters Rules and Regulations," which are the universally accepted code of ship operations. Crew members are required to sign a copy when they begin service. Here are typical rules and regulations:

- ◆ No drunkenness will be tolerated.
- ◆ No crew member shall have illegal drugs or offensive weapons in his possession.
- ◆ No indecent language will be used on board.
- ◆ No crew member is to be involved in a fight.
- ◆ Crew members off duty, below a specified rank, must not be seen in passenger accommodations or public rooms.
- ◆ Respect must be given at all times to all officers.
- ◆ Respect and a courteous manner must at all times be given to passengers.
- ◆ All crew members will attend boat drill.
- ◆ All crew members must report punctually for duty.
- ◆ Crew members will not miss the ship.
- ◆ Gambling is prohibited for all crew members.[2]

Some captains focus their attention on administrative matters and have little time or interest in meeting or interacting with passengers. Others enjoy socializing and tend to dine often with passengers and invite them

---

[2]Every ship has its own Masters Rules and Regulations. These are extracted from a pamphlet titled "Shipboard Hotel Personnel Information Booklet," published for its employees by Royal Caribbean Cruises Ltd.

to visit the bridge. Like other CEOs and presidents, their behavioral priorities have much to do with their individual personality. Some are customer oriented—outgoing and gregarious ambassadors for their companies. These individuals are frequently seen by the passengers throughout the ship at all hours of the day and night. Some seem to wish to be photographed as often as possible, while others quietly observe the activities and entertainment to ensure quality control. Without question, the captain's position is critical to the entire operation of the vessel. The captain is the key to the morale of the vessel. If morale is high, the crew is happy and productive, and the guests immediately recognize it. A good captain, in addition to all his nautical and legal requirements, is a good manager of people, a good listener, and a team builder who motivates and inspires the officers, staff, and crew. The ideal captain knows most, if not all, the crew and calls them by name if known, but always smiles and greets all crew members. He encourages his direct reports and department heads to do the same, thus creating a warm, hospitable environment on board.

A good captain recognizes the diverse cultural background of the crew. He creates and nurtures an atmosphere of civility and respect for all the crew irrespective of position, race, nationality, political, religious, or sexual persuasion. He doesn't abide bigotry, hatred, favoritism, and intolerance.

The best captains rarely, if ever, need to pull rank. They are quietly effective. They exude confidence based on their knowledge, competence, and people skills. These captains don't swagger, don't ignore the crew, and don't shout or talk down to them. They operate with the calm assurance of someone who is in charge yet has the complete respect of his team. They create an environment where many hundreds of folks, from all walks of life, *want* to work with him and for him. They cherish his leadership and will do anything for him. When mistakes happen (and they invariably do), these captains don't rant or rave; they don't need to. Rather, they point out the error with the purpose of explaining why it was wrong and what the better behavior would be. They use this as a positive learning experience for the crew, who appreciate the captain's role as educator and motivator.

A good captain builds a strong senior management team, incorporating all the department heads of the vessel. He holds frequent meetings to encourage good communication among the departments and to build bridges of understanding. To the extent possible, he engenders a participative management style, encouraging the best insights and ideas from all participants. Importantly, he encourages his department heads to nurture and advance this same management philosophy within their respective departments.

In years past, a captain was a great seaman and navigator—and that was pretty much all that was necessary. Today, he is a navigator, statesman, diplomat, and CEO of a strictly regulated, culturally diverse business that operates around the clock. He runs a service business where the consumers are a captive audience who must have their many expectations about their cruise purchase met every hour, every day. The selection, training, nurturing, and retention of good captains is critical to the success of any cruise line!

The staff captain is the captain's right-hand man. Officially, he is the captain's deputy and second in command of the ship. When the captain is not on board the vessel, even in port, the staff captain must be on board to ensure that someone is in charge at all times. The staff captain is responsible for all maintenance, radio communications, security, and normal ship's discipline. For example, his job description on NCL ships says, "The staff captain shall receive all reports of misconduct and take appropriate action or make recommendations to the captain in accordance with the procedures established by the captain. He shall maintain a log of such actions as required by the flag state."

Safety, too, is his top concern, focusing on passengers, crew, and equipment. Staff captains ensure that the lifeboats work, that fire equipment is all in its proper place, and that the crew is well trained and frequently practices all emergency procedures. Royal Caribbean, as a typical example, requires every member of the hotel staff who has been on board less than three years to complete a sixteen-hour course including first aid, CPR, firefighting, and lifeboat handling. Staff Captain Tom Strom, second in command of the *Nordic Empress,* talked with us about his job and career:

> I started as a deck boy, working on freighters and tankers. I lived in accommodations you wouldn't think of offering to any crew member today. My quarters today are the same as second-class passengers used to get on transatlantic crossings. I am in charge of all the navigators [people on the bridge], security officers, safety officers, and the doctor. That's security as in sheriff, and safety as in lifesaving. Our chief officer is a navigation officer—he has the 4:00 A.M. to 8:00 A.M. watch on the bridge and assists me with the maintenance outside. The outside maintenance work is supervised by the boatswain— he's like a sergeant, and all the able-bodied seamen, the ordinary seamen, and the deck boys—the guys on the deck— report to him. Of course, I worry most about fire. We had a fire in the 1970s on the *Skyward* and had to evacuate all of the passengers, but no one was hurt and the ship was back in service in a week. Security didn't used to be a problem until the hijacking of the *Achille Lauro* in the 1980s. That was

an eye-opener for us—we realized that ships were no safer than other places from possible terrorist activities. So we have to be prepared for them. Of course, we have no way of knowing if passengers bring weapons on board. So we X-ray luggage on a selective basis depending on the threat that is most evident at any given time. For example, we're influenced by whether there is peace or war, our itinerary, and the nationality of our guests. Any of those can trigger security concerns that we address. [In the post-9/11 environment, ships X-ray all luggage and carry-on items.]

Among the crew, we have occasional friction. So we have set up rather strict rules and go over them with crew members when they join the ship. Fighting is a bad case—or being late for work repeatedly. We have weekly attitude adjustment meetings where we take these people in who seem to have a little problem adjusting together with their supervisors. We go through the issue at hand. If they feel they have been treated unfairly, we look into that as well. But the idea is to correct the situation so that it doesn't happen again.

Sexual harassment and gay rights are not a problem aboard our ships. We have heterosexuals and homosexuals, and they all get along. I've never encountered a sexual harassment problem. We do have a policy against it. But you know, the people who work on ships are a special kind of people. We all live off the same hallway. We share cabins. It's much more intimate than an office, where you see each other from 9 to 5. Maybe that's why we don't have as many problems. If you are a single person without family ties, it's a good place to be. There's a sense of belonging. When people do fight, it's usually because two people are trying to do the same job and bump into each other accidentally. They almost never fight for personal reasons.

Passengers sometimes confuse the staff captain with the captain; both are addressed as captain and may perform duties generally associated with a ship's captain. The two uniforms have different stripes, however, which makes it easy to tell them apart.

Doctors and Shipboard Health Care

The medical facilities, under the direction of the ship's doctor, are sometimes quite extensive, although they are designed to take care of minor problems only or to stabilize passengers until they can be evacuated safely to a suitable hospital ashore. Medical professionals would characterize them as being infirmaries rather than hospitals. Cruise lines experience different frequencies of medical emergencies. For example, an older passenger base and longer cruise itinerary would predictably result in a higher incidence of medical emergencies than, say, a three- or four-day getaway itinerary. Cruise ships must be prepared for the unexpected, which can and will happen both at sea and in port.

Over the years, the industry has had to deal with intestinal diseases, both on ship and at ports of call, norovirus outbreaks, Legionnaires disease, and SARS. Against the backgrounds of tens of millions of cruise passengers, these instances, fortunately, are quite rare. It's important to remember that cruise lines are obligated to report breakouts of diseases to the Centers for Disease Control. This protocol immediately generates media attention. Our primary land-based competition, on the other hand, is under no such obligation. In fact, because on land, guests are continually checking in or out of properties, it's frequently difficult to determine that there *is* an outbreak!

When the norovirus first gained notoriety in 2002, its virulence made it difficult to bring under control. The cruise lines worked together and in cooperation with the CDC to develop protocols for killing the virus germs on the many surfaces of guest contact. Guests were screened by shipboard medical staff at embarkation and sent home rather than contaminate their would-be fellow passengers. For all the media hype at the time centering around a few thousand cases of norovirus on cruise ships, the U.S. Public Health Service had reported 28 million cases in the United States in the prior year! We guess the cachet of cruising cuts both ways: The glamour of cruising creates much higher consumer word-of-mouth than more mundane land vacations. On the other hand, when something goes wrong at sea, even a commonplace stomach virus, there is huge, out-of-proportion media coverage.

Legally, there are no American or international requirements concerning the level of cruise ship medicine. Because cruise lines are in the hospitality business, it makes eminent sense for them to provide necessary and adequate medical care. *Condé Nast Traveler* boarded ships belonging to twelve major lines to examine their medical facilities and reported the results in their February 1994 issue. One of their key findings was that the quality of care depended, in part, on the ship's itinerary; the farther away it went from ports where passengers could be evacuated, the higher the level of preparedness. Another variable is the average age of the guests. Beyond that, facilities and credentials of doctors varied widely. Some ships had doctors from such countries as Denmark, the United Kingdom, the United States, and Canada. Other ships had doctors from Colombia and Mexico. Some ship doctors had been trained in primary and emergency care medicine and cardiology, while other lines employed those whose specialty had been dermatology, gynecology, and radiology. Some of the ships had X-ray machines and said they could and would perform operations such as appendectomies, if necessary, while others preferred to send the patient to the nearest hospital.

We should note here that ship doctors are hired by medical directors ashore. Sometimes they are semiretired and enjoy traveling. More often, they are career ship physicians. Apart from emergencies, their routine work (for which they are paid directly by the passengers) frequently consists of treatment of minor ailments like the flu or sunburn. Another problem is that sometimes people leave their medicine at home, and while ships make every effort to accommodate, obviously they cannot carry (nor do they try to carry) a fully stocked pharmacy. The bottom line, as with other shipboard services, is that cruise lines make judgment calls based on their perception of the needs of their guests and a cost-benefit analysis. All well-run lines realize that the health of their guests is critically important and pay a great deal of management attention to this complex issue.

Technical Matters

The second key officer reporting to the captain is the chief engineer. A ship is a large and sophisticated complex of machinery. It contains a power plant, consisting of diesel engines and electric generators; a heating plant, which produces steam for water heating; an air-conditioning plant; a desalinization plant to produce water; a sewage disposal plant; intricate plumbing; electrical systems; fire and safety systems; a closed-circuit TV system; and a host of computers to monitor, regulate, and operate all of this equipment. Everything on a ship can and does break down—frequently when the ship is at sea. Modern ships have a variety of redundant systems so they may operate uninterruptedly in case of a system failure. When things do break down, it's critically important that the ship have the technical competencies as well as materials to repair or replace defective parts or systems. Sometimes it is as simple as a toilet getting clogged in a passenger's cabin, but it can be as complicated as the malfunctioning of one of the main generators that supply all of the electric power to the ship. In any case, when you are in the middle of the ocean, there are no outside repairpersons to call; everything on the ship must be able to be fixed or replaced immediately for the comfort and safety of those on board. Erik Bakken, chief engineer on NCL's *Seaward,* points out that he is responsible for power, waste management, lights, telephones, air conditioning, and refrigeration on his ship. He has a staff of thirty to assist him. The heart of his operation (which passengers never see) is a control room in the bowels of the ship filled with gauges, dials, and computer displays. Engineers on the *Seaward* work four-hour shifts. The key, says Bakken, to being able to take care of any emergency on board is to carry enough inventory of spare parts. The *Seaward,* for instance, carries 11,000 different items worth over $3 million—everything from light bulbs and TV sets to major machinery components and even a spare sauna heater! Ninety percent of these are tracked in one of Bakken's computer databases and replaced as needed.

Waste Disposal at Sea

The waste disposal plant of modern cruise ships is a good example of the kind of high-tech machinery operated by the engineering department. It shows how the art of modern shipbuilding and operation has had to adapt to changing societal needs and a changing business environment. Historically, waste disposal was never a concern in the cruise business or the shipping business at large, for that matter. After all, it's a very big ocean out there! So disposing of the waste from ships—beer and Coke bottles, paper plates, newspapers, human excrement, and bilge water was considered "pissing in the ocean"—in other words, of so little impact as to be without any significance.

Our growing awareness of our environment and our own effect on it and our quality of life has changed that thinking forever. It didn't begin with cruise lines, of course. Automobile emissions have been an issue for more than three decades now, railroads no longer discharge waste onto their tracks, and fast food restaurants have had to abandon Styrofoam packaging, for the most part. But because ships sailed out of sight of land much of the time, no one really cared what they did with their waste.

As the world became more ecologically aware, the prevailing thought that the oceans were virtually indestructible changed. With the understanding of the reality that the oceans are a critical part of the human environment, international agreements were negotiated to safeguard the seas. The London-based International Maritime Organization (part of the United Nations), for example, put forth a policy of zero tolerance of the discharge of any plastics into the sea, and that policy had the force of the laws of 140 member nations behind it. Even the equipment for trapshooting, a popular activity off the sterns of cruise ships, and the driving of golf balls had to be redesigned because shotgun ammunition and golf balls contain plastic!

It was a rude awakening for many cruise operators. Although they certainly agreed in principle with the need for keeping the oceans clean and were willing to comply, their existing equipment simply wasn't adequate for the job. Space, as we have pointed out, is at a premium on a ship. A modern ship carrying 2,700 passengers and a crew of 900 can easily generate a ton or more of garbage daily as well as other kinds of waste. There simply was no place to put all those empty cans, plastic and paper cups, discarded wrapping from shopping expeditions, and old Bingo cards until the ship completed its cruise. Even if there was space for ordinary garbage, the ships had no holding tanks for toilet discharge; this had always been dumped at sea and was believed to be good for the fish.

Well, it turned out it wasn't good for the fish, and soon it was clear that there were only a few viable options. The first, of course, was to reduce whatever waste you could—replace paper napkins and disposable plates and cups used for hamburgers and Cokes around the swimming pool with cloth where possible and dishwasher-proof plastic. The problem with that was that you needed additional space for dishwashers, to say nothing of fresh water, which the ship either had to carry or make on board to do the extra washing. Moreover, that would produce dirty water that itself would have to be recycled before it could be discharged. Of course, you could stick with paper and incinerate it instead of throwing it overboard, but that too would require a good deal of space for an incinerator that would be both safe (remember, fires of any sort are highly undesirable on ships) and smokeless (passengers don't like soot on their bathing suits). A third alternative was to off-load the garbage in various ports of call, but this assumed that these ports had the infrastructure able to handle this stuff, and many small Caribbean islands didn't. The problem was exacerbated by a sense of urgency. New rules were being promulgated all the time, and ships that could not adapt would have to be withdrawn from service. In the future, virtually all waste would either have to be processed on board to a point where it could be disposed of without environmental impact or brought back home.

Today's newest cruise ships incorporate complete waste disposal systems that are more efficient facilities than those found in most towns. They easily cost $10 million or more and can be up to three decks high. The purpose of these systems is to grind, incinerate, shred, compact, and treat every form of waste so it can either be converted into an acceptable form for incineration or discharge, or stored compactly until the ship returns to home port, where it can be recycled or transported to landfills. On a large cruise ship, there may be as many as ten crew members whose full-time job is to handle waste disposal.

Passengers, too, are now enlisted to do their part. It usually starts with announcements and posted notices requesting them not to throw anything overboard. Royal Caribbean, for example, has a highly visible "Save Our Seas" program that includes a film shown on board and buttons worn by crew members. On ships of all major lines, separate trash cans in guest areas for plastic, glass, and metal are clearly marked to assist in the sorting process. Cabin stewards are asked to sort waste into metal, glass, and burnable materials. Metal such as aluminum is shredded into small pieces for recycling. Beer and soda cans are placed in compactors that form them into large blocks for recycling. Plastics and Styrofoam materials are compacted for storage and subsequent recycling. Paper and cardboard is also shredded and then incinerated. Leftover food is placed in cold storage until it can be processed in a pulper/grinder that squeezes the pulp and extracts the water. A sewage treatment plant breaks down waste into water and purified waste, which can be discharged after treatment in specified areas of the ocean. Even bilge water has the oil separated out and recycled before the residue water (with oil less than 15 parts per million) is discharged. And the use of plastics on board has been eliminated as much as possible. Many cruise lines do not supply small plastic shampoo bottles to avoid the problem of disposal; they either package cabin amenities in cardboard or use shampoo dispensers. Virtually all major cruise lines have instructed their crews that throwing *anything* overboard is cause for immediate dismissal. Signs to that effect are posted in crew quarters as gentle reminders.

Cruise lines have been working with state and federal authorities to work out regulations for virtually every waste stream. One of the more interesting items is ballast water. As a ship sails from its home port, its fuel and freshwater tanks are full. As the fuel is consumed, at certain points ballast water is pumped into the vessel to maintain proper trim and stability. This ballast water must be pumped from the ship to allow for the bunkering of replacement fuel and fresh water. The ballast water is lifted in one place and returned in another. Seems innocuous, right? The reality is that there are millions of tiny organisms in the water that was lifted but may not exist or belong in the place where the water is to be pumped out. These microscopic organisms could contaminate the water in that area and disturb the ecological environment. This is most prevalent in warm waters, where these organisms thrive. States like California have worked out ballast discharge zones that are sufficiently offshore (3 miles) to avoid risk. This degree of environmental sensitivity and care was unheard of in the 1970s.

 ## The Hotel Manager

The third senior officer reporting directly to the captain is the hotel manager (on some ships, the title is hotel director). The hotel manager has the largest staff on the ship because his crew is directly responsible for providing the vacation experience the line offers. The key department heads in the hotel manager's area typically include the chief purser, who is the ship's banker, information officer, complaint handler, and person responsible for clearing the ship through foreign ports. As we pointed out earlier, on British lines such as Princess, the chief purser *is* the hotel manager. Indeed, it is worth noting that the very title *hotel manager* is relatively new on cruise ships; in earlier times, the chief purser managed many of the hotel functions on most lines. Carnival made this transition in the early 1990s to reflect the new functional responsibility that encompasses food and beverage management, hotel operations, entertainment, gift shops, spa, and the casino operation. The food and beverage manager, who runs the restaurants and bars, reports to the hotel manager on most lines (although not all), as do the executive chef and housekeeping manager (sometimes called chief steward). Finally there is the cruise director and his or her staff. On a large ship, this may number as many as seventy people, including entertainers, musicians, port lecturers, children's counselors, and aerobics instructors.

The hotel manager is often responsible for a group of other services such as the casino, photography, beauty salon, and gift shops. On some ships, many or all of these services are provided by outside concessionaires. On others, the cruise line owns and manages some or all of these services directly. For instance, Royal Caribbean uses a concessionaire to handle its onboard photography (a highly profitable venture) but runs its own gift shops. Carnival handles its own photography, but its gift shops are a concession. Both lines operate their own casinos, and both lines use the same concessionaire, Steiner Leisure, to run their beauty salons and spas. Steiner Leisure has the concession for these services on a majority of the North American–based cruise lines. Carnival, Norwegian, and Royal Caribbean run their own food and beverage operations; however, a few lines use concessionaires to provide the food and beverage services (often referred to as *ship's chandlers*).

Many hotel managers on today's ships come from the hotel industry, although that is a recent development. Most of them have spent their careers at sea, working their way up through the purser's, food and beverage, or housekeeping department. Hotel manager Gunnar Mikkelsen, who we met on NCL's *Seaward* (currently operating as the *Superstar Leo* for Star Cruises) had been with the line for eighteen years and before that was a chief steward at RCCL. Mikkelsen spends four months on board a ship, followed by two months off—a typical schedule for a ship's hotel manager and other senior officers. Like many others, Mikkelsen is married and has children. His family makes their home in Florida. Johannes Moser, hotel manager of the *Seabourn Spirit*, on the other hand, is an Austrian with a food and beverage background who grew up in the hotel business. His Irish wife is the housekeeper on board (a position equivalent to chief steward on other lines). Her family owns a hotel in Dublin. Jacques Bourguignon, a Royal Caribbean hotel manager, has a degree in hotel and restaurant administration from Jean Drouant School in Paris. His credentials include the Ritz in Paris, the French Novatel hotel chain, and food and beverage director for Westin Hotel and Resorts. In recent years, as capacity has expanded, more and more hotel people have been attracted to the business, and many lines now have hotel managers who were trained at hotels in either the rooms or the food and beverage division.

Typically, the hotel manager's job is to orchestrate the vacation experience the cruise line has promised to deliver to its passengers. To do this requires coordination of all passenger services and ensuring the line's standards are maintained. Everything that has to do with guest satisfaction is his bailiwick. If a vessel has a low guest satisfaction rate, the hotel manager is held accountable long before the captain unless problems are due to mechanical failures or marine operations. Control of onboard revenues and expenses is the hotel manager's second major function (more about that later). He is also responsible for the human resources function for all of the departments that report to him. This includes everything from mundane tasks like scheduling work (or approving schedules) to communication and morale. Finally, a number of reports must be submitted to shoreside management after each voyage so management is aware of performance and problems that must be addressed.

Managers, by definition, accomplish their jobs through other people, and so perhaps the best way to describe how hotel managers get their job done is to examine each of the departments and see what it does. It will be quickly obvious that while these departments function similarly to their land-based hotel counterparts, there are profound differences.

The Purser's Office

The purser's job doesn't exist in a traditional hotel. In some ways it is similar to the front office or rooms division, except that passengers rarely check in or check out on the ship. The purser's staff does, however, operate the reception desk found in the central area of every ship. This is the place passengers go to ask for information, register complaints, and deal with money matters. In the absence of the hotel manager, the purser is the chief financial and administrative officer on board. The purser's primary duty is to take care of accounting—that means keeping track of what is spent by each passenger as well as the revenues taken in by every department. The purser holds all of the money on board the ship, usually in a large safe located in his office. Passengers are constantly converting travelers' checks and needing cash for the casino, duty-free shopping, and other activities such as bingo. In addition, the crew is typically paid in cash on board twice a month. Funds are needed in ports to buy supplies, pay tour operators, and for other expenses. The amount of cash a large ship carries can be substantial; more than $500,000 for just a week's cruise is not unusual. Most cruise ships today use a credit system on board to handle guest accounts. This minimizes the handling of cash by crew members. If passengers don't have credit cards, they may be required to deposit cash with the purser at the start of the voyage if they want to buy anything on board, and when that deposit is used up, credit is cut off. The purser's office is responsible for establishing individual passenger credit at the beginning of the cruise and settling accounts before debarkation at the end of the cruise.

The purser's office, like a hotel's front desk, is the place folks go to make requests, look for solutions to problems, and ask questions. Passengers may decide to upgrade their stateroom from an inside cabin to outside (ocean view, as we say at Carnival). Or there may be a mechanical or plumbing problem with their stateroom, or lost luggage (usually it's found, but sometimes the airlines failed to deliver it). Then it must be located and arrangements made to pick it up at the next port of call. The purser's desk functions as the lost and found department as well as the focal point for passenger questions such as "What time is the midnight buffet?" (frequently asked—honestly!) and "Which elevator do I take to the front of the boat?"

Another major area of responsibility handled by the purser's office is customs and immigration. All passengers and employees must pass through U.S. Customs and Immigration before getting off a cruise ship. Moreover, every time the ship pulls into a foreign country, specific paperwork must be handled before local authorities will clear the ship so passengers and crew can disembark.

On the major lines, the purser's staff is often American because these jobs appeal to U.S. citizens and aren't regarded as servile. They share a cabin with another employee and are allowed to be in specified public areas when off duty, provided they follow the ship's rules and regulations.

Food and Beverage

All of the preparation and service of food and beverages on the ship is under the direction of the food and beverage manager. Because food is considered one of the most important components of the cruise experience (the most important, to some folks), the job of delivering a high-quality product to more than 3,000 passengers on a major ship is monumental. Passengers are more likely to comment on and remember details about foodservice than any other part of their cruise. The miracle of the cruise dining experience is creating the feeling that guests are eating gourmet food presented with personal service in an elegant restaurant when in fact they are being fed banquet style in large numbers at a time. It is an enormously complicated process that works amazingly well. The key, of course, is that at a banquet ashore, guests have no choice in the food selection. On a contemporary ship like one of Carnival's, guests can choose from three soups, two salads, a pasta, seven entrées, a cheese course, and six desserts. Being able to offer an extensive choice to so many people, given the constraints of time and storage space, is possible only because of a precise and accurate forecasting system. If it's Italian Night on the *Ecstasy,* Carnival's management knows exactly how many of the 2,400 passengers on board will order the steak Genoa, the veal Parmigiana, the pollo novello alla diavola, the poached filet of sole, and the other three entrées. Their storerooms carry just what they need; there is little room for extra. They have baked exactly the right number of cappuccino pies and amaretto cakes. The preparation of the food is usually under the supervision of an executive chef, who has a set of recipes, developed onshore, that must be followed exactly. Often the recipe's are accompanied by an album of photographs showing the visual presentation of each menu item.

Because of safety, sanitation, and health requirements, the galley is one of the most disciplined areas of the ship; everything must be done by the book, and there is no room for exceptions. The dishes are timed to be cooked just before they are served. For example, if the first sitting is at 6:15 P.M., the waiters will have the orders in to the galley by 6:30 and begin serving the appetizers. The first of the main entrées will start coming off the line at 6:40. By 7:15, the first dirty dishes will be coming in (to be immediately washed and reused for the second sitting), and desserts and coffee will start coming out. By 8:00, people will begin to leave (they have to if they want to catch the first sitting show—a graceful way to empty the dining room!). This leaves time for the waiters to reset the tables with clean linen and tableware for the second sitting at 8:30. Waiters are well trained and highly motivated. While their salaries are nominal, their tips can be substantial—waiters on the three major lines average around $3,000 per month tax free, and as all of their meals, accommodations, and medical expenses are provided, that's money they can take home. Top waiters make $3,400 or more—a small fortune in countries like the Philippines and the Czech Republic.

We should note here that the food and beverage department is also responsible for feeding the employees, who number 900 or more on larger ships. This is no small task. Unlike the passengers, who are a homogeneous group, the crew can come from 50 to 70 different countries. They do not all eat at the same time, and they do not all like the same food. Also, they use different dining rooms depending on their rank (three is average—one for the officers, one for the staff, and one for the crew). There is always a separate galley to feed shipboard employees and a wide choice of dishes to satisfy the cultural diversity of the crew.

Perhaps the best way to capture the problems and solutions of living and working aboard a cruise ship and feeding a shipload of passengers with high expectations is to interview the food and beverage manager on a major highly rated cruise ship. We picked Dedrick Van Regemorter of the *Star Princess.* Dedrick comes from a hotel background; before joining Princess he spent fifteen years with Marriott working in properties all over the world, from Amsterdam to Marco Island, Florida. He decided to move to the cruise line business when the hotel business slowed and with it the number of opportunities for promotion.

> There is a tremendous difference between food and beverage service on land and on board a ship. The ship is a closed environment. You work with the people who you have to live with, and you live with the people you have to work with. Therefore, it's extremely important to develop good interpersonal skills. Because you have to live with your people, it's not like on land, where you go to work in the morning and if an employee is not doing his job or if things go wrong, you can get upset or take disciplinary action. You know that in the evening you can go home and leave all that behind you, and the person who you got upset with also goes home, and in the morning all is forgotten. You see everyone all of the time, so you have to be very positive, but at the same time you have to keep their respect, and you have to keep very strict discipline. One of the things I noticed coming from the outside is that the number of stripes you carry on your shoulders is very important. It makes a big difference in the amount of attention you get from others on the ship.
>
> Aside from the living conditions, the responsibilities of my job are very different from when I worked in a hotel. While I do all of the ordering for our ship as far as items and quantity, I don't have to get involved at all with the financial details I did on land. When I worked in a hotel, there was tremendous pressure on me as well as all managers to control wages, overtime, and other costs as well as generate income. I do have a consumption budget I need to watch, and some other expenditure guidelines, but that's all. I don't worry about food costs; I don't even know what it costs to feed a passenger. Ninety-five percent of my energy and all of my staff's energy goes to making our passengers happy.
>
> When it comes to the differences in the way we do our job, we have to remember to view a ship, from the customer's point of view, as entirely different from a hotel. On a ship, the primary reason for being there is to have a good time. There are no business meetings, faxes, or phone calls—there is nothing to remind you of home. When you walk across that gangplank, the ship sets off a psychological switch that allows you to escape into another world, a world where there are no worries and where everything is taken care of.

Those of us who work on a ship are in a different world as well. When you work at a hotel, the influence from outside never leaves you. You might worry about your baby who is sick at home, for instance. But we never leave the ship, so we tend to have fewer distractions. Our transmission didn't break down on the way to work; the landlord isn't threatening to kick us out. The atmosphere is very positive. Moreover, a lot of our employees come from countries where the hospitality business is highly respected, where being a waiter is an important job, so they like their work. Because we're an incentive-based industry, the majority want to keep their jobs, and they realize that the better they are at doing them, the more money they will make. Finally, everyone has made a commitment for a certain period of time, six months or a year, so they feel they might as well make the best of it. If they are poor performers because of lack of experience, then we try to help them. In the dining room, we might put together a smaller station for a week or two supervised by a head waiter, or assign them to work with a more experienced waiter until we can bring them up to the same level as our regular staff. But if they have a lousy attitude, then we simply suggest they go home and find something else to do.

Serving tables on a cruise is different than in a hotel. The group of people being served stays the same for a whole week. This enables the waiter to develop a relationship with the guests so he can improve his service to them. For example, after the first night, when the waiter asks you whether you prefer coffee or tea, he should not have to ask you again. The experienced ones remember whether you want a single or double espresso, or decaffeinated coffee with cream, or regular coffee with sugar. A hotel waiter doesn't have that opportunity and so doesn't even focus on it. The only people at the hotel who remember preferences are bartenders because they try to develop a local regular clientele. So, on a ship, remembering details, developing a relationship with passengers, and having a real service attitude become the most important thing. In a hotel, waiters have other concerns that they don't have on a ship that distract them. They have to worry about the handling of cash, they have to worry about how many people they have to serve at one time—sometimes they have their hands full, and other times they have nothing at all to do. Here our waiters know exactly how many people are going to be coming to dinner and what time they're going to arrive. So everything is planned and organized; there's no idle time. It is hard work—our waiters may work as many as twelve hours in a sixteen- or eighteen-hour period. Because it's in shifts, they get an hour or two off in between. But we all adapt to the routine—we wake up at the same time, we take the same time off, we eat at the same time—the structure of the routine removes some of the stress from our lives.

Another difference from a hotel is in the way we do our cooking. The majority of our galley crew is European. They are all trained cooks. The levels and positions are different. To be a first cook, which means to be responsible for a station in the galley, like the fish station, takes quite a few years. It is more than on land because we still use the traditional French culinary setup. We do everything from scratch, when in hotels the move to convenience and prepared foods is accelerating. For instance, on land many kitchens use powders to make their stocks. We make our stocks from bones. Nothing goes to waste. On land, we often bought our meat pre-portioned and vacuum packed. On a ship, you buy a whole hindquarter and cut it down.

We use a lot more labor, and that is what accounts, in part, for the high quality of our food. We even make our own bread. In many hotels we would buy fresh bread, or brown and serve bread, or frozen bread. Here I buy 5,000 pounds of flour, add yeast and water, and put a baker to work, and he will produce 12,000 fresh rolls.

That brings up another interesting point. In hotels, you might use leftovers to make a new dish the next day. You won't find that on a ship. We don't have leftovers. We have limited storage capacity and a strong tradition of no waste. Remember, there are no trucks to come by daily and take away what we don't use. Unlike a hotel, where they forecast how many people are going to show up and order a certain item and if they don't there are some things left over, we know exactly how many people are coming and exactly what they are going to order. That's because even though we have a lot of choices, we serve the same menu on every cruise, and while we can't forecast individual demands, human beings are creatures of habit, and we're dealing with a large group of them. Sometimes we have an odd week or two where it's possible to run out of an item. Sometimes produce and fruit like strawberries, at certain times of the year or under certain weather conditions, can spoil faster than anticipated. And if that happens I can't pick up the telephone and ask someone to send over some more. But if we should have a problem like that—

and it hasn't happened to me yet—I would talk to the printer who would change the menu on the computer and we could get the press rolling and turn out a thousand new menus in twenty minutes. We are self-sufficient, and we must be able to react.

Our passengers expect quite a bit when it comes to food. They do not expect to eat the same foods they would have at home or even in an ordinary restaurant. I like to compare the food we have to serve daily to the food you might order when you go to that one extraordinary restaurant you go to for special occasions every four months. That's why lunch consists of four or five courses, and dinner is a six- or seven-course event. Moreover, the stress of what to order is relieved because price is no consideration—you've already paid for it. At home, your eyes go immediately to the right side of the menu before you order that lobster or rack of lamb, but on a cruise there is no right side at all.

Part of that quality dining experience is, of course, service, and on land it is not possible to give 800 people a really first-class dining experience in an hour and forty minutes. When I was at Marriott, we thought, "Wouldn't it be great if we could go to a meeting planner and offer a menu where the guests would have a choice of four entrées?" But there was no way to pull it off in a hotel banquet kitchen, which has only a few people and a small space because everything is prepared earlier in the main kitchen and most of the work and manpower is focused on the restaurants. On a ship, everything we do is different. I have 107 people in our galley, and they don't have to worry about what people are going to order or when to prepare it. All they have to worry about is taking orders and cooking them individually from 108 waiters and assistant waiters. Our food goes right from the oven to the plate to the passenger. You know, having a ship that's consistently full removes a lot of uncertainty and allows us to produce really fine food and serve it with style.

The Steward's Department

The steward's department (on some lines called the housekeeping department) is charged with the cleaning and general maintenance of all of the cabins and interior public areas on a ship. It is also responsible, in most cases, for cabin foodservice. In addition, the department handles the laundering of all of the crew's uniforms as well as linens, sheets, and towels for the dining rooms and cabins. George Drummond, who was chief steward on NCL's *Seaward,* told us:

> I've been at sea nineteen years. My job is to see that we have a clean ship. Our passengers are entitled to spotless cabins. I'm also in charge of getting the luggage into and out of cabins. On three- and four-day cruises, passengers may bring as many as three pieces of luggage on board; multiply that by 1,600 and you can see I have my hands full every time we embark and disembark the ship. It takes three to four hours to get everyone's luggage on board and delivered on a ship this size. We can unload it in thirty to forty minutes because we collect it the night before and load it on pallets.
>
> I enjoy making the passengers happy—the pool attendants are in my department too, and we send them around to spray the passengers with water to cool them off, which they really appreciate when they're lying in the sun. I expect my cabin stewards to give their passengers service, not just make up their rooms twice a day. They need to tell them to have a nice day, ask them if they need anything, and get it if they do. I expect them to offer to press their clothes for the captain's party and to make sure the passengers know them by name. It takes a lot of training—many of my people come from places where the word *clean* doesn't mean the same to them as it does to me. I have to show them, and I personally go around with every new steward to show him what I expect.

Drummond, now deceased, was speaking of luggage movement on a ship carrying 1,600 passengers. Imagine the logistics of handling luggage on a cruise ship with 3,000 or 4,000 passengers. This could result in 10,000 to 12,000 pieces of luggage! To assist in this seemingly daunting task, the newer, larger ships are designed with more elevators to move luggage and more space to sort and deploy it. Moreover, some lines like Carnival offer self-assisted guest luggage handling both at embarkation and debarkation. This is a natural change that has met with high guest approval. (All one needs to do is watch an airline boarding process to realize that many folks simply do not wish to part with their luggage!) On shorter three-, four-, and five-day itineraries, more than half of the guests opt to wheel their own luggage, which greatly relieves the burden on the ship's crew.

Cabin room service is yet another area that has become far more complex with larger ships than in those of Drummond's era. A shore tour can return 600 hungry passengers to a ship after the lido and dining room lunch hours. With experience of oft-repeated itineraries, the ship knows to anticipate these peak demand times and has extra staff poised to handle the food and drink requests. As was pointed out earlier, the routine of a ship, not felt by the guest, helps provide a superior level of service that a resort or hotel has no hope of matching.

The Cruise Staff

The cruise director is another job that doesn't exist in a traditional land-based resort. Many resorts have social directors, but they have an entirely different function from that of the cruise director on board a ship. Unlike social directors, who typically work alone, a ship's cruise director has a good-size staff to manage—entertainers, musicians, shore excursion managers, youth activity directors, aerobics instructors, a newsletter editor, and, on some ships, a print shop and television studio. On Royal Caribbean's *Sovereign of the Seas,* the cruise staff numbers seventy. Like the food and beverage department, the cruise staff can and does make a huge difference in how people feel about their cruise. Remember, the product customers are buying is a vacation experience, and the persons responsible for all of the activities on board and ashore hold the keys to making it a memorable and satisfying occasion.

The most visible product of the cruise director's work is the daily schedule of activities, which is usually placed in the passenger's stateroom the previous night. If the ship is going to be in port the next day, the schedule lists the tours that are available and when they will be leaving. If there's going to be a port lecture, a dance lesson, a bingo game, or a tour of the bridge, it's in the schedule and will be run by one of the cruise staff. Youth activities are listed here as well as parties for singles and grandmothers. The idea is to have a wide variety of activities and entertainment choices for every age and to see that every activity starts and finishes on time and is run in a fashion consistent with the line's standards.

Cruise directors check out possible new shore excursions and monitor existing ones. They may arrange for a local group to come on board and provide entertainment before the ship leaves—a Mexican mariachi group with folk dancers, for instance, in Acapulco. At night, cruise directors are all over the ship—checking on the two big shows presented in the show lounge (which they usually introduce), the pianist at the piano bar, the DJ in the disco, the comedian in another lounge, and the teen party going on in the teen club. In fact, they may be the stars of a show or two themselves! They may be the first person up in the morning and among the last to go to bed. It is a grueling job to see that 2,000 to 3,000 people are enjoying themselves and having fun, for as many of the twenty-four hours in a day they can handle, for three, four, five, or seven days or more. And then start all over again with a new group within a few hours on the same day the old group departs.

Cruise directors come from a variety of nationalities and backgrounds. While many started as entertainers, others come from the ranks of cruise staff and various shoreside walks of life. The best ones exude a star quality that guests enjoy. They genuinely like people and get along well with them. They're adept at handling temperamental artists as well. Good cruise directors are hard to find but can make all the difference in how passengers remember their vacation, and they have a profound influence on the on board revenue.

A good cruise director schedules activities in such a way to maximize both guest satisfaction and onboard spending. If a lounge band is hot, the lounge is packed with happy guests and the bar revenue is strong. Conversely, if the band is so-so, the lounge is lightly attended and revenue suffers. It is a curious but serendipitous axiom that happy guests spend more—which makes the cruise lines happy, too!

The challenge is that a cruise vacation experience has a significant number of components (some of them, such as entertainment, quite complicated) that must be assembled, packaged, and coordinated in an effective manner to satisfy guests. The solution lies in the advantage a ship has because it is a controlled and confined atmosphere—a cocoon, if you will—in which a well-trained staff following a tested and standardized routine can deliver a superior food, entertainment, and service experience with little opportunity for error. It takes the teamwork of a number of specialists, from chefs to captains, supported by a strong infrastructure, to pull it off, but the results justify the efforts.

The Other Side of Life on Board

We had the opportunity to do an in-depth interview with Shannon Cannon, the CFM coordinator on board Celebrity's *Constellation*. The celebrity family member coordinator is responsible for the crew's welfare on board, including crew activities and morale. Here are her insights on life on board:

> Life on board the ship is a lifestyle that you have to be prepared to change into. You have to be prepared to come on and work. It's hard to leave. It's different than home. At home you work five days a week, thirty-five to forty hours a week maximum, weekends off. Here you work ten hours a day, seven days a week, no overtime, no holidays off, no days in lieu. You don't notice it. It's a small community, like your community dorm rooms. In my position, at some point, I meet everyone.

No matter how busy you are, it's the people that keep you coming back. You can never say no. I've been very fortunate to be on the *Constellation*.

My days, most mornings, start at 8:30 or 9:00, depending on what activities are going on. Sometimes I have to be up at 7:00. You work through. You might have a few hours to run off at port to run around or take a nap. Activities run every evening until one, two, or three in the morning. We try to run activities every evening, so there's always something available to them whether they want to participate or not, and a variety of those activities.

It's a busy day, but when you go home you miss it. It's hard; I spend more time here than I do with my family and friends at home. It's difficult; you keep in touch with those few friends and family at home. You keep in touch with the people here when you are at home more than you keep in touch with the people at home when you are here.

In relationships, many of them form. I mean a lot of the time people will take a relationship for what it is. You are here for a certain period of time. Then you leave, and you never know if you are going to be on the same ship together or not. It's company, really. You look for that closeness while you are here. We have married couples that are on board and working together. The company tries to do its best in keeping them together. It does tend to be a little bit difficult, as it is a small community.

There's heartbreak, too. It's so hard to come on board and pretend to be somebody you aren't. It's a switch between *Friends, Sex and the City,* and *Seinfeld.* Really, you know, there's a lot of heartbreak. There's a lot of promiscuity. There are a lot of safe moments that happen. There are a lot of good things that do happen. I have a girlfriend who met her husband on board. He's from England and they are living in Canada now.

It's a shame, there are a lot of things that happen. It's not an emotional connection. It's a physical connection. Sometimes I'm their mother, their psychologist, or their psychiatrist. A lot of it just happens. You just don't know somebody. You spend a lot of time with them, but your life is just in this small area. If your vacations don't correspond, they go one place, I go one place, and so you never really know who that person is. There's a lot of dishonesty, but there are a lot of good things that go on.

We have parents on board who leave their children with a family member, so they are supporting their families. Some are supporting parents and brothers and sisters and their children as well.

You see both sides, people who will come and have the experience and travel and then go. They stay for three or four contracts. Sometimes they come on and it's not what they anticipated, the work life. They weren't told what the workweek would consist of and what their life would be. Sometimes it's not quite for them.

Some people I know are lifers. They will never leave. I love them because if they are lifers, I can come back and visit them and I can just cruise, just on vacation.

I never anticipated staying for six years. I thought I'd stay for two or three years and leave. I am from Halifax, I started late, I was twenty-seven. You see so many people coming on who are twenty or twenty-one.

I'm thirty-three now, and I'm still here. I thought I would leave last time, and I had made plans to leave—and I'm still here. The last time something happened, they called me and said, "Can you come back in four days?" How do you say no? All of my girlfriends are here. You come back and you are so fortunate to be here on the *Constellation.*

I came back and felt so welcomed and loved. I met crew members on the airplane at the airport from San Juan and they didn't let me touch my luggage. They didn't let me do anything. They wanted to take care of me. They were so happy to see me. I was so happy to see them. There were people in the terminal waiting for me. They were waiting for me in the gangway. People kept coming by, saying, "We're so glad you are back." It gives you a warm feeling. That's what keeps you coming back. It just sucks you in.

A lot of the time, I am the crew mother. I get cranky like mothers do. You learn a lot about people. I'm very outspoken, so I don't have qualms or quarrels telling people off. However, I listen to them too. I've sat in my room until 2:00 in the morning talking to someone because they needed someone to talk to.

In St. Petersburg, there are extracurricular activities at the Seamen's Center there. What I mean is there is prostitution. I hand out condoms to ensure they are practicing safe sex. They are always in my office for them to take, but some of them don't make it into my office to take them. I will sit in the gangway and make sure I hand condoms out to every bloody one of them who is going out the door. If they tell me they don't want one, I say, "You're taking one."

I like to know what's going on and what they are doing. In most places, I know where they'll go for those things and I know where they will need them, you know. I don't like to tell them where to go. I just say, "Your friends will tell you."

You get close to people. A lot of them don't have places to turn to. You know, there are a lot of times I have to tell a crew member there's bad news at home. "You have to contact home." We've had to do emergency leaves. We've had crew members arrested for drugs. I've been interviewed by the FBI. I had to clean out rooms where I've found baby shoes that they've bought for children. You make that connection. You know a lot about them. A lot of times you don't know who you are face to face with and you think they are the best in the world and the next week they are arrested for whatever reason. I like to think I am a fairly good judge of character.

HOME ON THE ROLLING DEEP

4

Case studies in
backstage management

It is not within the scope of this book to give the reader an in-depth feel for the actual cruise product offered by all the major industry players. Several of the guidebooks on cruising, such as Berlitz and Fielding, do an excellent job of this. However, we thought it might be interesting to dissect some of the elements of how the cruise experience is managed on board. We purposely picked two examples to contrast differences and show similarities, a smaller ship and one of the major mass-market vessels. Our choice for the smaller vessel was the *Seabourn Spirit,* based on a fourteen-day cruise from Istanbul to Venice. While Seabourn has only three ships, the *Seabourn Pride, Seabourn Spirit,* and *Seabourn Legend,* they have been consistently ranked by travel agents, journalists, and consumers as among the world's best cruise lines.

Cruising with Seabourn

Seabourn was founded by a young Norwegian industrialist and entrepreneur named Atle Brynestad, a self-made man who started his first business at age sixteen, knitting and marketing his own line of Norwegian sweaters. After gaining success in diverse areas of business, Brynestad sensed a growing market for cruises and, knowing that Norwegians seemed to have a knack for running them well (there have been a number of Norwegian-owned companies over the years, such as Norwegian Cruise Line, Royal Viking Line, and Norwegian American Line, and of course Royal Caribbean Line was started by a Norwegian), Brynestad decided to develop a new concept for cruising. He was attracted to the luxury end of the vacation market because of his personal lifestyle and experience.

By the mid-1980s, several concepts of luxury cruising were in the market. Cunard's *Queen Elizabeth 2* was a 66,000-ton dual-purpose ship built for both transatlantic crossings and cruising. The first purely premium line was the Norwegian American Line, which operated the

Sagafjord and the *Vistafjord.* Built for long-range cruising to resemble elegant European hotels, these smaller, 24,000-ton ships carried between six and seven hundred passengers. Royal Viking Line, another luxury cruise line of the time, was founded in 1970. Warren Titus, its first president, felt they could differentiate their product successfully by providing a larger number of deluxe cabins and suites. These ships were constructed using a new, modular prefabrication system that allowed for greater freedom of design and considerable cost savings. The line had three 22,000-ton, 500-passenger ships by 1974, the *Royal Viking Star, Sky,* and *Sea* (these were later stretched to 28,000 tons and 700 passengers). At the opposite end of the scale was another Norwegian company, Sea Goddess Cruises, with two ships launched in 1984. These ships were designed to have the ambience of large luxury yachts. At 4,253 tons each, they had a passenger capacity of only 116.

In 1987, Brynestad recruited Titus from Royal Viking, and the two men, along with a group of associates, set out to design a cruise line that would be both better and clearly different from the available luxury offerings. They reasoned that while Royal Viking's facilities and service were undoubtedly the finest afloat, their ships were too large to provide the kind of intimate and exclusive quality of service they felt luxury-minded clientele would demand. While Sea Goddess was able to satisfy this expectation, for the most part, their two ships were so small that they lacked many of the amenities the market also expected (such as a full-sized spa); moreover, they didn't behave as well in choppy waters as a larger ship would. Their solution was to design a new kind of ship—10,000 tons in size—that would accommodate 208 people, all of them in 104 suites of 277–575 square feet each. By contrast, Royal Viking ships had some cabins as small as 138 square feet, while Sea Goddess suites were 205 square feet, excepting the owner's suite at 475 square feet. They believed this new Seabourn design would offer the intimacy of a small yacht while providing the amenities and spaciousness of a larger ship. Another important consideration was that this size ship could accommodate a galley large enough to prepare all meals on an *à la minute* basis rather than banquet style. The greater size also allowed for a large enough crew to provide the highest crew-passenger ratio in the industry (better than two crew members for every three passengers), thus ensuring top-notch service. Their first ship, the *Seabourn Pride,* made her maiden voyage in November 1988. Her sister ship, the *Seabourn Spirit,* was launched a year later. In 1989, *Travel and Leisure* magazine, in a lengthy cover story on Seabourn, described it as "the one to beat." In 2006 the readers of the same magazine voted it the world's best luxury cruise line.

From the beginning, Brynestad recognized that he was not selling a cruise but, in his own words, "a unique vacation experience." Because Seabourn's all-suite ship would only carry 200 passengers on a hull that might carry 400 or more passengers in a standard configuration, and because it offered a very high crew-passenger ratio, Seabourn would have to be priced at the very top of the market. Seabourn's Mediterranean cruises today cost an average of $750 to $924 per day per person, with most cruises designed in seven-day patterns; these can be combined for longer cruises of up to five weeks without repeating ports. There are, of course, other itineraries (the three ships sail all over the world, including to China, Vietnam, and the Amazon). About half of the line's cruises are available in itineraries of seven days, and about half of the guests on board combine two or more cruises to stay aboard longer. In this way, Seabourn is able to attract and satisfy new, younger, affluent travelers who seldom vacation for more than a week or ten days at a time and at the same time satisfy their traditional clientele who like longer cruises. Given virtually any itinerary, however, Seabourn is among the most expensive cruise products on the market. With the high price tag come extremely high expectations. Market studies show that the average household income of Seabourn clientele is $250,000. According to Deborah Natansohn, Seabourn's president, "Our clientele have every vacation option in the world, and they are quite accustomed to partaking in the finest accommodations, service, and cuisine around the world. But those are just the basics, meeting their expectations. To truly attain their loyalty, we have to exceed those expectations—to surprise and delight them. That is the art form."

Indeed, "delight" is an important part of Seabourn's corporate culture. It is a part of their branding. They use the term "Signature Delights" to define the sorts of pampering extras they weave into guests' shipboard experience. To that end, the line is continually searching for small, not necessarily expensive touches that add to the overall sense of pampering that keeps guests coming back for more. In terms of impact, probably no element is as potent as the open bar policy, which provides complimentary wines and spirits throughout the cruise. This not only represents tremendous value to the guests but also contributes to a relaxed, club-like social atmosphere on board. In recent years, Seabourn has introduced a "Pure Pampering" menu of luxury bathing oils from the prestigious British firm Molton Brown. Guests can request one of these from their stewardess, and, if they wish, the stewardess will draw and prepare the bath for them. Another example is the innovative, complimentary "Massage Moments" offered to guests sunbathing on deck. A free five-minute neck and shoulder massage does more than simply relax the guest—it signals, in a singularly tactile way, the company's intention for the guest's pleasure. As meaningful as these added touches are to the guests already on board, they also serve the company as concrete examples of added value that are used in marketing and selling to prospective clients. They help "define the indefinable."

Another innovation Seabourn created for its guests is the option to have their luggage picked up at their homes and delivered to their suites on board the ship, a program they dubbed "Personal Valet" luggage shipping service. Seabourn partnered with DHL Worldwide to create and provide this service, which is very popular with its upscale guests. It is not inexpensive, but for Seabourn's guests, it removes one of the most unpleasant parts of their journey: manhandling their luggage through airport terminals, security checks, and customs clearances.

Once guests arrive at the ship, embarkation procedures are completed quickly and with little or no waiting, because so few guests embark at a time. They are handed a complimentary glass of high-quality French champagne (such as Heidsieck Monopole nonvintage Brut) as they are greeted by name by the hotel manager and his white-gloved staff and escorted to their suites. A complimentary bottle of properly iced champagne is waiting in every suite along with the luggage. Within a few minutes, a cabin stewardess appears, introduces herself, and orients the guests to their suite, offering a selection of designer soaps (Hermes, l'Occitane, Bijan) to complement the Molton Brown toiletries in the bathroom. Unlike a hotel room or even an ordinary cruise line cabin, Seabourn accommodations do require some orientation. Their standard 277-square foot suite seems more like a small studio apartment. The décor is muted pastels, with either a 5-foot picture window with electric window shades or a double sliding glass door that opens onto a narrow, step-out balcony. There is a convertible dining/coffee table with a sofa and two chairs, a queen-sized bed, a desk with personalized monogrammed stationery, a large walk-in closet with a combination safe, a TV with DVD player and a Bose Wave stereo CD player, a bar and refrigerator stocked with favorite alcoholic beverages and soft drinks (personal preferences Seabourn collected several weeks earlier), polished glassware, a marble bathroom with two sinks, a tub and shower, fluffy Egyptian cotton towels, terrycloth robes and slippers, and more. Playing on the TV is a DVD entitled "Welcome to Your Suite," which points out all of the special features and how to use them. Room service is provided twenty-four hours a day (including caviar and champagne at no charge). During meal hours, complete dinners from the restaurant menu are served one course at a time in the suite by regular waiters for those who wish a private, romantic candlelight dinner or simply don't want to dress up and dine in the restaurants. Unlike many other cruise ships, where important announcements are automatically piped into cabins periodically, on Seabourn announcements are broadcast on only one of the four channels; it remains silent most of the time.

The ship is spacious but small by contemporary cruise ship standards, so it does not take long to tour the public areas. The spacious main dining room, called The Restaurant, is open from 8 to 10 for breakfast, 12:30 to 2 for lunch, and 7 to 10 for dinner. Seating is open. Passengers can come in any time they want without reservations and be seated wherever they want and with whomever they wish. We consider this a defining feature of true luxury cruising. There are plenty of tables for two as well as larger tables for groups of four to twelve who wish to dine together. No one ever sits alone unless the individual so chooses; single passengers are invited to join other guests or dine at tables with officers and senior hotel staff members. Dinner menus feature cuisine designed by celebrity chef Charlie Palmer, one of America's most successful and acclaimed chef/restaurateurs. Most dishes are prepared to order—à la minute. All dishes are characterized by bold flavors, fresh ingredients, and playful, aesthetic presentations. Favorite dishes, according to the company, include grilled lamb loin with roasted morels, parmesan flan, and sweet peas; pan-roasted halibut with spring asparagus risotto; and, for vegetarians, soy-glazed shiitakes and gingered greens, Crunchy Vidalia onions, and onion soubise. Lighter fare includes crab lasagna with tomato basil coulis and aromatic braised sea bass with fennel and tomato bouillon. In our opinion, Seabourn's restaurants would merit at least one and probably two stars if Guide Michelin were to rate them.

In addition to the Restaurant, the ship offers the Veranda Café, which has indoor and outdoor seating and serves buffet breakfast and lunch. While it is buffet style, waiters stand by to carry plates to the table or serve passengers as well as handle special orders. In the evenings, the Veranda Café is transformed into two, a more casual alternative to The Restaurant, serving innovative tasting menus of paired small plates.

The ship has three public lounges where entertainment consists of a small musical group with one or two soloists and one or two other cabaret-type entertainers. There is an intimate casino featuring slot machines, roulette, and two blackjack tables. There is also an enrichment lecturer, usually either a college professor or an expert on the area the ship is cruising. On the particular Seabourn voyage we were on, the enrichment lecturer was Dr. James Bill, director of the Center for International Studies at the College of William and Mary and an expert on Mideastern affairs.

Other shipboard amenities include a spa with treatment rooms, sauna, and steam baths, and a spacious gymnasium complete with free weights, treadmills, elliptical machines, bikes, rowing machines, and a complete beauty salon. There are three whirlpools and a swimming pool, a track that circles the vessel (fifteen times around equals 1 mile), a gift shop, and a library stocked with DVDs, music and books on CD, and a broad selection of recently published contemporary and classical fiction and nonfiction. There is even a self-service launderette for guests who don't wish to use the regular ship's laundry service.

More than most lines, Seabourn recognizes that in the hospitality business the passengers are part of the physical product; guests expect each other to behave and dress appropriately, but on Seabourn's ships, as elsewhere, different sorts of guests dress differently. Seabourn vessels therefore have abandoned strict dress codes in favor of guidelines that increase the options to adjust to the times. There are three kinds of dress suggestions: casual (no jacket required), elegant casual (jacket but no tie required), and formal, which is basically black tie optional. The ship's daily program lists the suggested dress for lounges and dining venues each evening after 6. Passengers understand that this is a matter of personal choice, as the ship always offers a more casual alternative for dinner, and those who do not wish to dress are able to dine in their suite, either with another like-minded couple or by themselves, to watch a movie or read. On formal nights, most male guests wear tuxedos or (a few) dark suits. However, any guests who wish a more casual dinner on formal nights can dine at 2 in elegant casual attire, with a jacket but no tie required for men; on other nights, 2 is always casual. Thus the mix of fashions found in lounges before and after dinner is broad enough to make everyone comfortable, but it is not too broadly diverse.

Seabourn's philosophy of how to achieve superior service is based on two main tenets. The first is that you have to take care of your internal customers (your employees) before you can expect them to take care of your external customers (the guests). The second is that the guests are Seabourn's most important asset—and that it is the staff's job to find out very quickly what each individual expects and to make sure that is delivered in spades, and if possible exceeded, so the guest will clearly be able to differentiate Seabourn cruises from the ordinary and articulate that difference to others when the voyage is completed.

The company does not just pay lip service to these concepts; they constantly reinforce them with a passion. Vice president of fleet operations Larry Rapp believes that this level of service starts with human resource management. "In order to provide superior service," he says, "Each employee must feel absolutely secure in his or her position. He or she has to feel, from a psychological standpoint, free to take whatever decision needs to be taken to satisfy our guests without constraint from a company system, a budget plan, or an organization plan. The crew member who is speaking to a guest has to have the power to provide satisfaction—no hierarchy should get in the way of that." The "Twelve Points of Seabourn Hospitality," a document that every employee has and that is posted in the hotel manager's office, contains several points aimed directly at encouraging this kind of behavior:

◆   Any crew member who receives a guest complaint "owns" that
    complaint. He/she is responsible for ensuring guest
    satisfaction.

◆ Always remember the importance of teamwork and service to coworkers.
◆ Communicate guest problems to fellow employees and management.
◆ Take responsibility for your own behavior.
◆ Do not be afraid to make a mistake as long as your efforts are sincerely intended to do your job in a better way.

To further ensure there is no misunderstanding of what is expected, the Seabourn Hotel Operations Manual specifically states that every Seabourn supervisor is to receive, *before* signing on the ship with their employment contract, a document called "Supervision of Hotel Employees." The document is very specific and states that performance evaluations will be based on the ability of supervisors to accomplish these tasks. Here are some relevant excerpts:

◆ It is the duty of each supervisor to find a way to motivate his or her team to:
— Find out what each guest wants.
— Give it to him or her.
◆ Supervisors have the responsibility to encourage open communication by creating in their employees:
— Self-confidence
— Empathy
— Respect

Below is an outline of the management style Seabourn Cruise Line expects of its supervisors:

I will support front line employees, not try to control them.
I believe that *every* employee wants to do the best job he or she can.
I fully realize that my employees' attitudes and feelings affect their performance and that my supervision can affect those attitudes and feelings.
I will give positive feedback to my colleagues as often as sensible.
When I need to give negative feedback, I will only refer to facts, *not* to people. I will say, "The ashtray needs cleaning." I will not say, "You don't take proper care of the ashtrays," or, worse yet, "You are a sloppy person."
I will listen to the ideas of my employees and give them full credit when they contribute to a success.
I will give each of my colleagues all the respect that is their right as a human being. This means treating them as they want to be treated.

Every week there is a waiters' meeting after the dining room closes at 11 P.M. during which guest comment cards from the previous week's cruise are reviewed. In attendance one evening when we were there were the hotel manager, the maître d'hôtel (who chaired the meeting), the chef de cuisine, and all seventeen waiters from ten different countries. The meeting began with the chef reading aloud the negative comments from the previous week concerning the food. He commented first that negative comments were not negative but constructive. "We want to maintain our reputation for the best food," he told the group. The first comment he had was that the "pasta was not done correctly." A waiter pointed out that this comment was from an Italian family. Italians are particular about their pasta. But the same comment card went on to say that "the food improved the second week." The waiter added, "By the second week we knew this family. They liked spicy food and we gave it to them." The maître d' complimented the waiter for being on his toes. Another comment stated that "the pastry needs improvement." A member of the group commented that he had tasted the croissants that morning and they were horrible. The chef agreed and noted that the baker had become ill in Istanbul and left the ship. A new one was due the next day. The only other negative food comment was that "the menu was too Americanized." The chef told the waiters he needed more feedback from them as to what their European and Asian clientele liked. Then some of the positive comments were reviewed. They included "great selection," "superb meals," "good cuisine and variety—better than before," "my kind of food," "I blame you for the weight I gained," and "all our special requests were handled with no problem." Overall, the score on cuisine was 9.81 out of a possible 10. The chef noted that 87.3 percent of the responses gave the cuisine a perfect 10, and no one gave it below an 8.

The maître d' then reviewed the comments on the waiters' service. There were only three negatives. The first dealt with slow dinner service on the Veranda. The maître d' recommended that waiters concentrate more on their stations. Another guest mentioned that their wineglasses had been removed before the end of the meal and said this was not a good idea, as there was always the possibility that someone would want more. Everyone thought that was a good comment. "From now on we won't do it," said one of the waiters. Finally, a guest wanted to know why he couldn't order full room service by the pool but had to return to his suite to get it. The hotel manager noted that in truth they didn't have enough manpower on board to offer this. "But," he added, "People paying $35,000 ought to be able to get it." A discussion was held in which several waiters contributed ideas. It was decided that the full room service menu would be offered from one of the bars on deck and that trays of sandwiches would be passed around at lunchtime so guests would not feel the need to order room service. They then turned to the positive comments they had received. "You have given a new meaning to class and superb service." "We are used to traveling on a private yacht, but we like this cruise so much we're spending an extra $25,000 to stay another week." "All your waiters are as adorable as my two sons." Several waiters were mentioned by name, and the others applauded or cheered whenever one of these comments was read.

The meeting ended with a review of the known likes and dislikes of the guests joining the ship in Athens in a couple of days. One liked certain cheeses, and a note was made to check with the provision master to be sure they would be on board. Another liked bran cereal and skim milk for breakfast every day. One was known to like fresh fruit juice brought to him while exercising on the treadmill—this turned out to be one of us authors; talk about a small world! And, yes, I did receive my juice each day! Everyone made notes so he or she would remember.

The meeting was highly participatory. After every negative comment, several suggestions were offered as to how to improve things. No one was criticized directly, and there were no recriminations. A similar meeting took place the following morning in the housekeeping department. Every negative comment was reviewed, and the tone of the meeting was always "How can we solve this problem?"—never "People don't understand that we can't do this." As a result of this continuing process, Seabourn is constantly refining and fine-tuning its service. "The whole secret is getting everyone involved in producing the product," said the hotel manager, who was part of the original group that developed the Seabourn concept and was their first food and beverage manager. "Then it becomes theirs and they own it and are proud of it. I not only solicit their ideas, I try them out when I can. If they work, I adopt them." When I asked how he could do this with such a demanding clientele where mistakes can be fatal, his answer was, "We hire good people we can trust and then we train them. God is in the details, said Frank Lloyd Wright."

Training goes on continually at all levels. Hotel managers are supplied with a series of management tapes used in business schools and training seminars. These are shown and discussed on a voluntary basis regularly. The company also offers all supervisors the opportunity to attend courses at the hotel school of their choice when they are off the ship on vacation. The sommelier gives monthly tastings and lectures on wines and the regions they come from, and the chef briefs the waitstaff every night before dinner, using a waiter's manual that gives a brief description of the ingredients of each dish on the menus, describes how they are cooked, and lists common allergens, such as nuts, garlic, and alcohol. Waiters regularly are quizzed in writing to improve their knowledge of food and wine. Questions include, "What do you know about sabayon?" "What ocean or sea does the turbot come from?" and "Name three types of caviar." In keeping with Seabourn's nonthreatening, nurturing atmosphere, the quiz, along with the answers, is posted a week in advance so everyone has a chance to study and learn the answers before the test.

Many of Seabourn's staff don't see the *Seabourn Spirit* as a cruise ship at all. "We're a small hotel that floats." We heard the same sentiment echoed later in the voyage by another crew member. "I would never work on a cruise ship," he said scornfully. In truth, as we have pointed out earlier, we believe cruise ships are not floating hotels but floating vacation experiences. Nevertheless, it serves Seabourn's purpose from a recruiting, training, and motivational standpoint to encourage that kind of thinking.

Compensation aboard Seabourn ships for service personnel is unique. Tipping is neither required nor expected. While staff may accept a tip if offered, they must not solicit tips under any circumstances, and in fact they commonly refused them. The hotel staff is compensated by a salary plus a revenue-sharing plan based on the number of guests on board each cruise. The theory is, "If we do a good job, people will take more cruises and tell their friends. If they do that, the company makes more money, and so the people responsible for creating that experience should share in it." Longtime Seabourn guests, of which there are many, have learned that they can give money to the Crew Welfare Fund, which pays for parties and excursions for the entire crew.

Seabourn's method of getting the crew involved in producing the product combined with eclectic itineraries where different ports are visited every week (unlike mass-market ships, Seabourn cruises do not go back and forth between the same destinations on a regular schedule) offers unique opportunities as well as problems. The most important opportunity is to forge a lasting personal relationship between the customers and the company. The morning after the *Seabourn Spirit* departed from Istanbul with ninety new passengers joining the passengers continuing from the previous voyage, the dining room waiters met to examine pictures of all of the new folks and memorize their names. In the lounges, dining room, and Veranda Café, whenever a crew member recognizes a person, he or she repeats the name out loud so other crew members can hear it, so they too can greet the guest by name. The payoff becomes most obvious in the dining room; even if you sit at a different table each night with a different waiter, you are greeted by name.

Rapp points out that Seabourn's cuisine is another opportunity to provide a distinctive experience. Their policy is to buy fresh regional products at ports where they are available. On the voyage we were on, the chef purchased fresh strawberries in Odessa, fish in Istanbul, and goose liver in France. During one stop in the Greek Islands, he headed off to the local fish market to buy some of that day's catch, which appeared on the menu that evening. Often, guests are invited to come along. This provides a personal connection with the chef, who is able to teach the guests a bit about the ingredients and get to know more about them. Freshness is an obsession on board. The orange juice is squeezed fresh daily—yesterday's fresh juice is consumed by the crew! Even the sommelier and head bartender buy many of the wines used on the ship in their countries of origin. "Because I am involved in the wine selection, I can explain the wines and sell them enthusiastically," the head bartender told us.

One of the prime motivations that brings guests to Seabourn is their expectation of having unusual travel experiences ashore. Because of their size, Seabourn's ships can visit places that larger ships can't. Some guests choose Seabourn for that reason. And even in popular ports visited by lots of ships, Seabourn can create exclusive and intimate experiences that are not possible for hundreds and hundreds of participants. The challenge is that the shore excursions, the very aspect of Seabourn's product that attracts many of its guests, are also, to a certain extent, beyond its direct control. Unlike a seven-day Caribbean cruise, where the ship visits the same port every week, a Seabourn ship may visit some ports only a few times a year. That means that they have to work harder (and usually pay more) to ensure the availability of best equipment and tour guides for their shore excursions, as the infrastructure in some areas is dominated by the larger vessels that call more regularly. Moreover, things often change—museums and other sites close for renovations, new ones open, and the recommended shopping and dining venues can change. Seabourn's method of dealing with this is to differentiate their versions of what is offered as much as possible from the run of the mill. Buses and vans are only half-filled to give guests more comfort while touring. Members of Seabourn's own travel staff escort each vehicle. Bottles of water and soft drinks are carried on board, and a complimentary refreshment stop is included. The company auditions the guides that will be used, when possible, and requests the best ones by name whenever possible. Detailed written contracts are given to all tour operators that specify, among other things, that all admissions are to be included, the hours at which the buses will arrive and depart at each stop, and any other requirements such as, "After lunch the guide will be stationed by the bell tower on the square to answer questions."

Seabourn's guests have clearly declared the importance of unique shoreside experiences in their travel decisions, and the company has acted on that knowledge by adding a specially created, complimentary "Exclusively Seabourn" shoreside experience at one port of call on every cruise. It would be difficult to overstate the importance of this amenity to Seabourn's guests. In one such event, Seabourn's guests are welcomed at dusk into the ruins of Ephesus in Turkey, after the site has closed to the general public. Torch-bearing guides dressed as ancient Ephesians lead them down the marble road to the Library of Celsus, where candlelit, linen-draped tables await them. In the Library façade itself, a string quartet plays classical music as Seabourn's guests enjoy cocktails in this fantasy setting. It is an experience they will never forget, and one they will brag about to their friends and families for months and even years afterward. That is not only brilliant product design, it's also very smart marketing.

At some destinations, it is possible to offer tours unavailable to other ships. These tours are usually quite expensive because the operators must do a lot of research and development for relatively few visits and small numbers of participants. One example is a horse-drawn carriage trip through vineyards and châteaux in France. In Venice, guests enjoy a private tour of the Guggenheim Museum hosted by one of its curators after closing hours; wine, of course, is served. Again, these tours are often the unique creations of the ship's travel office, which gives the staff a feeling of ownership and thus an internal mandate to see that they succeed.

Seabourn's success can be attributed to a complex and carefully orchestrated corporate culture based on values shared among the management, employees, and guests. "The key to Seabourn's success is listening and adapting; we need to understand the vacation attributes that our customers value most and then, almost invisibly, adapt our product to their changing lifestyles and needs," says Natansohn. "The market views us as having a consistently excellent product," she adds. "But it's not the product itself that's necessarily the same over time: It is the fact that we consistently anticipate service and fulfill our customers' desires." That is, for Seabourn, a key point. Everyone who works for the company understands what counts. The passengers, who are paying more than $800 per diem, know they are buying a distinctive and personal experience, and that's what counts for them. They expect uniqueness and customized service; indeed, they demand it. The company shares the same value.

"It doesn't matter what you want—the company will get it for you" is a reality in Seabourn's service delivery system. Guests frequently bring their own recipes on board, which the chef gladly prepares. It gives the company a chance to further customize and thereby differentiate their product. In some cases, special ingredients are flown to the ship to fulfill these requests. Natansohn boils down the reasons why people choose Seabourn to a deceptively simple-sounding formula. "First, they come to us for the travel—because they want to go where we can take them in the style we provide. Then they come for our service, because that is how people experience luxury. There's nothing as luxurious as the sense of being served by skilled and dedicated professionals. And third, they come for the society on board, for the relaxed, club-like social atmosphere on board our ships."

To satisfy those expectations, the company relies on highly trained and motivated people—people who are motivated not by money (although they are well paid) but rather by a genuine pride in what they do. That is one of the most striking things about the service staff on board

Seabourn: the frank sincerity of their desire to please their guests. This pride is reinforced regularly. After a spectacular party on the cruise we were on, the following memo from the hotel manager was sent to every manager on the ship and posted in the crew quarters:

> To Everyone Involved in the 4th of July BBQ Yesterday, thank you all for the effort you have put in to make this special day a SUCCESS. Many guests commented how much they appreciate your hard and professional work. *Some people dream of worthy accomplishments, while you stay awake and do them.* Congratulations.

The company shows genuine respect and empathy in dealing with its employees on every level. The easiest way to lose your job at Seabourn may be to lack that empathy for fellow employees and for guests. If the company had a song, it would be that old Broadway number "You Gotta Have Heart." *Heart* translates into a recognition that everyone on the ship is literally in the same boat and that it is a special boat where dreams come true for the guests and the employees.

Finally, there is empowerment. The Seabourn product is no longer the sole creation of Brynestad and Titus. As a result of investments beginning in 1992, Seabourn is now a part of Carnival Corporation. "It shows you that these [small luxury ships] cannot make money on their own," points out Carnival's chairman and CEO Micky Arison. "However, by being linked to the Carnival family, they have the opportunity to use our purchasing power and sales force, which has been instrumental in making them profitable."

Atle Brynestad sold his remaining interest in Seabourn in 1998. On 1 September 2001, he bought the original Sea Goddess ships (then called *Seabourn Goddess I* and *II*) from Carnival and extensively renovated them, creating a new cruise line, SeaDream Yacht Club. Taking advantage of their small size, SeaDream concentrates on the charter market, with the result that 47 to 61 percent of its revenue is from full ship charters.

When all is said and done, what drives Seabourn is that it is a creation of the people on the front line who interact with the guests and together shape the experiences for the benefit all of the parties. Larry Rapp adds, "Everybody in this industry talks about moments of truth, when your intention touches your customer and things can go either way. There is no place on earth where a company has more moments of truth than on a cruise ship. When guests wake up in the morning, they meet their stewardesses. They go to breakfast and see our waiters. From there, they go to a lecture on the next port of call or to an aerobics class. Every time they turn around, they encounter a member of our staff. There are hundreds of moments of truth every day. And obviously, every one of those has to be positive or we lose."

We believe the techniques that have won Seabourn its top ranking as a service experience are equally applicable to other segments of the hospitality and travel business, such as hotels and restaurants. They are simple to enumerate but difficult to accomplish:

1. Affluent guests don't buy rooms or food or seats. They buy experiences. The more personal the experience you provide, and the more distinctive it is, the more customers are willing to pay for it. Value is not merely a function of dollars. Satisfaction is an equally important dimension.
2. Treat your employees with the same kind of respect you expect to receive. It goes without saying that managers need to understand what respect means.
3. Involve your employees in shaping your product and empower them to deliver it, so they share in the pride and rewards that come with accomplishment. Give them constant feedback so they can see how they are doing. People want to work in organizations because they want to accomplish more than they can alone. Companies that can mesh the personal goals of employees with an organization's overall goals will succeed and prosper.

Cruising on Carnival

Cruising on a Carnival Fun Ship is a very different experience than a Seabourn cruise. Yet, as we will see, there are many points of similarity. If Seabourn is delivering an expensive and exclusive vacation, Carnival is focusing on high-value vacations for the mass market. The average price point is $150 a day, a fraction of the Seabourn per diems. The target market is adults ages twenty-five to fifty-four with household incomes of over $50,000. As Seabourn targets less than 5 percent of the population of the United States and Canada (ignoring its truly global affluent market for the moment), Carnival aims at 50 percent—more than ten times the target market of Seabourn! As truly remarkable as the Seabourn product is (both of us would kill or maim to sail on Seabourn again and again), the reality is that most folks not only can't afford it but also would not appreciate (or perhaps even like) the experience. Perhaps that's why Carnival owns Seabourn, not the other way around.

As a mass-market vacation provider, Carnival is challenged to find about 3,350,000 passengers in 2006—and that number will grow to close to 4 million vacationers by 2009, as three additional Fun Ships come on line to fill out a twenty-four-ship fleet. Of course, it's not enough to spend billions to provide a fleet of sparkling white ships. As many other travel providers have sadly realized, investing in capacity doesn't always mean that capacity will be utilized. In our opinion, like Seabourn, it's the software that makes the difference and that has made Carnival so successful.

But the hardware does contribute! After being electronically processed at the port of Miami, the cruise capital of the world, folks are greeted at the gangway by cruise staff members and stewards who direct them to their staterooms. Their first impression is typically one of awe at the soaring, dramatic ten-story atrium. This isn't Kansas, Toto! It's fun to watch people's reactions. There's excitement in the air as they realize this will be no ordinary vacation.

Carnival's standard stateroom is large by industry standards, larger than other contemporary lines. Individual twin beds convert to king size (and stay that way, even under battlefield circumstances)! The inside staterooms measure 165 square feet; the ocean-view staterooms are 190 square feet. They come equipped with telephones, televisions, wall safes, ample closet and drawer space, and a vanity table. The bathrooms feature a large shower area and are large enough to move around in comfortably. The ocean-view rooms have large picture windows, not the small pizza-shaped portholes of yesteryear. Balcony cabins offer a spacious private verandah to the sea with deck chairs and a table. Many staterooms feature one or two fold-down upper berths. A number also provide space for a rollaway bed, thus accommodating up to five people. No wonder Carnival typically sails in excess of 113 percent occupancy!

Embarkation hours in Miami are 12:30 to 3:30 P.M., with the ship sailing at 4:00. Eager vacationers begin to arrive before noon, and embarkation generally starts earlier to accommodate them. Luggage is delivered to the stateroom by 6:00 P.M., but in truth, most arrives an hour or so after the guests check in. As noted previously, many guests opt to roll on their own luggage. After locating their stateroom and meeting their cabin steward, most folks consult the Carnival Capers daily shipboard schedule and either head for the lido restaurant for the embarkation lunch or explore the vessel. Some, of course, immediately take to the open decks and begin working on their tans.

The lido lunch is an informal buffet style set up with a full salad bar, pasta stations, hamburgers, hot dogs, barbecue chicken, and so on, augmented by a pizzeria, a New York–style deli, Chinese cuisine, and a daily changing international menu. Waiters circulate to take beverage orders and assist guests with their trays. During the week, food stations are set up at breakfast and lunch to offer greater variety. Varying choices include customized omelets and fajitas for breakfast and grilled chicken or shrimp with fresh-tossed Caesar salad and a carving station for lunch.

At embarkation, each guest receives a sail-and-sign card with a magnetic strip that enables them to make purchases and board without using cash. This is convenient for the guests and probably contributes to a slightly higher level of onboard purchase. This card acts as the guest I.D. and includes the dining room table assignment. Conquest-class vessels like the *Valor* feature two comparable appointed restaurants seating between 800 and 1,000 people. Each features a second-level balcony to create more intimate spaces. Tables range in size from two to twelve and are reserved for the length of the cruise. There are four sittings for dinner: 5:45, 6:15, 8:00, and 8:30. Breakfast and lunch are open seating, with the majority of the guests opting for dining on the lido for those meals. Typically, senior citizens and families with small children prefer the early sittings; most of the rest tend to gravitate to the late sittings. Additionally, there's a continental breakfast service in the stateroom each day, including cereals, the aforementioned lido for breakfast and lunch, and complimentary twenty-four-hour room service featuring a selection of sandwiches, fruit plates, and the like. A twenty-four-hour pizzeria offers eight kinds of pizza and calzone, including exotica such as goat cheese with sun-dried tomatoes.

Dining each night presents myriad choices ranging from appetizers, soups, pasta, at least seven entrées, including a vegetarian selection, cheeses and fruit, and a variety of desserts. Lunch and dinner menus also feature Spa Carnival cuisine, which offers low-calorie, low-fat, low-salt, low-cholesterol choices—including desserts!

While obviously not à la minute, the food is invariably better than that found in Orlando or Las Vegas at all but the highest-priced restaurants. In the view of at least one of us—possibly biased—it's equal to or better than all other cruise lines out of Miami.

Because of the Fun Ship positioning, vacationers come on board expecting to have a good time however they choose to define it. It's a sort of self-fulfilling prophesy: They want to have a fun time, and they do! In fact, the Carnival sales force tells agents *not* to send curmudgeonly clients on Carnival. Let's face it: Some people are happiest being sour and carping about everything; they seem to perpetually wear overstarched underwear! If there's a sourpuss assigned to an otherwise affable, convivial table of six or eight, how pleasant will that be for the majority? Therefore, it's not a luxury that Carnival can tell agents who not to send but rather a necessity. Perfection is in the details—including garnering the appropriate clientele and winnowing out those who wouldn't fit. (While on this somewhat delicate but critical subject, Carnival also instructs agents not to send those few folks who would be most pleased to travel with others, just as long as they're just exactly like them!)

The crew is oriented to refer to the passengers as "guests" through Carnival's training programs offered under the banner of Carnival College. The whole idea, of course, is to put the emphasis on treating their customers as guests in their shipboard home, with the full gamut of hospitality implications the term implies.

The shipboard staff, as well as all shoreside Carnival employees, are oriented to the fact that purchasers of Carnival vacations have made a highly discretionary decision to spend their time and money to experience a Carnival cruise. They therefore have a reasonable level of expectation regarding the food, service, ambience, entertainment, and activity choices the cruise will provide. They expect to have an enjoyable, hassle-free vacation and take home lifelong memories. Individually, they may anticipate meeting new friends, rekindling romance, finding romance, rest and relaxation, quiet and solitude, or pretty much nonstop partying—and every possibility in between.

The core of this product delivery is summed up in Carnival's vision statement: "To provide quality cruise vacations that consistently exceed the expectations of our guests." All employees know this vision statement and are motivated to execute it. It's interesting to note that Carnival's vision statement wasn't defined and articulated until 1994. In fact, that was the first year that fleetwide and shoreside hospitality training was instituted. Before that, for several years, there was an extensive shipboard program lasting several weeks. The problem was that so few crew members were trained that when they went back into the shipboard environment they were literally outnumbered and overrun by the vast majority of crew who hadn't had this training and could not therefore relate to the concepts and ideas proffered by the recently trained minority. Without an environment of positive reinforcement of the newly learned attitudes and behaviors, there was, if not total atrophy, a strong propensity to not have these new skills reach full fruition.

When one considers the success Carnival achieved *prior* to fleetwide training, one's mind boggles! The suggestion is that the natural corporate culture was sufficiently well oriented and focused to ensure reasonable levels of passenger (the term used before *guest*) satisfaction. A kind of street-smart communal mentality was able to do an effective job without formal training. (Guest satisfaction has greatly increased and, perhaps even more important, the crew and even many of the guests are verbalizing this experience.) It's one thing to experience good service and warm, caring hospitality. It's even more powerful if you become consciously appreciative of the service as you encounter it. This leads to enhanced enjoyment—somewhat like savoring a wine rather than just unconsciously drinking it. This greatly increases the likelihood of Carnival's guests becoming fiercely loyal to the brand and enthusiastically telling others about the experience. Remember, positive word-of-mouth from returning cruise passengers is the industry's most powerful tool of market expansion.

Carnival's strategy is to enhance the product experience, to deliver a better food, service, and entertainment product than other cruise lines at higher price points while, at the same time, maintaining and fine-tuning its Fun Ship cruise ambience. The enormous economies of scale that accrue to Carnival due to its dominant size, combined with its powerful economic strength, which allows it to enjoy the lowest capital costs in the industry, provide Carnival with ever-increasing nonproduct cost savings and the healthiest profit margin and return on invested capital in the industry. Over the years, the strategy has allowed for a continual reinvestment of a portion of these cost savings in a steady stream of onboard product enhancements. This approach has been contrary to the industry's tendency to take cost out of the cruise product to partially offset the adverse profit effect of declining yields in a maturing, expanding industry. The subtlety of Carnival's strategy has been to effect widespread product enhancements with virtually no fanfare so as not to raise the expectations of its guests beyond the minimum threshold required for purchase, thus creating the highest probability of ensuring the implementation of its vision statement.

Moreover, like Seabourn, Carnival upholds the concept of internal guests, which allows each member of the crew and shoreside staff to view his or her work as important in itself and integral to the success of the entire team. The theory is that to the extent employees can understand the big picture of the company and can view themselves as contributors to the success of the organization, they'll take more pride and derive more personal satisfaction in their day-to-day job. Add empowerment, which is the ability to deal with problems and situations on the spot (with great latitude, as practically any situation has some unique aspect to it), and you have a surefire formula to exceed guest's expectations. Waiters are trained to ask guests how their food is and offer a different selection if necessary. The purser's desk personnel strive to quickly resolve whatever may go bump in the night in a caring manner—how they would like to be treated, if the roles were reversed, is an important litmus test. The golden rule truly has universal applications.

Because of the dramatic growth of Carnival from one ship in 1972 to twenty-one in 2006 and because of the company's belief in promoting from within, practically all shipboard management positions have been filled from within the ranks. This fact certainly contributes to a happy, motivated crew. Crew members realize it's not enough to do a good job to just keep the job. They understand that if they do a great job, above and beyond the norm, and demonstrate sound team-building, communications, and conflict resolution skills, they enhance their probability for earning promotions with correspondingly higher compensation and benefits. They realize an ever-growing number of positions must be filled. With new ships coming each year, these folks should not (and do not) consider themselves in dead-end jobs! The twin phenomena of sustained growth and home-grown promotions also serve to satiate Carnival's never-ending quest for new crew. The obvious Carnival advantage, in terms of career opportunities, acts as a huge magnet that attracts folks from around the globe. A modest percentage of these have worked on other ships but were motivated (on an unsolicited basis) to switch because of perceived better career possibilities. At last count, sixty-four countries were represented in Carnival's crew manifest.

A big part of the Carnival Fun Ship experience is choice. Like successful land-based competitors, such as Orlando and Las Vegas, Carnival strives to offer activity and entertainment choices broad enough to satisfy just about everybody. Look back at a short list of some of the activities offered—to show the diversity—that appeared in chapter 2.

Club 02, designed in conjunction with the folks at Coca-Cola, offers a unique cruise experience for teens ages fifteen to seventeen—from outdoor activities like basketball, volleyball, ping pong, and pool parties to high-energy dance parties lasting late into the night. During the day, activities are more relaxed. Teens can come and hang with their friends while watching a movie, listening to the latest music, or playing video games. Karaoke jam sessions are also popular for our rising stars and star wanna-bes. Even teen-only shore excursions have been set up so teens can enjoy the sites and sounds of our beautiful ports with their peers.

Club 02 lounges feature comfy seating, video monitors, state-of-the-art dance floor and lighting equipment, and an area where teens can enjoy Coca-Cola products and other nonalcoholic specialty drinks.

Club 02 directors are specifically hired and trained to catalyze the Club 02 program. They create the spark that gets all the teens involved. Each director brings his or her own unique style to Club 02. The motivation and dedication to the program of each ensures the teens' cruise experience is unlike anything they have ever done before. Many directors act as hosts, entertainers, and DJs for the teens.

Activities for Club 02 teens include:

◆   Teen activity schedule
◆   Board games
◆   Card games
◆   Music hangs
◆   Theme parties
◆   Lido deck activities
◆   Reality game shows
◆   Trivia and scavenger hunts
◆   Pool parties

Without question, fitness is a huge and growing aspect of today's lifestyle, and Spa Carnival provides the exercise and training options folks are looking for. At 15,000 square feet on Conquest-class vessels (and proportionately smaller on the other classes in the fleet), these spas are among the largest afloat and far larger than at the typical resort. They are equipped with treadmills, stair machines, bicycles, rowing machines, free weights, benches, and enough progressive resistant weight training stations to satisfy the most earnest devotee! Additionally, there are separate high- and low-impact aerobic areas, saunas, steam, whirlpools, and a cushioned outdoor jogging track. The spa offers a complete array of treatments, from mud packs to aromatherapy to radio cathadermy (don't ask us, but spa fans will understand). The spa facilities, technician staff, and variety of treatments are fully comparable with the finest on land.

Wide choices for entertainment options are also important. Each seven-day cruise, for example, includes two lavish original production shows such as be-bop, with fast-paced singing and dancing featuring the music of the 1950s and 1960s, to the best of Broadway, which reprises show tunes from hits ranging from *Miss Saigon* to *Phantom of the Opera*. Other nights feature cruise staff introductions with audience participation, a variety of stand-up acts such as singers, comedians, musicians, jugglers, acrobats, and dancers, and the invariably popular guest talent night. (When you have up to 3,600 people on board, chances are excellent you've got a terrific pool of talent to draw from.) In addition to these shows, which take place in the main lounge, there's another show lounge on each vessel that features a dance band with one or more singers and late-night cabaret entertainment. There's a state-of-the-art high-tech disco that pulses with the latest sounds but also fulfill requests for blues, country and western, and golden oldies.

Another dance band performs each night in a highly visual themed lounge. An expression of Carnival's entertainment architecture format, this lounge may be based on the movie *Passage to India* or evoke memories of an endless summer or the exotic Orient. Similarly, the library, a quiet retreat, may be patterned after Tara in *Gone With the Wind* or a senior naval officer's study in Admiral's library or an Englishman's club in Churchill's cigar bar. Singalong piano bars are also themed, ranging from ancient Egypt to Rick's Café American with its sultry Moroccan setting.

The casinos on Carnival are the largest afloat, featuring blackjack, craps, roulette, Wheel of Fortune, Caribbean stud poker, and Texas hold'em. The casinos on Conquest-class vessels offer 218 slot machines ranging from nickel slots to progressive mega cash, which has paid out jackpots of over $1 million.

The Carnival crew is also trained to provide extra little touches or unexpected surprises. A room steward, for example, will arrange towels in the shape of a different animal each night. A waiter may offer magic tricks to kids of all ages or do napkin tricks—and show interested guests how it's done. At most dinners throughout the cruise, the waitstaff may sing and parade through the dining room. A Carnival Caribbean favorite is Bob Marley's "Hot! Hot! Hot!", practically guaranteed to get a sizable portion of the guests joining in the dancing as guests and staff weave through the dining room. Waiters with trays of drinks balanced on their heads lead the parade while performing amazing limbo contortions.

The stark contrast to hotel or restaurant dining is vivid. The electricity of folks laughing and enjoying themselves is quite different than the somber, library-like atmosphere on land. Part of the difference is the Fun Ship crew, who truly enjoy making guests happy; part is the guests' expectations of having fun and enjoying a good time; and part is the unique shipboard opportunity (certainly not limited to Carnival) that allows people to dine together and make new friends. Let's face it: In a land-based resort restaurant, most folks stick to themselves and have little meaningful interaction with others. Couples may nod to others or exchange pleasantries in a hallway or elevator, but the typical hotel experience is one of social isolation. We believe people today, more socially isolated than their parents or grandparents, welcome the opportunity to meet others. Friendships and romances formed on ship can be most gratifying and frequently last a lifetime. In fact, we think this is one of the key reasons cruise vacations enjoy higher levels of customer satisfaction than land-based vacations.

Carnival's Quality Control

Imagine the challenge of consistently delivering a uniform, high-quality cruise experience within a twenty-one-ship fleet comprising five classes of vessels, of which some are more than twice the size of the others. Add in the complexity of 26,000 shipboard employees from some sixty-five countries, and you have a daunting quality assurance task. Carnival's approach to this challenge is through disciplined, periodic shipboard visitations by a quality control committee (QCC) of senior shoreside executives. The QCC includes the president and CEO, the senior vice president of corporate training, the senior vice presidents of hotel, cruise, and technical operations, the vice president of food and beverage, the vice president of cruise programming, the vice president of casino operations, and the vice president of corporate training. This core group is augmented by other senior shoreside management so they too can have a feel for the process, problems, and opportunities involved with such a vast operation—the largest in the industry.

The QCC visits each ship of the fleet at least once a year. It is a scheduling challenge of the highest magnitude to coordinate busy executives' travel schedules, flights, and hotels as well as the shipboard participation. This task is made practical by the use of the Carnival corporate jet, a ten-passenger Global Express. Trips are carefully coordinated, where possible, to allow for the visits of two or three ships per trip for added efficiency.

Each QCC visit includes a three-hour meeting with the shipboard department heads (twenty-five to thirty-five people) and an inspection of the guest and crew areas of the vessel. These are not surprise visits but rather are carefully communicated in advance; thus, shipboard management has the opportunity to conduct meetings with their respective staffs so all the crew can relay questions or concerns. Additionally, notice of the meeting is posted in public crew areas with a suggestion box to encourage crew feedback. Every other year, the president gives a PowerPoint presentation to the crew that includes ample time for crew Q&A. No subject is taboo, and dialog is encouraged through a relaxed, informal style: "Call me Bob!"

The presentation covers an update on major company events and initiatives since the prior meeting. It includes the current status of crew benefits such as the crew retirement program and the employee stock purchase plan. It also provides a big-picture look at what our competitors, such as Las Vegas and Orlando, are doing to fight for share of the vacation market. In recent years, the overarching emphasis with the crew has been the importance of hospitality training and execution. Of course, having Carnival's senior management on the ship for a full day gives plenty of opportunity for them to walk the talk by smiling, greeting, and acknowledging all crew members, whether encountered in the crew or guest areas of the ship. It also allows the shoreside management to quickly size up the degree of hospitality exhibited by the crew. If the president is walking with an officer and a crew member acts surprised when the officer says "hello," then you can be certain that's not his normal behavior!

Shipboard visits and meetings allow the shoreside senior management to observe the interaction among the senior shipboard management. You may have a terrific captain, for example, who is paired with a competent hotel director, but perhaps their personalities don't mesh well. This would be difficult to detect and correct without direct observation. Conducting three department head meetings in three back-to-back days makes it easy to recognize a ship that has low morale or a low degree of participative management. The comparisons starkly show the contrast in shipboard team chemistry.

Carnival also conducts extensive crew comment card evaluations twice a year on each ship; these provide crew feedback in measurable form so that trends, both positive and negative, can be noted. The captain and hotel director organize a department head meeting after the crew comment cards are tabulated, analyzed, and compared with prior data. The detailed minutes of this meeting are circulated among the QCC members so they have a feel for the current issues and opportunities among the crew. Some of the crew issues result from situations outside the vessel, such as lack of banking facilities in a given port on a Sunday turnaround day or severe limitations on when Customs and Border Protection (CBP) allow crew off ships in some ports (so-called crew windows).

It's important to understand that whether a ship is small or large, luxury or mass-market, or anywhere in between, the entire focus of the cruise product is the guest experience. The old adage is more true than ever: The customer is king.

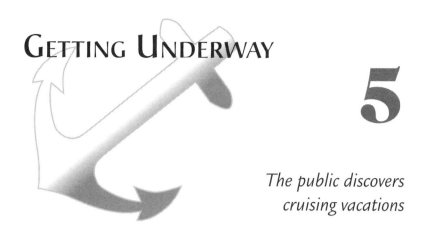

GETTING UNDERWAY

5

*The public discovers
cruising vacations*

We might as well call the 1980s the halcyon days of cruising—the period when the industry really got underway.

The consumer demand to try out this new kind of vacation was pushing ahead of the supply, and there was a dramatic growth of new passengers. In 1970, only half a million people a year were cruising—two-tenths of 1 percent of the American public. Growth was slow at first because capacity was limited and ports of embarkation were few and remote. But the pace accelerated as new cruise lines and cruise ships were launched. By 1979, the figure had doubled to one million, and it reached two million in 1985 and three million in 1988. By 2006, slightly more than ten million folks per year were cruising—a twenty-fold increase in thirty-six years, making it the fastest-growing segment of the travel business. This explosive growth was the result of the cruise industry redefining itself from a narrowly focused niche product to a broader-based mass-market vacation experience. New cruise lines that docked for the first time in Miami and other ports around the world included Carnival, Monarch, American Hawaii, Chandris Fantasy, Sea Goddess, Seabourn, Pearl, Renaissance, Premier, and Celebrity. There were few barriers to entry—almost anyone with a modest amount of capital or credit could start his own line. The low cost structure was appealing. New operators could lease or buy from a selection of previously owned (a euphemism for *used*) ships retired from transatlantic crossings or other service and laid up. Or, if they wished, they could build new ones at relatively low levels of investment. Back in 1970, a ship like the *Skyward* could be leased for as little as $2,500 a day or built new for $11 to $12 million. At least some profits were pretty well assured at the time because of the small capacity of the industry and high consumer demand. All ships rose on the strong tide of that demand. With this dramatic expansion, not surprisingly, like other oligopolies with a small number of suppliers and large number of consumers, many lines were forced to close, including some of the newer ones. In fact, the table on the following page lists seventy-three brands that were marketed in North America since 1970 and are now defunct!

Defunct Cruise Brands since 1972

Number	Line	From	To	Notes
1	Blue Star Line	1910	1972	Discontinued passenger service.
2	American President Line	1947	1973	Luxury liner service ended in 1973 but the line still operates modern container ships.
3	American Export Line	1948	1974	Ships were laid up. Independence and Constitution later went to American Hawaii.
4	Flagship Cruises	1971	1974	Ships were sold to the P&O group for Princess Cruises
5	French Line	1894	1974	Condemned by airline competition. s/s France decomissioned.
6	Prudential–Grace Line	1970	1974	Renamed Prudential Line
7	Greek Line	1939	1975	Company fell on hard times after death of owner Basil Goulandris.
8	Incres Lines	1951	1975	Their ship Victoria was sold to Chandris after the line collapsed.
9	Swedish American Line	1925	1975	Last two ships were sold to Karageorgias Lines and Flagship Cruises.
10	Italian Line	1927	1976	Ships were laid up.
11	Matson Lines	1882	1976	Sold off passenger vessels. Freight only line.
12	Italia Cruises International	1976	1977	Line managed by Costa offering Miami–Nassau overnight cruises. Ship was laid up in Italy.
13	Monarch Cruise Lines	1975	1978	Monarch Star and Sun went back to Holland America as Veendam and Volendam
14	Prudential Line	1974	1978	Ships sold to Delta Line
15	Venture Cruise Lines	1978	1978	Ceased operations and declared bankruptcy. This line only lasted ten days.
16	Carras Cruises	1976	1979	Ship was sold to Delian Artemis Cruises S.A. and was charted to Costa.
17	Strand Cruises	1977	1979	This company offering 14 day Med cruises for Americans and Canadians went out of business.
18	Ulysses Line	1973	1979	Brand dissolved when UK tour operator Thompson did not renew their charter contract.
19	Norwegian America Line	1913	1983	Ships Sagafjord and Vistafjord were sold to Cunard
20	Bahama Cruise Line	1975	1984	Became Bermuda Star Line
21	Paquet	1863	1999	Purchased by Louis.
22	Scandanavian World Cruises	1982	1984	Cruise-Ferry service NY to Freeport discontinued.
23	Astor United Cruises	1981	1985	Ceased operations and ships were sold.
24	Eastern Cruise Line	1970	1985	Merged with Sundance to form Admiral Cruises.
25	Sundance Cruises	1984	1985	Merged with Eastern Cruise Line to form Admiral Cruises.
26	Western Cruise Lines	1980	1985	This subsidiary of Eastern Cruise Line became part of Admiral Cruises.
27	Chandris Lines	1915	1986	Renamed Fantasy Cruises.
28	Club Sea	1986	1986	Company never became a reality. Although brochures were printed and were open for booking.
29	Admiral Cruises	1985	1987	Merged with Royal Caribbean.
30	Helenic Mediterranean Lines	1972	1987	Declared bankruptcy.
31	Lauro Lines	1912	1987	Fleet sold to Mediterranean Shipping Company. Renamed Star Lauro.
32	Norwegian Caribbean Line	1966	1987	Name changed to Norwegian Cruise Line.
33	Signet Cruise Lines	1987	1987	Original name of Seabourn before a Texas company owning the name "Signet" objected.
34	Home Lines	1946	1988	Company sold to Holland America. Homeric became Westerdam and Atlantic sold to Premier.

118

#	Company			Notes
35	Sitmar Cruises	1928	1988	Purchased by Princess
36	Aloha Pacific	1986	1989	Company folded and their one ship, Monterey, was laid up.
37	American Star Lines	1988	1989	Unsuccessful Greek owned company operating Betsy Ross. Ship went to Star Lauro.
38	Bermuda Star Line	1984	1990	Merged with Commodore.
39	Ocean Cruise Lines	1984	1990	Merged with Pearl Cruises.
40	Pearl Cruises	1981	1990	Bought by Paquet.
41	Crown Cruise Line	1991	1993	Two of three ships were sold to Cunard. Became known as Cunard Crown Cruises.
42	Fiesta Marina	1993	1993	Ship, Carnivale, went back to Carnival.
43	Frontier Spirit Cruises	1990	1993	Their one ship Frontier Spirit was sold to Hapag–Lloyd and renamed Bremen (VI)
44	American Family Cruises	1993	1994	Unsuccessful joint venture between Costa and Bruce Nirenburg. Ship went back to Costa.
45	Fantasy Cruise Lines	1986	1994	Chandris phased out the Fantasy brand and continued operating the Celebrity brand.
46	Cunard Crown Lines	1993	1995	Ships sold to Star Cruises.
47	Epirotiki Lines	1954	1995	Joined with Sun Lines to form Royal Olympic Cruises.
48	Regency Cruises	1984	1995	Ceased operations and declared bankruptcy.
49	Star Lauro	1987	1995	Renamed Mediterranean Shipping Company.
50	Sun Lines	1958	1995	Joined with Epirotiki to form Royal Olympic Cruises.
51	Diamond Cruises	1992	1996	Merged with Radisson Seven Seas.
52	Royal Cruise Line	1974	1996	Became part of NCL.
53	Dolphin Cruise Lines	1984	1997	Became part of Premier Cruises.
54	Majesty Cruise Lines	1991	1997	Ships were sold to NCL.
55	Manhatten Cruises	1996	1997	Short lived company offered overnight party/gambling cruises from New York.
56	Seawind Cruise Line	1991	1997	Joined with Dolphin Cruise Line to form an enlarged Premier.
57	Royal Viking Line	1970	1998	Became part of Cunard and then Seabourn.
58	Sea Goddess Cruises	1984	1998	Became part of Seabourn.
59	Tall Ship Adventures	1988	1999	Ship Sir Francis Drake was destroyed by Hurricane Lenny in 1999.
60	Cape Canaveral Cruise Lines	1997	2000	Cape Canaveral Tours discontinued their cruise division. Dolphin IV was sold for scrap.
61	Commodore Cruise Line	1966	2000	Ceased operations. Filed Chapter 11.
62	Crown Cruise Line	1999	2000	Filed Chapter 11. Not related to the original Crown Cruise Line bought by Cunard in 1993.
63	Marine Expeditions	1999	2000	Went out of business following the collapse of their sister World Cruise Company.
64	Premier Cruise Lines	1983	2000	Ceased operations and declared bankruptcy.
65	World Cruise Company	1999	2000	This company was affiliated with Marine expeditions and offered year round world cruises.
66	American Hawaii Cruises	1979	2001	Ceased operations when AMCV went Bankrupt.
67	Delta Queen Coastal	2001	2001	Ceased operations when AMCV went Bankrupt.
68	Great Lakes Cruises	2001	2001	Ceased operations after their ship, Arcadia, failed sanitation inspections several times.
69	Renaissance Cruises	1989	2001	Ceased operations shortly after September 11, 2001.
70	United States Lines	2000	2001	Ceased operations when AMCV went bankrupt.
71	Regal Cruises	1993	2003	Ceased operations after Regal Empress was arrested in Port Manatee.
72	First European Cruises	1997	2004	North American branch of Festival Cruises. Festival ceized operations.
73	Royal Olympia Cruises	1995	2005	Ceased operations in early 2005. North American operations shut down in 2004.

Defunct Cruise Lines

In truth, the business was so small it *had* to grow; its embryonic state assured its growth, especially considering the unusually high rate of consumer satisfaction cruising was generating. The product was simply so good, compared with land vacations, that growth was inevitable despite spates of mismanagement, underfunding, and inept marketing. Moreover, for the rising middle class, which was anxiously collecting every new status symbol it could lay its hands on, the cost efficiencies of cruising created a true vacation value compared with land alternatives. This was—and still is—difficult to match.

The Target Audience

The demographics and psychographics of the target audience for cruises in the 1970s were different from today's cruisers as well. Because cruises then cost far more than today in today's dollars, they were far above the range of the average household where Mom stayed home and took care of the kids while Dad worked as a bank teller or the head buyer in the shoe department of a large department store. Most cruises were seven and fourteen days long, so if you were going to go on one you had to wait until the kids were old enough to be left with a sympathetic aunt or grandparents who could control them. In fact, most cruisers in those days were themselves grandparents! A cruise was not a place to take a young child; the facilities for them, if there at all, were basically babysitting and offered only at times when school was out—mid-June to Labor Day. The majority of passengers considered other people's children an unwelcome intrusion on their golden years' vacation. The majority of folks who had the time and the money to take a cruise were over fifty-five. That age group set the tone and ambience for the whole cruise industry—the country club set who were at least fifty-five in 1975 were born in 1920 or earlier. Many were World War II veterans—folks who had made it. They represented a new generation of American wealth rather than old, inherited money. They still liked to Charleston and dance to tunes like "Sentimental Journey" and songs from "Your Hit Parade" such as "Don't Fence Me In" and "Slow Boat to China."

There were, of course, some younger cruisers—lawyers, doctors, and top managers—but they could not help noticing that most of the other passengers were older than they were. If they did bring their children, the kids were bored at sea; it was only in port, where there were old forts to explore and beaches to snorkel off, that activities were available for the whole family. Not only were there few families, there were few honeymooners. Cruises were more appropriate for silver and gold wedding anniversaries. Many of these cruisers were either living in Florida or snowbirds—visitors who regularly came to South Florida. The ships could easily be seen, dominating the port of Miami and thus providing some degree of consumer awareness. In the trade, these passengers were either called "condo commandos" or "condo dragons."

Early Marketing Maneuvers

Royal Caribbean had thirteen or fourteen air gateways to Miami (compared to 155 today), and Rod McLeod recalls that 35 to 40 percent of their passengers were from California, linked to Florida with special air charters. California was considered a ripe market because a lot of people there had taken cruises—principally to Mexico from Los Angeles. They hadn't been to the Caribbean and wanted to go there, but it had been too expensive. McLeod remembers the exact date of RCCL's first California departure. It was 1 January 1971, at 1 A.M.—New Year's Day. The plane was a Boeing 707 stretch 180-seater, and it was completely sold out. "We were reaching out for a new market," McLeod told us, "and offering round-trip air from Los Angeles, a B deck outside stateroom with two lower berths on the *Song of Norway* to Nassau, San Juan, and St. Thomas. Our price, including all port charges, transfers, and a quick sightseeing tour of Miami and lunch on Key Biscayne before boarding the ship, was only $368." As this price was only $50 or $60 higher than RCCL's brochure cruise only, it was a tremendous bargain by any standard.

In contrast, Carnival relied heavily on the local senior market and tour operators during its early years, 1972–1974. This was logical because the local market was cheaper to mine from an advertising standpoint (remember, Carnival started on less then a shoestring!), and Carnival's owner at the time was AITS, a large nationally recognized tour operator. It wasn't until 1975 that Carnival adapted the marketing strategy that would ultimately result in its unparalleled growth. Two problems existed with their first strategy. First, the local South Florida market was subject to frequent price dumping as cruise lines endeavored to pick up last-minute business. The fact that the condo commandos were close by and largely retired meant they could react to a favorable price offer with a few days' notice. In fact, it was not unusual to see septuagenarians milling about the embarkation area, bags in tow, hoping to take advantage of a standby rate or a last-minute cancellation. In the early to mid-1970s, last-minute rates were *very* negotiable! It wasn't uncommon to hear stories that a seven-day cruise regularly selling for $225 could be had for $75 to $100 per person at the pier. In some instances, shenanigans occurred where the embarkation supervisor or purser pocketed "gratuities" in exchange for the cabin gratis or for a favorable rate. In those early days, there was a great deal of entrepreneurship on the vessels. While not universal, many cruise directors, pursers, maître d's, cruise staff members, and waiters had their own deals going. These could range from a per-head payment for passengers delivered to shore tour operators to a percentage of the revenue from an island store. Additionally, anybody who handled the ship's money had the possibility of becoming a "partner"—the euphemism used in the cruise industry to describe someone who is diverting corporate funds to their own pocket. These abuses have been largely curtailed today thanks to onboard computers and credit card purchases. With current stringent cost controls, every penny is accounted for. Partnering is a thing of the past for most lines.

The problem with the tour operator market sourcing strategy was that Carnival could not control the efforts of the tour operator. For example, if a tour operator took a block of eighty-five cabins a week on a year round basis, it didn't mean that he *had* to sell them, only that he would *try*. Consequently, if the tour operator encountered difficulty and could sell only half the cabins, then Carnival was stuck with the remainder—usually with only fifteen to thirty day's notice prior to the sailing. It used to drive Bob Dickinson, then Carnival's vice president for sales and marketing, bananas—especially when you consider that he was dealing with as many as eight tour operators at a time! Some days he faced an inventory of 200 unsold cabins two weeks prior to sailing on the *Mardi Gras,* which had only 457 cabins to begin with.

"Where were the tour operators getting those passengers?" Dickinson asked himself. Obviously, from travel agents. The solution was patently clear: Carnival would have to deal with those same travel agents directly. That way it would at least know which cabins were really booked with customer names and deposits and which ones represented wishful thinking. Consequently, Carnival became, in effect, its own tour operator by packaging round-trip airfare, transfers between the airport and pier, overnight or day hotel rooms as necessary, and the cruise. The program began in 1975 with ten gateway cities operated in conjunction with Delta Airlines and the now defunct National Airlines. This allowed Carnival to deal directly with travel agents through its field sales force, which at the time consisted of just eleven folks! Today, Carnival operates from 172 cities throughout the United States and Canada and is covered by a field sales force numbering eighty.

While dealing directly with the travel agents was an improvement over the tour operator system, one more hurdle had to be overcome. Twenty years ago, the strong winter and summer seasonality of the vacation business was such that tour operators, cruise lines, hotels, and airlines had a love-hate relationship with travel agents. They loved the agents in the shoulder season (soft periods, such as the fall and spring); they would break (not just bend) their own rules, wheedle, cajole, pamper, feed, and entertain them in an unabashed attempt to get agents to send them business. On the other hand, in the winter and summer, when there was a strong consumer demand for vacations, these same companies typically became extraordinarily inflexible; no rules were bent, let alone broken. Moreover, these vacation vendors paid travel agent commissions with great reluctance during high season because they reasoned they would have gotten the business anyhow. They figured it hardly made sense to pay a travel agent what amounted to a windfall for consumer demand that the hotels, airlines, and cruise lines had generated, not the travel agent.

It was obvious that the supplier-agent relationship was fragile at best and certainly dysfunctional. Rancor and suspicion was rampant on both sides. Depending on the time of year, agents and suppliers talked out of both sides of their mouth. Dickinson recognized that if Carnival was to break through the clutter of thousands of travel suppliers and win the hearts and minds of travel agents, it would have to both act differently and make sure travel agents knew and could see they were acting differently. He felt the logical course of action to grow the cruise business was not only to rely completely on the travel agent community but to treat them with respect, cordiality, and candor at *all* times. "After all," says Bob, "We were selling an intangible product that only 1 percent of the U.S. and Canadian population had any experience with. Clearly we needed travel agents to explain the cruise experience to a largely unfamiliar audience. Our challenge then was to tell the agents that we were a different sort of supplier and back up those words with action. It was a high-risk game, because if we failed to follow through, the agents would never have forgiven us." He remembers many travel agent speeches in which he reminded agents, "Suppliers bend over backwards for you in the fall and don't know you from a hot rock in the winter." This level of candor was uncommon at the time, but it did get agents' attention. No doubt some travel suppliers were angry that a colleague would point out this flawed relationship, but they couldn't and didn't dispute the veracity of the claim. In the short run, it undoubtedly cost Carnival money to be a reasonable partner to travel agents on a year-round basis, but that turned out to be money well spent because long-term agent loyalty and support are virtually priceless.

By 1979, almost all cruise lines were operating at 100 percent of their revenue capacity. Few, if any, berths were being offered on a complimentary basis or at reduced rates to travel agents to stimulate business or even as incentives or perks for company employees. In those days, it was so difficult to get aboard a ship without advance planning that Sitmar was running consumer newspaper ads with pictures of the *Fairsea* and *Fairwind* in Alaska and the Caribbean headlined: "If you want to be in this picture next year, see your travel agent today."

In many circumstances, this kind of emotional advertising appeal works. It plays on people's desire for status by possessing or experiencing something scarce. But it can also produce exactly the opposite effect; consumers may think to themselves, "If it's so hard to get, I won't even bother. I can do without it." And that's exactly what frequently happened in this instance. While going on a cruise was a status symbol, it was also to most people an unknown and untested experience, one they could easily forego if it was perceived to be difficult to acquire. Travel agents felt the same way. Why try to sell your customers something you may not be able to book for them, even after you make the sale? Talk about frustration! The result was what the cruise lines called the sold-out-syndrome in both consumers and travel agents' minds. There was little probability you could, on an impulse for a honeymoon or anniversary for example, book a cruise for next month or even the following one, so few cabins were available.

Consumers who were sufficiently motivated to try anyway visited their travel agents, who dutifully called for reservations and were generally told, as they anticipated, that no space was available. Their reaction was natural. When other clients suggested a cruise, unless it was for the following season, they discouraged them from even trying to book. They would tell prospects inquiring about a proposed cruise, "Don't even bother to think about it for now—there isn't any space."

After a while, when enough agents began to develop this mindset, an unanticipated problem arose. Five to 10 percent of these long-term bookings, those made many months or even a year ahead, were canceled due to normal attrition (personal tragedies, illness, scheduling conflicts, etc.). Berths that were not previously available went back on the market. The second time around, however, they were not readily resold because of the wide spread perception of already being sold out. For years, intermittently, industry marketing executives gave interviews to the trade press and speeches to travel agents decrying the sold-out syndrome and reminding agents that berths were indeed available for close-in sailings.

However, as the cruise industry continued to expand, the inevitable happened. The berth supply began to catch up with consumer demand. Take a look at Exhibit 5.1. You can clearly see the dramatic increase in the number of cruise passengers, fueled by a significant increase in capacity. As a result, occupancies dipped slightly and then firmed up by the new millennium. By design, the graph is calibrated at five-year intervals to eliminate the temporary drag after 11 September 2001.

Capacity growth jumped dramatically after 1995 as new ship construction was a net add to the industry, for the most part. In 1990–1995, a number of vintage vessels were retired from the North American market, thus softening the effects of new ship construction. That the industry passenger carryings more than doubled between 1995 and 2005 is a direct result of net new capacity. The shipbuilding industry, concen-

EXHIBIT 5.1 **Cruise Passengers Marketed/Sold from North America, Industry Capacity and Occupancy**

Year	North American Capacity[a]	Passengers Sold[b]	Estimated Occupancy[c]
1970	n/a	500,000	90%
1975	n/a	690,000	95%
1980	40,000	1,431,000	96%
1985	56,771	2,152,000	93%
1990	83,533	3,640,000	89%
1995	105,161	4,378,000	87%
2000	166,201	7,214,000	90%
2005	225,400	9,600,000	103%

[a]Source: Cruise Line Industry Association lower berths at year-end.
[b]Source: Cruise Line Industry Association
[c]Author's estimates/Cruise Line Industry Association

trated in Italy, Finland, Germany, and France, was churning out larger, more economical, and more fuel-efficient ships, and the North American cruise industry was filling them!

Occupancy rates slowed temporarily in the mid-1990s but rebounded nicely as a result of newer, more competitive ship products making inroads in the broader (i.e., land) vacation industry and sophisticated revenue management systems that began to be established within the cruise lines.

Failure to fill a cruise vessel with paying guests is a costly proposition for the cruise lines. When a passenger is lost to the industry—when a ship sails with an unoccupied berth—the financial effect to the bottom line is the difference between total net revenue the line would have received and the variable cost of carrying the passenger. This is the economic profit per guest. A composite industry average unit economical profit is estimated as in Exhibit 5.2.

As Exhibit 5.2 illustrates, assume that a passenger buys a cruise for which the brochure price (similar to the rack rate in the hotel business) is $2,100, including round-trip airfare from point of origination. Cruise berths, like hotel rooms and airline seats, are perishable commodities. If they are unsold today, they are worth nothing tomorrow. The problem, however, is exacerbated in the cruise business, where an unsold cabin stays unsold not for a few hours or one day but the entire length of the cruise. To give consumers an added incentive to buy, most cruise lines offer so-called permanent discounts off the brochure rates. Carnival

EXHIBIT 5.2   **Estimated Average Industry Economic Profit/Passenger**

Gross Ticket Revenue*	$2,100.00
Discounts	−600.00
Less Commission 14%	−213.00
Air Cost	−330.00
Transfers	−25.00
Credit Card Fees	−25.00
Plus On Board Revenue	+350.00
Less On Board Cost	−150.00
Less other variable cost:	
Reservation/Documentation	−30.00
Food	−77.00
	$1,000.00

*Air/Sea Guest

brochures point out that savings can be achieved through their Super Saver programs and say, "See your travel agent for details." Princess puts a card in its brochure advising consumers that Love Boat Savers may be available, and Royal Caribbean calls them Breakthrough Rates. Special group and other promotions by either travel agents or cruise lines may also reduce fares even further on some sailings or in specific cabin categories. For the purposes of our example, we've assumed the discounts on our cruise amount to $600, bringing the net rate paid to $1,500. From this, the cruise line has a series of expenses to be deducted, starting with travel agent commissions. These vary, but we're assuming about 14 percent here, or $213. Next is the cost of the airfare the line must pay—in this case, $330—and transfer fees (getting the passengers from the airport to the ship and back), which are $25. About 80 percent of passengers pay for their cruises with credit cards today, so we need to allow $25 to cover the credit card fees. Once the passenger sails, he or she spends money on board—buying drinks, souvenirs, gambling, shore excursions, massages, and more. We call that onboard revenue, and we're pegging it on this hypothetical cruise at $350. There are costs involved, however, so we need to deduct $150 to cover those. Then there are other variable costs as well—those involved with reservations and ticketing, which are $30, and the cost of food which for this seven-day cruise we're calling $77. This works out to an economic profit per passenger of $1,000. The economic profit per passenger is, in fact, the marginal net profit because all other costs, shipboard and shoreside, are fixed in the short run. This substantial incremental profit spurs the industry to fill its ships to the greatest extent possible.

In 1995, for example, a lost percentage point of occupancy translated to 50,600 passengers. If the industry achieved the 1985 occupancy level (93 percent) in 1995, the incremental profit would be 7.5 points of occupancy, or 379,500 incremental guests, generating an incremental profit of $379.5 million! As occupancies dipped in the 1990s, there was speculation that the cruise industry would become more like the airline industry in terms of pricing, decreasing product differentiation, and even financial losses. When the level of capacity utilization drops, there's a marked disparity between supply and demand. Pricing becomes extremely volatile as anxious suppliers chase after hesitant buyers. The relatively perishable aspect of an airline seat or a cruise berth simply doesn't tolerate take-it-or-leave-it pricing. While unused hotel rooms are also perishable, a room unsold at 6 P.M. on Monday may still sell by 10 P.M. or even on Tuesday, but the moment a cruise ship sails, her unsold berths remain unsold for three, four, or seven days. The fixed costs are spent; *any* revenue is found revenue—and practically all the revenue is profit! How volatile can pricing be? Remember peanuts fares? half-price sales? penny fares? The airline industry has shown a great deal of imagination in the business of setting prices for its products because they're in a similar situation as cruising: When the plane goes, it's gone!

Airline pricing became so confusing after deregulation in 1978 that for a period of twenty years or so consumers were driven to travel agencies to purchase their tickets in the hopes that they could ferret out the lowest price fares. Fifty-nine percent of domestic airline tickets were purchased through travel agents in 1978. By 1998, the agent share had grown to 89 percent. Today, the share is back down to roughly 60 percent, primarily as a result of robust airline website booking engines.

More important than the shift in purchasing patterns, however, is the unseen, negative marketing force that price instability generates. People don't want to make poor purchase decisions, especially with discretionary purchases such as leisure and visiting friends and relatives (VFR) travel. They don't want to appear foolish. They don't want to feel ripped off. Unstable pricing with widespread consumer perception of myriad pricing schemes acts as a drag on discretionary purchase decisions. There is a perception that someone else will be offered the same thing for a lower price ten minutes from now. Business travel is less affected by ever-changing pricing because most of that form of air travel is not viewed as discretionary but necessary. Moreover, the user of the travel doesn't normally pay for it; the company does. Leisure and VFR travel are adversely affected by price instability because people can opt out of the purchase decision—and in fact do, in many cases—rather than run the real or perceived risk of paying too much.

Unused capacity, perishable capacity, inevitably, inexorably drives pricing lower in an effort to attract discretionary purchasers. Pricing has an elastic effect on demand, especially in travel and tourism. Typically, the lower the price, the greater the demand. When downward price pressure becomes institutionalized in an industry because of overcapacity over a long period, then product costs get squeezed. This leads to commoditization. In other words, products are seen as interchangeable commodities, blurring their distinctive differences. This certainly is evident in the airline industry. A coach seat between New York and Los Angeles is purchased on the basis of price, not the perceived differences among carriers. This has led Bob Crandall, former president of American Airlines, to suggest on more than one occasion that American's pricing is dictated by the cheapest operator in the market. While there are product differences between American and Southwest, for example, the differences aren't significant enough to override even a few dollars' difference in the purchase price. The perception, then, at the consumer level, is that an air seat is an air seat. With brand differentiation meaning little or nothing, the industry can only jockey price and availability (convenience). And, for that matter, they can't push convenience too far because many people will greatly inconvenience themselves—change aircraft, fly at inconvenient times, forgo a meal—for a few dollars in savings. What a shame! The domestic airline industry can't afford to be dazzling, creative, innovative, and exciting. These things cost money and, with severe long-term overcapacity, consumers are simply unwilling to pay that cost. Stripped-down, utilitarian commodities inevitably win out over uniquely differentiated style and class when it comes to mass transportation.

Just imagine what the cruise industry would be like if it follows the airline industry model of protracted overcapacity. Volatile pricing, commoditization, and financial loss would indelibly change the face of cruising forever. This specter is enough to make at least one of us consider early retirement to the Home for the Bewildered!

Why did consumer demand for cruising grow more slowly in the 1990s? The principal reason for this deceleration, in our view, is the diminishing number of first-time cruisers as a percentage of total berths occupied. Throughout the 1970s and 1980s, when industry growth was even more dramatic, some 65 to 75 percent of cruise-industry passengers were first-timers. Since 1990, however, the percentage of first-time cruisers has been declining. The Cruise Line Industry Association estimates that no more than 40 percent of the cruisers in 1995 and subsequent years were first-timers. In other words, as many as 1.5 million folks should have tried cruising in 1995 alone but did not do so. Imagine if they had. We wouldn't have had enough capacity to carry them!

There are a number of reasons for the decline in the percentage of first-time cruisers. First of all, as more and more people cruise for the first time and come back satisfied, they book additional cruises, which of course raises the number of repeaters. On a recent Princess cruise to Alaska that one of us took, there were 600 members of the Captain's Circle (repeaters) out of 1,600 passengers on board. Many cruise lines offer incentives to repeat passengers in terms of lower prices and cabin upgrades. Seabourn, for instance, has a series of cruises that, when booked by Seabourn Club members, are offered at a 10 percent discount. If members bring guests who occupy a suite on the same sailing, the guests receive a 5 percent discount. Club members are also entitled to substantial fare reductions for accumulated days sailing with Seabourn. After twenty-eight days aboard Seabourn ships, they're entitled to a 25 percent discount on their next fourteen-day cruise. After seventy days, the discount goes to 50 percent. Royal Caribbean's Crown and Anchor Society members receive savings of as much as 30 percent on some cruises as well as a quarterly magazine that often contains other savings certificates as well as early booking information about upcoming cruises. Norwegian Cruise Lines Latitudes Club members get as much as 50 percent off on their next cruise plus certificates for onboard savings. Just about all of the lines have special onboard recognition events hosted by the captain for their repeaters. So cruise lines have effectively been wooing repeat passengers, and thus you would expect their numbers to increase.

Moreover, many cruise line executives feel it is getting progressively more difficult to attract new cruisers as the market matures and vacation options increase. One former executive puts it this way: "Our greatest opportunity was to take people out of hotels within our destination areas. And if we could empty out some Miami Beach hotels, some Puerto Rican hotels, some in Jamaica—all the better. We were so small [years ago] that we needed relatively few new passengers every year compared to the overall size of the travel market in our destination areas." As the industry expanded its fleet capacity, it could no longer rely on tactical regional marketing but had to compete in the larger national and global markets.

Then there is the question of sluggish economic growth. Says McLeod, "It is not a market share battle—it's an economic battle. For the first twenty years, when we were growing, we really didn't feel the economic downturns. We might have felt the economic upturn because the demand strengthened and the prices went up. But we didn't feel the downturns. We were dealing with people who, as a percentage of total population, had higher levels of household income. Today we're in a discretionary income battle. We're competing with land-based resorts; we're even competing with the automobile industry!"

While all of these reasons are valid, we tend to believe the problem can more directly be attributed to marketing and advertising maneuvers within the industry itself. A continuing economic battle is being fought for discretionary dollars. The price of a seven-day air/sea cruise today is about the same as a new home computer, complete with a CD-ROM, a laser printer, and the most enticing software, including broadband Internet access. There is a substantial segment of the market that, when forced to choose, would rather have the latest computer or HDTV than take a vacation.

In a marked turnaround, after years of wooing first-timers, cruise lines had unintentionally but effectively turned their backs on them. As these lines attempted to position themselves as upscale, they had relied on Alice-in-Wonderland advertising to justify high prices. Inadvertently, they had reduced the industry's appeal to first-timers as customers. With the exception of Carnival, no cruise line back then wanted to even appear mass-market. There seemed to be far more interest in selling image to the relatively few past cruisers rather than selling substance to the much larger universe of potential first-timers.

There are several plausible motivations for that strategy:

♦ By setting significantly higher pricing for its product, a cruise line's projected profit, budgets, and business plans look more appealing, at least on paper. This has great appeal for the new executive trying to justify bigger cost budgets as well as for the tenured executive trying to cover up past sins.

♦ It is undeniably easier to market a cruise product to known past passengers than to identify unknown vacation customers and persuade them to become first-timers.

♦ Cruisers typically have found their first cruise vacation highly satisfying and therefore want to cruise again; that's the vast majority of previous cruisers, because of cruising's high satisfaction levels.

The irony of this upscaling was that while the image lines had raised brochure prices and glorified their advertising, they had not materially changed their products. The actual onboard experience for the Miami-based lines, for example, in the mid-1990s was still largely the tried-and-true contemporary formula: casual dress, unstuffy atmosphere, an abundance of activities, and lots of good food. While it's true that the contemporary cruise experience had evolved and improved (with more sophisticated menus, larger vessels, more activities and entertainment options, more elaborate spas), the personality and atmosphere of these contemporary lines are still dramatically different from those of a truly upscale, traditional line such as Crystal or Holland America.

Yet the industry doubled in size between 1985 and 1995 and doubled again between 1995 and 2005. This is an enormous accomplishment against the background of declining percentages of first-time cruisers and a dramatic shift in the cruise brand landscape. Exhibit 5.3 shows the

Exhibit 5.3   **Positioning in the Cruise Industry, 1996**

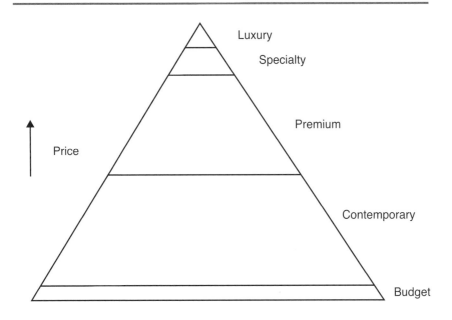

Budget	**Contemporary**	**Premium**	**Specialty**	**Luxury**
Commodore	Carnival	Princess	Windstar	Sea Godess
Fantasy	Royal Caribbean	Holland America	Club Med	Seabourn
Seawind	NCL*	Celebrity	Pearl	Cunard – NAC
Dolphin	Costa	Crystal*	Orient	Silversea
Regal	Majesty	Delta Queen		
	Premier			
	American Hawaii			

*Straddling luxury

brand positioning in the cruise industry in 1996, when the first edition of this book was published. Exhibit 5.4 shows the pyramid just ten years later.

In just ten years, the entire budget segment of the marketing disappeared! Why did this happen? Perhaps the biggest reason is the consolidation that's occurred during that same time frame. Royal Caribbean acquired Celebrity, and Carnival acquired Costa and Cunard and Seabourn. Finally, in 2003, Carnival Corporation purchased P&O/Princess, picking up six brands: Princess, P&O UK, Ocean Village and Swan Hellenc in the U.K., AIDA in Germany, and P&O Australia.

EXHIBIT 5.4   **Positioning in the Cruise Industry, 2006**

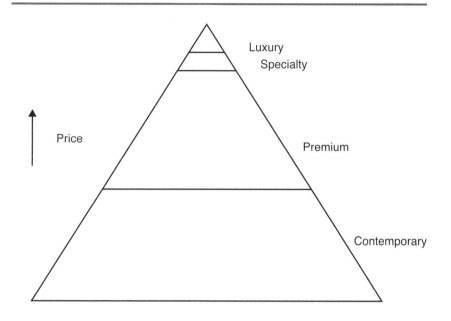

Contemporary	Premium	Specialty	Luxury
Carnival	Princess	Windstar	Cunard
Royal Caribbean	Holland America	Delta Queen	Seabourn
NCL	Celebrity		Silversea
Costa	Crystal*		Radisson
NCL America	Disney		SeaDream
MSC	Oceania		
	Cunard		

*Straddling luxury

The lines that fell by the wayside were smaller lines with older tonnage. They lacked the capital to compete in the arms race of new ship construction. Their older, smaller ships had been able to compete on price for years with some success. But as lines like Carnival and Royal Caribbean retired their older ships and replaced them with new, larger ships with more features and amenities, competition became fiercer. When the larger scale of their operations drove cost efficiencies, the budget lines could no longer compete even on price. With price parity and product inferiority, the result was inevitable.

When the budget lines disappeared, cruising's position in the overall marketing was, surprisingly enough, unchanged. Why? Because the surviving lines in effect matched the old budget lines price points, meaning the contemporary lines filled the price volume sector of the old budget lines as well as their existing segment. This was accomplished primarily by way of the aforementioned cost efficiencies and a proliferation of shorter three-, four-, and five-day itineraries, which reduced the price point for many consumers. At the same time, the contemporary lines greatly expanded the number of home ports, adding New Orleans, Tampa, Galveston, Houston, Mobile, and Jacksonville as year-round gateways and expanding capacity in Orlando, New York, Los Angeles, Seattle, and Baltimore. Because more cruise vacation options were brought to the market, consumers could purchase cruise vacations with considerably lower transportation costs than in the past.

Remarkably, in the last ten years or so, the cruise industry substantially reengineered itself, casting off marginal tonnage and adding state-of-the-art cruise ships that better appeal to the ever-changing and ever-demanding vacation public.

To put the cruise industry in perspective, one should look at its positioning in the overall vacation pyramid (Exhibit 5.5).

In other words, so-called mass-market cruise vacationers are already in the upper middle of the overall vacation pyramid. Consider the myriad budget-oriented accommodations and eating places available to land-based travelers: Days Inn, Holiday Inn, the no-tell motel, Denny's, Burger King, McDonalds—you get the picture! There are thousand of hotel rooms in the United States priced at $50 a night or less on every highway and rooms priced below $100 a night at some fine beachfront resorts.

Contemporary cruise lines start at about $80 per night per person. That's $160 per night per couple. If you comparably equip a budget land vacation with a low-price cruise, you see that a hotel room in the price range of $100 per night equates to the entry level of cruising (Exhibit 5.6).

To check out where cruising sits in the vacation pyramid, figure that the land-based hotel rooms priced at $100 per night or less are occupied 65 percent of the time (the industry average). Too, figure the average length of stay as 4.5 nights—reasonable for a budget vacation.

◆ 200,000 hotel rooms × 65% occupancy = 130,000 fully utilized room equivalent

EXHIBIT 5.5   **Overall Vacation Positioning**

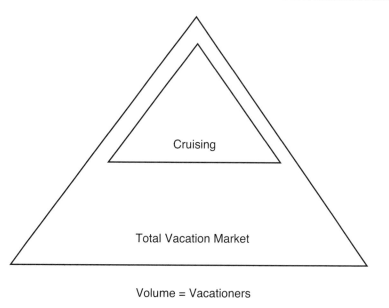

Volume = Vacationers

◆ 130,000 fully utilized rooms × 365 days a year = 47,450,000
   room-nights
◆ 47,450,000 room-nights ÷ 4.5 nights average stay = 10,544,000
   leisure trips × 2.2 persons/trip = 21,088,000 annual vacationers

The low end of the cruise industry amounts to roughly two million passengers a year. Therefore, the land-based hotel vacation market that forms
the base of the cruise/hotel-based pyramid, below entry-level cruising, is
ten times larger! This supports the claim that cruising, even at the lower
end, pricewise, is well into the middle of the overall vacation pyramid.

Moreover, cruising is purchased in discrete increments: three days,
four days, seven days, ten days, etc. This, in effect, makes cruising more
expensive because of the absence of one- and two-day possibilities.
(Granted, on occasion cruises of these odd lengths are offered, but in diminished quantities.) In other words, there is a whole spectrum of land-
based vacations that are less expensive than cruising, not just on a per
diem basis but on an absolute basis because of their shorter duration trip
possibilities.

EXHIBIT 5.6   **Budget Cruise/Land Comparability
(per diem per couple data)**

	Cruise	Land	Comments
Transportation	n/a	n/a	Presumed comparable
Room	$160	$100	
Port Charges/Taxes	$28	$11	
Breakfast	Included	$10	Well, we did say budget!
Lunch	Included	$12	
Dinner	Included	$30	
Drinks	$6	$8	Duty-free on cruise
Tips	$10	$5	
Activities	Included	$16	Putt-Putt Golf, Wax Museum, etc.
Entertainment	Included	$12	Movies
Total	$204	$204	

Cruise line marketing strategies aimed at the repeat passenger are, by definition, market share strategies. They do absolutely nothing to expand the cruise market. With a market share strategy, a cruise line is saying, "My cruise line is better than your cruise line." With a market *expansion* strategy, a cruise line is saying, "My cruise vacation is better than your land vacation." A market expansion strategy is definitely more difficult to execute. It forces the line to explain their cruise product as a splendid vacation experience to someone who has not experienced it, may have difficulty grasping the concept, and who, very likely, has misconceptions or concerns about cruising.

Market share strategies have none of these challenges. When the audience is made up of highly satisfied past cruisers, the cruise line is preaching to the choir. By personal experience, this audience knows how terrific a cruise vacation is. No, the challenge of market share is simpler and more focused: The line just has to say it's "better" in a fashion that will convince sufficient numbers of past cruisers to purchase *its* product—because, after all, they are going to purchase *some* cruise product. Past cruisers do repeat, with growing frequency. CLIA data suggest that the majority of first-time cruisers plan to take another cruise within the next two years; the majority of frequent cruisers plan to cruise again within the next year.

How can a market share strategy possibly keep pace with dramatically growing cruise capacity? It can't, unless the industry can induce repeaters to cruise more often. Of course, given the low cruise prices generated by lack of broader (need we say first-timer?) cruise demand, some of these folks can save money by cruising more. It's becoming less expensive than staying home!

The problem is that each individual line, if it so chooses, can justify a market share strategy, especially if it's trying to justify high brochure rates. After all, check out the rates in cruise brochures these days. They don't bear much resemblance to the reality of the marketplace. Any way you slice it, two-for-one pricing says that brochure tariff is twice what the company is really offering to the public. However, taken collectively, the individual efforts of two dozen lines, each acting independently, means the industry is simply thrashing around and setting a course that leads nowhere. Not only does the primary message of the advertising focus on repeat passengers and ignore the needs and concerns of first-timers, but, we might argue, the messages are actually demotivating to a large number of potential first-timers.

In the mid-1990s, cruise line advertising and brochures featured Calvin Klein–style, sexily clad models with about 4 percent body fat lounging on the decks, dancing in the disco, or watching the sunset. How intimidating is that to the average American woman who may consider herself overweight? But it gets worse: The cost of the breast augmentations, collagen-enhanced lips, and mouthful of perfectly capped teeth would wreak havoc on the average American family's budget. And what about the clothes? One cruise line ad showed six people in an idyllic scene waiting at a small Caribbean island dock for the return of the ship's tender. Typically average middle Americans, they're dressed in white linens, white wide-brimmed straw hats and immaculate white yachting shoes. They look like they matriculated from places like Groton or Briarcliff and have names like Muffy and Biff. And while we're at it, just where would you have found such a cozy little scene in the first place? After all, this line featured some of the largest ships in the industry, carrying thousands of passengers. Only six people on a dock? They must have missed the ship!

Sure, we're biased, but let's take a serious look at what the industry is suggesting it is offering to people who have no idea what a cruise is. Start with the names of the companies operating ten years ago: There was Cunard *Crown* Cruises, Cunard *Royal* Viking Line, *Majesty* Cruise Lines, *Princess* Cruises, *Royal* Cruise Line, and *Royal* Caribbean Cruise Line. These names, to consumers who know nothing about them (and remember, 82 percent don't), suggest they are offering experiences akin to spending a week at Buckingham Palace. (Interestingly, only two brands survived.) The royal impression is reinforced when we look at the names of the ships sailing today. The *Majesty of the Seas, Grand Princess,* and *Queen Mary 2* all sound like they could be the queen's royal yacht. Contemporary cruisers are, for the most part, North Americans who not only don't relate to monarchies but fled Europe two hundred years ago to escape them!

There are, of course, those who do seek this kind of social validation; they are the same ones who purchase their family heraldic seals from mail order companies located in London that advertise in the *New Yorker*. Sure, the names of the lines and ships suggest royal treatment, and many do want that. There's an implied promise that on board you'll be on a floating palace, a special place where you will be treated like a king or queen for the length of the cruise. We're not knocking the promise—that is, in fact, the experience everyone is selling. But that particular analogy is much less resonant with today's lifestyle than it was thirty years ago. It's too formal. Take a look at modern homes being built versus those our parents or grandparents bought. The formal living room (which those who still have it seldom use) has been replaced by the informal family room. Believe us, developers are no dummies. If their research showed that people wanted formal rooms, they'd be building them. The point is that most people want a more relaxed, unpretentious lifestyle. And what about contemporary furniture? Our mothers had reproductions of Chippendale chairs, if they could afford them. Go into any popular furniture store at any price range and try to find one of those today. Bloomingdale's has a few, but they're not the hot sellers. How many homes in any issue of *Architectural Digest* look like royal palaces, either inside or out? We couldn't find any in recent issues!

Now this may seem like a small matter to some, but marketing history is full of products whose names may well have contributed to their downfall. Sapolio and Lava, with their medicinal-sounding names, were the most popular soaps in America until Ivory came along. Eastern Air Lines had a hell of a time getting consumers to remember that it also flew west, and Pan American World Airways was rarely the first choice on the majority of its domestic routes. What your name is says a lot about who you are, especially if I don't know anything else about you. If you doubt that, try introducing yourself to strangers as a Rockefeller, Rothschild, DuPont, or Vanderbilt, and watch their reaction—even today!

This image of exclusivity and formality is strengthened when you look closely at the photographs and words used by many lines in their marketing communications efforts. All of the major lines (including Carnival) boast about their expensive art or antique collections. Brochures refer to luxurious staterooms, elegant dining rooms, five-star service, and gourmet food served on exclusive china (Wedgwood and Rosenthal are hot names) accompanied by polished silver and crystal goblets. And everyone's executive chef is a member of the "prestigious international Confrèrie de la Chaine des Rôtisseurs," which assures that your soup at dinner is more likely to be crème prigourdine with truffle rather than chicken soup with noodles. Female models wear fashions by Thierry Mugler, carry purses by Gucci, and wear three-karat diamond rings.

Men are dressed casually by Ralph Lauren or Versace or wearing the latest styles in formal dinner jackets. Are these symbols valid? To some extent, some of the time, yes. But some scientific evidence says they are not. Sociologist John Brooks, in *Showing off in America* (1981), points out:

> The most effective status seeking style is mockery of status seeking . . . thus the well-to-do wear blue jeans, even worn and threadbare, to proclaim that one is socially secure enough to dress like an underpaid ranch hand.[1]

Even more important, we should ask whether these symbolic representations reflect what the majority of prospective cruisers are looking for. We think not. More important, is this what the average vacationer really wants in a vacation? We do believe most past cruisers, with their first-hand experience, can penetrate the hype and fanciful advertising. They know that liberties are being taken. Liberties? There must be a stronger way to say that! But what about those inexperienced folks who don't have that advantage? How can they possibly interpret these elitist symbols and make sense out of all of this?

Before we tackle that question, let's consider what people seem to want when they take vacations. The two most popular vacation destinations in the United States are Orlando and Las Vegas. Some 35 million visitors each year go to Las Vegas, and the Orlando area attracts nearly 50 million vacationers. For the most part, the hotels, restaurants, resorts, and attractions in these two areas are not luxurious or gourmet. Operators try to provide good food and service in a comfortable, inviting, and imaginative setting. Do people plan a trip to the Walt Disney World Resort or the MGM Grand with a great deal of concern about wardrobe? about whom they'll be with? what social situations they'll encounter? If there is any concern at all, it's about the weather: What if it's too hot? What if it rains? These mass-appeal land-based vacationers simply aren't concerned about fancy clothes. Vacationers more than likely have been to similar destinations and resorts and therefore have a good idea what to expect—and it's not precious.

---

[1]Cited by Richard P. Coleman in "The Continuing Significance of Social Class to Marketing," in *Perspectives in Consumer Behavior,* 4th ed., by Harold H. Kassarjian and Thomas S. Robertson (Englewood Cliffs, N.J.: Prentice Hall, 1991).

And that's the point. Because the vast majority of vacationers have not been on a cruise, they don't know what to expect from first-hand experience. No, they form their opinions from other people, old movies, *Love Boat* reruns, and cruise line advertising and brochures. Because only 18 percent of the population has ever cruised, chances are that other people's cruise experiences have not played a part in the non-cruiser's perceptions of cruising. What do you think the influence on movies has been? Probably nothing good! How many late-night movies show glamorous people in white tie and tails prancing about in first-class suites and grand public areas on magnificent prewar ocean liners? Or you have something slightly more recent like *Titanic*—not the most positive of experiences. And, along with the disaster scenarios, the passengers themselves are depicted as upper-crust society types, not the common man.

How about *Love Boat*? A television staple for ten years, this show did much to publicize modern-day cruising. Most industry watchers agree that this program, an iteration of *Love, American Style,* helped create top-of-mind awareness of this new vacation alternative. But not without a price. Talk about the beautiful people! Everyone on the show was gorgeous or handsome or famous—certainly glamorous. The few characters that weren't moneyed were either buffoons or crooks or gigolos preying on the swells. This show presented cruising in a way that had to, at least subliminally, alarm the average middle-class American. After all, why would anyone want to spend his vacation worrying about whether he or she will fit in? People run the rat race fifty or so weeks a year. When they go on vacation, they want to relax and enjoy experiences that are different from their normal work and community environment. The last thing they want to do, especially the male of the species, is to pay good money and "pay" good time to be in a socially threatening environment. It puts you down rather than builds you up!

In our forebearers' primitive society, men were the hunters who brought home the kill for the consideration and approval of the wife and family. Their self-esteem depended, in large part, on their microsocietal acceptance. If the man was considered a good provider by his family, word would spread throughout his tribe or clan, and his stature would be enhanced. Cultural anthropologists tell us that man today has these same deep-rooted drives; consequently, he is loathe to present a vacation choice that won't meet with acceptance of his wife and family—and, of course, himself. A bad vacation selection today is akin to bringing home a tainted kill in ages past.

Therefore, male vacation purchasers tend to move with extreme caution; their vacation purchases tend to be careful, subtle iterations of previously acceptable vacation choices. Of course, now we're back to cruising's fundamental challenge: As most people have not cruised, the choice to leave familiar land-based vacations and take a cruise is anything but a subtle variation on the land-based vacation theme. To the uninitiated, cruising is perceived as a departure from the normal vacation pattern—requiring a giant leap of faith.

Curiously, most women have absolutely no problem taking the plunge, but then, they descend from gatherers, not hunters. Women are far more intuitive than men. They can see the value of something they haven't experienced much more easily than men. When a woman enters a room full of people, she takes in the whole scene at once, seeming to grasp every detail in a flash. She'll notice immediately, for example, that the woman 25 feet away, in a cluster of folks, has an orange-red purse that clashes with her blue-red knit suit, or that the coffee table needs dusting. The man, on the other hand, is a linear thinker, absorbing details from point A to point B to point C. He enters the same room thinking: "I'm now looking at a fuzzy mass of people. I'm now discerning woman A." And so on. You get the picture! Most women know they are going to enjoy cruising; it just feels right to them. That's why, in our experience, many women would kill or maim to be on a cruise. Yes, the problem is clearly with the males! Their linear thinking presents an enormous obstacle to trial. Any additional obstacles, feeding negative perceptions, merely make the task of converting men to cruising even more daunting.

Against this background we have all the inappropriate images for today's cruising that have been developed from watching movies and television. One would think, then, that cruise advertising on television and in print would work extra diligently to break down the old stereotypes and present the cruise product as an approachable, realistic, inviting, and unintimidating product. The sharp decline in first-timers over the years attests to the industry's collective failure to induce trial. We argue that the cumulative effect of individual lines' advertising—sending confusing messages that not only may not help overcome the obstacles that selling cruises face but may inadvertently reinforce negative perceptions—has contributed to this situation.

Whoa! That seems harsh, doesn't it? With so many factors at work, why do we give advertising so much of the blame? Because, as we have seen, it's the only thing the industry can truly control. This works two ways: When advertising is effective as a market expansion vehicle, it brings in large numbers of first-timers induced to try this exciting, satisfying vacation choice. These first-timers, in turn, sparked by their personal discovery, tell others about cruising with excitement and relish. This positive word-of-mouth and third-party endorsement causes other non-cruisers to try the product. (Remember, we know this is so because cruising has both the highest customer satisfaction of *any* vacation and the cachet of being a new experience—unlike ordinary land-based vacations.) On the other hand, when advertising is *not* effective in bringing in a sizable number of first-timers, third-party endorsement is also proportionately reduced.

The industry therefore loses twice: fewer immediate first-timers and fewer secondary first-timers are induced to try the product. While this would be difficult to prove, it's our view that the power of word-of-mouth endorsement diminishes disproportionately as cruisers take more cruises. While there are no doubt exceptions to this rule, the explanation for the phenomenon is as follows:

1. The more people cruise, the less excited they are about their discovery. It's old news after a while; people get jaded and take it for granted. (To test this theory, remember what happened a few years after you learned to ride a bike or make love!)

2. With subsequent cruises under their belt, people seem to acquire (and display) too much knowledge, which is off-putting to prospective first-timers who are overwhelmed by their own lack of knowledge of the subject. Many potential first-timers frequently become intimidated and withdraw from the arcane discussions of seasoned cruisers.

Savvy travel agents today recognize this situation and counteract it by promoting cruise nights exclusively for first-time cruisers, stressing that experienced cruisers are *not* welcome. Agents learned this by observing what was happening when the crowd at a cruise show was mixed: The experienced cruisers told war stories of a can-you-top-this nature and the first-timers clammed up. It's pretty intimidating to hear someone expound on the sixty-four ships he's been on, stressing the *Lusitania, Merrimac, Graf Spee,* and *Bismarck*! Or, worse yet, a novice asked a "dumb question" (of course, it wasn't dumb, just perceived that way by experienced cruisers), and the cruisers in the audience rolled their eyes in disgust at what they view as verbal flatulence. Trust us, this was immediately discerned by all the prospects in the audience, who experienced subtle but very real discomfort. Is this a positive environment to sell cruises?

Cruising's high-falutin image, propelled by market share advertising strategies designed to increase a line's share of existing cruisers, not only runs counter to the successful, inviting, down-to-earth appeal of most land-based vacation products but also reinforces the non-cruisers' concern about price.

But, you ask, if the industry is aggressively pricing its products with myriad discounts, and these prices are widely promoted via advertising and other promotional means, how can industry advertising be blamed for fueling the misconception that cruising is too expensive? Remember, all of the research shows that for the majority of consumers, the biggest obstacle to cruise trial is the perception that cruising is too expensive. For any cruise line's advertising to produce results, it must effectively deal with and negate this misconception. Shrinking percentages of first-timers attest to the failure of the advertising. That the market share strategies have failed is unarguable. The cause of the failure (with particular focus on the "too expensive" issue) is pretty straightforward. First of all, the beautiful people with their fancy clothes and accompanying bodies imply a degree of affluence—suggesting and reinforcing consumers' negative perceptions on the issue. Second, and just as important, the market share advertising strategy, by definition, speaks to an audience of past cruisers. Therefore, these ads and brochures have no need to, or reason for, proactively explaining the experience of cruising: As a result, the non-cruiser cannot understand or interpret the value of a cruise vacation on the basis of this kind of advertising. On the contrary, if consumers realized the true value of cruising, they would flock to the product because it is the superior vacation value.

Larry Pimentel, the president of SeaDream Yacht Club, is fond of saying, "Consumers are used to unbundled, tip-of-the-iceberg pricing when encountering practically all land-based vacations." In other words, consumers know from personal experience that the advertised price of a resort is only a fraction of what they will end up paying. All-inclusive resorts, like Club Med, where the advertised price includes everything, amount to less than 1 percent of the U.S. and Canadian vacation market. People know even less about all-inclusives than they do about taking a cruise! We know from experience that non-cruise consumers assume that the advertised price of a cruise is similar to a conventional resort. They don't realize the great number of included features in a cruise price because market share advertising doesn't address this issue. The plain fact is that virgin cruise shoppers, when apprised of the price of a cruise, compare it to what they are familiar with—resorts and sightseeing vacations. They don't realize they are comparing apples to oranges. The lead cruise price, even after the deal, seems, and frequently is, much higher than the lead land price, which includes far less. The industry, as previously mentioned, claimed 40 percent of its passengers were first-timers in 2005. We believe the industry first-timer figure is probably no more than 35 percent. But, take Carnival's 33 percent market share out of the industry calculation, and the rest of the industry generated less than 30 percent first-timers.

We believe a business strategy designed to capture a larger share of the existing cruise market is a poor one, not just for cruise lines but also for the cruise industry's primary distribution channel: travel agencies. Like many cruise lines, too many agencies ignore cultivating the greater vacation opportunity (the larger land vacation part of the pyramid). Instead, agents take the path of least resistance and sell most of their cruises to repeat cruisers. The better approach would be two-pronged; it would at least equally include promotion and sales to first-timers.

There is a widespread belief among marketing executives that not only is it easier to sell cruises (or anything else, for that matter) to people who are already users then to go out and create new customers. That is true in most cases, and we do not dispute it. The value of a loyal customer is much more than most people suspect; marketing experts often say it costs four times as much to win a new customer as it does to keep an old one. This approach is especially appropriate with a product category in a mature market where the number of new customers is limited, and therefore the probability of obtaining them is relatively constrained. Take toothpaste or laundry detergent. Marketing executives at Proctor and Gamble know there are not a lot of people out there who seldom do their own laundry or mind wearing dirty clothes and who, all of a sudden, after being exposed to a powerful sales message on television, are going to go out and start washing three loads a day instead of one a week! The name of the game, therefore, is to increase their share of the estimated market among those who already do three loads of laundry a day—mothers who stay at home caring for young children, for example.

The market share strategy is not the best one, however, in a young industry, where there is a good chance of attracting a whole lot of new people who have never used the product—as is most certainly the case with the cruise industry. What about Marketing 101, where you were taught that you can't create a new market—you can only satisfy the needs of an existing one? Marketing gurus Kevin Clancy and Bob Schulman call this "death wish marketing." They cite Professor Frederick E. Webster Jr., who teaches at Dartmouth's Amos Tuck School of Business. Webster says that people who believe this misread Professor Theodore Levitt of the Harvard Business School, who, in his classic article "Marketing Myopia," which many feel started the modern marketing revolution, said, "Selling focuses on the needs of the seller; marketing on the needs of the buyer." These executives who favor a market share strategy interpret Levitt to mean *existing* consumer needs and wants, says Webster, and that's wrong. It's a myth, say Clancy and Schulman.[2]

It's a myth "because it assumes that consumers (individual people, business executives, and government officials—everybody who spends

---

[2]For a complete discussion of this and other marketing myths, we highly recommend Kevin J. Clancy and Robert S. Schulman, *Marketing Myths That Are Killing Business: The Cure for Death Wish Marketing* (McGraw-Hill, 1994). "A company cannot *create* markets" is Myth #50.

money for products or services) can always identify their needs and wants. What made Fred Smith (Federal Express), Ray Kroc (McDonald's) and Steve Jobs (Apple) so extraordinary is that they identified needs people did not know they had. They created whole new industries."

Remember what we said earlier about women's intuition? We were not being chauvinistic. Many scientists who have studied the brain know that right-brain thinking consists of hunches rather than logic, and women, who tend to think more with their right brain, are generally more willing to take risks and to explore uncharted territory because it just feels right. Left-brain thinkers, on the other hand, need sound logical reasons to try anything new. However, men also can think intuitively, given the right incentives. How many men wanted a personal computer twenty years ago? How many people wanted to be connected to the Internet ten years ago? Not a lot—these were new markets created by a simple understanding of the fact that people wanted better access to more information, but they didn't know how to get it, or where. It's not surprising that many travel agencies have been influenced by the cruise lines' marketing misdirection and attendant co-op money. *Co-op money* refers to the widespread industry practice of giving travel agencies cooperative advertising and promotional funds to jointly promote the specific cruise line and the co-operating agency as the retail point of purchase for that line's products. (More about this later.) Unfortunately, lucrative co-op money serves as a distraction that draws the retailer's attention to the underlying marketing strategy of the cruise line that supplies it—a market share strategy that inevitably causes negative repercussions for the agency.

To ignore the first-timers is an enormous missed opportunity for travel agencies because:

◆ First-timers are generally buying the concept of cruising and are not aware of the myriad available brands. They are less concerned about the subtle and frequently confusing market positioning of the various cruise lines. They either have a strong brand preference (because of effective market expansion advertising and positioning or strong word-of-mouth endorsement) or no brand preference at all—viewing a typical cruise in a more general way. Either way, the only sales effort required may be to match desired itinerary, dates, or destinations with available cruises. Repeat cruisers, on the other hand, can put travel agents through their paces for hours, querying them on the nuances—and deals—of dozens of cruise lines.

◆ The net profit of a cruise sale is five to fifteen times higher than a land package, yet the typical travel agency sells ten land packages for every cruise. A booking of two people on a cruise can equal the profit for a group of thirty people on a comparable land vacation.

♦ First-timers are less aware of the practice of rebating, where travel agents voluntarily give back a percentage of their commission as an inducement to make or keep the sale. Many experienced cruisers, on the other hand, relish the task of securing the largest rebate. Perhaps it makes great table conversation on the cruise: bragging rights for the couple that negotiated the best deal for the cruise. Could this be the adult version of King of the Mountain? The winners are reinforced by their victories to try to win again with even greater rebates. The losers, stung by their defeat, are galvanized by their determination never to be placed in that position again. Consequently, they demand rebates on their next cruise purchase. Anecdotally, agents have told us they have even had clients who demanded a rebate *after* the cruise as an inducement (bribe) to keep their continued patronage. In some communities, the practice of securing deep rebates is carried to ridiculous extremes. Prospective cruise purchasers will waste their time and gas money to drive a good distance to save an extra $10 or so on a $2,000 cruise.

♦ Cruising enjoys the highest customer satisfaction of any vacation, satisfied customers are far more likely to return to the same agency to book again. Roughly two-thirds of all agency business is repeat business—the backbone of the enterprise. Secure first-timers and they become annuities, paying off for many years.

♦ Cruise vacations are easier to book because the cruise line handles many of the details of air scheduling, transfers, accommodations, meals, and so on. Also, cruise and air/sea pricing is generally available one to two years in advance of the travel date—not so for most land vacations. Therefore, a travel agent can quote a price on an air/sea cruise when no comparable air/land price is available.

♦ Without sufficient numbers of first-timers, cruise prices will fall, rebating will become more rampant, and the profitability of selling cruises for the agency distribution system will be weakened.

The sobering fact is that unless this market share trend is reversed, the cruise industry runs the risk of becoming the same sort of boutique, out-of-the mainstream vacation it was thirty or more years ago. To prevent this, cruise lines must back up their image with substance and focus their marketing once again on the substantial group of potential cruisers who don't know what they've been missing.

When we first wrote of these concerns ten years ago, our position was that the industry would continue to sail at less than full occupancies and at lower than appropriate prices due to the prospect of overcapacity and underdemand. Today, the picture is surprisingly different. First of all, as shown in Exhibit 5.2, cruise line occupancies bottomed in 1995 and corrected themselves. In fact, by 2005, CLIA reported the industry averaged 103 percent occupancy, an unprecedented level.

What happened? Were we wrong? Were we crying wolf? Let's take a look at the factors contributing to the turnaround:

1. Beginning in the late 1990s, cruise lines began to adopt sophisticated revenue management programs that allowed the lines to price in more dynamic fashion to maximize occupancy (more about this later).

2. Within a year after the first edition of this book was published in late 1996, the two most offending (in our view) TV ad campaigns were dropped. These were the campaigns that were alluded to earlier—showing gorgeous models in expensive clothes in dreamy, unrealistic settings.

3. The concentration of the industry into fewer and larger players created a far stronger opportunity for the cruise industry to fill ships. Eight cruise lines closed their doors, as they were unable to compete. Their low occupancies brought the industry average down.

4. The surviving cruise lines grew; remember, the industry more than doubled the number or passengers carried between 1995 and 2005. The surviving lines had more scale, bringing more resources (advertising dollars, sales effort, etc.) to bear on filling ships. Carnival, as an example, was 26 percent of the industry in 1995 and grew to 33 percent by 2005.

5. The physical product changed dramatically in the intervening ten years. Not only were the old ships of the marginalized cruise lines removed from the market but also the surviving lines sold off their older ships or shifted them outside the North American market. As a result, the average age of the industry's fleet became younger during this period, not older.

6. At the same time, the surviving lines were adding huge amounts of new tonnage in the form of sophisticated, state-of-the-art floating resorts. The industry doubled its capacity in this period with the introduction of new ships that created a great deal of hoopla and favorable press.

7. The sheer size of the vessels created a great deal of ink: In turn, the introduction of the *Carnival Destiny,* the industry's first 100,000 grt ship; the *Grand Princess,* at 110,000 grt, the

Voyager of the Sea, at 138,500 grt; the *Queen Mary 2* at 150,000 grt; and the *Freedom of the Seas,* at 158,000 grt, each raised the bar in terms of size. No doubt these ships and the dozens of others represented by these classes of vessels brought renewed interest in cruising by experienced cruisers.

The intervening ten years ago represents a sort of Darwinian evolution. The weak brands became extinct, and, in many cases, the surviving brands were succeeded by making significant changes in their products, their communications, and, in many cases, their senior management teams. During this period, only Carnival was able to grow and prosper without making significant changes in senior management. Every other line has made major management changes, especially in marketing. New thinking and new skill sets have made our industry stronger and healthier, as evidenced by robust occupancies and record profits.

YOUR CRUISE LINE GPS

6

Positioning and differentiation of cruise lines

When Al Ries and Jack Trout wrote their classic treatise on positioning, the last thing they had in mind is the modern Global Positioning Satellite (GPS) System, which establishes and tracks a ship's position by means of satellites placed in orbit by the United States government originally for defense purposes. Nevertheless, a parallel can be drawn. Ries and Trout were concerned with how consumers "positioned" products in their minds and used that information to make buying decisions. GPS instruments assist sailors in viewing their position on the earth's surface and setting their course. Like sailors, consumers set their course as well—the routes they will follow to satisfy their needs and wants. They do this by assessing their own position relative to their environment and thereby deciding what they need to do (purchase) to improve it.

There are several ways consumers go about making choices when they are planning vacations. The principle ones (in order of importance) are recommendations of friends and relatives, recommendations of a travel agent, travel brochures, travel advertising, and editorial material such as they are likely to find in the Sunday travel section of their local newspaper or *Condé Nast Traveler.*

Up to the 1980s, the cruise industry was relatively small. Because the most influential source of new business for vacation products is recommendations of friends and relatives, the general public knew little about what it was like to take a cruise or the differences among the various lines; they simply were unlikely to know anyone who had ever been on one. At the same time, travel agents were equally uninformed. Most of them had never sold a cruise, much less set foot on the deck of a real live cruise ship. Only those agents who lived near cruise ports (principally Miami) had seen a cruise ship even from the outside. They did have an ample stock of colorful and often expensive brochures that they could and did distribute to customers who asked about them. Few cruise lines did much advertising, and none of them used television. When Aaron Spelling Productions first introduced *Love Boat* on television, the Princess brand name was played down considerably because they wanted a generic cruise ship and Princess was not sponsoring the show— they simply provided the facilities. Indeed, one of the sponsors of the series was Norwegian Caribbean Cruise Lines—the first and, at that time, the only line with a sufficient advertising budget to employ television advertising. However, while aspirational, the program did not project a realistic image of what the cruise product was about. It appeared, for example, that the main duties of the principle characters' (the captain, purser, ship's doctor, and bartender) consisted of mending broken hearts, matchmaking, and generally acting as social directors for the passengers. The staterooms were large by hotel standards, outrageous by ship's standards!

Because it was a case of the blind leading the blind when it came to purchasing a cruise, agents typically handed the few customers who were bold enough to inquire about a cruise a few brochures and told them to take them home and give them a call if they wanted to book one. Very often, agents didn't even do that. Many agencies had a wall full of brochures (many still do), and if the agency owner had acquired some cruise brochures (usually by sending for them) in the hopes that someone might actually want to see one, they were out there on display next to a Cosmos Tour of Europe (eleven countries in ten days) or a week at the Hilton Hawaiian Village on the beach at Waikiki. At the time, agents displayed hundreds of brochures and Carnival simply didn't garner much shelf space.

The image people had about what a cruise was like—or, if you will, the position the cruise vacation experience occupied in the mind of the general public into the early 1980s—was as a costly, stuffy, maybe even pretentious holiday best suited for affluent, sedentary middle-aged and senior citizens—in short, the country club set. Those who did not fit that mold and took a cruise anyway did so because they perceived it as a status symbol. Paul Fussell, in his classic book titled (as you might expect) *Class,* observes, "The middle is the class that makes cruise ships a profitable enterprise, for it fancies that the upper-middle class is to be mixed with on them, without realizing that class is either peering at the minarets in Istanbul, or hiding out in a valley in Nepal, or staying home in Old Lyme, Connecticut, playing backgammon and reading *Town and Country.*"[1] Cruise lines had little top-of-mind awareness as vacation destinations, as they had little combined capacity, were not advertised visibly, and were not sold often.

---

[1] Paul Fussell, *Class* (New York: Ballantine Books, 1983).

Back to Ries and Trout and their explanation of positioning. While, they pointed out, positioning starts with a product or a service, it has little to do with what you do with that product. *Positioning is what you do to the mind of the prospect.* Not that changes to the product or service itself aren't significant; they can be. Cruise lines, like other hospitality products and services, do change their physical appearance, food, features, and price. But from a communications point of view, these changes are made for the purpose of securing a higher degree of awareness—in other words, a stronger position in the prospect's mind. Ries and Trout pointed out several ways to accomplish this. One is by being first. Everyone knows that the first man to climb Mount Everest was Sir Edmund Hillary. But who was the second? Who was the first person you fell in love with? the second? It takes a little longer to answer those follow-on questions because, as Ries and Trout pointed out, the mind is like a ladder, and for every product category there is one at the top of our minds—the one we think of first.

Now, if you can't be first, the idea is to find another way to establish a meaningful position in your prospect's mind. Avis faced that problem years ago when it grew large enough to compete on a national basis with Hertz, the pioneer in the rental car industry. Hertz was number one, and everyone knew it. It advertised the fact heavily. Avis couldn't say, "We're number one too." First of all, it simply wasn't true, and even if they had pursued a business strategy of building more locations than Hertz, it wouldn't have mattered because Hertz had firmly established its position in people's minds as being number one. So what did Avis do? It positioned itself against the leader by saying, "Avis is only number two in rent-a-car, so why go with us? We try harder." The campaign turned Avis from a company that had lost money for thirteen consecutive years to one that made a profit the very first year after their new campaign was launched. Did they try harder? Sure. Their cars were very clean. Their people were very nice. But they offered all the same cars other companies rented. People who rented Avis cars reported that they received good service but there was nothing wrong with Hertz's service either. The real difference had nothing to do with what Avis did to its cars or how accommodating its rental agents were but rather how it was able to reposition itself in the minds of the prospects. If you got off a plane in Chicago and there was a long line in front of the Hertz counter, you went to the Avis counter. If Hertz only had small cars and you wanted a big one, you went to the Avis counter. You didn't go to the National counter or the Budget counter. Why? Because Avis was number two. Avis successfully positioned itself as an alternative to Hertz; it occupied the heir apparent or crown prince position.

Cruise lines never had to wrestle with this problem at the beginning. In the early years, no single company occupied the position at the top of the ladder of cruises in the consumer's mind, although NCL promoted itself as "America's Favorite Cruise Line" until 1984, when Carnival began billing itself as "The Most Popular Cruise Line in the World." Because there were so few ships, there was plenty of business for everyone. Moreover, cruising was primarily destination-oriented back then, and so while there may have been more than one ladder in consumers' minds, these ladders were for different destinations. In those days, people went on cruises mainly as a way to visit and sample new destinations. Because different lines visited different ports, one easy way to pick a cruise was to decide where you wanted to go or what you wanted to see. Some lines promoted Bermuda, others the Bahamas, different ports in the Caribbean, the Panama Canal, or Alaska. Carnival, Royal Caribbean, and Norwegian Caribbean cruised in the Caribbean. Holland America and Princess cruised to Alaska and Mexico. The preferred line was the one with the most awareness for each of these destinations.

But positioning became an issue as soon as the industry grew to a size where many ships visited the same destinations, and it became even more of an issue when the lines began to realize they were selling vacation *experiences*. Surveys began to show that more and more passengers were looking at the ship itself as the primary destination. One factor in determining possible positions is the kind of growth you can realistically expect to achieve. If, for example, you are 99 percent confident that the number of new cruisers will continue to increase at the same rate it has and if you are one of the leaders in terms of market share, then you can be reasonably certain that if the number of new cruisers to the industry grows 10 percent, then your new cruisers will probably grow by the same percentage—providing you have the existing capacity to absorb the growth or are building ships to provide the needed capacity. Remember, in the 1980s, when this evolution was occurring, the industry was operating at very high occupancies—over 90 percent. The implication of this assumption, if you buy into it, is that you need not position yourself as a better alternative to any competitor's line because there will be enough business for everyone (unless your capacity is going to grow by an increment larger than the industry growth in a given year). On the other hand, if you are not confident of growth, then you must take the view that "marketing is war" (a common view among marketing executives in some industries) and that your growth is going to depend on increasing your market share by stealing customers from other cruise lines.

Back in the mid-1990s, former Royal Caribbean executive vice president Rod McLeod viewed the situation as a little of both. To begin with, he was not entirely comfortable with the forecasts of growth in passengers supplied by CLIA although he points out that he has been its chairman on two occasions.

CLIA is a promotional association, not a research institute; CLIA is responsible for promoting the growth of the cruise industry and for positioning the cruise industry as a dynamic, growing, and profitable business. We didn't pay a lot of attention to their figures—we had our own fleet model. I suspected CLIA's forecast in growth of passengers is "optimistic." Remember, we're not selling open heart surgery. The question we're asking is: Are you interested in cruising in the next five years? We're not asking are you interested in having coronary bypass surgery in the next five years. This is something a lot of people would like to do; sixty-percent said they would. Thirty-nine percent said they definitely would; I don't think that number was overly optimistic. I do look at it as an enabling statistic. It's basically saying we're not selling bypass surgery—people want to do this. There's a predisposition out there that cruising is something they would like to do. That doesn't speak to the reasons they haven't, or may not at this point. They may have barriers to entry and this is one of the problems. I'd like to have a Rolls Royce. There's a barrier to entry. I think we have to understand that better and we have to shape and form our product to take advantage of that potential. There are a lot of people out there who are willing to work with us.

Some of that potential is people who say, "Yes I'd like to take a cruise—you know, when I get old enough. Maybe for my twenty-fifth wedding anniversary. That's what old people do, my parents do that." We've got to overcome that. I agree with Bob Dickinson that we do have a story to tell. The median age on Royal Caribbean's short, three- and four-day cruises in the summer is somewhere between thirty-eight and thirty-nine years of age. That shows that we are tapping into that younger market.

The CLIA market research proved reasonably accurate. As the industry added huge increments of capacity from 1990 onward, the industry occupancy utilization figures dipped in the mid-1990s—but, as shown earlier, rebounded to recoup breaking levels by 2005. Prophetically, McLeod went on to say:

A lot of [future] growth depends on how smart we are and how we alter the product. The one marvelous opportunity we have—that marketers in this industry have—is the ability to shape and form the product like nobody else in the travel business can. You look at Bermuda or Hawaii or Miami Beach—they talk about average length of stay. We don't talk about it. We determine it!

Market Segmentation

Once the cruises lines had a fix on the growth of the market, whether through their own research or that supplied by CLIA, they began to focus on market segmentation and differentiation. One major way the industry segments its products is by price. Security analysts, travel agents, and others talk about the luxury market, the premium market, and the contemporary or mass market. Radisson, Silverseas, and Seabourn are luxury. Princess, Celebrity, and Holland America are premium. Royal Caribbean, Norwegian Caribbean, and Carnival are contemporary. These classifications are based mainly on price and amenities. However, as Rod McLeod points out, "There is a good deal of disagreement between the major lines as to how the market is segmented by product. We all have our own way of looking at it. I don't subscribe to the standard classifications; unless your consumer and principal distribution system agree with those particular labels, I think they are irrelevant." He adds, "I don't think the world looks at us that way. Take the automobile industry. Look at the players. If I say Mercedes to you and I say Chevy to you, you now associate those two names certain specific attributes with them. These are related to price, style, and comfort. But people don't know enough about cruises to make those same kinds of associations. For the most part, if you mention the names of various cruise lines to consumers, they can't make the same connections you just did in your mind with automobiles."

Consumers do recognize luxury lines, McLeod concedes. But he believes cruise prospects are not able to draw a hard line of differentiation between premium and contemporary lines. McLeod has his own product segmentation system that he uses internally. He calls it "the drinking man's guide to cruising Segmentation."

> We have the champagne and caviar lines. Champagne and caviar lines would include Radisson and Silversea. Then there are the Evian and granola lines. These are the specialty operators. In that I would put Windstar. Next we have wine and cheese lines, which I think we can further segment into imported and domestic. Crystal would contend that they belong in the champagne and caviar but I would contend they belong in the imported wine and cheese segment. Holland America and Princess are in the domestic wine and cheese category. Next down on the scale after wine and cheese lines there are beer and pretzel lines. Finally at the bottom there are bread and water lines. We are in the domestic wine and cheese segment, but we're also in the imported beer and pretzel segment. Carnival falls into the domestic beer and pretzels category.

Note that the budget or bread-and-water lines faded away within a few years of McLeod's positioning.

Although Carnival and Royal Caribbean are often considered similar, McLeod says, "Do I believe Royal Caribbean is better than Carnival? Sure I do. Why? Because we cost more. You pay more and you get more."

Would that it were so simple. RCCL may charge more on some cruises some of the time, but with all of the discounting, rebates by travel agents, regional fares, and special promotions that are an inherent part of the cruise industry today (and probably always will be), it is difficult—if not impossible, in our opinion—to make a generalized statement about who charges more for cruises. It depends where, when, as well as on what ship and with what itinerary. In this respect, the cruise industry is like the airline and hotel businesses, which also deal with perishable commodities. Can you say that American charges more or less than Delta? Or that Hilton charges more than Marriott? Sometimes they do, and other times they don't. Even more to the point is the issue of product cost. While there are surely instances of paying more to get more, it's not always the case. We haven't been able to buy a new Mercedes yet for the same price as a new Pontiac, but we've noted that Red Lobster restaurants sell fresh lobster for less than its competitors. That's because they buy more lobsters and serve them to a larger customer base. It's a simple matter of economy of scale.

As you might imagine, several other cruise line executives we talked with (as well as one of us) did not agree with McLeod's segments or necessarily where he placed them in the hierarchy. McLeod understands this and readily concedes that his analysis is "one man's opinion of market segmentation." But he thinks it is a useful way of approaching the problem. He noted that with the trend toward consolidation, there will be fewer meaningful players. This may result in some more niche marketers. As long as they have a valid niche the consumer is looking for and recognizes, he believes these lines would succeed. But to do this you have to understand what a niche is, and he believes many operators don't.

"If you have an old, small ship that is not competitive in the volume market, that in itself does not define you as a niche player. You can't go off saying, "'I have an old, inefficient ship and therefore I am a niche player and I deserve to be here." From a consumer standpoint, you're irrelevant. They'll say, "You have an old, inefficient ship and we don't need you. If your prices are low, you're a bread-and-water line, but you're certainly not a niche player." To me, the niche players are up near the luxury segment in the Evian and granola segment. To me, the niche players are providing a unique service the consumer is looking for, and they do it very well. When we get into this rapidly consolidating industry, in terms of major marketing players, what we have to communicate to our prospects is our points of difference.

What we have to understand is that we're standing on the edge of what is, in effect, a new industry. We've come from an industry that ten to fifteen years ago had fifteen horses across the track, all of them running abreast. Maybe some a little ahead, others somewhat behind, but most clustered around each other. What has happened over those past ten years, particularly in the last five, is that a couple of the big horses with stamina—stamina being resources—have moved away from the pack. And in doing so the big horses are getting bigger. If you are a consumer in the grandstand, you don't necessarily need binoculars to know who the fifteen players are; you're now seeing three or four horses, and they're big ones. And their jockeys are wearing very distinctive colors. And they're coming around the track and you can't miss them."

Royal Caribbean Cruise Line

Fast-forward to 2006. Consider president Adam Goldstein's view of the positioning of Royal Caribbean:

> I'm a strong believer that especially in this decade we have distinguished ourselves in ways that resonate with customers and travel agents. Our marketing approach and the level of activity and energy that we convey around the Royal Caribbean product experience with our campaigns and how we marry that up with the features that we have onboard the ships with the rock walls and ice skating rinks and now the surfing machines. There's no question in my mind that it has set us apart.
>
> Travel agents absolutely reinforce that notion because they say, "You're the brand these days that makes our phones ring." So, I feel quite strongly that consumers understand that if you want an active, upbeat, multifaceted cruise vacation experience at a high quality standard, Royal Caribbean is your choice. I don't think there is another choice.
>
> We have a product marketing department [that thinks up ideas like the surfing machines]. That's the way Dan Hanrahan structured the department in his tenure in marketing, and we still have it that way. There's a very strong partnership between the product marketing people and the operations leadership and the new building people. That's the group. People ask me who came up with the idea for the surfing machine. I have no idea, but it came out of our mix.
>
> So, I really feel that Royal Caribbean has absolutely emerged from the past. I don't mean to denigrate anybody else. All the big cruise lines generally speak and deliver a very high level, all of them, whether they are regarded as contem-

porary, premium, what have you. It's a very high satisfaction delivery business. We really feel we have a space in our brand that's not only defensible but is on the offensive. We are pretty focused on convincing land vacationers to come on a cruise. That's still our primary focus. We need to continue to generate first-timers to our brand. We are still running about 40 percent first timers. They are also recommending it to their friends and families.

The management team here fifteen years ago came out of the Royal Caribbean merger with Admiral and needed a strategy to go forward. That was a big change. It began in 1989. Richard Fain asked me if I would drive a strategic planning process forward, but the challenge for me was simply to glean from the management team: What did we believe? What was our situational assessment? How could we go forward? With all due respect to Carnival, we should not overestimate the effect of their brand positioning on what we needed to do. Although they had gone public and everybody saw that they were fantastically successful financially, they were still one of many players in the business. Princess was its own company. Norwegian was its own company. Holland America had just stopped being its own company.

We thought that Royal Caribbean in that day had inherently a tremendous potential. We combined an ability to deliver quality with a versatility to do that in many different ways. That was when we pushed into short cruises for the first time. That's when we pushed into Europe and Alaska [cruises] for the first time. As we did those things, what we saw, what we experienced, was whether it was three nights to the Bahamas on Nordic Empress or twelve nights to Northern Europe on Song of Norway or seven nights to Alaska on Viking Serenade, the experience resonated with our customers across all those dimensions. Whether our customers were coming from Iowa, the proverbial Bert and Ethel, or whether they were coming from the United Kingdom or whether they were coming from Australia or Chile, they were all really enjoying the Royal Caribbean experience.

So we thought, "Wow, we have a broad parameter of cruise lengths, a broad parameter of deployment, a broad parameter of sourcing [customers]. There's a lot we can do with this brand." Not only that, it's not clear that there are other brands that have that bandwidth. I'm speaking fifteen years in hindsight, but I'm summarizing a thought process that came to the conclusion that Royal Caribbean International could house a large number of berths in a relatively large number of ships and profitably deploy those berths under one brand name.

We had a lot of debate about generalization versus specialization. We still do, to some degree. There was a lot of debate in marketing circles in those days about how successful marketers and successful brands pick one or two things out and that's what they focus on and say, "You've got to get those right." You've got to be prepared to sacrifice other opportunities if they aren't consistent with those one or two things. It's understandable, because the textbook thinking is there for a reason. There are a lot of examples of single-minded companies being very effective and fuzzy-minded companies losing their way. That's fair.

But what was going on at ground level, if you will, was that a remarkably diverse group of people were having remarkably different vacations at the same time on the same ship, and they were loving it. So, the reality of the situation was that these ships are amazing assets in their ability to house diverse experience. And so, if you are an older customer oriented to enjoying our publicized entertainment program, liking to get a cocktail before dinner, see one or two shows and go to bed before the midnight buffet and then get up at six or seven in the morning and do it again, you are going to have a great time.

If you are a teen, you're probably not going to get up for lunch, never mind breakfast, and you just hit your stride at midnight, then you really don't want to come home until 5:00 A.M. and you just want to spend time with your peers, well, you can do that too.

The two don't get in each other's way that much. It happens sometimes, but mostly it doesn't. We have the physical plant and the staff support to enable that. Larger ships allow us to offer a diversity of experiences that is multifaceted not only for quite different kinds of guests but also for multigenerational family travel. It's not at all unusual for people to tell me, "You know what? You guys are the only vacation I know where every generation of my family can go there and have a great time. Every other place that we go, somebody's not going to be happy."

We paint a pretty broad brush. Our marketing is generally toward thirty-five- to fifty-four-year-olds, which most cruise lines are. The household income is upscale, because it's an upscale purchase. What happens is that through the great work travel agents do for us and the great reputation we have and the marketing work we do, we are able to convey activity, energy, and quality for all ages. That's what we are. It's not to say that smaller brands that might be more focused can't be successful. Of course they can be successful, but they are more targeted. There are customers they can attract, and there are types they are going to repel.

Norwegian Cruise Lines/NCL America

Colin Veitch, the president and CEO of Norwegian Cruise Lines, weighs in:

We had to change and do something different. There was no point in clinging on to the traditional model because it wasn't working for us. We had a me-too product on ships that were unattractive compared to the new ships that were being introduced. So, while we waited for new ships to come, which would take a number of years, we said, "Let's at least do something with our product that gets people's attention and get a different mentality onto our ships and perhaps get some preference on the purchasing, because you know our industry's pricing systems are quite complex. We wish to sail with every cabin full. We capture more of peoples' discretionary spending once they're on vacation than the typical hotel does as well. We can't scale back our staffing in the way a hotel does, depending upon how full it gets. There is a very high fixed cost. There is no marginal cost to the last passenger on the ship. In fact, there's a marginal utility to the last cabin because people spend money on board. So, in principle, it's better to give a cabin away to get people with money in their pocket into those beds than to sail with an empty cabin. Inventory is perishable. It's really a sad sight to see a ship sail away with an empty cabin. So, in the pricing model, to get a good overall yield, you really have to have people who want to buy your product for some reason other than that you have the cheapest price. If you are only getting people because you have the cheapest price, you aren't going to do very well, unless you are also the lowest cost producer. That's a certain strategy in any industry. There's no room for three lowest cost producers and there's no reason to be the second-lowest cost producer because then you are selling on price and you don't have the best margin. It's fairly clear who the lowest cost producer in our industry was, and we said we aren't going to copy that strategy, so we have to differentiate ourselves and have consumers choose our product in preference to somebody else's product, and that way we will get at least the price everyone else is trying to get. That's how we chose to use our space. If you took the other argument to extreme, you would have a ferry with a canteen in it. There's a tradeoff between space for cabins and space for people to enjoy themselves. In the end, if we have a ship with the highest density of cabins but we don't have a product that people care to buy, then we are back to selling on price again.

It's nice to think what we did turned the industry upside down. Certainly people were skeptical to begin with, but I do see quite a few changes in what the other cruise lines are doing as a result of the success we've had with this. The truth is not going to be seen until we have our entire fleet replaced and we are offering the youngest fleet in the industry with purpose-built, freestyle cruising ships.

We are a relatively big brand already. The NCL brand is about 9 percent of the market. We are essentially a one-brand company. The Hawaii–U.S. flag operation is called NCL America, and our international flag brand is Norwegian Cruise Line or NCL, so everything we do is built off the recognition of the basic core brand of NCL. As a single brand, therefore, we are quite sizable compared to other brands. There are only two brands that are bigger than we are in our domestic market here. Other brands have some overseas markets that we don't replicate. We are very much focused on homeland cruising, as we call it, and sailing out of North America. We carry more passengers out of North American home ports than any other brand except for the two mega-brands of Royal Caribbean International and Carnival, the Fun Ships. But in carrying North Americans from North American ports, we're bigger than Princess, Celebrity, and Holland America. That starting point is driving our pace of ship ordering and our pace of growth. It is our intention to continue to be a strong number-three brand in the industry. There's a big difference between corporate scale and brand scale. Consumers don't know who owns these different brands, and they don't go to travel agents asking to buy a Carnival Corporation cruise or an RCCL cruise. They go in and they want to buy Holland America or a Fun Ship cruise or a Royal Caribbean International cruise or an NCL cruise or a Princess cruise. So in the consumer's mind, NCL always has been and will continue to be a big brand.

Our ambition is to be a strong number three. I think it's a good place to be. There's no point in getting into an arms race with Russia and the United States. The best thing is to support and form a strategy and recognize which space is already occupied and don't simply look at the theoretical textbooks and say, "Well, I'm going to be the low cost producer." The low cost producing position is taken. The high-end luxury position is taken. But, there are several spaces for brands of a sufficient scale to make a good living if you have a reason for people to make sure that:

◆   We maintain our brand scale and replenish our fleets so that at least on the basis of hardware we aren't disadvantaged, but beyond that . . .

◆   . . . we develop a differentiated strategy so people will actively ask for and pay a premium price versus an RCCL cruise or a Princess cruise.

We're building beautiful ships, but everyone else is building beautiful ships as well. We have already benefited from freestyle dining because we learned to manage the crew differently because there wasn't the same incentive there was before. We have moved from the model where individuals in the crew were acting much more as individuals seeking individual rewards from passengers in the form of cash tips to an environment in which we have genuine teamwork and crew members supporting each other. We no longer have recommended flat tipping. We have a recommended service charge that we put in everybody's bill. If they aren't happy with the service, they can take it off, but generally people are and leave it on and that money is then the basis for the compensation for all the crew responsible for maintaining the service.

The other lines haven't introduced the really important part of freestyle dining, which is that the main dining room doesn't have a first seating and a second seating. The other lines have introduced more alternative restaurants. But the alternative restaurant is not the essence of freestyle dining. The alternative is what makes freestyle dining work. The essence of freestyle dining is you don't have a fixed time for dinner. You eat when you're hungry, not when we tell you. The choice of 6:30 P.M. dinner or 8:30 P.M. dinner is not something that belongs in a modern vacation, in our opinion.

Not only will you be eating at the same time [on other contemporary lines], if you're lucky you'll meet people you've never met before and you like and get on with. If not, you'll starve with them, and that's not any experience you find in any other vacation option we are competing with. It's anachronistic. But it's there for physical, structural reasons. My theory is that the initial pleasure cruise ships in the Caribbean were converted transatlantic liners that had been built for first seating, second seating and a first show entertainment, second show entertainment regimen to keep people occupied with lengthy meals and lengthy shows for the bulk of this straight line voyage between Europe and America. You take those ships and say, "Now you are going to go cruising in the Caribbean," but the hardware you have is configured for first seating and second seating dining. Then you find your passengers will pay your crew by stepping back from the wage process and tipping them, and then your crew is not a wage cost to you. Then you go and build new ships and look at what you've got and make a nice conversion from what you've already built. All the ships that have been built for forty years are built on that model—the transatlantic liner converted into a Caribbean cruise ship. If it started the other way and somebody had taken a resort hotel and said, "Let's take this and go to sea," ships would have been built differently, which is why Star Cruises built their ships differently. They said, "We aren't starting from ships, we're starting from hotels. That's our competition." So we need to look at hotels. That's our competition.

I think one of the striking things you'll notice [on our Hawaii ships] is that the interaction between the crew and the passengers is different than on the rest of our ships or on anybody else's ships. It's an American crew and an American passenger base. When we announced that we were going into this, of course, the conventional wisdom again was that an American crew is a negative. We've said from the beginning that we think it will be a positive, and it may be such a positive it will actually be our greatest strength. I am convinced with the people we've got going on the *Pride of America* that it's going to be our greatest strength. I've sailed on the *Pride of America,* and I've seen the interaction, and it's a greater quality than on the international ships. Everyone on the international ships is very service-oriented. It's a great product, but it's a meeting of different cultures.

It's also very striking that you watch the American passengers sit at the bar, and they are having a conversation with the bartender that's a conversation of equals. They are talking about baseball, and the bartender knows about baseball. Every interaction with a crew member and an American passenger is one more standard social interaction in our standard cultural setting. The passengers appreciate it. The highest scores we have on all the things we measure are for crew hospitality on the American ship, ahead of the quality of the ship, the meals. They are higher than for the itinerary. They are higher in service relative to the other scores. The gap in crew hospitality is relatively bigger than on the [international] ships. The score for hospitality is high on all the ships, but on an international ship it is only marginally higher than many other things. On the American flagship, it's far and away the thing that stands out for the passengers. The crew scores in Hawaii are not higher than the ships in the Caribbean, but it's a larger gap. They will be higher. I see the momentum from when they started until now. I look at the crew on the *Pride of America*, and my prediction is that when people will look back at this at the end of 2006, when the book is published, the real secret weapon of U.S. flag cruising is the U.S. crew."

Carnival Cruise Lines

Andy interviewed Vicki Freed, Carnival's senior vice president of sales and marketing:

Carnival is the largest, most popular, and most profitable cruise line in the world for a variety of reasons. I think the first reason is the fact that years and years ago our company agreed that we are not in the cruise business; we are in the vacation business. So, as a result, rather than looking at nine or ten million people that cruise every year (or, back then, a much smaller number, less than a million people), we looked at the much larger vacation market, which today encompasses 300 million person-trips in the United States and Canada taken for three nights away from home or longer and involving a stay at either a hotel or cruise ship.

So, by casting our net at the much larger vacation market, it forces us into the discipline of saying, "What do vacationers want? Forget what cruisers want." Over the years, as the needs and desires of vacationers have changed and become more sophisticated, it has forced our product to change to anticipate the trends. Today, 18 percent of the United States and Canada have cruised before. There's another 35 to 45 percent who could cruise and should cruise and haven't yet, which means the undeveloped cruise market is twice as large as the existing market.

So we are just looking at the tip of the iceberg. Obviously, if we can move people who should be trying cruising to try it, then all cruise lines will be beneficiaries and all ships will rise on that tide of incremental demand.

People would say, "Where is it written that they have to cruise or should cruise?" The answer to that is you can triangulate it in several ways. One is that we know from all consumer research, no matter who has funded the projects, that when people have cruised and compare it with land-based resorts and sightseeing destinations, cruising enjoys a higher customer satisfaction.

The satisfaction level with cruising generally is in the mid- to high 90s, whereas with hotels it's in the mid-80s. So, there's at least 10 percentage points more satisfaction in cruising. That is a significant difference. If this was Economic Man and there was perfect knowledge among consumers, they would be cruising like crazy. But they don't know the product, and it behooves us as the cruise lines and as the industry to explain our product.

By anybody's metrics, Carnival does the best job. As a result of that, in 2005, 48 percent of our guests were first-timers. They had not cruised before on any brand. In the industry, it was 40 percent. But, if you took Carnival out of the industry, the rest of the industry was more like 33 percent. The industry, while they may claim 40 percent, the reality is they don't have any good statistics on it. My best guess says that the rest of the industry is probably no better than 30 percent.

There's market research every year that does a query of people who are thinking of cruising who have never cruised, and the intention to purchase Carnival as their first cruise is a *multiple* of the next two mentioned brands. In terms of passengers carried in 2006, roughly 32 percent of all North Americans who cruise anywhere in the world will cruise on Carnival. We are the 8,000-pound gorilla.

On the other hand, the surest way to achieve mediocrity is to try and be all things to all people. So, our mantra since the early 1970s has been "The Fun Ships of Carnival."

We own fun. Fun is not a demographic characteristic. It's a psychographic characteristic. One of our earliest and most loyal patrons was Ray Kroc, the billionaire founder of McDonald's Restaurants. He wanted to have fun. We could have secretaries two years out of junior college, and they want to have fun. We could have families, with or without their children, and they want to have fun. We could have senior citizens like you, Andy, and they want to have fun.

The two most popular land-based destinations in North America are Las Vegas and Orlando. All of their cues, all of their messages are about fun. Fun for kids, fun for adults, what goes on here stays here, whether it's sexy fun or what have you.

The other cruise lines don't emphasize fun. Many don't go after fun. Many cruise lines seem to offer a posh, restricted vacation. It's not saying *fun* but rather *elegant* or *exclusive* or *elitist*. The land-based counterpart in this country would be places like Palm Beach or Palm Desert. These are not hugely popular resort destinations. They don't have anywhere near the vacationers in a year as Orlando or Vegas have in a month. They are much smaller, and that's fine, but it's not a brand that welcomes most people. It's not a vacation for everyone. Most people would feel out of place in Palm Beach. You don't find 1,000-plus room hotels in Palm Beach or Palm Desert. But you do find them in Las Vegas and Orlando, because there's a demand for them.

Fun is in most people's recipes for vacations. They want to have a good time. That's what we are promising, and that's what we are delivering.

Carnival's approach, from the standpoint of Carnival Corporation, is that we have a portfolio of brands, each one sharply defined and delineated so people can determine what's what and where. Anyone can tell the differences between Holland America or Princess or Costa and Carnival, and that's good, because we aren't trying to have one size fits all.

We carry more families than any other cruise line. But look at our competition: tons and tons and tons of families in Orlando. It's all by design, because we put Carnival squarely in the middle of the mainstream vacation market.

Royal Caribbean's advertising is all about adventure, rock climbing, ice skating. Now they have the wave machines on board, and boxing rings. Royal has chosen a position that defines them sharply versus the other lines.

Carnival is not only the low cost provider with the lowest prices, but travel agents have said that Carnival is the best value in cruising for over twenty years. We are the best value with the best pricing, and therefore we carry more people.

We watch our costs. We are happy to spend money on features the consumer appreciates. We buy TV media and magazine media, and we buy it better. Our shipboard operations are more efficient. We negotiate tough. Our mentality is not, "If that's the price, then we'll take it." If a vendor tells us what the price is, we say, "That's a starting point. Now we'll negotiate."

If I'm on a cruise, my cruise isn't going to be better or worse because I bought advertising more or less efficiently, but the price of the cruise will be higher if I bought advertising inefficiently. The price of the cruise will be higher if I bought my provisions inefficiently. The cost of the cruise will be higher if I have a lot of waste, unexpected cost, too many people in the home office. The cost of the cruise will be higher if I am throwing out hundreds of thousands of brochures because I printed too many or they were out of date too quickly. None of those things will make the cruise any better, but they will either drive the price of the cruise higher on the one end or reduce the profits on the other end.

So, even though we sell cruises for less than our competitors, because our cost structure is rigorous and careful, we end up with higher margins and higher profits. At the same time, we've been successful in taking many of those cost savings over the years and reinvesting them in the product—things like Carnival Comfort Bedding, Celebrity Chefs, and upscale menus. Why do we spend the money on these things? Because these features accrue to the benefit of our guest.

We generally turn down expensive product exposure opportunities because they don't enhance the cruise experience. It's just money to feed executive egos. We prefer to put our costs in areas that our guests appreciate. That's why Carnival is the best value in cruising.

Disney Cruise Lines

Tom McAlpin, president of Disney Cruise Line, delineates Disney's positioning:

"Disney Cruise Line started as another way to vacation with Disney. We knew that many people vacationing at Walt Disney World Resort typically coupled their time at the resort with some type of beach vacation. We also knew that the cruise business was growing rapidly and had a very high satisfaction rate. Knowing these two things and the fact that we were certain that we could create a product that was specifically designed for the niche family market, we took Disney into new waters with Disney Cruise Line.

Using storytelling, what Disney is known best for, to immerse guests into a product, we set out to differentiate everything and specifically designed the experience for every member of the family. This is what we call the no compromise

vacation. That means that every member of the family is going to have a great time. The children have an entire deck just
for them with tons of programs and activities, the teens have
their own dedicated space and adults have areas and activities
that are just for them too. We used the assumption that if you
take care of the kids, this gives the parents peace of mind and
the opportunity to have fun as adults.

Again, everything we do is differentiated.

From an entertainment perspective there are nightly
Broadway-style live stage shows, with Disney characters and
spectacular talent. Our shows are a bit different from other
main stage shows in that they are produced by Disney
Creative Entertainment and incorporate more cast, technology and special effects. Making all of this happen within the
confines of a cruise ship is a delicate task, which is why working very closely with the Creative Entertainment team during
production is extremely important for us.

Aboard, guests not only get to see the Disney characters,
but they get to cruise with them! This means there are a lot
more opportunities to have a more personal experience with
them. Each evening the characters hold meet and greet and
photo opportunities in the atrium lobby and additionally there
are character breakfasts aboard our seven-night itineraries
along with other unique character experiences.

On the dining front, we have an innovative rotation dining
experience which gives guests the opportunity to rotate each
evening to a different restaurant and dining experience, all the
while, keeping their same tablemates and servers. Again,
something that isn't easy to do. . . First of all, each dining
room must be the same size and secondly you have to set up
the rotation and communicate to guests where they will dine
each evening and what time. Essentially it is like making their
"reservation" for them. On seven-night cruises, we do have casual dining as an option for those who want more flexibility.
On all itineraries, there is quick service food such as hot dogs,
hamburgers, pizza and wraps all day long on the pool decks.
Additionally, adults can indulge in the reservation-only restaurant, Palo.

Castaway Cay, our private Bahamian island—is the quintessential beach experience for families, not just a private island. In order to capture this experience, we had to insure
several priorities. One, it had to be convenient for guests
to get from the ship to the island and back to the ship. So we
were the first cruise line to actually build a dock on the

island, eliminating the need for tendering and allowing guests the ease of walking right off the ship to Castaway Cay. Secondly, just as our ships were designed, we wanted to make certain every member of the family had something for them at Castaway Cay. There's a beach for the family, one for the teens and a secluded beach just for adults, called Serenity Bay. Lastly, we didn't want to interrupt the guests' day by having them go back to the ship for lunch, so we created Cookie's BBQ, which offers guests the ultimate island BBQ lunch.

What I hear all the time is, 'I didn't know there were that many children aboard,' and that's by design. With an entire deck just for children, there's plenty of areas and activities just for them, likewise, there are adult specific areas aboard that children are not allowed in. Even the way we schedule the dining room seating and rotations tiers up to this design. We put those adult families together and those families with teens together and those families with smaller children together.

We don't think of ourselves as a floating theme park, rather a way for guests to immerse themselves in vacation and have a quality experience and enjoy Disney. We do this by taking the elements of relaxation and Disney and interspersing them throughout the cruise. Scheduled onboard age-specific activities, entertainment options and shore excursions combine with relaxing spa treatments, pool lounging or reading a favorite book in a lido chair on the promenade deck to make for the ultimate cruise experience.

We have talked a lot about differentiation and I will tell you the number one differentiator of all of the things we do is our cast and crew members. The quality of service they provide to our guests is known throughout the world. We train them on guest service guidelines and intermix this with something we call aggressive hospitality. Those words sound like they do not fit together but the way we think about it is that you only have a short time to build a meaningful and special relationship with guests. I'm not going to tell you the secrets of the trade, but I can tell you we have a primary focus on finding the best crew members that are out there, and investing in training them.

When I talk about differentiation and building a market I have been talking about what we have to have to be successful. But sometimes you have to say what am I going to give up in order to differentiate myself? The answer for Disney was casinos onboard. What we found were two things: one, gaming and the Disney brand did not fit. Two, we also found that the people who want to go on a family vacation are not really that interested in gaming. And three, this was the right thing to do. Sure we could have made more money, but not having casinos aboard was the right thing for us to do. The people who praise us the most are the moms, because if we had casinos where would the dads be?

You know the Disney brand is very well known. When people walk into a travel agency they know what they want. They want Disney and they ask for that upfront. Our goal is to make that product so powerful and so appealing so that they won't take anything less. We make it easy for the travel agent.

We have talked a lot about the family market, but let's not forget that 33% of our guests are traveling without a nuclear family—they're not traveling with children. So this product appeals to empty nesters, it appeals to grandparents, to the newlyweds. When we first started this business, we thought we would have to market to the adults separately from the family. We do not market to the adults anymore, we market to families, and the adults come. We have three couples that have been on our ships more than 30 times.

When we launched this business we had to create awareness to make ourselves well known. So we enlisted a big campaign to let people know what Disney Cruise Line was all about. Once we started operations we relied, and still do rely on the word-of-mouth from our guests.

Moving forward, our goal is to continually invest in the product making it better and better, so each guest debarks ranting and raving and telling their friends how wonderful it is—even booking another cruise themselves. This is our biggest form of marketing today.

Our theme is: 'When you wish upon a star your dreams come true.' We even designed our horn around it. It goes back to the philosophy of Walt Disney—how hard he worked. You have to believe in it and you have to be able to try."

© Disney Enterprises, Inc.

Costa Cruises

Lynn Torrent, president of Costa Cruises, North America, outlines her product:

Boasting a rich Italian history that began over a century ago, Costa Cruises is the fifth-largest cruise line in the world and the number-one cruise line in Europe. Ranging in size from

30,000 tons to 112,000 tons, the eleven Costa ships provide an ambience that is distinctly Italian—from the progressive architecture and stylish design to the unforgettable cuisine and gracious hospitality. This signature Italian style of cruising brings the Costa experience to life on cruises that span the globe on more than 300 departures throughout the Caribbean, the Mediterranean, Northern Europe, South America, Asia, and transatlantic.

Based in Genoa, Italy, with offices in fourteen countries, Costa Cruises has become a billion-dollar global company. With eleven ships and two on order, Costa continues to grow at a rapid pace as one of the international brands of Carnival. The company is highly regarded for its program consistency and itinerary diversification, the latter of which includes new routes in Dubai and the Far East. These new itineraries in China marked the first time an international tour operator was authorized to operate in the Chinese market and depart from the country's ports. In 2008, the company will celebrate sixty years of cruising—another milestone.

Costa's highly experiential cruises offer a signature Italian-style cruise vacation for the mainstream market. Shipboard activities include some of Italy's favorite pastimes—everything from bocce ball to driving a Grand Prix simulator car. Friendly staff use phrases with Italian words that have a universal understanding, such as *buon giorno* and *buona sera*. While this international flair is apparent throughout the complete Costa fleet, it differs between North American and European routes.

Travelers who cruise Costa's Caribbean rave about the line's Italian ambience of "great friends, great food, and great fun." Because Americans make up approximately 90 percent of the passengers aboard Costa's Caribbean sailings, the experience on these sailings offers a mix of Italian flair and American comfort. Cruises begin with a *buon viaggio* celebration and progress to include Roman Bacchanal parades and festive toga parties, both of which are marked by the zesty and warm personality of Costa's staff, who encourage guest participation. Other signature elements include tarantella dancing and pizza tossing during Festa Italiana, an onboard Italian street festival. Also popular is Notte Meditteranea, featuring entertainment vignettes from popular Mediterranean countries. While these experiences encompass the Italian romance of the cruises, North Americans can also rely on familiar favorites including pool games, trivia, bingo, and nonsmoking areas in dining rooms and show lounges. Most beloved are the Italian comfort food selections offered throughout the ship. Specialties from various Italian regions are infused with classic Italian-American offerings, giving North American guests varied menu items from which to choose. Perhaps the company's North American tagline best sums it up: "Cruising Italian Style ... That's Amore!"

With numerous itineraries available throughout the year, travelers can explore some of the world's most exciting destinations in an authentic European atmosphere with Costa. North Americans constitute between 5 and 20 percent of passengers on these sailings, making the experience a true European immersion for those guests. While English is still widely spoken, the Romance languages are very prominent on these routes. For many, this offers an authentic European element to their vacation. Also attractive to guests on these sailings is Costa's long history of cruising in Europe, coupled with its extensive reach throughout the continent. The company boasts nearly sixty years of cruising history, with more itineraries and ports than any other cruise line in Europe, providing the ultimate way to explore the Mediterranean, Northern Europe, and other destinations. Of special note is the newly inaugurated *Costa Concordia,* the largest ship in the Costa fleet, with the largest spa at sea. Featuring the youngest and largest fleet sailing throughout Europe, the company offers a variety of itineraries and the most seven-night options. From the ice-carved fjords of Scandinavia to the sun-kissed ports of the Mediterranean, Costa brings its Italian way of life in a true European immersion experience.

Costa is also South America's number-one cruise line, with numerous routes on the continent and an international clientele. New to the company are routes in the Far East—introduced by popular demand. Throughout all itineraries, Costa guests are made to feel at home with an unforgettable vacation experience through impeccable and spontaneously friendly service aboard and ashore.

Costa is the first and only shipping company in the world to obtain the BEST 4 certification for the quality of its products and services. The categories include environmental compliance, workplace health and safety standards, as well as assurance and safeguarding of core labor rights.

In March 2005, Costa was the first company in the world to be awarded by Royal Institution of Naval Architects with the voluntary Green Star notation. The Green Star certifies that all of Costa's vessels are operated in an environmentally responsible manner and help protect the air and sea in the areas where they sail.

Mediterranean Shipping Company (MSC)

Rick Sasso, MSC's president, discusses his new and growing cruise line:

Beautiful. Passionate. Italian.
Those three words are the true essence of MSC Cruises. MSC Cruises is a cruise line inspired by the strong personal vision and commitment of its Italian owner, richly endowed with the traditions, warmth, and flair of its Italian heritage, and backed by the financial and technical resources of one of the world's largest shipping companies, Mediterranean Shipping Company (MSC).

Allow me to provide some historical perspective. MSC was founded in 1970 by Gianluigi Aponte, who took one secondhand freighter and turned it into what is today a fleet of almost 300 cargo ships, including the world's largest (*MSC Pamela*) and more new builds on the way, calling at more than 200 ports on five continents. In addition, the company operates SNAV, a high-speed ferry company in Europe that is the fastest growing in terms of both size and transportation capacity—in fact, it carried 3.8 million passengers in 2005.

With the same determination and vision that led to his success in the shipping industry, Mr. Aponte acquired half of a small cruise line in 1988. Over the next few years, he purchased three cruise vessels, and MSC was well on its way to becoming well known in the European cruise market as well as the shipping industry.

With its fleet of three classic vessels, MSC Cruises had little name recognition in the North American market and was, at the time, admittedly a small player on the world cruise stage.

The company's owner, however, was passionate about his commitment to change all that. In 2001, the line ordered its first new cruise ships with increased passenger capacity. The multibillion-dollar expansion program kicked into high gear in 2003 with the introduction of the first new build, *MSC Lirica*. As part of the plan to establish itself in the North American market, MSC Cruises opened a new North American headquarters with a new management team of experienced U.S. cruise executives in Fort Lauderdale.

The line's second new build, *MSC Opera*, debuted in 2004, and the company added the newly purchased *MSC Armonia* and *MSC Sinfonia* (formerly Festival ships built in 2001 and 2002). By 2005, the fleet had more than doubled. Two more newbuilds—the Panamax ships *MSC Musica* and *MSC Orchestra*—joined the fleet in 2006 and 2007 respectively, bringing the fleet to nine vessels.

But that is far from the end of the story. In 2006, the line contracted to build another *MSC Musica*-class Panamax ship (to be named *MSC Poesia*), with an option for a second, and two 133,500-ton post-Panamax vessels. With the post-Panamax ships *MSC Fantasia* and *MSC Serenata* on the order books, MSC Cruises stands as the world's largest and fastest-growing European cruise line.

As you can see, this unprecedented move from a company this size to build so many ships in such a short period of time shows just how very serious—passionate, if you will—MSC Cruises is about its commitment to growth. It is also a company that is passionate about and committed to success and a company that knows the cruise experience should be as beautiful as the ships.

For MSC Cruises, it is an experience that can be best described as *Beautiful. Passionate. Italian.* MSC Cruises' well-appointed and spacious ships offer travelers experiences that reflect the heart and soul of Italy, with an ambience comparable to that found at the best Italian hotels. Whether in the Caribbean, the Mediterranean, Northern Europe, South America, or South Africa, guests onboard an MSC Cruises ship will find an authentic Italian/European cruise experience, from the cuisine featuring regional Italian specialties (as well as perennial all-American favorites and gourmet delights) to the warmth and generosity of the Italian officers and international crew. Plus, its European-style entertainment, suitable for the entire family, has been called the best at sea, earning standing ovations each evening.

The hallmark of MSC Cruises is the ability to recreate the art of cruising through the personality and spirit of its ships and crew, with an emphasis on the cruising experience and a high level of service and hospitality. That means white-glove service, being greeted at embarkation and escorted to your stateroom, fresh food on board every day, and warm Italian service and hospitality.

The rich Italian character of MSC Cruises is reminiscent of lines such as Sitmar Cruises and Home Lines, which were renowned for the warmth, charm, and attention to detail of their Italian crews. While embodying the timeless understated elegance of those famous lines, MSC Cruises also offers onboard features that today's vacationers want, such as stylish staterooms with balconies and complimentary twenty-four-hour room service, spacious public areas, luxurious spas and fitness centers, casinos, Internet and coffee cafés, miniature golf courses, and children's facilities and programs.

And who better to represent MSC Cruises than Italian film icon Sophia Loren? Ms. Loren epitomizes all that is MSC Cruises—*Beautiful. Passionate. Italian.* We are honored to have the Academy Award–winning actress and incomparable beauty serving as our spokesperson and godmother to both *MSC Lirica* and *MSC Opera.*

A cruise vacation with MSC Cruises is a true cultural experience. While each sailing features onboard ambience with a true Italian flair, guests can select from itineraries that feature more than 100 ports of call. MSC Cruises takes guests to some of the world's most exotic lands and locations featuring picturesque beauty, historic landmarks, and tropical getaways, as well as ever-popular destinations.

As MSC Cruises grows, it continues to expand opportunities for travelers to experience cruising that is *Beautiful. Passionate. Italian.* With grand new ships on the horizon and year-round sailings throughout the world, MSC Cruises reaffirms its position as a global player in the cruise industry.

Celebrity Cruises

President Dan Hanrahan positions his brand:

Celebrity Cruises has been recognized as a leading premium cruise line since its inception in 1989. Since that time, we have consistently built on a great foundation while introducing new and innovative ships and onboard experiences. We have communicated those products and our core brand attributes in a variety of ways using a quickly changing array of media.

But within this fastest-growing segment of the travel industry, even with impressive innovations, distinguishing one cruise line from another has become an increasingly formidable challenge. All cruise lines have spas, all cruise lines have dining, and they all provide reasonable staterooms. Finding the nuances is becoming more difficult as every line tries to outdo all others with the experience they deliver. Meanwhile, every year brings new ships presenting enticing new products and services. So how, exactly, do we distinguish our brand?

In 2005, we took a step back to think about that and applied that thinking in establishing our new brand position. That, in turn, inspired an integrated brand communications platform designed to clearly communicate to the right audience what separates Celebrity from the pack—and we believe it's the outstanding service experience we offer onboard every Celebrity ship.

Our distinction comes from that special something that only we can offer, so we gave it a memorable name, and it's no accident that our brand name is part of it: Celebrity Treatment. It's a level of service tailored to our guests' individual needs. It's not intrusive; it's not forced. It's relaxed—which is exactly how we want our guests to feel when they sail with us.

We believe it's our extraordinary service and onboard experience that sets us apart, and we know that is what has led to such a large and loyal following of repeat guests. So, our communications are designed to creatively convey that message. Granted, communicating intangibles can be a challenge, but we chose to build our campaign around the core attributes of our onboard product:

1. *Extraordinary service.* Celebrity offers highly personalized, anticipatory but unobtrusive, and memorable service, with a guest-to-staff ratio of two to one.
2. *A culinary experience that is best in class.* From the inviting design of the venues to the gourmet menus created by Europe's renowned master chef Michel Roux, Celebrity's dining experience is second to none.
3. *A stylish, inviting environment.* The ambience throughout every ship in the Celebrity fleet is one of understated elegance. It's sophisticated, but never stuffy.

While shaping our creative campaign, we also sharpened our target and conducted extensive research geared toward homing in on who our communications will resonate with and who the Celebrity vacation experience is best suited to please. We determined that the right audience for us is the baby boomer audience—more experienced travelers, guests ages forty-five to sixty-five, who enjoy a comfortably sophisticated, upscale cruise experience in which their every need is anticipated and met, often in wonderfully surprising ways.

To communicate the Celebrity experience to the boomer audience in a meaningful, impactful way, we launched a new creative campaign built around our theme line, the Celebrity Treatment. Within the TV and print advertising, we playfully position Celebrity as a leading premium brand and distinguish ourselves with a promise to offer a unique and better cruise experience through exceptional service—the Celebrity Treatment—which only Celebrity can offer. The campaign was designed to show how Celebrity's service and experience as a whole makes our guests feel like celebrities and conveys the emotional connection our guests feel from the minute they step aboard until the moment they reluctantly leave.

In terms of where we advertise, we naturally look for opportunities where we can both increase our visibility and differentiate the Celebrity brand from the competition, and we determined that a network schedule would be an outstanding way to do that. We found it to be the perfect stage upon which to launch our new campaign, utilizing high-profile appointment TV programming that targets our audience very effectively. It also separates the Celebrity brand from our core competitive set in an unexpected medium, which helps drive greater brand differentiation and preference.

Our broadcast campaign consists of two thirty-second ads, which we launched in a very visible way—marking the first time in five years that we advertised on network TV, and on some of the top-rated shows of the season, along with buys on select cable channels that reach a significant percentage of our target throughout the year.

Early reaction from consumers has been exactly what we hoped for. Testimonials confirm they understand what Celebrity offers, with comments ranging from, "When you are on Celebrity, you are a star," to "This is the way you want to feel on a cruise."

Two print campaigns—one each geared for consumers and trade—played with the Celebrity Treatment theming as well ("Ahhh, the Celebrity Treatment. How will it affect you?"), and were similarly designed to stand out versus the competition, with creative executions and, for the trade, a clear call to action.

A new and decisive twist we took with our TV campaign was to clearly acknowledge within the TV spot the vital role that travel agents play in our business. While several lines report increases in direct bookings today, Celebrity still sells about 95 percent of cruises through the trade—one of the highest percentages in the business. We depend heavily on travel agent support to sell our brand. So, we acknowledged them in the body of the ad versus just the tagline. And the response we've received from agents has been nothing short of phenomenal.

For example, one agent wrote, "So many travel vendors claim to be the travel agent's partner, but this is the first time I have seen an ad that actually promotes travel agents. . . . Most of our travel partners depend on us for the biggest percentage of their business, but only you did something about it." Similarly inspired by our public recognition of trade, multiple agents have said their offices now "will do more than ever to sell Celebrity." It's very much a mutually beneficial relationship, and we plan to continue to place heavy emphasis on it.

Finally, as PVRs (Personal Video Recorders) and the Internet are changing the way consumers take their entertainment and gather information, a differentiated message becomes more important than ever. However, a differentiated message is no longer enough. Figuring out where you can reach your audience with the differentiated message is the new challenge facing marketers today.

Holland America

Stein Kruse, president and chief executive officer, Holland America Line, discusses Holland America's positioning:

I would say Holland America Line is a cruise line that has a global footprint. We go almost everywhere. We are a little bit higher priced, but you get a whole lot more for what you pay. We deliver a value proposition rather than a price proposition. We believe that there are the small nuances that our product has that separates us from other cruise lines. So we aren't a luxury cruise line or a mass-market cruise line; we're in the middle. We're a premium cruise line, and those many subtleties that we believe are unique to a brand are what distinguishes our brand.

Everybody's a competitor of Holland America, of course. But I'm not so overly concerned about other brands per se. I'm more concerned about reaching out to a broad audience of potential vacationers, people who are looking for a respite from daily life. Those may be people considering another cruise line, but they may just as well be people considering going to Hawaii or taking a resort vacation in the Caribbean or going to Las Vegas or going to a beach house in Cabo San Lucas. It's a big universe.

We focus on five key pillars of our brand. It's in our accommodations, it's in our services, it's in our dining, it's in our destinations, and it's in our onboard activities. I can drill down in any one of those areas.

When you talk about destinations, I could be wrong, but I don't think I am. We go to more places with our ships than any other company. We go to seven continents, including Antarctica. We have nearly 300 ports of call in any given year. We have cruises from as short as two and three days to as long as 116 days. So, in terms of the destinations and the availability of different types of trips, we are really unique.

In terms of accommodations, what is unique to us is the fact that we have, by most people's definitions, relatively large vessels. But they are actually very intimate in terms of the number of people that the ships can accommodate. Other cruise lines, except for the luxury operators, do not have as generous a space ratio as Holland America does. Our space ratio varies by ship a little bit. It's in the high forties. That's a very comfortable proposition for ships of our size.

In today's world, which of course has changed much over the last five, ten, fifteen years in terms of ship design and ship outfitting, our ships are now medium-sized ships, yet they have very generous space rations, both in the public rooms and in the individual staterooms. The cabins are staterooms, larger by comparison to most of the other non-luxury cruise lines. We offer more suites and more mini-suites. The outfitting in the cabins, particularly with our Signature of Excellence initiative, is very generous and comfortable and is a part of our subtleties.

Dining is another area where we constantly try to evolve what we do. First of all, because we are a destination-focused company and go to so many places, we try to incorporate some local fare in our cuisine when we go to far away places. We change our menus, for instance, when we go to Alaska. We feature a lot more seafood, Alaska salmon, things of that nature. In the Caribbean, we would have different menus. When we are on a world cruise, we pick up specialties when we are in the Far East, and so on and so forth. From time to time, we do buy from local suppliers when we traverse those routes.

We have Rudi Sodamin, who is our master chef and who works with us on creating most of our menus and in most of our food management. Rudi Sodamin is probably one of the best-known, if not *the* best-known, chef in the cruise industry. I would say Rudi is just as good as those other guys [Michel

Roux or Georges Blanc]. Their claim to fame is that they run one restaurant, you know. They have a name; that's all. We have a guy who's been out there delivering consistently over twenty-plus years, literally millions of meals in this kind of environment, who knows exactly how this operation works. For instance, this year when we were in Alaska, we had a fantastic program that Rudi created, "Holland America Goes Wild on Salmon." Essentially, it was about using wild Alaskan salmon in myriad ways—in appetizers, in main courses, in salads, in sandwiches, in barbecues, all kinds of different ways. So, those things are found very exciting and very much appreciated by our clientele.

I believe if you look at Holland America run ships today you see our Signature of Excellence initiative throughout; when you come into our main dining room, it's all white crisp linen, all silver, no stainless there; the china is beautiful Rosenthal china. The whole experience, we try to make sure it's one of elegant dining, again with the limitation that you are dining simultaneously with another thousand people. You should, when you sit at your table, whether you are with your spouse, a friend, or a large party, feel that you are having a dining experience that was something that you not only looked forward to but where you are actually pleasantly taken with the experience. To do that three times or more a day, whether it's in the dining room, or a specialty restaurant or room service, on the lido, and doing that many times a day, day in and day out, it becomes a consistent hallmark of a brand—or, as we like to say, "HALmark," to play on Holland America Line.

We are known as a line with an Indonesian crew, and we are very proud of that. We have predominantly Indonesian and Filipino crew members in our service roles. We have large training facilities in those countries. We have our own school, our own dormitories. We train with our own staff, which has been with us years and years. We have a very set way of training. They learn the Holland America way from the beginning. That allows us to have the consistency that I talked about and also have a fundamental sort of standard that you can adhere to and everybody can align behind.

It would be easy to say our market is everyone, but the reality is I don't think everyone is a Holland American Line customer. We are clearly a choice cruise line for people who have cruise travel experience. It doesn't mean that you can't travel with us as a first-time cruise traveler or as a first-time international traveler, but we certainly see more experienced travelers/cruisers than other companies.

In Holland America Line's case, we have a high repeat percentage of business. It varies by the type of product, but it's easily in the 35, 40, 45 percent range in various products. That means that, obviously, 60 percent or so are not former cruise customers of ours. They may be former cruise customers of other companies, but some of them have not cruised before, so we are attracting first-time cruisers. A lot of our older customers (not specifically by age, but meaning they've traveled with us before) are bringing friends. A lot of them are bringing the next generation, their kids or their grandchildren. In order for us to appeal to such a broad audience, we have to have onboard activities and shoreside activities that appeal to these multigenerational travelers. We as a company have spent a lot of effort and significant amount of capital, both onboard and shoreside, to ensure these new customers like our product.

I can give you a couple of examples. For example, Half Moon Cay, which is without a doubt the most popular destination that Holland America Line goes to, and the highest rated and arguably the best private island in the Caribbean in the cruise industry, has seen many, many new types of activities put on that island over the last few years. You can go on that island now, and you can literally do so many things that you can't do them all in a day. You can go parasailing, you can go scuba diving, you can go horseback riding, you can swim with the stingrays. So, the type of activities on that island, our own island where the quality is controlled and assured by us, is very impressive and very, very appealing to both existing and new customers alike.

On our ships, another example is we used to have a few years ago zero kids' facilities. You made your own fun out of whatever you could find, whether it was playing in the pool or playing hide-and-seek in the public rooms. Today we have multimillion-dollar children's facilities with lounges and video machines and computers and arts and crafts facilities, etc., etc. So, whether you are three or thirteen, you will come onboard and you will be immersed in activities suitable to your age. If you are traveling with a grandparent or parent, you are very much entertained by the things we do and by peers your age who are also doing those things.

The age of our average passenger is going down very, very slightly. That's actually very good, because it's not going up, which means that as we've grown as a company and have more destinations and as we have longer voyages, we are seeing, for lack of a better description, more baby boomers becoming Holland America Line customers.

Princess Cruise Lines

Jan Swartz, senior vice president of marketing for Princess Cruises, weighs in:

Princess offers a premium cruise product for affordable prices. We take passengers all over the world on beautiful ships that are, by design, tailored to give a vast array of amenities, while the passenger never feels lost in a crowd.

Princess has many points of distinction versus the competition. We believe that Princess offers a unique proposition in cruising—a contemporary, upscale, yet comfortable cruise product you can experience almost anywhere in the world, as our cruises visit all seven continents. Let me outline what we see as the key differences.

First, Princess is the leader in the balcony revolution in cruising. As the cruise industry has evolved, balconies have become the de facto standard in the industry. Princess has the youngest fleet in the industry, with an average age for our ships of 5.6 years. Princess offers more affordable balconies than any other cruise line, with now 53 percent of our cabins offering balconies. A balcony offers a stunning and memorable way to experience your vacation, especially as you travel some of the most exciting and exotic places in the world, like Alaska, Europe, or Asia.

The second point is that we have designed our ships to deliver what we call "big ship choice, small ship feel." Princess broke the mold of the traditional cruise model where there was one large theater, one large dining area, and you basically split the passengers into two groups. Everybody went to the theater or dining, and they switched at 6:00 or 8:00 P.M. Instead, Princess offers many dining and entertainment venues, often seating at most 500 people, so the impact on passenger flow is quite significant. The restaurants, bars, and theaters are intimate gathering places with sophisticated décor. The scale of the ship allows you to have a wide breadth of activities, but the actual layout and passenger flow distinguishes us from the competition. Our passengers never get the sense that they are lost in a crowd.

The typical passenger articulates the experience by saying, "I feel really comfortable on Princess, and I would never guess there are that many people on the ship." Everybody finds their own intimate spaces that they claim as their own. That's a characteristic unique to Princess.

This design also supports our unique dining concept of personal choice dining, which offers the choice of anytime dining or traditional dining. As you know, in the cruise industry, for many years dining has been modeled off the traditional dining pattern where you dine at fixed early or late seating. What Princess said is, "We have a proportion of our passengers, typically 40 percent, who still prefer traditional dining, so we'll still offer that, but we're going to offer anytime dining as well."

Anytime dining is similar to what you would find at any restaurant on shore. You can make reservations, or you can come as you wish and be seated. It offers our passengers total flexibility in designing their own cruise experience. You can take a late shore excursion and come back and shower and catch dinner at 8:30, and then the next day perhaps get up early and take a fishing trip and then dine at 6:00. So you are not locked in at a specific time to a specific place or even with specific people. We find there are 60 percent of our passengers who prefer that flexibility, and so we were able to evolve our dining experience to what travelers expect when they vacation today.

We found it was a mix—that some of our passengers still prefer traditional dining. There are benefits to traditional dining, as our passengers build a relationship with other passengers and their waiters while on board. Structurally, we were able to support these dining concepts because we can assign smaller venues to one concept or another—a feat other cruise lines cannot replicate easily.

Then, of course, we would say our cruise product is distinguished from the competition by our Princess service. We have a very well-known customer service program called C.R.U.I.S.E., which stands for "Courtesy, Respect, Unfailing In Service Excellence." It's a training and motivational program we have in place for the crew and also our shoreside staff in our various offices and throughout Alaska in our wilderness lodges.

This program has been in place for ten years now, and I believe it's the most longstanding customer service program in the industry. Many customer service programs come and go, but ours has stood the test of time and is more vibrant today than it has ever been.

Our primary target market is experienced cruisers, past passengers of Princess and past passengers of competitive cruise lines.

Why is that our target market? It is because we are a destination cruise line. We offer cruises all over the world. This kind of rich deployment with a wide variety of itineraries tends to appeal to an experienced cruiser.

A first-timer usually tries out cruising closer to home. So, the diverse nature of our product offering has more appeal to experienced cruisers. However, the broad appeal of our product also attracts first-timers as well.

Oceania

Oceania's president and CEO, Frank Del Rio, offers his view of Oceania's place in the cruise market.

While not a luxury or ultra-luxury line, Oceania Cruises offers a luxury experience with most of the elements and amenities associated with the luxury lines, at a premium price point. Yet our definition of luxury is one that has great appeal to our guests. The true measure of luxury is feeling completely comfortable in your surroundings. Being looked after by an unobtrusive staff who are genuinely warm and caring and anticipate your needs, rather than being fawned over or having staff hover around you.

And the size of our ships grants us an enviable advantage and distinction. It allows us to deliver a level of personalized service—not possible aboard ships that carry thousands of guests—without sacrificing the amenities and creature comforts that guests expect, such as a luxurious spa, expansive suites, and staterooms with private teak verandas.

At the very outset, we defined our product with a succinct vision and absolute clarity. We have remained true to our Points of Distinction, which are the pillars of our brand, and the resulting brand definition and distinctions are very clear to guests.

- ◆ The finest cuisine at sea, served in four distinctive, open restaurants.
- ◆ An acclaimed culinary experience created by world-renowned master chef Jacques Pépin.
- ◆ The exclusive Tranquility Bed, featuring luxurious Euro-top mattresses, plush duvets, down pillows, and the finest Egyptian cotton linens.

◆ An elegant country club casual ambience.
◆ Midsize ships that feature large-ship amenities.
◆ Voyages to the world's most alluring destinations.

Our three 684-guest ships provide for a much more personal experience, as we have more than 400 staff members onboard whose singular focus is to provide our guests with the most memorable experience possible. Our unique brand of hospitality transcends the rich décor, the finest cuisine, and the most comfortable beds at sea. It's the familial bond that quickly forms between the guests and the staff. It's being treated as a lifelong cherished friend more than an honored guest. It's the genuine warmth that you feel and the sincere smiles you see every day.

You see the difference in the way we serve our guests and the way we make them feel. You taste the difference in the cuisine. Each and every meal is prepared to order, cooked à la minute instead of the mass, banquet-style preparation that is required to produce 2,000 to 3,000 meals at a time. Our chefs are true culinary artistes, and they take great pride in creating memorable meals. And our menus are a study in culinary diversity. Featuring more than 200 menu items each and every day, they are the most diverse and creative menus you'll find at sea. An extraordinary dining experience is one of the pillars of our brand, and we have quickly made our mark by transforming the evening meal into the evening's event. And the level of comfort we provide our guests defies description. Little things like cashmere blankets, complimentary garment pressing, and complimentary cappuccinos and espressos say a lot about the line's dedication to providing a superior guest experience.

As extraordinary cuisine is the single most important element in differentiating Oceania Cruises from all other cruise lines, our superb five-star menus are crafted under the meticulous, watchful eye of world-renowned master chef Jacques Pépin, our executive culinary director. Talented chefs, under his tutelage, create daily gastronomic events that surpass all expectations. Only the finest and freshest ingredients find their way into these amazing culinary creations. And in our wine cellars is a vast collection of vintages from around the world to please even the most demanding palate. Each evening, dinner is a highly anticipated occasion accenting each day's discoveries with an impressive selection of gourmet entrées as memorable as the unforgettable destinations visited.

In the evening, guests may dine at any of our exquisite restaurants, each one unique and radiating its own special ambience. Our open seating policy allows them the freedom to decide when, where, and with whom they wish to dine. Guests may choose from the Grand Dining Room, Toscana, or Polo Grill, or dine under a canopy of stars at Tapas on the Terrace. For lunch, there is our sunlit Terrace Café, or Waves, serving a mouthwatering array of barbecue fare, pizzas, and daily chef specials poolside. For a more traditional breakfast or lunch experience, the Grand Dining Room provides a daily cornucopia of classic offerings to tempt the palate and test the willpower. Of course, should guests wish to dine in the privacy of their suite or stateroom, an extensive room service menu is available around the clock.

And a culinary experience is more than just fine food and wine. Our most recent corporate initiative was the creation of the Perfect Table, which blends all of the key elements necessary for the ultimate dining experience. The finest cuisine, complementing vintages, deft service, a dazzling display of Versace china, Riedel crystal, and Christofle silver, and a sophisticated ambience all combine to elevate the dining experience from extraordinary to one that is a virtual culinary fantasy.

A great meal should always be followed by a good night's sleep, and with that in mind we set an industry trend with the introduction of our trademark Tranquility Bed in 2003. As they say, imitation is the sincerest form of flattery; many other lines were quick to follow in Oceania Cruises' wake and spent hundreds of millions of dollars to upgrade their bedding. Once again, the adroit and astute executives of Oceania Cruises have signaled "catch me if you can" to their respected competitors with the third generation of the Tranquility Bed. Featuring custom-made Imperial Mattresses, up to 11½ inches thick with a cap of memory foam and dressed in even more luxurious Egyptian cotton linens, the new beds are topped with the finest down pillows and sumptuous silk-cut Italian duvets.

In addition to our leadership position in providing a superior shipboard experience, Oceania Cruises has quickly established itself as the leader in destination cruising. Offering the most overnight port stays of any cruise line in Europe, Asia, and South America, Oceania Cruises presents each destination in glorious detail. Our destination-rich itineraries feature few, if any, sea days, which affords our guests the opportunity to immerse themselves in the destination. They do not just see the sights; they experience the culture, cuisine, and history of the destination. It's a rewarding, enriching, and enlightening experience that is possible only when traveling with destination experts.

All of these elements add up to an extremely appealing value proposition, one that discerning travelers were quick to recognize and embrace. For the same price or a few dollars more than what you would expect to pay for a cruise aboard one of the leading premium lines, Oceania Cruises offers a truly extraordinary experience with many of the luxury elements offered by the ultra-luxury lines. The value for money simply cannot be surpassed.

Cunard Cruises

Carol Marlow, president of Cunard Lines, discusses her product:

Cunard offers its guests the opportunity to sail "The Most Famous Ocean Liners in the World"—and, by doing so, to join a 167-year legacy of royalty and celebrity traversing the world's oceans aboard legendary ships that are themselves iconic and celebrated. In an ever-changing world, the Cunard experience remains uniquely authentic—a voyage conducted not just as it always has been but as one *should* be—solidifying the line's appeal to tradition-minded travelers.

The brand's particular elegance of style, service, and society has been constant throughout its history, keeping the Golden Age of Ocean Travel alive and vibrant. As in our heyday, today's Cunard voyage is still a stimulating suspension in time—laden with British tradition and service, shared with fascinating like-minded individuals, conducted amidst sumptuous settings of a grandeur found nowhere else on the sea. Sailing Cunard remains a pinnacle travel experience, a rite of passage separating the sophisticated and adventurous traveler from the mere vacationer. Our guests' sense of aspiration and achievement is perhaps the core benefit to them of choosing Cunard—consistent with the badge appeal of luxury brands in general, yet stronger and better defined than most of our luxury cruise competitors.

The classic liner experience we offer aboard our three Queens attracts a mature, refined customer. While, on average, our guests are somewhat older, with median ages in the low sixties, we attract a wide range of guests—with a large, growing component in their forties and fifties as well, a trend noticed by many luxury lines. With our Queens' global fame, our passenger base is also global. Unlike most cruise lines, who source mainly from their home market, Cunard's liners attract a diverse international audience on most voyages and overall sail as many Europeans as Americans.

Most guests are quite affluent, especially in our Grills suites categories, and many are experienced international travelers and cruisers. However, there are many aboard each voyage enjoying a once-in-a-lifetime celebration for which they have saved for many years—such is the mark of distinction the brand conveys. Cunard is often seen as a special-occasion voyage for experienced cruisers, though each of our liners maintains a strong following who sail her regularly.

Our diverse audience is defined far more by their outlook than by their demographics—an appreciation for (or aspiration to) a more traditional, more intellectual and highly social environment. We think of our target as civilized adventurers—refined individuals who seek meaningful, emotional experiences through elegant travel. The typical Cunarder exhibits conservative tastes and traditional style—fashionable, perhaps, but rarely trendy. They tend to be courtly and outgoing, eager to join in onboard activities and events, and excited at the prospect of meeting new people. As Cunard is a badge brand, our guests are more likely than some to be status-aware and status-conscious—looking at their Cunard voyage as an opportunity to earn new bragging rights at home or as confirmation of their position or achievements.

From its inception, Cunard has sailed distinctive, adventurous voyages. The line launched with the first scheduled service across the Atlantic, first carrying mail, and then ferrying nineteenth- and twentieth-century emigrants to America while providing the ultimate excursion for well-heeled adventurers. Most of Cunard's many great liners have plied this classic route, the epitome of the Cunard experience. *Queen Mary 2* maintains this tradition today, with twenty-plus transatlantic crossings each year between New York and Southampton, England, the line's home port. Similarly, Cunard led the way in offering an annual world cruise, sailing the first round-the-world passenger voyage over eighty years ago. We continue this annual occasion today, setting the industry standard for these exotic journeys. Maintaining these unique deployments reinforces Cunard's special place in maritime history.

Our liners themselves have also made history—the largest, fastest, grandest ships of their times. Today's Cunard fleet continues the tradition of majestic and celebrated ships, unique and unmatched on the seas, combining the hypnotic allure of the past *and* the finest today has to offer.

Each of Cunard's Queens—*Queen Elizabeth 2*, *Queen Mary 2*, and the soon-to-launch *Queen Victoria*—is built with liner strengths and imbued with liner style. Their modern technologies and hull designs enable swift, safe sailing through open seas—the classic liner voyages. Each ship's public rooms carry the brand's hallmark style, with soaring spaces and elegant details creating magnificent one-of-a-kind venues, where everything feels more special. Their size allows them to offer a range and caliber of onboard amenities that cannot be found on smaller luxury ships, yet still of the quality that sophisticated travelers expect and demand—from spacious spas to top-notch shopping.

Accommodation is equally distinctive and tasteful. Here our liners offer a distinct product advantage—perhaps the widest breadth of accommodation categories available, from the deluxe comfort of our standard inside staterooms to the exclusive opulence of perhaps the most luxurious suites of any ship sailing today. This allows Cunard to offer a range of luxury service levels to prospective guests—a unique combination of accessibility and aspiration. Our Grills product provides the higher-end guest with exclusive dining and lounges, more personalized butler services, and a range of added amenities—the only ultra-luxury product that offers access to all the entertainment, enrichment, and excitement of a top-quality larger ship.

While the three Cunard ships share many common elements, from classic venues and Royal Nights events, to—most important—the line's White Star Service[SM], each has its distinct charms as well. *Queen Elizabeth 2,* the longest-sailing Cunarder of all time, with over thirty-five years captivating the world—serves as the standardbearer for British elegance and decorum, offering the most classic and formal experience on the seas. *Queen Mary 2* updates this tradition as the most modern exponent of the large liner experience—a grandeur of space and décor beyond any ship built to date, an instant classic and worldwide celebrity, carrying a host of updated features. When *Queen Victoria* launches in 2007 (the first time in history that three Cunard Queens have sailed together), she will offer a third alternative to Cunard guests, combining traditional British elegance, a robust onboard experience, and a host of her own seagoing innovations—like every great Cunard liner. With her classic style and service traditions, offered in the breathtaking glamour of a true Cunarder, *Queen Victoria* will surely add her own distinct chapter to the line's great legacy in years to come.

Crystal Cruises

Gregg Michel, president of Crystal Cruises, on defining his brand:

An uncompromising commitment to service, space, quality, and choices has defined more than a decade of award-winning excellence for Crystal Cruises. Our company was founded in 1988 with a clear vision of combining the hallmarks of small-ship luxury cruising—personalized service and exceptional quality—with the special benefits of a large ship offering more venues for dining, entertainment, health and fitness, and enrichment. Today, Crystal sets the bar on luxury cruising, enjoying a reputation of consistent and unprecedented acclaim.

For the past ten consecutive years, Crystal has been voted "World's Best Large-Ship Cruise Line" by the readers of *Condé Nast Traveler* and *Travel + Leisure* magazines—the only cruise line, resort or hotel to have achieved such distinction. And in the February 2006 issue of *Condé Nast Traveler, Crystal Serenity* and *Crystal Symphony* were awarded with the coveted number-one and number-two spots in the magazine's sixth annual "Best Cruise Ships in the World" readers' poll.

The Crystal Difference starts with our most important mission: "To be the best in the luxury service business, not just the luxury cruise industry." Every aspect of the cruise experience—service, accommodations, dining, entertainment, enrichment, spa and fitness, and shoreside discovery—is attended to with this commitment and delivered with passion and a creative flair.

Service begins with one of the highest staff-to-passenger ratios in the industry. Our European-trained staff hails from more than forty nations and is selected based on a winning and friendly personality as well as expertise in providing Six-Star service. Through an intensive training program, our employees embrace the Six-Star Crystal Basics, a multipoint credo that addresses attitude, communication, competence, style, safety/environment, security, and execution. Our high service standards are maintained through a significant investment in staff recruiting and training, and a genuine commitment to staff's well-being. At just 9 percent, the line boasts the industry's lowest turnover rate and one that is virtually un-heard of in most luxury hotels and resorts.

By industry standards, Crystal ships are very spacious. Carrying 940 guests and 545 staff members, *Crystal Symphony* is less than half the size of mass-market mega-ships. Yet, at 50,000 tons, she is large by luxury ship stan-dards, with considerable space dedicated to innovative spa and learning facilities, stimulating entertainment options, creative dining options, spacious decks, generous amenities, and sumptuous staterooms. These are features valued by luxury-loving cruisers, especially those who find yacht-like ships too cozy or limited in activity options. With the launch of our 68,000-ton *Crystal Serenity* in July 2003, we raised the bar with 655 crew members for 1,080 guests and 63 tons of space per guest, one of the highest space ratios of any luxury ship.

For discriminating travelers, choosing among the wide se-lection of staterooms and suites is the first step in creating the ultimate travel experience. More than half of our staterooms and suites (85 percent on *Crystal Serenity*) open onto private roomy verandas—a must among all segments of the cruise industry.

Luxury, as they say, is in the details. From design to ameni-ties, every Crystal guestroom is a sanctuary of luxurious ap-pointments. Beds are dressed with plush duvets, feather toppers, and 100 percent Egyptian cotton sheets, comple-mented with mohair lap blankets and a pillow menu. From the Frette bathrobes to the multiple hair dryers to the spe-cialty bath products, every detail is attended to with care for the ultimate in guest comfort. These are just a few of the luxuries that are standard with every stateroom. The luxury experience is further elevated in Crystal's Penthouse state-rooms and suites, with personal butler service and other amenities.

Extraordinary space has been allocated not only to the staterooms and suite accommodations but also to the public spaces. Throughout, similar to the smaller luxury vessels, Crystal boasts very high ratios of space to guest. Yes, unlike the limitations of smaller luxury vessels, the unique size of Crystal's ships allows us to offer a wide range of entertainment options. We built our larger luxury ships with a commitment to the space for a variety of entertainment—from grand lounges to intimate cabaret rooms and piano bars to learning centers. A lavish casino, a late-night disco, and a purpose-built movie theater provide additional options for our guests. The cornerstone of our entertainment philosophy is our commitment to offering a diverse and high-quality variety of programming that appeals to a range of guest preferences. Our award-winning reputation and onboard product is also well known, so we can attract a mix of world-class stars and up-and-coming talent.

Long in tune with the varied interests of our sophisticated clientele, Crystal has launched revolutionary enrichment programs. For example, our Creative Learning Institute (CLI), featuring an alliance between Crystal and carefully selected quality enrichment partners, brings experts aboard to share their knowledge through a series of interactive classes on arts and entertainment, wellness, business and technology, lifestyle, and wine and food. Among these stimulating opportunities are keyboard lessons by Yamaha, language immersion with Berlitz, and wellness seminars from the Cleveland Clinic and the Tai Chi Cultural Center. For guests who want to stay connected or learn new computer skills, our innovative Computer University@Sea® offers twenty-four-hour e-mail and Internet access and complimentary classes in Windows and e-mail, Photoshop, digital video editing, and web page design. This program is the most extensive in the luxury cruise industry.

The Crystal Visions® Enrichment Program taps the intellectual curiosity of guests with popular speakers including celebrated authors, guest chefs and renowned wine connoisseurs, ambassadors and diplomats, historians, television journalists, celebrities, and noted business and financial leaders, including experts from the Smithsonian Associates and Sotheby's.

For more active onboard pursuits, guests can swim laps in one of two swimming pools, play paddle tennis (two courts on *Crystal Serenity*), jog or power walk on the wide 360-degree promenade deck, work out in a well-equipped fitness center, enjoy instruction from Professional Golf Association pros with Taylormade equipment, or pamper themselves in the lavish Crystal Spa and Salon—the only spa at sea designed in accordance with the principles of feng shui. As always, our emphasis is on choice, quality, space, and service.

Certainly, the dining experience of any luxury vacation must showcase creativity and quality. At Crystal, we add ambience, choices, and gracious, anticipatory service, all of which contribute to our extraordinary success in this area. Gourmet cuisine is served in as many as seven evening venues, including the spacious Crystal Dining Room, casual eateries, and intimate specialty restaurants with menus designed by celebrity restaurateurs such as Piero Selvaggio and Wolfgang Puck in connection with his Chinois on Main venue. Two of our most lauded dining venues, the Sushi Bar and Silk Road, boast the exquisite cuisine of world-famous Nobu Matsuhisa. With the most extensive wine cellars at sea (some 20,000 bottles), we offer guests a comprehensive choice of wines, plus a new reserve list of twenty rare vintages. Our intimate vintage rooms aboard each ship play host to the ultimate gourmet experiences with celebrated winemakers' dinners.

At Crystal, we do not believe that luxury travel and family travel need be mutually exclusive. We welcome children with dedicated facilities that are unusual on luxury ships. On select cruises, and when we have larger numbers of children, junior activities directors create imaginative activities and age-appropriate programming for children ages three to seventeen.

The same care extends to our compelling, carefully crafted shoreside Crystal Adventures. While our ships traverse the world on rich itineraries, it is how we deliver the destination that is key to the Crystal experience. Today, Crystal offers innovative options varying from the adventurous, such as flying in a MiG fighter jet over Moscow, driving a Formula 1 race car in Monte Carlo, or diving the waters of Rhodes's recently opened Kalithea Bay, to exclusive cultural opportunities at the legendary Hermitage and the Vatican. Through Crystal Private Adventures, guests can enjoy the assistance of a dedicated land programs team to plan the most personalized excursions ashore.

Whether our guests are enjoying a seven-day Crystal getaway or our unparalleled hundred-plus-day world cruise, they will find a consistently delivered experience of impeccable service, extraordinary space, superb quality, and abundant choices. It is this consistency—performing precisely as promised—that builds trust and loyalty. These are the elements, along with meaningful innovations, that define the Crystal difference.

At Crystal Cruises, our ships travel the world in search of the new, the treasured, and the exciting. Extensive itineraries in the Mediterranean, the Baltic, Western Europe, North America, Panama Canal, Mexican Riviera, Caribbean, South America, Asia, and Africa range from seven days to over one hundred, offering our guests a world of opportunity to experience the service, space, quality, and choices that define the Crystal difference.

Regent Seven Seas Cruises

Mark Conroy, president of Regent Seven Seas, positions his product in the luxury segment:

Regent Seven Seas Cruises [formerly Radisson Seven Seas Cruises] is a wholly owned subsidiary of Carlson Companies, one of the largest privately held hospitality companies in the world, with annual gross revenues of over $30 billion and comprising five hotel brands (Regent, Radisson, Park Inn, Park Plaza, and Country Inns and Suites), two restaurant brands (TGI Friday's, Pick Up Stix), travel consortia in both corporate and leisure segments (Carlson Wagonlit Travel, Carlson Leisure Group), Carlson Marketing Group, and others.

The cruise line was launched in 1992 with one ship, the 350-passenger *Radisson Diamond.* Then, in 1995, the line merged with Seven Seas Cruise Line (another one-ship operation with the 200-passenger *Song of Flower*) to form Radisson Seven Seas Cruises. In 2006, Carlson Companies decided to merge their two luxury brands, Regent International Hotels and Radisson Seven Seas Cruises, to form one brand under the Regent banner.

On the hotel side, there are currently eight Regent hotels in operation and another nine properties under construction or in development. The hotels are located in Asia, Europe, and the United States. New properties are set to open in each of these areas of the world.

The line now consists of four luxury cruise ships—the *Seven Seas Voyager,* the *Seven Seas Mariner,* the *Seven Seas Navigator,* and the *Paul Gauguin.* RSSC carries around 100,000 passengers per year and offers a worldwide deployment, visiting over 300 ports on all seven continents, including Antarctica (for which the line offers a series of chartered sailings of the upscale exploration ship *Explorer II*).

RSSC guests are typically cruise-experienced (85 percent having previously cruised), sophisticated affluent travelers who are seeking a high-quality vacation that does not compromise their lifestyle. They are looking for a vacation experience that is exclusive, provides unique access to interesting destinations, and where they can enjoy attentive personal service in the company of like-minded guests. They prefer to be one of few versus one of many. They are typically forty-five-plus years old, with a household income of over $200,000 or a high net worth. They are often very active in their communities and philanthropy, and enjoy the performing arts. They are initially attracted to RSSC through the recommendations of friends or their travel agent and because of the line's reputation for personalized, friendly, and professional service, world-class suite accommodations, superb cuisine, and interesting itineraries. The repeat factor on RSSC ships is currently around 45 percent and growing.

RSSC enjoys a strong relationship with its travel agent partners, who recognize the high income potential of selling the inclusive product, who appreciate the partnership opportunities offered by the line, and who love the fact that their clients return happy from their cruise, having received great service before, during, and after their vacation.

Regent Seven Seas Cruises is firmly established among the luxury lines and has been able to differentiate itself through features such as the Regent Travel Concierge, which allows guests to fully customize their vacation arrangements ahead of time with unique shoreside access. The line has also created special Circles of Interest cruises, which allow guests to enjoy unique and memorable experiences by exploring the destinations they visit through their own personal lens, based on their special interests or passions such as food and wine, photography, architecture, performing arts, wellness, and others. In addition to these innovative concepts, RSSC has also undertaken a multimillion-dollar investment to upgrade the soft furnishings in guest accommodations and public areas, upgrade bedding and suite amenities, and improve communications technology.

Last, but surely not least, the entire staff of the Regent Seven Seas fleet, from the captain to the night cleaner, live by the Tao of Regent, which is:

> To serve others is to serve oneself.
> To hear without being told.
> To see without being shown.
> To know without being asked.

Silversea Cruises

Albert Peter, chief executive officer of Silversea Cruises, positions his product:

> Silversea is the first travel company, and the only cruise line, to have twice topped *Condé Nast Traveler*'s list of one hun-

dred best travel destinations, placing us above not only all other cruise lines but also the world's finest land-based resorts and hotels. This achievement is exceptional, but not surprising, when you understand that Silversea has always considered our competition to be leading luxury hotels like the Four Seasons, Ritz-Carlton, Mandarin Oriental, and Villa d'Este, to name a few.

We started making waves in the cruise industry with the launch of our first ship, *Silver Cloud,* in 1994. At 16,800 tons and accommodating only 296 guests, *Silver Cloud* was the first cruise ship to offer yacht-like intimacy blended with spacious, all-suite, all ocean-view accommodations, a majority of which featured a private teak veranda. *Silver Cloud* offered a guest space ratio (the gross tonnage of the ship divided by the guest capacity) of nearly 57. This compared with 48 for the Seabourn ships and 37 for the Sea Goddesses. In fact, only the German *Europa* had a higher ratio, but it did not have a single private veranda. And *Silver Cloud* also had plenty of space to incorporate the favorite amenities found on larger ships, such as an elaborate show lounge featuring nightly entertainment, a casino, a spa, and state-of-the-art fitness facility. Though spacious from the guest's perspective, *Silver Cloud* was small enough to slip into ports and inland waterways that were inaccessible to the larger, mass-market ships—opening up a world of unique and exotic travel experiences.

But in developing our luxury brand image, one that would go head-to-head in competition with the world's leading resorts, we knew Silversea had to go beyond offering revolutionary ship design. From the outset, our focus was on providing a highly personalized level of service. This was accomplished by staffing *Silver Cloud* with 210 crew members, providing a crew-to-guest ratio that was virtually one to one. This also meant recruiting and retaining staff of the highest caliber who demonstrated a sincere commitment to excellence and who would ultimately play a significant role in helping Silversea to develop a sterling reputation with our guests and to continually win awards from influential travel publications around the world, including *Travel + Leisure* and the *Robb Report.*

Over the years, our fleet has grown to four ships, each offering an award-winning, ultra-luxury experience. But what exactly is "ultra-luxury"? For one thing, it is not a static concept, but one that is continually developing to reflect innovations in product and service.

In the early days, the hallmarks of ultra-luxury cruising included offering a single, flexible, open-seating dining option, plus an all-inclusive shipboard environment where guests never had to sign tabs for drinks, as all beverages, wines, and spirits were complimentary, and they never had to worry about gratuities, as none were expected.

These initial product innovations were based on a realization that sophisticated, affluent travelers consider freedom and convenience among the most important components in the luxury travel equation. However, there is an aspect of luxury that has become even more precious to the affluent consumer, and this is the ability to control the time they spend on a cruise vacation. We recognized this need as an opportunity to further tap into the affluent client base of resorts, and in 2003 we rolled out Personalized Voyages®.

This groundbreaking program, unique in the cruise industry, enables guests to check in and out from their cruise with the same ease and flexibility they would find at a hotel. Instead of being locked into a fixed number of days aboard ship, our guests are able to customize their voyage by selecting their port of embarkation and disembarkation. For the harried business executive who can rarely find time for an extended vacation, a rejuvenating Personalized Voyage of just five days to the Italian or French Riviera can be the perfect complement to a routine business trip in Europe. Or, for the newlywed couple seeking a luxurious honeymoon experience that fits their tight professional schedules, a Personalized Voyage offers the flexibility to design a romantic adventure completely tailored to their particular interests and needs.

Silversea ships have been sailing the globe for over a decade, and while our company's history reflects many exceptional achievements, giving us a strong sense of pride, we have no desire to just rest on our laurels. As we have matured as a company, the overall cruise industry itself has further evolved. What were once considered luxury amenities, like private verandas and open-seating dining, increasingly have been adopted by more mainstream cruise operators.

In 2005, we took a decisive step to further differentiate Silversea from our competition by launching a new print advertising campaign prominently featuring actress Isabella Rossellini as our new ambassador. We selected Isabella, internationally renowned for her timeless beauty, elegance, and sophistication, to spearhead a global communications initiative designed to create greater awareness of our company's appeal for the international traveler and to express our unique concept of luxury, one that is closely linked with our Italian heritage.

As a result, we are seeing a significant shift in our demographics toward a younger clientele. Plus, we are now attracting a broader international spectrum of guests from previously untapped luxury markets in places like Asia, Russia, India, and Mexico. These developments indicate that we are attracting a growing segment of guests who identify with the face of our marketing campaign—and those ineffable qualities of elegance and luxury that Isabella represents for Silversea.

In tandem with our rebranding efforts, we have forged new marketing partnerships, or leveraged existing alliances, to further enhance the uniqueness of our luxury product. For example, through our exclusive partnership with FAI—Fondo per l'Ambiente Italiano (the National Trust for Italy), Silversea guests can now extend their voyage with optional land extensions to Milan, Lombardy, and Lake Como. These new land programs give our well-heeled guests a rare opportunity to explore some of Italy's most revered artistic and architectural treasures that are now under the care and protection of FAI, plus enjoy accommodations at some of Northern Italy's poshest resorts.

And our successful collaboration with Relais and Châteaux, undertaken in 2002 to develop an exclusive collection of signature dishes for Silversea, along with a program of culinary enrichment cruises featuring celebrity chefs, is taking a new direction. Our alternative restaurants, Saletta (aboard *Silver Cloud* and *Silver Wind*) and Le Champagne (aboard *Silver Shadow* and *Silver Whisper*), are now the setting for the first-ever Relais and Châteaux wine-themed restaurant at sea, featuring a new collection of dishes designed specifically to celebrate and showcase some of the world's finest vintages.

We continue to break ground with innovative itineraries and specially tailored shore adventures that are the perfect complement to our all-inclusive shipboard experience. Our in-house destination experts have designed more than 2,500 optional shore excursions in cities spanning the globe from Auckland to Zanzibar. In a typical year, Silversea ships call in more than 300 ports in 100 countries, offering nearly 150 itineraries that combine fresh and intriguing worldwide experiences—such as the option to take a flightseeing tour over Moscow in a MiG fighter jet—with destinations that are traditional favorites.

In short, Silversea is continuing to refine its luxury brand image while charting a course of innovation tailored to our discerning guests' desire for unique travel experiences and in-depth cultural enrichment.

So there you have it. Fourteen major cruise brands explain their unique positions in the cruise market—and in the vacation market, in some instances. Personally, we think the latter approach makes the most sense, as the success of the various cruise lines is highly dependent on their ability to draw from the larger overall vacation market. In any event, each line takes great care to cater to its target customers. The lines do an outstanding job of this. Why else would guest satisfaction be so superior for cruising?

NOW HEAR THIS

7

*Marketing
communications—
A view from the bridge*

Imagine, if you will, that we have just started a new cruise line. For the purposes of this discussion, let's call our new line Hospitality Cruises. Our new line will have a fleet of five large ships in the 85,000-ton class and thus compete for passengers with the major cruise lines for business. Our job as the vice president of sales and marketing for Hospitality Cruises is to formulate a marketing communications strategy. In this chapter, we take a closer look at the elements that might go into coming up with such a plan—the situation we are facing as we enter this new business, our communications channels, our target market, our positioning, our competition, their creative strategy and advertising messages. By doing this exercise, we have an opportunity to focus on what the major players are (or should be) doing, why they are doing it, and assessing as best we can their effectiveness—thereby gaining an understanding of promotional strategy within the cruise line industry.

The Situation

The place to begin, as with many such plans, is the situation as it exists in the marketplace today. Even though we have not yet designed our own product, we do know quite a bit about the cruise market using data obtained from research done by the Cruise Line Industry Association (CLIA) and other sources. We also have published speeches as well as off-the-record comments made by the CEOs and marketing and sales officials of the major lines and their advertising agencies in which they describe their own assessments of the situation they face, their positioning, and their advertising strategies. Much of this was delineated in the previous chapter.

Market Size/Potential

Since 1970, the industry has had a compound annual growth rate of 8 percent. The prospect for continued market expansion is favorable. In the past thirty-five years, an estimated 58 million passengers have taken at least one deep-water cruise of more than two days. Nearly 30 percent of the total passengers carried have been generated in the last five years alone. Of those who have cruised in the past five years, the average number of cruises per person has been 2.4 in the same time frame, or slightly more than one every two years.

According to the 2006 CLIA Cruise Marketing Profile Study, 97 percent of the cruise market meet the criteria of being twenty-five years of age or older and live in households with annual earnings of $40,000 or more. This group represents 44 percent of the U.S. population, yielding 127.2 million prime cruise candidates. Thirty-nine percent of the target market have cruised before—49,608,000 folks. By the end of 2005, 51 million people had cruised before. The target represents 85 percent of the total North American cruise population. The other 15 percent is folks either under twenty-five or from households with an annual income less than $40,000. Reflecting the dramatic growth of the industry, 55 percent of these who have cruised before have done so in the past three years.

The study goes on to point out that based on a nationally projectable survey of 2,000-plus core households, the most likely market projection for cruising within the next three years is 31.0 million folks of the core market, or 36.4 million total passengers. This certainly triangulates well with planned capacity increase in the 2006–2008 period. In this same projection, 46 percent of the intended cruisers have never cruised before. If previous history is taken into account, however, experienced cruisers will cruise more frequently than they have indicated in the study thus pushing out two to five million non-cruise cruise intenders as capacity is always fully utilized. Due to capacity limitations, this will give a result of 35 to 40 percent first-timers in the 2006–2008 period. The industry would be thrilled to have 49 percent first-timers, but it hasn't seen that high a level in nearly twenty years. This miss of two to five million non-cruisers who intend to cruise in the next three years and don't is enormously costly to the industry, even if we safely assume it will sail virtually full during the period. As emphasized before, a lost first-timer fundamentally impedes industry growth and creates both lower cruise revenues and higher acquisition costs.

As shown in Exhibit 7.1, cruisers tend to be older, with higher household incomes and higher levels of education attainment. Both groups are predominately married and have a similar racial composition.

Customer satisfaction with various vacations is shown in Exhibit 7.2.

EXHIBIT 7.1 **Demographics Summary**

	Cruisers	Non-Cruise Vacationers
Median Age	49	42
Median Household Income (000)	$84	$73
Full-Time Jobs	57%	56%
Retired	16%	11%
College Grad	57%	50%
Post-Grad	23%	20%
White	91%	88%
Black	4%	5%
Other	5%	7%

Source: 2006 CLIA Cruise Market Profile Study

There's a large satisfaction gap between cruising and land-based vacation. The only vacation that comes close is the all-inclusive resort. However, cruisers who have done both vacations rate cruising 13 percent higher than all-inclusive resorts.

EXHIBIT 7.2 **Level of Satisfaction with Types of Vacations**

	% Extremely Satisfied	
	Non-Cruise Vacationers	Cruisers
Cruise Vacation/Ocean Sea Voyage	—	45%
Vacation at All-Inclusive Resort	44%	40
Visit to Friends/Relatives	40	41
Resort Vacation (own arrangements)	40	36
Vacation House Rental	36	33
Resort Vacation (package)	34	32
Trip (non-package)	34	32
Camping Trip	32	27
Land-Based Escorted Tour	31	30
Land-Based Package	29	30
Vacation: Part of Business Trip	29	27

Note: Data are based on a 5-point scale where 5 is "extremely satisfied" and 1 is "not at all satisfied."

The research goes on to point out the amount vacationers spent on their last trip or cruise.(Exhibit 7.3)

EXHIBIT 7.3 **Average Amount Spent per Person per Week— Total Vacation**

Category	Average per Segment
Cruisers	$1,690
Destination	$2,020
Luxury	$2,320
Premium	$1,900
Contemporary	$1,690
Non-cruise vacation	$1,180
Rep Sample 2006	$1,410
Rep Sample 2004	$1,303
Rep Sample 2002	$869

The average cruiser spent $1,690 per week, or about 43 percent more than the average of non-cruise vacations ($1,180/week). Within the contemporary segment, however, the gap varies: Carnival has the narrowest premium, if any, versus non-cruise vacations because of its strategic decisions to limit the number of Alaska and European itineraries, offer the most short-cruise itineraries, and offer the most U.S. departure cities. Nonetheless, the table clearly substantiates that cruising is positioned in the middle to upper section of the vacation pyramid. Note the volatility in vacation pricing as shown by the dramatic rise in the representative samples in the post-9/11 era (2002 versus 2004 versus 2006).

Exhibit 7.4 describes the travel companions across the cruiser and non-cruiser vacation segments. The two biggest variances between the two groups are the children and friends categories. Land vacationers travel with children under eighteen 39 percent of the time, while cruisers only do this 30 percent of the time. While this percentage has improved dramatically over the years, family travel still represents a growth opportunity.

Traveling with friends, on the other hand, is a big plus for cruising. Cruisers are 38 percent more likely to travel with friends than land-based vacationers (25 versus 18 percent). This speaks to the superior collegiality and bonding that cruising affords—a hassle-free environment, where women are not tasked to work on their vacation and alpha males can't easily dominate.

The primary growth opportunity, at the moment, is among younger prospects ages twenty-five to thirty-nine, families with children, and sin-

EXHIBIT 7.4   **Description of Vacation Traveler Companions**

Category	Non-Cruiser Vacationers	Cruiser
Spouse	77	81
Children under 18	39	30
Other Family Members	22	23
Friends	18	25
Adult Children 18 or Older	13	14
No One Else	3	1
Partner/Companion	10	10
Members of Organizations/Group	3	4

BASE: Cruises/Vacationers

gles. However, with the graying of America, the size of the market for older cruisers should increase rapidly. In 1990, only 17 percent of Americans were over sixty years of age. By 2025, that figure will stand at 27 percent. Older individuals typically have more disposable income, and those that are empty nesters or retired have more time for travel.

 The Target Market

The demographics of the cruise passenger are extremely broad, with potential cruisers coming from all ages and walks of life with the economic wherewithal and inclination to spend at least $100 per day per person. The longer and more expensive the cruise, the older and wealthier the passenger.

On the whole, however, differences in age, sex, and income are not as great as one might expect among those who have expressed an interest in cruising. For example, 57 percent of men are interested in cruising, while the figure for women is 63 percent. When viewed by household income, cruise prospects comprise 56 percent of households that earn between $20,000 and $39,000, 62 percent of those between $40,000 and $59,000, and 66 percent of those that earn more than $60,000. Cruise prospects comprise 60 percent of singles and 59 percent of married folks. Various sources indicate that, at most, only 18 percent of the population has taken a cruise. Therefore, most of the growth in passengers will have to come from first-time cruisers. According to CLIA, 40 percent of cruisers are first-timers and 60 percent are repeat customers. As a new entrant into the marketplace, we must decide whether to depend heavily on first-time cruisers or, if we do a good job of positioning ourselves, focus on repeat cruisers from other lines. Based on reasonable capacity gains over the next ten years (4–6 percent annual increases), all the large lines must continue to attract a significant number of first-timers to their brands to survive and thrive. We can expect them also to try to retain their current customer base through relationship marketing efforts.

It should be noted that these prime prospects are regular vacationers—that is, they are not stay-at-homes but like to travel and take trips involving air flights. They are, for the most part, adventurous people who like to see new sights, have new experiences, and meet new people. Travel researchers have characterized them as more willing to take risks than those who prefer to stay at home. We know that among those who have expressed an interest in cruising, significant numbers take at least one vacation per year, periodically travel internationally, prefer to travel with friends, and have typically stayed at resorts.

We believe that, ultimately, land-based resorts are the enemy. That's where we need to look for our customer base—not just among existing cruise lines. There is evidence that the resort business sees it the same way. In a story in the *Miami Herald* about a $12 million renovation program of the pool area at the Bal Harbor Sheraton on Miami Beach, David Fine, their director of sales and marketing, was quoted as saying, "The Sheraton improvements are aimed at pulling leisure travelers away from cruise lines and other major resorts." The story continued, "The hotel plans to hire a cruise director to orchestrate outdoor entertainment, including games, jugglers, food, and music."

Now there's a new concept for you: a hotel with a cruise director! But then, why not? They tried to turn the great *Queen Mary* into a land-based resort. Unfortunately, no cruise line has been able to pull off converting a cruise ship to a land-based resort.

The late Gilbert Trigano, who founded Club Med, told us that his original concept was based on the idea of providing guests with "a land-based cruise." The Club's GOs ("gentil organisateur," in French, or "congenial host," in English) handle all of the tasks at a typical Club Med except housekeeping and maintenance, mingle freely with the guests (GMs, or "gentil members"), and, in fact, perform many of the same duties the cruise staff on a modern ship handles.

It should be noted here that not all non-cruisers represent an equal potential. First, there are the requisite economic and leisure time requirements. But even within the appropriate profile, there is a spectrum of propensity to take a cruise. At one end is the non-cruiser who will never cruise. Just because people say they would like to take a cruise doesn't mean they ever will. Both of us would like to climb Mount Everest. We'd also like to own a vineyard in France and a château to go with it. But we probably won't.

At the other end of the spectrum is the non-cruiser poring over brochures, deciding which cruise to take next month. That person you can count on being afloat on someone's line somewhere in the very near future.

In between is that large group of people who would enjoy a cruise and can afford one but have one or more barriers to entry that we have heard discussed at length in earlier chapters by industry executives. The four of these most often cited are price, boredom, confinement, and seasickness. From a realistic point of view, there is some degree of reality in all of these, among even some of our best prospects. For example, maybe they can afford a cruise now, but if they are working for a company that is in the midst of downsizing or reengineering, they might believe they're better off putting their vacation dollars in the bank until the storm blows over—if it does! Confinement? We don't feel confined in a ship that's fourteen stories high and longer than three football fields in length, but we won't deny that some people would perceive they might. Boredom? If you're a couch potato and your idea of high-quality fun is watching every football, baseball, and basketball game broadcast, you're going to be bored on just about any cruise ship sailing the seas right now. The beer and pretzels you can get, but many of the games you can't. Finally, a few folks really do get seasick even when the ship is docked at the pier—and we won't be able to change their minds no matter what we tell them!

So, as we contemplate a marketing and communications program for our new cruise line in the current, increasingly competitive environment, it is toward the latter end of the spectrum that the near-term battle must be waged for the potential vacationer who already has a strong propensity to try cruising, not for the one who must be convinced of the merits of a cruise vacation. The others may cruise in the future as their friends come back and tell them what great vacations they had.

More About Cruise Appeals and Impediments

Studies have consistently shown that taking a cruise is appealing to most people. Indeed, among those who have done both, it is considered superior to a land-based resort. For example, in a CLIA study among persons who had taken both a cruise and a resort vacation in the previous five years, 32 percent reported that they were more pampered by the staff, and the same percentage said their cruise vacation was better organized. Twenty-nine percent said they were more satisfied with the dining experience on the cruise, while 13 percent found their cruise vacation more hassle-free and 11 percent reported that it was more relaxing. Fifteen percent said it was a better value for the money. About the only negative was accommodations. A cruise cabin is, by necessity and design, smaller than an average resort room, and 15 percent of vacationers who had taken both a cruise and a resort vacation found the resort accommodations superior. However, it is not really fair to compare a ship at sea with a building on land; if customers understand that their cabin will not look like the ones in movie sets and on television, which are in fact Hollywood sound stages, there is ample evidence that they will not be disappointed.

After vacationers take their first cruise, they report a high level of satisfaction. As we've pointed out, the industrywide figure is beyond 90 percent. In truth, virtually all vacation types create a high level of satisfaction—in other words, most people report being satisfied with their vacation, whether they take a cruise, stay in a resort, rent a condo for skiing or a cottage by the sea, take a package tour, or simply visit friends and relatives. That's one reason why vacations are so appealing. But when CLIA asked these same vacationers to state which kind of vacation they were "extremely satisfied" with, 41 percent said a cruise— which was the highest score received by any of the types of vacation mentioned. Package tours and visiting friends and relatives both received 29 percent "extremely satisfied" ratings, while resorts received 24 percent. Eighty-five percent of those who have taken a cruise in the last three years expressed an interest in taking another one, and the mean time frame was within one to three years! It is worth noting that since the first-time cruiser has only been on one ship, he or she defines the experience as highly satisfactory irrespective of whether the trip was a three-day *Fantasy* weekend cruise or a three-week *Crystal Symphony* South America cruise. Price, amenities, and even ports of call have little to do with satisfaction levels. This is an important point to consider when we think about positioning our new company.

Among those who have never taken a cruise but would like to, expectations are high. These are often the result of what they have heard from previous cruisers and from travel agents, as well as what they have seen and read in editorial material and advertising messages. Focus groups held among prospective cruise passengers indicate that people who are interested in taking a cruise like the idea of abundant food, visiting exotic locations, pampering service, nightly entertainment, getting closer to nature while at sea, and having time and space to themselves.

Now, when we look at people who have never taken a cruise and ask their reasons for not cruising, we see an entirely different picture. A study by CLIA showed that price and a concern about the economy are major barriers to trial. Among those with some interest, the disinclination to mix cruises and children and seasickness were secondary reasons. Other concerns were "Won't be able to change plans once on ship," "If ill or injured, might not get the best medical attention," "If I took my children, there would be no chance to do anything on my own," "Little or no sightseeing on a cruise," and "Couldn't be by myself because there are too many people." In fact, as we have seen, many of these are pure misconceptions. Passengers seldom get seasick on cruises; not only do modern ships have elaborate stabilizing systems but also they tend to cruise in protected waters. Moreover, cruise ships have access to elaborate satellite weather forecasting systems and can easily outrun any storm system. Even in the hurricane season, cruise ships continue to sail on schedule, for the most part, simply diverting to other ports when necessary and thus avoiding most, if not all, of the bad weather. As for not being able to change your plans once you get on a ship, when you board a plane going from New York to Los Angeles, or the Orient Express from London to Venice, or a Cosmos Grand Tour of Europe, you can't change your destination plans either. Good medical attention is available *within minutes* on a cruise ship twenty-four hours a day—try that in hotels, resorts, or any other form of vacation we know of. A few years ago, when Public Broadcasting did a documentary on a round-the-world trip aboard the *Queen Elizabeth 2,* the ship's doctor said many of the people aboard were either in fragile health or sick and were on the ship to recover or because they knew that if they needed help the vessel had, among other resources, a completely equipped operating room. As for things to do, take a look at the daily calendar of any cruise ship on a day at sea. On one daily calendar from an NCL cruise aboard the *Norwegian Jewel* in the Caribbean there were dozens of activities, including a wide range of dining options, onboard shopping, casino games, shows, dancing, movies shown on closed-circuit TV in the cabins, the bliss of enjoying the open sea, and an extensive range of shore tours.

Nevertheless, we have to recognize that not everyone sees things the way we do. Take the matters of the economy and price. If people are nervous about keeping their jobs or having enough to pay the rent, they do postpone vacations and delay buying big-ticket items. That's the way it is, and that's the way it has been during times of economic uncertainty. Moreover, a cruise is paid for up front—typically sixty days in advance. People are not used to charging or writing checks worth a few thousand dollars for their vacation in advance, even when it's a terrific value. Besides, the concept of value is subjective. There is no universal standard as to what constitutes value. Harold Kassarkian and Thomas Robertson, in their book on consumer behavior, point out that in one study consumers defined value in one of four ways:

1. Value is low price.
2. Value is whatever I want in a product.
3. Value is the quality I get for the price I pay.
4. Value is what I get for what I give.

Kassarkian and Robertson conclude:

These four consumer expressions of value can be captured in one overall definition: perceived value is the consumers' overall assessment of the utility of a product based on perceptions of what is received and what is given. Though what is received varies across consumers (i.e., some may want quantity, others high quality, still others convenience) and what is given varies (some are concerned only with money expended, others with time and effort), value represents a tradeoff of the salient give and get components. Handbook of Consumer Behavior. Robertson T. and Kassarkian H (Eds) New Jersey, Prentice Hall 1991.[1]

Whether or not a cruise is a good value does not depend on what we believe a good value is but rather on what the customers believe (always keep your eyes focused on the customer), and that depends on *their* idea of value. So we must make certain to explain why our cruise is a good value using *their* frame of reference. We think, and we believe people who have taken cruises also think, that you get a lot of high-quality services for a low price compared with what you would have to pay if you bought those same services (transportation, lodging, dining, sightseeing, and entertainment) à la carte instead of packaged together on a cruise vacation, and that's what makes it a good value.

Segmenting the Market

In 1995, CLIA released the results of a cruiser segmentation study, the purpose of which was to identify and profile distinct consumer segments within the cruise market. While CLIA has not updated this segmentation study since, the segments aren't likely to change much from a psychographic point of view. We have not adjusted the average age or income data of the various groups, as these segments tend to repopulate themselves as some move out due to death, infirmity, adverse financial circumstances, etc., while other folks move into them as they become older and more affluent. You could posit, however, with extended lifespans, that the average age may have drifted up a year or two in the intervening eleven years. Similarly, due to inflation, there's some upward drift to the household income data. Bureau of Labor Statistics data show that the average U.S. net compensation gained 16.4 percent between 1995 and 2004. Because of the shifting segment populations noted above, the real number may be less. The important factor is that, directionally, all segments should maintain their relative positioning.

Segmentation studies are useful because if you can get a better fix on what kind of people already enjoy cruising (or any other product or service) and what percentage of the total market they represent, it is easier to decide which segments you should target for future marketing efforts.

---

[1]Thomas Robertson and Harold Kassarkian, eds., *Handbook of Consumer Behavior* (N.J., Prentice Hall, 1991).

You can also create different marketing messages for each segment stressing the appeals and benefits that are most important to them. If you also learn something about their media habits, then you not only know what to say but where to place your message where they are most likely to see it. The sixteen-page questionnaire, which was mailed to 2,800 recent cruisers and returned by 86 percent of them, sought to answer these questions about people who had already taken a cruise:

What are these segments like in terms of demography, lifestyle, and general attitudes?
What is their cruise behavior?
What are their perceptions and needs with respect to cruising?

The segmentation study identified six distinct segments of past cruisers. Members of each segment resemble each other (and are different from members of other segments) in many respects that have to do with how they approach cruising.

The two largest segments are the Restless Boomers (33 percent) and Enthusiastic Baby Boomers (20 percent). Both include those roughly between the ages of forty and sixty-five. This group comprises one-third of the population. Other segments are Consummate Shoppers (16 percent), Luxury Seekers (14 percent), Explorers (11 percent), and Ship Buffs (6 percent). Let's take a close look at each of these segments and see what we know about them.

Restless Baby Boomers are newest to cruising. They have enjoyed their cruise experience and would like to cruise again, but cost may be an impediment because they are price conscious, at least for now. The average age of this group is forty-four, more than half are college graduates, three-quarters are married, and their median household income is $58,990. They are also at a point where they are still inexperienced travelers are trying different vacation experiences. They vacation as a family and see themselves as average Americans, thrifty, family-oriented, and not particularly fashionable or cultured in their own opinion. They also like outdoor camping and attend pop/rock concerts. They do not read newspapers or magazines as much as other groups.
Enthusiastic Baby Boomers are somewhat older than their cousins (forty-nine years), not as well educated (only 38 percent are college graduates), and not quite as affluent (their household income is $55,000). They live intense, stressful lives and look to vacations for the escape and relaxation that they offer. While they shop for value, they are willing to spend to get what they want. They see themselves as fun-loving, willing to try new things, physically

active, and fashionable. Other leisure activities they enjoy are sporting events, video games, and attending clubs and discos. Like their restless cousins, they read newspapers and magazines less than other groups.

Consummate Shoppers are constantly looking for the best value (not necessarily the cheapest) in a vacation and in a cruise. They definitely enjoy cruising, as long as they can get a good deal. As you might expect, they are somewhat older (fifty-five years). Almost half are college graduates, 71 percent are married, and their average household income is $60,000. They see themselves as well traveled, average on most characteristics, and, of course, thrifty. They spend their leisure time reading for pleasure and attending the theater. They are heavy television viewers as well.

Luxury Seekers can afford and are willing to spend money for deluxe accommodations and pampering. They are somewhat younger than consummate shoppers (fifty-two years old), 61 percent are college graduates, 73 percent are married, and their average household income of $95,000 reflects their ability to pay for what they want. They are often last-minute planners, extravagant, and willing to pay for quality. They view themselves as very well traveled, ready to try new things, successful, physically active, and cultured. Their leisure activities include going to concerts, boating, sailing, skiing, and golf, as well as visiting museums and attending classical concerts and sporting events. They watch television and listen to the radio less than other groups do.

Explorers are next in line. They are well-educated, well-traveled individuals with an intellectual interest and curiosity about different destinations. They are an older group (average age sixty-four), educated (69 percent graduated from college), and are fairly well off, with an average household income of $81,000. They like to visit different vacation places; they are not looking for a rest, nor do they want pampering. Their leisure hours are spent somewhat in the same manner as the Luxury Seekers, except that they are not into physical activities to the same extent. They watch TV, read books, and read newspapers.

Ship Buffs are the last group. They are the most senior segment (sixty-eight years old), educated (60 percent college graduates), able to afford to travel ($78,000 household income), and 67% of them are married. They have cruised extensively, like it, and intend to continue cruising. They are not particularly physically active, family oriented, or fun loving, and they are reluctant to try new things. They spend their leisure time reading and attending the theater. They watch TV and read both magazines and newspapers.

From this information, we can formulate some reasonable ideas about the marketing messages that would appeal to each of these groups. For example, we would want our message to Ship Buffs to recall and reinforce the onboard experiences they enjoyed in the past. We would be wise to tell Explorers about new destinations. Consummate Shoppers will pay attention to special rates and promotions. Luxury Seekers must be reassured that their expectations for a pampered experience will be met, and Baby Boomers must be told about the fun and excitement of cruising as well as its affordability.

The Competition

When thinking about marketing communications programs, it is a fatal mistake to assume you are advertising in a vacuum. There are others out there as well, and whether their messages are in the best interests of the vacation industry or not, their messages do appear in newspapers, magazines, and direct mail, on television, and in other media. Consumers may see those messages and formulate judgments from them as to whether they prefer a cruise or land vacation or which cruise they prefer. Note that we used the word *may,* because if the advertising is not effective, there is ample evidence that no one will see it or no one will be influenced by it. Collectively the cruise industry spends more than $300 million a year on measured advertising.

Perhaps a logical place to start is with the comments we heard their executives make in the last chapter about how they positioned themselves. In any communications program, the messages flow from the positioning. In other words, what advertisers should be doing is communicating their positioning—who they are, what they are, how they are positioned in the spectrum of vacation products that are out there for people to chose from.

Remember, true positioning focuses on the customer's needs and wants, not the product. Positioning has nothing to do with the product; rather, it has everything to do with what people think about the product. As suggested in the previous chapter, this can be readily seen by looking at package goods, such as laundry detergents, whose makers spend many millions of dollars jockeying for position. There are as many as forty detergents on supermarket shelves today. Some are positioned to get rid of grease. Others kill germs. Some work better in cold water. Others make your clothes come out whiter than white or smell fresher than fresh. Are all these detergents really so different? Do consumers really care? The answer is no on both counts. Most shoppers recognize that all of these products are very much the same—soap is soap. They also know that just about all of them make their clothes smell fresh, get rid of grease, and work in cold water. It doesn't matter. The positions and brand names are useful ways of marketing and advertising, but the differences are seldom crucial to making the sale *except when everything else is equal. Note: Everything else is seldom equal.* Some brands have superior advertising. In the history of selling laundry detergents, campaigns like "Stronger than dirt" and "Ring around the collar" have catapulted their brands into first place overnight. Whether or not you're a smoker, consider the Marlboro Man campaign, which positioned Marlboro cigarettes as a brand for "real men." Was this achieved by putting male hormones in the tobacco or shaping the cigarettes to look like cowboy boots? Don't kid yourself; Marlboro cigarettes are just like everyone else's. The positioning is something that happens in people's minds, not in the product.

To discuss the marketing of cruising, it is both useful and necessary to examine the advertising the different cruise lines use to create a brand image in the minds of their prospects. What is the one thing advertisers want prospects to remember about their cruise line after they read an ad or see a television commercial? One thing is enough—if you expect readers or viewers to remember two things, it's a stretch at best.

Moreover, that one thing must have an implied promise in it—"Buy me, and I will do this for you." Why would anyone shell out hard-earned money for anything if he didn't believe he was going to get something in return, something that benefits him in some significant way? Consumers have been described by some behaviorists as "creatures moving around all day trying to fill their needs." Everything—that's everything we do—can be said to fill some need. That includes buying cruises and other vacation products. Branding is the key to all of this. A brand is a personality. Leo Burnett, a great advertising man, created the Jolly Green Giant for his client Green Giant frozen vegetables. The Jolly Green Giant turned what was really a commodity into a distinct personality. Today, a quacking duck on television gives AFLAC insurance a personality. In travel advertising, personality is particularly important. Southwest and Jet Blue are two airlines that have been able to give themselves a personality that appeals to consumers.

In 2002, Royal Caribbean Line launched a new advertising campaign that had almost instant success in the marketplace. Recognizing that many non-cruisers perceived a cruise vacation as being locked up in a big steel container all day while it rolled around the ocean, their TV commercials showed consumers on cruises taking helicopter rides, dog sledding, rock climbing, and more while the voiceover suggested that cruising was more than a vacation, it was an adventure. "Get out there" was the tag line. The one thing RCL wanted you to remember when you saw one of these commercials was that a cruise was an adventure.

The print advertising at first followed a similar path. They showed it, they said it, and they asked for the order—"Get out there." By 2006, the campaign had changed somewhat. Instead of showing hard adventure, the ads offered a more intellectual or sublime adventure—appreciating the Sistine Chapel, for instance. "Be inspired," promised the headline. "You'll never know what seeing all this beauty will make you want to do. Luckily, whatever it is, you can do it when you get back on the ship. Europe. See it both by land and sea on a cruise or a cruisetour vacation. Find our more at royalcaribbean.com. Get out there."

From all visible evidence, the campaign worked. Dan Hanrahan, who was at the time RCL's marketing director, was later promoted to president of Celebrity Cruise Lines. But the urge to "Get out there" remained. It was, by all accounts, a good campaign.

Although we all like to think so, that doesn't mean it necessarily sold a lot of cruises. It means a lot of people remembered the campaign. There's a difference. Travel agents like to claim they are influential in getting people to decide what cruise to take. Advertising executives chortle over how many bars of soap or cans of soup successful campaigns have sold. We all like to attach positive results to projects we participate in. But the truth is, solid research shows that most people pick vacations based on recommendations from friends and relatives. We all consider ads, travel articles, advice from travel agents, and brochures, but when it comes right down to it, if your dear Aunt Zelda just returned home from a Costa Cruise she thought was the best thing since pasta was invented, chances are you'll book a cabin on a Costa Cruise too—unless you hate pasta, Aunt Zelda, or both.

The problem is that it's hard to build ships that are terribly different from each other, and so the classic marketing claim that almost always works, if it's true, —"My product is better than the others"—is difficult to prove. Ships haven't changed their design that much since Columbus sailed his across the ocean. The size has changed, the amenities have changed (Columbus didn't have a spa), the food has changed, but a ship is a ship is a ship. So what do you say if you can't say you have something unique?

Well, one thing you can do is to copy your competitor's claim, but try to do it with more panache. "Trade your commute for a more exotic route. Escape completely," says a Princess ad. The illustration shows passengers on a ship approaching Hong Kong. "Princess offers the widest variety of cruises to Asia. Let Princess transport you to the world of mystery and intrigue that is the Far East." Princess isn't offering a vacation or an adventure experience in this ad. It is selling destinations: Hong Kong, Singapore, Bangkok. In another ad, again headlined "Escape completely," the photo shows a sumptuous breakfast set on a balcony with a background of glaciers. "Leave your routine for an Alaska experience that's anything but," says the subhead. "Only Princess offers the Glacier Bay Champagne Breakfast, where your balcony becomes your front-row seat for one of the most breathtaking shows in nature."

What kind of promise is this? Promising us champagne and breakfast while watching the glaciers? What happened to the *Love Boat*? We know that many consumers were willing to run to their nearest travel agent, checkbook in hand, when they were offered love. But a champagne breakfast? Besides, that's easy to copy. Any other line, or all of them, can offer the same thing—and probably would, if they thought it would sell a few more cabins. There is, of course, a valid promise in this campaign—"Escape completely." There's nothing wrong with it except that it is the same promise Royal Caribbean makes when it says "Get out there." And, unfortunately the pages of *Travel + Leisure* and *National Geographic Traveler* are full of ads for resorts all over the world promising escape. The reality is that escaping from the drudgery of the rat race is a promise all ships and resorts can promise. It's not unique to Princess.

Holland America Line has an interesting campaign. One ad features their culinary arts center, presented by *Food and Wine* magazine; another, their outstanding service; a third, their luxurious amenities. Across the bottom of every advertisement are the words "Spacious, Elegant Ships—Gracious, Unobtrusive Service—Worldwide Itineraries—Extensive Activities and Enrichment Programs—Sophisticated Five-Star Dining." Every ad is signed "Holland America Line—A Tradition of Excellence."

These guys are all about selling excellence. They not only say it in their signature but also document it in their photographs and their copy. "Paradise need not be confined to a particular latitude or longitude," reads one headline. The copy continues, "Plush cotton towels. massage showerheads, Sealy Firm-Top mattresses. Private verandahs. The largest staterooms of any major cruise line and more space per passenger throughout the ship."

To begin with, the Holland America ads are not advertising puffery. They promise elegance, and they deliver excellence. Holland America is a premium line; they promise premium service, and they deliver on that promise. But again, we need to ask the question—is this an important promise, important enough to sell cabins? The problem is that to most cruisers, especially first-timers, all cruises are elegant. Even the informal ones like Windstar, which operates sailing ships, are elegant. So Holland America is more elegant? So what? Does everyone want a Ritz-Carlton experience?

For the people who *do* want an elegant experience at an affordable price, Celebrity is another alternative. Celebrity is a direct competitor to Holland America. They're both very good premium lines. As we're writing this, Celebrity is in the midst of launching a new campaign, but for the past year or two their promise has been that you can get away from the ordinary drudgery of everyday life and be treated royally, like a real celebrity, on one of their cruises. A typical ad shows a passenger floating in clear turquoise water with this headline: "Somewhere between Monte Carlo and Mykonos, Mom becomes Madame."

The body copy is the same in all of their ads: "Ahhh, the Celebrity Treatment. How will it affect you? There's only one way to find out. Come and experience for yourself the feeling of being completely relaxed, pampered, and, dare we say, indulged."

This is a good ad. The art direction is stunning, and the promise is delivered in spades when you board one of their ships. A TV commercial makes the same point. A couple is being pampered and says they feel like royalty. But how in the world is a first-time cruiser going to be able to tell the difference between Princess, Holland America, and Celebrity?

They all seem to be offering the same thing.

Norwegian Cruise Line has two separate campaigns at the moment. One series promotes their freestyle cruising—indeed, those two words appear under their name in every ad. These ads, and in fact their whole concept behind them, have worked very well for this smallest of the big three lines, with only 9 percent of the market. Their ships feature multiple restaurants—French, Italian, Asian, American, spa, and more. There are no assigned tables, and you can eat in any or all of them anytime you want with whomever you want. This concept of being able to eat in a variety of restaurants has caught on in other lines, but NCL created it, and the words "freestyle cruising" have become distinctively associated with Norwegian.

At the same time, Norwegian has entered the Hawaiian market with an all-American ship, the first new cruise ship to fly the American flag in more than fifty years. With its gaily painted patriotic hull, unique itinerary (seven days sailing the Hawaiian Islands), and freestyle cruising, NCL succeeded in creating an all-new, distinctive product that people who want to cruise, or do cruise, know about.

Another distinctive cruise product that currently uses little mass media advertising is Disney Cruise Line. As Tom McAlpin told us, "Disney is just out there in so many places in so many ways." Their cruise line is another venue for delivering the same Disney magic they deliver in their parks and their resorts. One ad shows Mickey Mouse on the deck of a ship with the headline, "It's never too soon to start dreaming." Their cruises were originally advertised in conjunction with a day or two at the Disney World resort. Everyone knows that Disney offers unique cruises because many of the Disney characters are present just about all the time, and they can expect the same quality of food they get in the Disney resorts. Every line seeks to get awareness; Disney has great awareness almost automatically. But, of course, their marketing is aimed at people who like Mickey Mouse and Donald Duck.

This brings us to the 999-pound gorilla of the cruise business, Carnival. We want to make it clear at this point that we are not writing these words together. The views on Carnival's advertising and marketing strategy expressed here are Andy Vladimir's.

Let's start with the fact that Carnival is and has been for a long time the world's largest and most popular cruise line. This gives them an enormous advantage when it comes to marketing, or virtually anything else they do. Their very size gives them more money to advertise—a lot more money—which also produces cheaper advertising rates, which in turn gets them even more exposure with more efficiency than any of their competitors can possibly afford. A second advantage is that Carnival started with a brand name and an image to go with it in 1979, when their first ship was launched, and they haven't changed it since then—not once. Someone at Carnival, and I suspect it's my co-author, understands a basic rule of advertising: You don't change your strategy as long as it is working. More often than not, advertisers get tired of their campaigns well before consumers do.

Third, Carnival got it right. For whatever reason, they settled on "fun" as their positioning at the beginning of the game, and by doing that they preempted just about everything you can say about a cruise. Visiting new destinations in far-off places is fun, right? Making love under the stars is fun, right? Having a dinner of baked lobster with a glass of champagne is fun, right? Watching Broadway-caliber shows is fun, right? Giving your child her first snorkeling lesson is fun, right? Getting yourself wrapped in seaweed is fun, right? It's all fun, just as Carnival says in its current campaign: "At any one moment there are a million ways to have fun. Carnival, The Fun Ships." Unlike the other lines, who for the most part use a two-page spread to make their point, Carnival does it with one page. The art direction is so good and to the point that, along with at least a thousand other advertising men and women, I, too, wish I had thought of it. It shows what appears to be a million ways—a collage of photographs of what could be a million ways to do anything. One major image dominates each ad—a couple walking on the beach, a boy playing with dolphins, a woman doing yoga on a deck, a roulette wheel. Then a second small photo of another activity is inserted. It's an art director's dream, but it's not artsy—it is very much to the point. The television commercials tie in with the print and include a memorable song: "Somewhere beyond the sea, somewhere waiting for me."

As in our last edition, we decided to go online and find out how the real world was reacting to all of this. We picked two sites, cruisemates.com and cruisecritics.com, and asked their webmasters Paul and Laura to help us by posting a notice that we were looking for help. This is not a scientific survey in any sense, but we were interested in knowing how the people on these sites picked cruises and what influenced them. The following quotes are all from these two sites:

> First I decide on an itinerary. If it's just my husband and I, we choose together. If we're taking the kids, everyone gets involved. We then have a family meeting for they want to go and why and the approximate cost. Everyone gets a vote (Mom and Dad's votes count more, though). Next we start researching which lines go to where we want to go and the cost involved. I book the lines based on cost. When we travel as a family of five or six, depending on school vacations, we have to plan carefully as we have to fly into a port, so not only do we have cruise costs, we have airfares as well. My last cruise was on Royal Caribbean, and I booked it solely due to cost. We got a great price, three ports and an onboard credit. The same Carnival cruise was almost $100 per person, only had two ports, and offered no onboard credit. Our upcoming cruise is on Carnival. This time Carnival had the best price."

This answer is consistent with a lot of other answers we received. Now, this person is not a first-time cruiser, and you can see that itinerary and cost are all she cares about.

Here's another one from a woman in Texas:

> I've only been on two cruises, one with RCCL and the last one with Carnival. I chose Carnival last time because the price was right and because it sailed out of Galveston, I could drive instead spending the extra money to fly to the port. But the main reason was because while I was sitting on the deck of the RCCL ship in Nassau, I kept looking over at all the activity on the Carnival ship docked next to us and wishing I was over there.

Doesn't she know the grass is always greener on the other side of the fence?

We asked if you had to pick one thing that influenced your selection what it would be. Here's how one woman answered that question:

> If I have to pick one thing, it would be Carnival's value pricing. IMO the best value for a fabulous vacation! I don't believe I am missing anything by cruising with Carnival! And I can cruise more often! As a business traveler, I know how much it costs

to travel. Carnival is the best bang for my buck and the best vacation for me!

I MUST add that I LOVE "Beyond the Sea!!" Every time I hear it, I can close my eyes and look forward to my next cruise with Carnival!

Here's another answer to the same question from another Carnival loyalist:

Seems we always get good pricing from our CruiseCritic Travel Agencies, and yes the Ship is the main reason I chose the last cruise.

Also I must add the "Beyond the Sea" commercial is awesome. Everyone in our groups talk about how they stop what they are doing to watch it every time, even in our cabins. We were even on *Liberty* a few weeks ago out on the lido deck and it would come on the big screen. Everyone raced out to get a better view of it AND we were all on a Carnival cruise!

Note that these last two mention the advertising specifically. So does this one:

Pricing is probably the biggest factor that gets us to choose Carnival. But if we weren't happy with the cruises, we wouldn't keep coming back. We have two Carnival cruises scheduled this year. Also, our last cruise was on the *Legend,* and we had previously cruised on the *Spirit,* and knew that we liked that class of ship. Every time the "Beyond the Sea" theme starts playing on some TV in the house, I start smiling and maybe dancing a bit. My spouse laughs fondly.

Here's one from a first-time cruiser:

We decided to take a cruise as a special present to ourselves from ourselves. While in Alaska we will be celebrating our tenth wedding anniversary. So that is the reason for the cruise to start with.

As for picking out the particular cruise line, we decided on Royal Caribbean. To us, from pictures and advertisements, etc., it seemed to have a LOT of elegance onboard.

Curiously, they picked Royal Caribbean for its elegance. Royal Caribbean doesn't advertise elegance—Celebrity and Holland America do!

Now here's someone who really likes Holland America, but not because of their advertising:

> We have always traveled as a three-generation family and want a cruise line that will please everyone's tastes and budgets. In the early 1990s, we started with Premiere Cruise Line . . . Then we found a fabulous price from a discount cruise broker on a Holland America ship and were hooked—the Holland America deep discounts don't seem to be as prevalent as other lines (especially NCL), but if you look, they're there. HAL's service is personal—it is always hard to leave these people because they've become friends—the food is hugely varied for all of our tastes, including our picky kids and Grandma—everyone finds activities that they like—or none at all—and the absence of lines for food, etc., is a blessing. So, in response to your question, first issue is—MUST be HAL, second is price, third is itinerary, and fourth is departure port—because we must pay for airfare as well.

Here's one from a cruiser who reports she has sailed on Royal Caribbean, Holland America, Celebrity, and Princess, and is about to go on Carnival:

> My choices of cruise line and destination have mostly been guided by my agent, whom I trust totally. I tell him when, and he suggests where (depending on season) and best ship for current needs and number of people I am traveling with. I prefer dealing with the same person who has always been accountable to me for information and in making recommendations in my best interests. So far, he has not let me down. Therefore, I have not hesitated to steer friends and associates to him for their cruise needs. He is experienced, knowledgeable, and honest—I think he knows that I can be a pit bull or a poodle depending on how I am treated. He has much to gain if I am satisfied and lots to lose if I am disappointed. I am a fair person with keen instincts; I ask only to be treated as I treat others—respectfully and honestly. I ask for nothing more, and I will settle for nothing less.

Wow! Talk about singing the praises of the value of a travel agent! Her travel agent gets it. He's a good listener who suggests a product, including destination "and the best ship for [my] current needs and the number of people I am traveling with." The agent has placed his client on five different brands in response to his changing vacation needs. If there were an Oscar for Best Agent of the Year, this gentleman would be a contender!

Here's another Carnival fan who has completely bought into the Fun Ships concept:

> Just returned from our fourteenth Carnival cruise today off the *Valor*. I am loyal to Carnival because they have provided a consistent experience. The Fun Ship experience is Carnival's and Carnival's alone. I have tried Princess and Royal Caribbean and have not been impressed to the level to which Carnival has impressed me. Every line has some good, some bad. Carnival's Fun Ship mentality has not changed since the Kathy Lee days—their brand has been the same, even though many improvements have and continue to change.

This one is from a Norwegian Cruise Line fan. Freestyle cruising really resonates with him.

> Our first cruise was on the *Majesty of the Sea*. We chose that line and ship because of the shore excursion to Tulum.
>
> Our second cruise was on the *Carnival Jubilee*. We chose that ship because it was the only ship stopping at Sitka.
>
> Our third—the *Carnival Destiny*. We went on this ship because we went in a group of eight and it was what everyone wanted to do. Personally, we didn't like the large ship very well. Spent a lot of time lost onboard!
>
> Our fourth—on the *Norwegian Sea*. It was an East coast cruise, and at the time of booking we thought it would be a nice getaway, but nothing special. This was in June 2001 and pre-9/11, but the cost is what swayed us. We paid $250 per person, total. It was a thoroughly enjoyable cruise, and we loved freestyle.
>
> Our fifth—on the *Grandeur of the Sea*. We chose it because of wanting to go out of New Orleans, as it was a closer port.
>
> Our sixth—on the *Norwegian Dream*, out of New Orleans. This cruise combined our favorite port to leave from with what has become our favorite cruise line.
>
> Our seventh—a thirteen-night on the *Norwegian Crown*. Since retirement, we were able to do a longer cruise. Again, it

was a smaller ship, which we like, and on Norwegian Cruise Line. It was a great time, and we could have stayed even longer!

Norwegian Cruise Line has become our cruise line of choice, so that is the first thing we look at. Itinerary is next, but we don't mind going back to ports we have already seen. Cost is a factor, but we have purchased our last four cruises on an auction site and have gotten such terrific deals that we would be crazy to say no to cruising.

NCL has a unique brand positioning, as no other cruise line offers the extent of alternative dining options they do. While this feature doesn't appeal to everyone, it clearly has a following. NCL doesn't spend anywhere near the level of TV advertising dollars of its two contemporary competitors, Carnival and Royal Caribbean. Nonetheless, because its positioning is so distinctive, consumers get the message. While there's no empirical data to prove it, we suspect that travel agents play a larger role in recommending NCL, as freestyle cruising is easy to explain to prospective cruisers.

Celebrity touts great food and service, and guests notice.

I chose Celebrity, and here is why: They had chilled towels waiting for you at the entrance of the ship when you are boarding after being on shore. They had staff eager to help with trays and drinks in the buffet lines. The food was a cut above RCL and Carnival. The dining room staff pampered you by making sure you got whatever you requested from the kitchen—they always accepted special requests like offering shrimp cocktails even when it wasn't on the menu. Embarkation was a snap, they greeted you with FREE drinks as you boarded. They offered high tea in the afternoon and had a wonderful selection of treats.

Now this is a critique on MSC, an Italian line that doesn't spend much on advertising in North America because most of its cruises operate in Europe for the European market:

I agree that MSC provides the BEST cruise value ever. I am glad you acknowledge that fact. Perhaps you should expect the quality of the cruise to be in accordance with the price you pay. That is far more realistic and honest. The good thing is that on MSC you get more than on other cruise lines where you pay three times as much.

However, going back to the value aspect. In New York this month I paid $62.50 plus service for two small glasses of sherry and one margarita. On another night, $54 plus service for two glasses very mediocre California pinot noir and a Mudslide. Then there was $286 plus $59 service for a meal for three comprising one green salad, one steak tartare, one grilled prawns with baby artichokes, and two pasta dishes followed by three disgusting espresso coffees. Not one food item came close to matching the great food we have enjoyed on MSC.

This consumer appreciates MSC's value, as their prices are frequently the lowest in the market for comparable itineraries. However, any cruise line looks great, value-wise, when being compared to prices in New York City!

Consumers often have trouble sorting out their own priorities. This consumer isn't sure what he likes or why:

How do I choose which line to travel on? It is a combination of these factors, pretty much in priority order. It is almost like an "AND" function in that any one of them could call off the cruise, but no single one would make me go (e.g., they all need to be true). Date—I have windows of opportunity to go; duration—I have a limited amount of time I can take for a cruise, and ten-, twelve-, and fourteen-day cruises aren't a possibility; proximity to home—As duration is a problem, adding travel days on to get to the cruise becomes problematic. It also impacts costs.

Itinerary—I dislike sea days, so I look for port-intensive itineraries; costs—I tend to look for bargains. I'm not so enamored with cruising that I won't take a land-based cruise if it is cheaper. I also consider the airfare as part of the cost (also part of the proximity factor); personal taste—the cruise lines have different personalities. I have found that RCCL and Carnival are most to my liking, Celebrity the least. I tend not to care for the elegant, formal poshness of some lines, and food does not factor into my decision (they all have acceptable food for me). Ship design—I like vaulted space, lots of activities, large ships, and don't want to feel like I'm on a ship. For that reason, RCCL Voyager class and Carnival Spirit class are among my favorites. *Sun Princess* has been my least favorite (although, what were they thinking when they created the dining room on Carnival *Miracle*?). Why I picked the last cruise line: It was Celebrity. I was looking at RCCL, but the same itinerary on RCCL was about 25 percent more for a comparable ship. Price won.

Because fewer people take the luxury lines, there is less discussion about them on Internet boards. But they do discuss them. Here's one passenger's take on Crystal:

> I too have been cruising Crystal since 1990 and will continue to do so. One of the key reasons we sail Crystal is their staff and their can-do attitude. A simple smile or a greeting does make you feel special. Of course, the food is wonderful.

At the start of this chapter, we tried to imagine what we would do if we were to start a new cruise line and how we would position and market it. You can see that it would be a challenge. The current players seem to have covered the waterfront. That doesn't mean it can't be done. Adam Aron, former president of NCL, told us, "I personally haven't had to give much thought to what is the next hole that is waiting for someone to drive a truck through. You have to assume, though, that there always is such a hole, if you have a talented client and a talented advertising agency working together with the clear intent of finding it."

Let's be honest. Neither of us can think of a new kind of cruise line we'd be willing to invest our own money in. If we could, Carnival would have already started it. In their own years of experimenting with concepts they have tried a non-smoking ship (the *Paradise*) and a Hispanic market cruise ship (the *Fiesta Marina*), but that was then, and this is now. The *Paradise* was perhaps ahead of its time in 1998. Maybe a new ship or cruise line for non-smokers would work. In fact, we could give it some more ecological flavor and make it the world's first organic ship as well. All the food would be organic, as well as the bed sheets and even the toilet paper. We could even fuel it with ethanol!

A Latin American line? Why not? There are successful Italian, German, Greek, and Chinese ships. The Hispanic market is huge, and there's a lot of money there. Carnival's mistake was perhaps in using an older ship (the ex-*Carnival*, built in 1956) when they tried it in 1994. A new ship targeted to this market may well be successful.

Another possibility is a line designed exclusively for gay and lesbian cruisers. Many gay and lesbian groups successfully charter cruise ships already, but they would probably feel more comfortable on a cruise line just for them. Hotels have done it. Why not cruise lines?

Another possibility is a cruise line exclusively for couples. Talk about the *Love Boat*! No children. No singles. Just couples of all ages. Do you think this line would likely corner the honeymoon market? We do! Imagine the promotional tie-ins, everything from *Romance* magazine to Victoria's Secret to WE TV. Imagine deck chairs for two (Balinese lounges); romantic tables for two throughout the restaurants; fantastic wedding chapels, the most elaborate at sea, for weddings and renewals of vows—one inside and one on deck for the under-the-stars treatment.

An exclusive singles cruise line is also a likely niche market to develop. Imagine an environment where singles or all ages had an almost surefire opportunity to meet other singles. One neat feature we would offer: matching the sexes on each voyage within 4 percent (that is, there would never be more than a 52:48 ratio) to create the best possible expectation on the part of the single consumer. There would be a significant number of cabins designed for single occupancy (perhaps 25 percent), but we believe that, to maximize value, most singles would book basis two to a cabin either on a share basis or with a same-sex friend. Undoubtedly, this line would attract the vast majority of singles now cruising among the 160-odd ships being marketed today. One percent of the total industry boarding would fill this ship year round—and singles are estimated to be 2 to 5 percent of the total market despite the lack of a suitable product for them.

Finally, there might be a market for an unbundled cruise—one with a very low fare, but where nothing is included but the transportation. The food would be extra, there would be a charge for the entertainment, towels at the pool would cost extra, and so forth. At this writing, this very concept is being tested by a European entrepreneur. The line is called EasyCruise.

But, our starting point is Hospitality Cruises with a fleet of five 85,000-ton ships carrying about 2,000 folks (basis two) each. While the above positionings are certainly plausible, none of them has the likely potential to absorb five ships. Each of these is a niche market that would probably not be able to absorb multiple ships, let alone five. In other words, the existing large lines already cover all the large multiple-ship markets. Gaining entry in the North American cruise industry today would be a daunting task for a five-ship fleet. There is an alternative, however: Hospitality Cruises could function as a holding company for five brands, each of which is focused on one of the niches discussed above. All the back office, sales, reservations, accounting, and purchasing would be centralized to maximize economies of scale. Who knows? It could be the next big thing in cruising!

Back to Branding

What have we learned from all of the perspectives we have looked at in this chapter? One thing is that while advertising resonates with some consumers, it is not always (or even very often) the deciding factor. Consumers are confused. Some think the food is the same on all of the lines. Others make a clear distinction. Many use price as the deciding fac-

tor and thus may choose one cruise although they say another is their favorite. But it seems that there are many loyalists—persons who have
tried one line and keep going back to it, no matter what the price or the
promises, made by other lines. The trick is to convert all of your passengers into customers that return and return and return. You do that by
building brand loyalty. Indeed, the differences between one line and another are often so ephemeral that one can argue that's the only way you
can do it.

In the words of Rogers and Hammerstein in "Some Enchanted
Evening," "Once you have found him, never let him go." That's why all
of these lines have clubs where repeat passengers are invited to special
parties on board where they can schmooze with the captain and other officers. That's why they give out pins and medals and even certificates.
That's why these loyal passengers get special deals no one else is offered.
That's the way you keep them, once you get them.

But what about getting them in the first place? Suppose they've never
taken a cruise but they like the idea. Here's where brand awareness does
make a difference. Ranchers still brand their livestock as a way of identifying that these are their animals—often unique from others because of
their breeding or how they have been fed or raised. That's what a brand
is all about—identifying the unique attributes that set your brand apart
from others. The best way to tell people about those attributes is through
advertising, public relations, sales promotion, web bulletin boards,
friends and relatives, and business associates. Successful lines do all of
those things. They remember that the man who built a better mousetrap
and then waited for the world to beat a path to his door starved to death.

One of the biggest challenges facing the cruise industry today is that
of differentiating brands in a meaningful and valuable way. It's easy for
Disney because of their recognized brand. It's easy, too, for the *Queen
Mary 2* because it's an ocean liner, which by definition is different from
a cruise ship. But for everyone else, it's still a bit of a scramble. The truth
is that beef Wellington is beef Wellington, no matter whose ship you get
it on. And there are charming waiters who will do as much as they can to
please the customers irrespective of which ship's dining room they are
working. Winning customers is a tough business, and the best brand
wins!

That's Andy's view, reflecting his advertising background. I don't totally agree. To me, the real differences among the various cruise line positionings is in the atmosphere, the ambience, the experience, not in the
beef Wellington or the great service from the dining room waiter. This is
hard to explain to someone who has not cruised on each line, but—trust
me—the differences are huge. More importantly, I believe that most all
the cruise brands today are well delineated and well positioned. They

have done a good job of describing the experiences they offer and have used words and phrases that resonate with their target audiences. So when Andy says "the best brand wins," he's right only in the sense that the best-known brand has the largest share of the market and is the most profitable. The "best brand" is the one that best meets the needs of a particular customer at a particular point. The superior guest satisfaction that cruising offers is testimony that *all* cruise lines do this branding business pretty damn well!

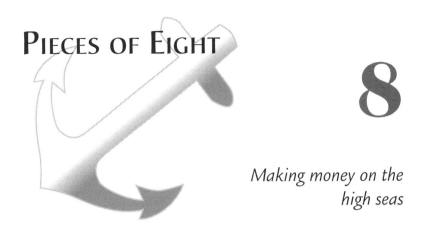

PIECES OF EIGHT

8

*Making money on the
high seas*

You and your spouse have decided to spend a week in a resort destination—say, Honolulu. You go to your travel agent or call your favorite hotel chain reservation 800 number; a rate is quoted on a per-room/night basis. The choice of room may be oceanfront, ocean view, junior suite, etc., maybe five or six choices in all. The rate of the room type selected times the number of nights is the price you will pay for the choice you make. Life is simple, yes? No, of course not. It just appears that way—which gives most land-based vacations a huge advantage over cruising. First, the room rate is expressed on a per-night basis, creating the lowest possible price (unless the place is called the Love Nest Motel and rents by the hour). Second, the purchasers know (or they think they know) exactly what they are receiving for their money: a room, maid service, and the no-added-cost amenities of the hotel such as the lobby, public spaces, beach area, and pool. If the hotel has a gym or spa, more often than not there is a per diem fee for usage.

The purchase decision appears to be small and totally manageable. The hidden costs, or costs that don't seem to count in the purchase, include breakfast, lunch, dinner, snacks, daytime activities, drinks, tipping, cover charges, taxes, cabs, etc. Why these items don't seem to enter into the perceived cost of a land vacation is curious. Perhaps people feel that many of these costs would be incurred anyway. After all, people do have to eat. Even staying home, one is likely to spend money on drinks and entertainment. Perhaps some vacationers don't include these costs because their inclusion might sway them not to make the vacation purchase. Remember, many Americans approach high-ticket discretionary purchases like vacations with a certain ambivalence. We are products of the Judeo-Christian-Puritan ethic. We are sinners who don't necessarily deserve to make nice-nice with ourselves. People are starving in India and Rwanda. We have to save our money for the proverbial rainy day. You get the picture! The self-delusion of not counting certain items as part of the vacation creates a low, and thus more justifiable, purchase price. In reality, the cost for food and drink is significantly higher in a resort than at home. Few people eat out for breakfast, lunch, and dinner, let alone late-night snacks. In the captive environment of a resort hotel, food prices for one breakfast could feed a family of four for a day's meals. A six-pack of beer bought at home is a fraction for the price of the same beer ordered at a resort. A Blockbuster movie rental is under $5.00, but an in-room movie rental may bring $10.95 plus tax. So while consumers can make the tacit argument that these costs shouldn't be included in the cost of a vacation, there is a distinct premium for these items at a resort or hotel. The premium is even higher when the property is seasonal or removed from mainstream commerce, as any tropical island is. In Bermuda, for example, where everything is imported, you can count on paying at least 25 percent more than in the United States. First, there is the shipping cost, which is calculated on bulk, not weight. This curious fact sends the price of potato chips through the ceiling!

Second, Bermuda has no income tax. The government's tax revenues primarily come from duties collected on all imported goods. This adds considerably to the purchase price of items for the hotel—everything from soap to napkins, from soup to nuts. Finally, there is the markup on the already inflated costs. Why? Because Bermuda, like all of the islands in the Caribbean, is small in size, and there is limited competition. You can't get it cheaper at Wal-Mart because there is no Wal-Mart, and if there were, it would probably have to charge the same as everyone else because there are only a few local residents—only 61,000, in Bermuda's case. The lack of competition merely compounds the problem, resulting in high prices to the consumer.

The paradox, then, is that the typical unbundled land vacation sports a low initial purchase price (the room) with high subsequent costs. Cruising, on the other hand, features an unavoidably high initial price because of its all-inclusive nature—but a much smaller number of subsequent costs—like drinks and shore tours—which are generally lower than on land vacations. Consequently, cruise pricing generates a high incidence of sticker shock. Given cruising's long-ago roots as an expensive, elitist vacation for the wealthy, high brochure prices seem to easily confirm a non-cruiser's suspicion that a cruise vacation is simply out of reach.

The cruise industry, through its marketing organization, the Cruise Line International Association, CLIA, attacks the apples and oranges comparison of land versus cruise vacation prices by giving seminars to travel agents in which the agents themselves go through the exercise of comparably equipping and pricing the two vacations. Since 1980, CLIA figures it has trained tens of thousands of agents; unfortunately, there are roughly 250,000 agents in the United States and Canada, and 10 percent or so enter or leave the industry each year.

Moreover, in the greater scheme of things, cruising represents about 7 percent of what the average full-service agency sells from a revenue standpoint, and only about 1 percent of the transactions. The infrequency of agency sales and the relative lack of importance of cruising in the full-service agency's big picture probably inhibit the agents' retention of CLIA training. In recent years, however, there's been a growing trend to cruise specialization, especially in the home-based and call center agency models. These specialists really get the message of the value of cruising and know how to explain what a cruise price represents.

Another factor that influences the way vacations are sold is that, in our experience, a good many, if not the majority of travel agents, have a foggy and unempathic view of their clients' vacation purchasing process. The reason is simple: They don't buy vacations the way everyone else does. When agents take cruises or stay at resorts, they travel either free or at significantly reduced rates. They expect and receive upgraded airline seats and accommodations when they are available. Indeed, most agents' knowledge of vacation products come from familiarization trips, where they are wined and dined at little or no cost to themselves. In many cases, their employer picks up the tab so that others in the office can get a first-hand briefing and the agency can say, "Our people have been there." The result of these freebies and VIP treatments is that when agents are sitting behind their desk quoting a room rate of $150 per night for a hotel in St. Thomas at a resort which they just visited and for which they paid the travel agent rate of $25 per night, they may question in their own minds whether the room is really worth that much or even feel guilty about selling it at that rate. Because agents don't go through the same thought processes as their customers, or pay the same prices when they travel, many of them are not, on the whole, as sensitive as they should be to the consumers' notion of pricing issues in general. They are often at a complete loss when comparing cruises and land vacations in particular because their own experience is so at odds with the real world.

All-Inclusive Vacations—Competition or Not?

A small but not insignificant portion of land vacations is the all-inclusive resort, such as Club Med and Sandals. It is estimated that some one million North Americans purchase all-inclusive vacations each year. That's only about one-tenth the number of people who took a cruise last year. Nevertheless, comparing these vacations with a cruise presents a problem—from the opposite extreme. All-inclusive land packages include tipping, virtually all daytime activities, and even alcoholic beverages and wine, in some instances. These items are not included with most cruises. Aficionados of this kind of vacation, and some travel agents, have urged cruise lines to emulate this approach. They believe that unless cruise lines become more inclusive, the all-inclusive land properties may erode cruising's popularity. This question is worth pondering for a few moments.

To begin with, offering everything at one all-inclusive price would be difficult for any contemporary or premium cruise line, if not impossible. First of all, it would exacerbate the perception that cruising is too expensive by necessarily increasing the initial purchase price to cover the extra cost. Instead of growing the business, it would probably shrink it. Second, we don't know how it would be possible to include all shore excursions, even if we wanted to (not even the luxury lines do that). These adventures ashore (whether it's landing on a glacier in a helicopter or snorkeling among reefs filled with colorful tropical fish) are important and memorable aspects of any cruise. Every port of call has a varied menu of choices of places to go and things to see. The prices of these tours vary according to costs involved and availability. Some tours are sold out almost as soon as the ship sails because tour space is limited, as is the ship's time in port. Except for small, exploration-type cruise products, such as the ones to Antarctica where everyone goes ashore in Zodiac inflatable rafts, pricing to include shore excursions is an impossibility. You can bet that you would have a shipload of unhappy people who couldn't see what they wanted to either because it couldn't be offered under such a system or everyone couldn't get on it. This is not a problem for all-inclusive resorts (which don't offer excursions off the premises for free either).

Then there's the question of tipping, another perceived all-inclusive advantage. While some cruise lines do include tipping in the price of the cruise, they're usually the expensive, luxury lines like Regent Seven Seas, Silversea, and Seabourn. The danger of a no-tipping policy, especially in service industries like hotels, restaurants, and cruise ships, where you tend to have a large number of low-salaried employees, is the inherent risk of poor service when the staff isn't motivated to perform at their highest level to earn tips and thus increase their income. The small luxury cruise lines manage to avoid this problem because they can afford, through higher ticket pricing, to pay substantially more compensation to their crew—higher, in fact, than they could earn virtually anywhere in the world on land or sea for doing the same job! As a result, crew members on these lines are highly motivated by salary continuation. If passengers complain about their hospitality and service levels, crew members can be and are easily replaced, as these positions are highly sought after.

Certainly, the cruise industry cannot and should not ignore all-inclusive resorts (remember, we quoted the founder of Club Med as saying he was inspired by cruises in the first place when he formulated his concept). We suspect these kinds of resorts tend to appeal to a person with a lifestyle somewhat different from the average cruiser and cruise prospect, and this fact suggests all-inclusives are not and never will be a meaningful substitute for cruise vacations. Nevertheless, travel agents and their clients are often tempted to compare prices of a week at an all-inclusive resort with a cruise vacation.

Commendably, all-inclusives have done a superior job of price stabilization. There is little discounting of the product, as operators are content to run their facilities at 50 or 60 percent occupancy, if necessary, to maintain their price integrity. It's much easier for them to do this because these kinds of operations have substantially lower fixed costs than cruise lines do. Moreover, because there are so few brands (Club Med, Sandals, and SuperClubs dominate the Caribbean, for instance), these companies can diligently enforce non-rebating policies at the agent level. Remember, a *discount* is a price reduction offered by the supplier, while a *rebate* is a price reduction offered by the travel agent from sharing a portion of his or her commission. Butch Stewart, the successful owner of Sandals Properties, says he simply refuses to accept commissioned bookings from agents who rebate any of their commission. The agent community knows this and respects his power to enforce the policy. Therefore, there is little or no rebating.

Because rebating is not illegal, and, in fact, is encouraged by the federal government as a pro-consumer policy to encourage lower purchase prices, cruise suppliers can control rebating only by exercising their individual rights to deal with any travel agent they choose, and, by implication, not choosing to deal with agents who operate counter to the cruise line policies. However, because there are so many cruise lines, with no one line capturing the lion's share of the market, as well as a perilous balance between cruise berth capacity and consumer demand, any widespread unilateral enforcement of an anti-rebating policy runs the risk of losing share of the rebating agent's business. While putting isolated individual agencies on no-sell status (meaning either not taking the bookings at all or taking them but not paying commissions) does occasionally occur among the lines (when, for example, the agency's sales tactics are judged to be anti-consumer and harmful to the line's reputation), no cruise line can afford, in today's competitive market, to put hundreds, if not thousands, of agents on no-sell status to stop rebating. Such an action may well stop rebating of the company's product, but it would also cause irreparable harm to its business. If an agency had a rebating policy and actively sold ten cruise lines, and a cruise line stopped dealing with it, the agency would simply move its business to one or more of the other nine cruise products. The company's product would be outpriced in the agency because of its rebating policy. Whatever price the company set for its products was in the context of the market affected by the other cruise lines' pricing. By not accepting rebating, the line may suffer a 5 to

10 percent price disadvantage (or to the extent of the rebates the competitive lines' products enjoy). In a price-sensitive environment, this situation wouldn't cost the company just 5 percent of its business but potentially much more. The line's competitive share of the rebating agency's business might drop from 10 percent to 2 percent—a decline of 80 percent—and that might be the best case! If the agency refused to stop rebating, the line would have no choice but a continued stop-sell, reducing its share of the agency's business to zero. Now, factor in the cumulative effect of a widespread anti-rebating policy unilaterally enforced by one cruise line. Perhaps one hundred agencies that account for 20 percent or more of the line's business could shift away 80 percent of their business on that line, costing the line at least 16 percent of its *total* business! No cruise line can afford to embark on an anti-rebating program that would put it at such risk.

Most lines, therefore, look the other way and ignore the rebating issue altogether. Some lines (Carnival is one) have a policy of prohibiting rebated rates from being advertised in public media. If the Carnival name is used in the ad, because it's the line's trademarked intellectual property, it can control the context of its usage. Offenders are sent cease and desist letters and almost always quickly comply with the policy. As a matter of interest, the policy also applies to advertising group rates in public media. The theory is that this restriction gives *all* agencies in the market a level playing field when it comes to promoting the prices of Carnival vacations via The internet, newspapers, radio, television, and outdoor media.

The Question of Rebating

This may be as good a time as any to address the question of why some travel agents rebate. With full commission retention, this is a low-margin business for travel agencies. To shave agency commissions by giving a prospect additional dollars off doesn't make a lot of sense from an economic point of view. The fact is that agents view rebating as a tool to help them increase their market share. If one travel agency decides to rebate, say, 5 percent of its commission on a given travel product, such as a cruise, and then other agencies in the area fail to match, the price advantage that the agency can offer consumers could result in increased cruise sales. This presumption is based on the perception (and, frequently, the reality) that most cruise purchasers, 60 to 70 percent of whom are experienced cruisers, will shop around from agency to agency to find the best deal. Consequently, an agency rebate can make the difference between a cruise sale and "I'll check with my husband." Once there is an indication that there is rebating in a market, even if it's been isolated and infrequent, many other agencies will begin to rebate for fear that otherwise they will lose business. The business that's at risk here is not simply the lost commission on the cruise sale but the even-more-serious threat of a lost client. If an agency has a long-term client who has presumably (remember, no one knows for sure) given the agency all of his or her travel and vacation business, not to mention referrals to associates, friends, and relatives, then all the client's future business, as well as those valuable past and future referrals, is potentially at risk because the agency, by not offering a rebate, never even gets a chance to match, let alone better, the rebate deal offered by a competitive agency. Even worse, many agents are concerned that this lost client may somehow get the idea that the agency they have been loyal to all these years has, in fact, cheated them or systematically taken advantage of them over time. Because the client receives a lower price from a competitor who uses rebates to make a sale on a cruise, it follows that maybe, just maybe, their former agency was over charging on *all* past business.

Another point to consider is that because cruising has a high initial purchase price due to the bundled nature of its product, the actual commission dollars received by agents when they sell a cruise are higher than when they sell a land vacation. Moreover, the rate of cruise commission, for most agencies, averages about 14 percent versus 11 percent for the combined commission rates for land vacations. Fourteen percent commission on a $2,000 one-week cruise for two people yields $280 commission for about an hour's effort. Rebating as much as $100 still yields net commission of $180 on the sale. By contrast, a $1,200 one-week land package at 11 percent commission yields $132, less than the rebated cruise commission. There's simply less commission for most land-based vacations, so there's a much lower tendency to rebate. In addition, as we mentioned earlier, the few high-priced all-inclusive land package operators have been able to effectively discourage rebating of their products.

Rebating of cruises is further encouraged by the nationwide marketing of so-called 800 numbers and Internet cruise specialists, many of which operate with rebating as part of their standard marketing toolkit. This can range from rebating "only when we have to" to a standardized rebate of a predetermined percentage on all business. To listen to some retail agents, however, you'd think the rebates are 100 percent or more!

This is really a case of perception versus reality. Because of their visibility, which is the result of aggressive cruise marketing, these national marketing operations appear through the eyes of local travel agencies to be a huge threat to the mom-and-pop agencies. As a result, the smaller agency frequently offers a rebate *in anticipation* of their prospects subsequently calling and succumbing to a national operator! Yet the truth is that the national marketers' actual volume simply doesn't warrant this concern.

For instance, an analysis of Carnival's individual booking statistics reveals that, on average, 65 percent of all cruise bookings fail to materialize. On the other hand, 95% of all deposited bookings do stick. Our best guess is that these data probably are representative of the entire industry. Our rule of thumb is simple: *The key to stopping the shopping is GTM* (get the money). The 75 percent failure rate of the nondeposited business is the result of travel agents who have not mastered the art of properly closing a sale and make the mistake of offering their prospects an option to avoid rejection. An option on a particular cabin at a particular price was originally designed to facilitate booking arrangements between the cruise lines and their travel agents. Options were never meant to be discussed with prospective customers. Why? An option means that the agency has the specific space reservation from the cruise line for a given period. A check or credit card number must reach the cruise line before that specified time expires. If it doesn't, the result is that the option is automatically canceled. Customarily, unless space is extremely tight or the booking is very close to the sailing date, options are generally given for seven days. After that time, the cabin goes back on the market. It is not unusual for a cabin to have as many as six or seven options on it before it is finally sold. Carnival, realizing that options are a crutch for many agents, has a very short option window, ranging from two hours to two days.

When an agent gives a prospective client an option, he or she is saying, in effect, "You have seven days to change your mind. You can shop for a better price here in town, or call those national 800 number agencies, or surf the Internet." Is it any wonder the cancellation rate of optioned bookings is so high? Getting a deposit, on the other hand, reflects a commitment on the part of the prospect. Once someone writes a check or gives a credit card for a deposit, the likelihood of changing that purchase decision is sharply reduced—reduced fifteen-fold, based on Carnival data.

Real estate brokers have understood this principle for years. They will willingly take a $250,000 house off the market, even during a busy weekend open house, for as little as $500 earnest money. Why is it called earnest money? Because writing such a small check—less than one-half of 1 percent of the purchase price—says the buyer is in earnest—he or she really wants the house and fully intends to buy it. Obviously, if this wasn't so in practice the vast majority of the time, brokers would demand and get a more substantial deposit. They don't have to demand more because when someone makes even a small deposit on a home, their purchase decision is made; they are emotionally committed, and they stop looking. Moreover, travel agents are often reluctant to recommend just one product to prospects (again, to avoid rejection), and so they like to provide a range of vacation options to consider. This is silly. In fact, shoppers put in a position where they are confronted with a host of purchase options are likely to discuss them with friends and relatives who, in turn, either add their own options—further confusing the issue—or send them to another agency to clear up the confusion!

Research of over 5,000 travel agents indicates that agents' primary fear in a consumer selling situation is the fear of rejection. They feel that if a client doesn't buy one of their recommendations, the agents themselves are somehow diminished, and that makes them feel threatened. This is hardly earthshaking news; just about everyone who doesn't like selling cites fear of rejection as the major obstacle to be overcome. Asking for the order—getting the deposit—is, of course, the moment of truth in any sale. At this point you find out whether your efforts as a salesperson pay off or not—whether your suggestions are accepted or rejected. If they're rejected, your fear of failure becomes real. It is a terrible moment!

In selling seminars around the country, we've consistently pointed out that these fears are without real foundation. No travel agent we know of has ever been killed, maimed, assaulted, or battered for requesting a deposit. If their client says, "I'll think about it," the proper response is "I can understand that. But it would be a good idea if you get back to me quickly, because that way we will improve our chances of obtaining the same or comparable space, and we have a really great cabin for you now." The implication is scarcity—cabins like this are not easy to come by. There is nothing deceiving in saying this—in fact, it is the truth. Every day closer to sailing, more cabins are sold, and thus there really are fewer choices remaining. (Remember, unlike hotels and resorts, cruise lines try to fill all of their capacity.) Trust us, scarcity sells. It is a proven technique that helps people make up their minds to buy because they do not want to lose out by delaying their decision only to find that the exact cabin they wanted or, even worse, the sailing date they planned on, is no longer available. The emotional power of scarcity is especially strong when dealing with high-ticket discretionary items, such as vacations, because of the deep-seated ambivalence we discussed in chapter 4. If a prospective purchaser does decide to take the plunge and opt for this discretionary purchase, the purchase better be available, or he or she will be terribly frustrated!

Cruise Commission Reductions?

The elimination of most airline commissions has led many agents and travel writers to suggest that the cruise lines might follow suit and reduce agency commissions on their products. Their reasoning is that the majority of cruise lines are highly motivated to maximize profits and may view this as a significant cost-cutting measure. For most cruise lines, travel agent commissions are either the largest or second-largest cost item. (Depending on its percentage of air/sea business, airfares could be the largest.) Perhaps just as important, a lower range of commissions would inhibit rebating altogether, or at least reduce the amount of the rebate to an insignificant level. Whether or not any of the cruise lines will take this tack remains to be seen, but the risk of unilaterally lowering commissions is great; it parallels the risk of curbing rebates. Given the sensitive balance between cruise berth capacity and consumer demand, most cruise lines pay higher commission percentages than their land-based competitors, not lower. While definitive data on the subject are lacking, our best guess is that average cruise line commissions climbed from about 12.5 percent in 1985 to about 14.5 percent in 2005. That represents an increase of 16 percent overall but an increase of 80 percent over the base 10 percent commission. Override commissions (those levels paid beyond the base 10 percent commission) have nearly doubled as cruise lines ferret out and reward cruise-producing agencies. Most cruise lines today typically have a sliding scale of commission payment percentages based on sales productivity (either measured in dollar sales volume or head count—that is, the number of bodies delivered by the agency). The concentration of cruise sales in a relatively small number of agencies—relative to the total agency count of 30,000 in the United States and Canada—suggests that these cruise-specializing agencies are not only benefiting from higher commission percentages but also their higher mix of cruise business is heavily influencing the individual cruise line's average commission payout.

Carnival is an illustrative example that probably is indicative of the industry pattern. Roughly 26,000 agencies did business with Carnival in 1995, representing nearly 70 percent of all U.S. and Canadian agencies. In other words, almost one agency in three produced no business at all! On the day when the airline commission caps were announced in February 1995, Carnival announced it would increase the commission it would pay to the 12,000-plus agencies that had not sold a Carnival cruise from 10 percent to 12 percent for a six-month trial period. The idea was to jump-start agencies that were financially affected by the cap situation to begin to sell cruises. Carnival even offered a sales call by one of its sales representatives within seven days of a call from any of these agencies. The sales call would produce not only product information and sales material but also sales training to help the agency convert from the order-taking mentality of an airline ticket agency. Remarkably, fewer than 400 agencies took advantage of this offer. Considering that Carnival is the largest and most popular of all cruise lines and thus, theoretically, the easiest to sell, we believe this example is a fair indicator of the inertia all vacation providers are experiencing even today.

The conclusion, then, is that while increased commission structures can and do motivate agencies to grow their cruise volume—if they are already cruise producers—they do little or nothing to motivate agencies that are neither oriented nor inclined to selling cruises—and, by implication, to selling any other form of vacation other than order-taking visiting friends and relatives (VFR) business.

Our Carnival story is not the only indication of agency inertia. When the airline commission caps were imposed, Rod McLeod of Royal Caribbean was widely quoted in the trade press expressing his opinion (shared by many leading travel agency business strategists) that the caps would finally force thousands of agencies to turn to the profitability of selling cruises to offset the financial effects of the caps. But then, a few years later, a disappointed McLeod reported to the audience of agents that the anticipated surge of cruise bookings from their agencies simply had not materialized.

While on the subject of commissions, it should be noted that three lines, Royal Caribbean, Princess, and Celebrity, acting independently of one another, abolished the Florida commission base. This anomaly, wherein Florida agents received a base commission of 15 percent rather than the industry standard of 10 percent, had its roots in the $19.95 and $29.95 one-night and two-night cruises offered from Miami in the 1950s and 1960s, before the modern cruise business was established. At 10 percent, the cruise commission was simply too low to attract agent's attention and motivate them to sell these new products. As a consequence, the 15 percent base Florida commission was created. Whether this initiative to create a level playing field among Florida and non-Florida agencies really accomplished any material change in the commissions paid in Florida is a matter of conjecture. After all, what difference does it make if a cruise-producing Florida agency had a base commission of 15 percent and an override of 2 percent or a base of 10 percent and an override of 7 percent? In both cases, the agency is receiving 17 percent commission for its efforts. Bear in mind the hotly competitive nature of the Florida cruise market; Florida is the leading cruise-producing state, accounting for 17.3 percent of overall industry sales.[1]

Given that this is a market share we anticipate Florida will at least maintain and probably enhance in future years, it's highly unlikely that any of these lines ultimately took an action that would make them uncompetitive as they vie for their share of this important market. In all probability, the net effect was to change the base for *nonproducing* agencies from 15 to 10 percent. In view of Carnival's experience after raising

---

[1] 2004 CLIA Passenger Industry Carryings Report.

commissions because of the airline cap, this probably was a non-event, akin to speculating whether a fallen tree makes a noise in a forest if no one is there to hear it.

Myriad Tariffs

Meanwhile, after the asides of rebating and commissions, we still have the vacation prospect considering the seemingly high initial cost of a cruise versus an unbundled land vacation. But there's a further complication: There's not just one brochure price for this cruise, not three or four like a typical resort hotel, but eight or twelve or twenty depending on the complexity of the cruise ship's stateroom breakdown. For most cruise lines, the vacation prospect is confronted with a grid of prices reflective not just of stateroom size (like a hotel room) but also location, with higher decks commanding a premium over lower decks. Then, consider the further complication of inside and outside staterooms. This gets even worse when some lines and travel agents refer to staterooms as "cabins." Don't you wonder what images pass through a prospective first-time cruiser's mind when he hears an agent ask him, "Would you like an outside cabin?" He may be picturing a gleaming white cruise ship steaming out of port with large ropes trailing behind, each attached securely to a rustic cabin, bobbing up and down on the briny deep. The cruisers are sitting in rocking chairs on the front porch, enjoying their cruise. Outside cabins, indeed! While old habits die hard, the trend in the industry is to emulate our land-based resort competition and refer to these accommodations as "ocean view." What other kind of view would you expect to find on a ship? Naturally, they sell at a premium over inside staterooms—those with no view.

When one factors in seasonality, wherein the entire tariff changes with the time of year to adjust for the ebb and flow of consumer demand, the complexity of prices is once again compounded. A hotel with four room categories and three seasonal prices generates twelve possible price combinations. A cruise ship with twelve room categories and three seasonal prices results in thirty-six possible choices. It sure seems like the cruise industry goes out of its way to make a cruise purchase as daunting as possible, doesn't it? Why have so many prices? The answer is that, with the exception of some small luxury and specialty lines like Windstar, Seabourn, and SeaDream, most lines want to have a large variety of stateroom prices to allow a blend of revenue possibilities. By having a few loss-leader cabins, cruise lines can have a low advertised lead price without committing too much inventory. Based on sufficient demand the line can, in theory, sell out all its staterooms at full tariff. If the demand isn't strong enough, the company simply keeps offering to resell the lower-priced categories that are selling and upgrade the existing passengers in those accommodations into the higher-priced accommodations that are not selling. More about this in the discussion of yield management.

Discounting

Although this price philosophy sounds simple enough, the real situation is more daunting. Why? Because brochure tariff for most mainstream cruise lines has little or no bearing on the real prices that cruise products fetch in the market place. If you have ever heard or been told that cruise brochure tariffs are overstated, you can be certain this is an understatement! In fact, the industry, already a victim of sticker shock because of the bundled nature of the product and carrying the burden of price complexity because of a dizzying array of accommodations choices, exacerbates the situation with unduly high brochure tariffs. How did the lines get in such a mess? In the late 1970s, when cruise berth supply was tight and demand vigorous (remember the Sitmar ads we mentioned earlier?), cruises generally sold at or near brochure tariff. Sure, some upgrading was going on—when someone paid for a category four inside stateroom on the lowest deck of the *Festivale,* for example, and ended up in a category seven inside twin/queen without paying the $150 per person tariff difference at the time—or where a consumer paid for a specific category with the guarantee that he would at a minimum be in that category but might well end up doing better. (In exchange for this guarantee the passenger was willing to forgo receiving a cabin number at the time of booking.) Most of the time, however, the brochure tariff price of the stateroom was the one that was paid for the cruise—and, in any event, on just about every cruise, some passengers paid the price published in the brochure, although not necessarily the price for the specific accommodation they received. But then came the huge capacity increases of the 1980s and 1990s, and brochure tariffs simply didn't get the job done. Ships weren't filling, and the industry embarked on a long and irreversible path of discounting. Now you may be saying to yourselves, "Whoa, aren't upgrades and guarantees a form of discounting?" You may think this is splitting hairs, but no, they're not discounts. Both pricing schemes are, in fact, sold at tariff, as we have said. Discounting, on the other hand, is a supplier-based pricing scheme that departs from tariff, creating a whole new lower pricing structure for the product.

The first widespread discounting scheme was NCL's Sea-Saver fares. These were capacity-controlled, cruise-only, run-of-ship (no stateroom numbers) rates that applied to bookings within thirty days of the departure date. This pricing scheme, introduced in July 1980 to deal with huge increments of unsold inventory resulting from the introduction of the *Norway* in June of that year, was soon followed by Carnival in January 1981.

Holland America introduced free air in the fall of 1980, in effect discounting their air/sea cruises by eliminating the air add-on charges that had compensated, partially at least, the line for the round-trip airfare between the passenger's home city and the ship's departure port. This was only applicable to the slow, fall season of 1980 to stimulate demand depressed by the national recession. Carnival too eliminated their air/sea add-on à la Holland America, but then compensated by increasing their base tariffs in 1983 and after to include the effect of the air add-on in the base. In other words, a winter 1983 weeklong cruise was priced from $950, including free air, versus $810 and an air add-on of $150 for a total of $960 for a comparable cruise in the winter of the previous year. As the company was able to recoup the entire air add-on (by 1984), the discount disappeared and a new tariff scheme was born. At the same time that free air was priced into the base tariff, Carnival also provided a cruise-only travel allowance so as not to penalize the passengers who did not purchase air and who, we assure you, had no interest in subsidizing the air cost of fellow passengers!

Free air pricing was quickly matched by the other year-round Caribbean operators. The reason this discount program was quickly changed to a new tariff scheme was simple: Agent feedback to Carnival in the fall of 1982 was overwhelmingly in favor of free air. At the time, about 75 percent of the Caribbean-based cruise lines business was sold on an air/sea basis. This was before the airline frequent flyer programs were established. Now, less than 25 percent of the industry's sales are sold on an air/sea basis, in part because more folks take advantage of amassed frequent flyer miles to provide them with free air. The proliferation of home ports, stimulating the drive markets, and low-cost advance purchase airfares contributed to the steady decline of cruise line–generated air/sea packages. Until free air, agents had to sell the cruise in two pieces: the cruise itself and then the air add-on. Free air eliminated the second step. Ironically, agents preferred to sell the more bundled, higher-priced air/sea product to the two-step process of cruise and air add-on.

The mid-1980s saw a plethora of discount programs offered by various cruise lines. Probably the most common was the market-specific promotion. If a cruise line needed a push for a few months to either top off a series of sailings or to prevent the total disaster of half-empty ships, it would select one or more cities to offer a city-specific air/sea deal. The cities would be selected not only on the basis of their ability to produce sales with a deal but also on the basis of a minimum amount of business already on the books from those cities for the sailings in question. The latter consideration assured a manageable level of dilution; with hardly any business already booked, the regional market was virtually undisturbed. Little or no refunding or upgrading of existing business, group or individual, was needed. Agents weren't upset that their group promotions were undermined because if there was any group activity, it had probably already proved fruitless. If there was a large piece of group business on a specific, isolated date or two in the series, then the cruise line would simply black out that date from the promotional offer.

This was a dangerous game, but if the line was careful it could be successful with a minimum of market disruption. Occasionally, the group would want to move to one of the non-blackout dates and the cruise line would take the dilution hit. Because this promotion (a euphemism for discount scheme) was capacity-controlled, the offer could be withdrawn at any time. This is an important feature of any discount program, as it protects the line from giving away the farm if the price set for the deal proves too low, resulting in higher demand at that price than the line is willing to provide in terms of berths.

Because the program is limited to specific markets, there is simply no disruption in the unaffected markets. If the program got underway in, say, eight cities and that proved insufficient to fill the needed capacity, then one or more additional cities could be added to secure the needed demand. Not without a cost, however: These city-specific promotions required city-specific advertising messages, generally involving the Sunday travel sections of the local papers but, on occasion, local spot television as well. Don't forget, though, those additional cities mean additional acquisition costs in terms of incremental advertising. Also, timing is always a consideration. These types of programs are typically developed relatively close to the time of the sailings—four months out—maybe six months out at the outside. The reason timing is crucial is that the early results of the promotion must be critically analyzed to determine what additional actions, if any, are necessary. Are more ads needed in the same cities? Are more cities needed? If so, which cities, and how soon can the ads be placed and run? (For a national advertiser, it generally takes at least ten days between the time an ad is ordered and when it appears in the travel section of the newspaper. When a vessel is sixty days away from a partially empty sailing, ten days seems like an eternity to a marketing executive! Because of these factors, prudent planning suggests a line have a contingency plan for their deals—a Plan B, if you will—that is on the shelf and ready to be rolled out quickly if necessary.

Market-specific programs allow the line the opportunity to test differing levels of discounts and differing advertising messages for relative effectiveness. Because these programs are market specific, whatever is done in a given city is limited to that city. It doesn't affect any other city-specific or national program the line is offering. A disadvantage of the program is more subtle: the disruption of the national advertising message of the line and the potential undermining of the prevailing national price structure. When a cruise line bombards Chicago, for example, with a great deal for certain sailings of certain ships in the fall, what message is it sending about:

1. Its other ships?
2. Its sailings during the rest of the year?
3. The validity of its normal (non-deal) price structure?

What is the long-term effect of seeing ads in the *Chicago Tribune* for a $799 one-week air/sea program, ads that may run for three months to the exclusion of any other advertising by the line, on the long-term pricing structure, which may call for a $1,099 lead price in the winter? Will consumers react and buy the $799 fall deal but, when it comes time to promote the higher-priced winter product, will there be a backlash? Intuitively, we know there will be. There is always a price to pay, in the long term, for quick-fix discounting—and that's true in most marketing cases. When department stores first decided to use television in addition to newspapers, they tended to advertise only the big sales, the rationale being that the medium was so expensive it should only be used for big events. It didn't take long for them to realize that consumer attitudes were changing as a result of this approach. Research substantiated this. Consumers get conditioned to buy at a sale price and reason there will always be another sale; all they have to do is have a little patience until it comes along. In the cruise business, as in the hotel group business, it's an issue of expediency: the soft sailings of today versus the unknown demand of tomorrow. One thing is certain: If the soft sailings of today aren't addressed effectively, there may not be a tomorrow for the cruise line marketing executive to worry about. Hence, in the cruise industry particularly, which is intolerant of the modest occupancy levels hotels accept, the needs of today—the next few weeks or months—always seem to take precedence over the unknown supply-demand equation of tomorrow. Up to now, in any case, the industry has been inherently and consistently optimistic about the future. Like Scarlett O'Hara, they believe that tomorrow is another (and better) day!

Other considerations that also affect pricing are the itinerary and the destination. For instance, Alaska marketing had its own peculiar pricing history, very different than the Caribbean. Here the practice has been to present an early booking discount that would expire on, say, 31 December. The intention is to create an up-front demand for this very limited (by both capacity and seasonality) Alaskan product—about eighteen one-week sailings a year. If the line was successful with its up-front pricing, it would revert to tariff. If the pace of the anticipated number of bookings needed to fill by sailing time was deemed inadequate, then the early booking deadline would be extended. When that happens, the cruise line's spokesperson might cite "popular demand" and the line's "inability to handle the onslaught of bookings." Later, if the pace of bookings fell short again, say, in April-June, to top off the summer Alaska sailings, then the lines would be extremely creative with all manner of last-minute discount programs—as they are highly motivated to fill this high-yield capacity. One of the favorites of Alaskan cruise marketers has been the special agency deal. These are special prices that only a limited number of high-producing agencies can obtain. These agencies, known for being aggressive promoters and marketers, were given these last-minute preferential deals with the thought that their very preference would motivate the agencies to provide extra business either by creating new business or converting it from other cruise lines. (The line offering the deal wasn't really too choosy as to where the business came from, as long as it materialized.) The smart cruise operators kept track of the incremental business that individual agencies would develop to determine whether it made sense to continue to allow them the preferential deal in subsequent years. As lines know from sad experience, there's no correlation between the promises of smooth-talking, charismatic travel agents and sales results! By their nature, preferential pricing deals work most effectively when they are kept quiet in the marketplace, not unlike private sales by a clothing retailer. Some agents seem to get more enjoyment out of telling the other agencies in the market about their special deal than spending the effort necessary to produce the actual business!

Most of the discounting schemes described above had the effect of rewarding prospective cruisers who wanted to make their cruise purchases close to the time of sailing. As cruise lines judge what market stimulation (discounting) is needed by the pace of bookings (how a particular ship and sailing date is filling in comparison with how it has booked in the past for that particular time of year), any delay in booking patterns makes this decision process problematic. (When you see enough of them, you notice that most cruise marketing and sales executives have gray or white hair.) First of all, the shift in bookings throws off the validity of the previous history—in effect, a new booking pace has developed with no comparable data to triangulate it with. Second, the new close-in booking pattern gives the line far less time to take corrective action to stimulate demand. When in doubt, the lines stimulated demand—on a close-in basis—thus perpetuating the problem by rewarding purchasers who delayed their purchase decisions with lower-priced cruises. At the same time, group business can suffer because these last-minute discount deals tend to undermine the once favorable group rates the agent may have obtained perhaps a year prior to the sailing. The groups, if they were promotional in nature, would tend to fall apart, costing the agent time and money. Frustrated, the agent would be leery of booking future group business. This system was not working, and something had to be done!

In 1992, something *was* done. Royal Caribbean successfully innovated a fleetwide, year-round advance purchase program called, aptly, Breakthrough Rates. This program was quickly matched in one form or another by the other large cruise lines. At the time, one company, Celebrity Cruises, held out and publicly opposed these programs for two years. Al Wallach, then their senior vice president of marketing, claimed in the trade press that it was presumptuous of cruise lines "to dictate to consumers when they had to purchase." Finally, with little fanfare, Celebrity succumbed to the industry trend and trotted out an advance purchase program of its own, rewarding those who purchased well in advance of the sailings with the best rates. Breakthrough pricing and its imitators start out with the lowest rates far in advance of the sailing, a year out or more, and then, based on how the sailing is filling, the rates are raised in discrete intervals. The discount is thus lowered until, on occasion—hallelujah!—tariff is reached. It's a sort of reverse striptease. The dancer starts off scantily clad and, as the performance goes on, dresses until she is fully clothed.

This kind of pricing makes eminent sense. It rewards those who have tied up their money the longest. It lengthens the booking pattern because it places the biggest discount in the hands of those who book earliest and, in general, restores a measure of much-needed price stability to the market—critically important for future market growth.

Pricing a discount is certainly an art. The cruise line must anticipate the response from the marketplace. This is a function of a varying price elasticity of demand—Economics 101. Some lower price point will produce the required increase in consumer demand necessary to fill that portion of the unsold capacity the line is willing to give away at that price. Too little a discount (too high a price), and demand will be insufficient. Too deep a discount (too low a price), and the unsold capacity quickly sells—but could have been sold at a higher price—and thus revenue is permanently lost to the line.

In the early 1990s, when demand did not react as anticipated, a number of cruise lines advertise two-for-one rates. This meant that one person could cruise for free if the second person in the stateroom paid the tariff price. Airlines did the same thing (indeed, they did it first). While these promotions were effective—they do catch the eye and make the phone ring—they also suggested to consumers that brochure tariffs are probably way too high. Undoubtedly, the lines maneuvered themselves into this position through a combination of optimism, survival, and ego. Optimism, as cruise lines figured that the next year will always be better and therefore the brochure tariff will begin to (finally) become realistic. Survival, as cruise line executives justified their existence (and next year's expense budget) on the corresponding revenue budget propped up by an increase in both tariff and net yields. Ego is the most subtle yet most powerful influence of the three. What cruise line wants to reduce its brochure tariff and thus send a signal to the marketplace that the line is somehow less in quality or stature than previously? Or, perhaps more importantly, that the line has, by repricing downward, reduced its ranking and positioning when compared to its competitors? (Never mind that the product was egregiously overpriced on its face and only sold because of an arsenal of discounting weapons.)

Proponents of high brochure tariffs argue that the consuming public is truly enamored of a great deal. No one wants to pay sticker price for anything! People want to save money. The more they can save, the more willing they are to buy. High brochure pricing provides the platform or base from which to deeply discount the product. Lower, more reasonable brochure pricing would reduce the discount levels, and the deal won't seem as attractive. Without an attractive deal, it is assumed, demand will lessen and lines will be forced to lower prices—that is, to deepen the discounts. Deeper discounts from lower brochure pricing, proponents argue, mean lower yields for the line. Hence, they advocate maintaining and even increasing brochure pricing!

The other side of the coin says that high brochure prices will frighten would-be cruise purchasers when there is no reference to the real prices. Remember, the all-inclusive nature of a cruise vacation already forces even realistic pricing to appear too high when compared with unbundled land vacations. We think the issue is not how much a person saves but how much he pays for the product he or she ultimately buys. If a prospective vacationer takes three brochures, a cruise brochure with ridiculously high pricing and two realistically priced resort or sightseeing vacations, which will appear to provide the best value? Which will seem unreasonable in comparison?

Some lines have addressed the problem in a somewhat Solomon-like approach. Their brochures feature discounted rates in a column right alongside the brochure tariff. With this approach, prospects can understand what they are paying (the discounted rate) without the products appearing too cheap relative to competing lines (as their high tariffs are consistent with those of direct competitors). The downside to this strategy is that it carves in stone the deepest discount. What if a line overestimated future demand and priced the discounted rate too high? Thus trapped with the published discount, it would have no choice but to obviate the brochure deal and peg a lower price. This is easier said than done. What do they do with those expensive brochures? Scrap them? If the line has a second, lower tier of discounts, it wouldn't achieve its goal of publishing realistic rates, as it would undercut its own published discounted rate. But if it underestimates demand with this published discount device, at least it allows an escape through capacity controlling the discount. This indicates that the discount in the brochure is, in fact, perishable, and suggests that the cruise price would move by discrete but unspecified iterations all the way to tariff if demand warrants.

 Groups

Group business is an important component of cruise sales, probably accounting for about a quarter of the entire business. Group business can be affinity groups like Kiwanis organizations, garden clubs, family reunions, and alumni groups, or it can be open promotions wherein agents block group space with a cruise line to secure a favorable rate and concessions and then promote the group rate to their FIT client base or to the general public through advertising and public relations. Either way, the agency books the space to ensure, as much as is practical, that the inventory will be available to sell when they promote the group. While this availability is the most important aspect of group development, group pricing and concessions are also important considerations. Agents need an attractive deal to provide prospects with an incentive to go on that specific ship and date. Locking in the lowest rates gives the agency confidence and enthusiasm when promoting groups. The concessions are equally important because they can help lower the price of the group cruise and thus make it a more attractive package.

The biggest concession, typically, is a complimentary berth for a tour conductor—or Pied Piper, as he or she is known in the trade. The Pied Piper is often the person who has organized the tour. Your priest, minister, or rabbi is organizing a trip to the Holy Land, and you decide to go along with him. He's the Pied Piper. For years, the industry standard has been one free berth for every fifteen base-paying passengers. In other words, the sixteenth person was free, equivalent to a reduction of 6.25 percent of the overall price of the group, if the tour conductor was prorated against the paying guests. Instead of being given away, some agents split the revenue from the earned tour conductors' space, giving some away to true group leaders and prorating the rest to further reduce everyone's cost. Occasionally, though, some cruise lines are *very* creative—offering tour conductors for as low as one free for six! Other concessions may include free or reduced-rate cocktail parties on board ship for the group, shore excursions, onboard credits, donations to a charity, and advertising dollars to promote the sailing—just about anything you can imagine!

Because group travel is an important segment of the overall vacation travel industry, it's critical that the cruise industry is fully competitive with its land-based vacation competitors. While we believe that group cruising is a superior value, it does suffer from the same handicaps, pricing-wise, that individual cruise products do: The perception of a high price because of cruising's inclusive nature, inflated brochure pricing—a practice not generally found in the pricing of land-based vacation products, which are more realistically priced with rare discounting, and price instability result from cruising's unique determination to fill every berth. Every few years, it seems, the cruise industry overestimates advance demand and inadvertently but frequently undercuts the group rates that have been promoted for the period. When that happens, our guess is it takes some time—one or two years—for many of those group-promoting agencies to begin to rebuild their confidence in group cruise pricing. The smart lines realize this and have developed group pricing that should ensure the situation won't occur.

A cataclysmic event like 9/11 simply wipes out all vacation providers' advance pricing schemes. It took a year to recalibrate advance pricing and three to four years to essentially get back to pre 9/11 pricing. When hiccups occur, it behooves cruise companies to stabilize group pricing quickly. But imagine what would happen if consumers truly understood the inherent value of cruising as we have explained it in this book? Demand would immediately exceed capacity, and price stability wouldn't be an issue!

Charters

A special form of group pricing is a charter hire. With a charter, the group or organization has exclusive use of the vessel for a contracted period. This exclusivity can yield a huge range of features unique to that cruise experience. These could include a one-of-a-kind itinerary or set of itineraries. A charter could take a ship out of its normal sequence or pattern, provided that, at the termination of the charter, the ship is in the right place and on the right day to allow it to return to its normal advertised schedule. Occasionally, the charter may take the ship and reposition it in another trading area—moving a Miami-based ship to New York for three weeks, for example. The charterer is expected to pay for the unsold positioning days when the ship deadheads (i.e., is without passengers) between Miami and New York at either end of the charter. If the ship is returned a day before its normal cruising pattern recommences, the charterer is expected to pay for the unused day.

Having a ship exclusively for the use of one organization results in a special feeling of camaraderie on board; it's the ultimate private party. All passengers have something in common—there are no strangers, and everyone feels special and "on the inside." As with large groups, it's common to celebrate such a happening with special customized T-shirts or other items that memorialize the event. Back home, these commemorative articles have a special cachet. "This was something we did that you could never do"—a one-of-a-kind experience! Religious groups and fraternal organizations are obvious choices for charters. Not so obvious are collectors of various kinds, Super Bowl attendees, Trekkies, and radio station promotions—all drawn by a strong common interest or hobby. In these cases, the charterer promotes the cruise in the special interest magazines and newsletters of the group, trusting that the appeal of being with like-minded folks, interacting and celebrating their hobby or special interest, will be a powerful enough draw to be successful. And many of them are—hugely so! We predict that people's growing thirst for affinity (which is less frequently quenched these days through the nuclear family and the community) will make special interest groups and charter cruising a larger component of cruise's business mix in the years to come.

Sometimes charterers don't charter the whole ship but merely a large part of it. As an example, Budweiser made a deal where it took over the entire second seating of a ship, which allowed them to have speeches and themed parties in the dining room as well as a special second seating show featuring their own entertainment. To compensate the other passengers who were all assigned to first sitting dining and the early show, Budweiser offered free beer to everyone on the ship for the entire cruise.

As a point of consumer protection, all charters must be legally contracted and then filed with the Federal Maritime Commission (FMC). Some unscrupulous promoters have advertised and sold charters they didn't really have secured, on a speculative basis, hoping to fill a ship. Of course, if they failed to hit the numbers, everyone who had already paid had their payments at risk. Sometimes all of it is lost, the promoter claiming the money was used up in administrative and promotional costs. While it's a federal offense to promote charters that haven't been contracted, occasionally an agent or travel broker will have a large group that could be sufficient to fill a ship if the group's response to the offer is strong. Some cruise lines will provide the mechanism of a partial charter for the initial size the agent is able to financially secure, with options to secure the balance of the space within stipulated time frames. Even here, though, the promoter can't advertise or imply exclusivity on the ship until the full charter agreement is signed and secured.

From the cruise line's perspective, the charter hire (price) should ideally reflect, at a minimum, the net yield of what the vessel would realize for that sailing date under its normal operation, plus pricing to recover any incremental cost of lost onboard revenue for the period. Chartering to a group of 2,000 teetotaling, non-gambling Polynesian frog worshipers can truly put a crimp in onboard revenue, so this must be anticipated and offset by a higher charter price. Some lines aggressively go after charters—with a very sharp pencil—because they like the demand compression a charter creates. They reason that the charter business is virtually incremental; forcing their normal demand for the sailing to compress—in other words, shift—onto other dates or other ships of the line's fleet. This fill-up of demand will result in higher rates for those sailings. As a result, those higher rates could theoretically justify a lower price for the charter hire itself. Normally, there is no incremental acquisition cost (advertising and sales efforts) for charters, another fact used by some lines to justify lower prices.

Frequently, two or more cruise lines with competitive ships on competitive routes are in competition for the same charter. It's not uncommon for a smart charterer to play cruise lines against one another. In the quest to get the business, lines can bid too low and end up with a case of seller's remorse. What's fascinating about this is that the demand compression caused by the charter also affects the line's direct competitors. If three lines, for example, offer one-week cruises out of San Juan on essentially the same itineraries, and there is competition on a charter bid, sometimes the two lines that don't win the low bid make more money than the lucky winner because, due to their greater availability of space in that same period, they were able to capture more of the compression of normal individual and group demand, at higher yields, than the winning line. This is because some travel agents as well as some of their clients view these lines, rightly or wrongly, as interchangeable. Sadly, some travel agents feel it's more appropriate to first offer their clients another line's product on the same date than the same line's product (the one they originally selected) on a different date or the same weekend but a different ship. This is obviously a result of the perception of the commoditization of the travel industry we spoke of in chapter 4 as well as the agent's inappropriate unwillingness to suggest an alternative date to the client.

Yield Management

Yield management, a business tool that emerged in the late 1980s in the airline industry, has application in the cruise industry. The focus is on yield rather than revenue because it gives management a much cleaner picture of the profit impact of pricing decisions. For example, the revenue of an air/sea booking, for comparable accommodations, will always be greater than a cruise-only booking. Yet, if the related cost of the airfare, transfers, and hotel (if occasioned by the flight connections) is greater than the revenue increment less the commission paid on the additional revenue, then the yield on the cruise-only booking is higher than the air/sea booking. Exhibit 8.1 gives an example.

To maximize revenue, sales from Seattle would be encouraged. To maximize yield, sales from Seattle would be discouraged, capacity controlled, or repriced, either by increasing the air add-on or, if free air, raising the cabin category that would be available for sales to Seattle-area residents. By raising the minimum category available from category four to category seven, the price would increase by $120. After 10 percent commission, the yield improves to $908—comparable to the other product prices in the illustration. Note we have used a 10 percent commission structure for ease of example. The proper way to calculate the yield is to use the weighted average air/sea and cruise-only commission costs the

EXHIBIT 8.1   **Seven-Day New York Cruise Booking (inside accommodations)**

| | Air/sea | | |
Gateway	Chicago	Seattle	Cruise Only
Revenue	$1,295	$1,395	$995
Less commission	130	140	100
	$1,165	$1,255	$895
Less airfare/transfers	260	455	0
Net yields	$905	$800	$895

line is experiencing. While individual lines differ, on average the industrywide commission is guesstimated at about 14.5 percent in 2005.

The objective is to sell the cruise to the right person at the right time for the right price. The revenue management departments of the cruise lines are tasked with maximizing revenue based on demand in the marketplace.

So the most important input to that equation is what demand is at any given point. Older models matched the pace of bookings to what was achieved historically, most commonly in the prior year. But the shape of demand changes from year to year, and the more sophisticated cruise lines in terms of revenue management—including Carnival, Royal Caribbean, Celebrity, and Princess—have developed mathematical models designed to predict the future shape of demand.

Based on unconstrained demand in the marketplace, the revenue management teams can manage pricing. The initial price for the cruise usually appears in the marketplace between twelve and twenty-four months prior to departure. Due to the nature of cruise inventory, the pricing varies by ship category. Given the mix of price programs typically offered by a cruise line, this can result in hundreds of price points even when the departure is initially open for sale.

The pricing is then manipulated up until departure. In an environment of strong demand, prices may be raised through several forms. The strategic price point of the cruise may be adjusted upward. Lower categories may be closed to avoid overselling the lower categories of the ship. Lower yielding price programs may be closed.

In an environment of weak demand, pricing is often used to stimulate demand. Price adjustments can take several forms:

Mild

Taking guarantees—This allows the line to ease pricing by selling unspecified higher cost inventory, if available, at lower prices.

Giving upgrades—This specifies a level of higher-priced inventory that will be sold at a lower price—for example, selling a category six stateroom at a category four rate—a two-category upgrade.

Adjusting the minimum rate—This applies to air/sea booking where the minimum stateroom rate available is a function of the cost of the round-trip air component. The normal minimum category might be category six for the Seattle market traveling to San Juan. If required, the category could be lowered to five or four to stimulate demand from that market (with many lines offering one hundred air/sea cities or more, obviously, a varying number of cities could be adjusted.

Moderate

Adjusting the level of the advance purchase discount rate—All advance purchase programs have stair-step price increments built into them that allow the line to reduce the discount (raise the rate—improve the yield) as demand warrants. In theory, once a new discount level is established, the line is not supposed to go back and lower it again. Under most circumstances, this is the case, but occasionally, lines misguess demand and the rates are adjusted down again (this is considered severe), causing a certain amount of disruption among agents and clients who booked earlier at a now higher rate. These guests either need to be protected at the new, lower rate or be upgraded to better accommodations. In any event, once the new discount level is established, changing the pricing structure, all the mild price manipulations can then be applied to the new base.

Market-specific deals—Discussed earlier, these programs, while severely discounting price in specific local markets, don't cause much of an effect on the overall market.

Severe

Best available stateroom—This is a first-come, first-served program that is based on one flat attractive price. The problem is the best staterooms sell first, giving the biggest savings to those who act quickly. But the line has to set the price low enough that the lesser accommodations also appear attractively priced, or the ship won't fill. Consequently, this type of program usually is a desperation, close-in move as it tends to reduce yield (on the better inventory) too drastically. A variation, without this difficulty, is a two-rate (inside, ocean view) best available program. On the other hand, the two-rate version has significantly less sex appeal in the newspaper.

Two-for-one—This is a sure way to stimulate demand, but the line has to content itself with no more than 50 percent of brochure tariff. It could be even worse, as all mild manipulations can be applied with this program if the sailing was a dog!

Lowering or eliminating air add-ons—Some advance purchase programs separately price the air component based on specific markets or regular zones. Reducing or eliminating the air add-ons,
which were a significant component of the initial (and, in theory,
the lowest) price, is a pretty severe action when done nationally,
but it is moderate when done in local markets, regionally, or for
specific groups, such as senior citizens.

Stand by fares—These are deeply discounted cruise-only rates that
are typically available within thirty days of departure. They tend
to be promoted in the local drive market, perhaps within 300 miles
from the port of embarkation.

Some cruise lines also capture spill data (or turndown demand) to understand patterns of behavior of those guests who called but did not actually make a booking. The combination of information about guests who did
book and guests who made inquiries but did not actually make a booking
helps understand the effectiveness of the pricing in the marketplace at any
given point. This information is modeled into some of the following:

Retention—This is a model that predicts which guests that book will
actually survive, or sail. The cruise lines use this to understand exactly how much and what type of inventory they have left to sell at
any point. Exhibit 8.2 shows the variability in the materialization
rate of the groups that are requested initially.

Booking profiles—This is a model that looks at the shape of the booking curve for a sailing. This model is then reviewed, and pricing action is often taken based on whether a sailing is ahead or behind
the curve. In Exhibit 8.3, the sailing is ahead of profile early on,
and prices should be raised accordingly.

Demand forecast—As previously mentioned, the demand forecast
predicts how much demand is remaining between that point and
departure. The demand forecast is used as an input to various
models.

Price elasticity—This model evaluates how sensitive the pricing is to
changes in demand. A price elasticity model suggests changes to

EXHIBIT 8.2 Number of Projected Cabins at Materialization

Departure Month	Group Offers	Sailing	Rate
January	2,000	500	25%
April	1,600	320	20%
July	1,200	180	15%
September	2,500	750	30%

EXHIBIT 8.3 **Sample: Booking Profile**

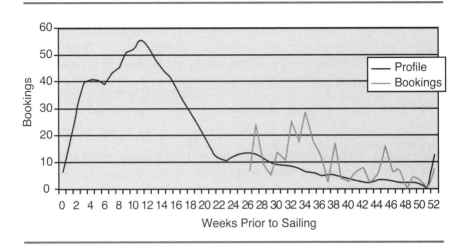

price points based on what the change in demand is likely to be. Exhibit 8.4 shows the expected bookings across various price points. When actual bookings vary versus the expected pace, the likelihood of consumers to buy at that price point may have shifted, and price points should be adjusted accordingly.

EXHIBIT 8.4 **Sample: Price Elasticity Model**

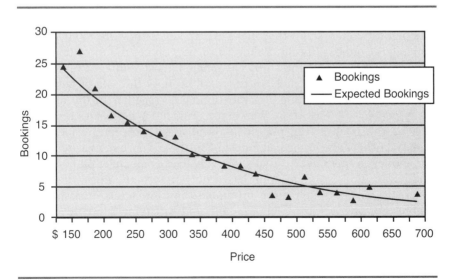

While ticket revenue is the lion's share of the revenue generated on a sailing, a sizable amount of revenue comes from the onboard spend. Hence, cruise lines are motivated to fill each and every cabin to maximize their total revenue per berth per voyage. Some lines have developed online pre-booking systems to provide their guests an opportunity to reserve some of their onboard activities, such as shore excursions and spa appointments in advance.

Whether demand is strong or weak, each decision to change a price and the amplitude of the change is critical to maximizing yield. As an extreme example, a few years ago one line faced a critical lack of demand in the spring for its upcoming fall season. The line selected a rate scale it thought would fill its ship and offered it to travel agents for both groups and individuals. The ship was sold out by early summer. However, the groups materialized faster and in far higher numbers than anticipated (because of the low rate), and the ship was actually well over sold by early fall. Obviously yield was not maximized, costing the line many hundreds of thousands of dollars in profit. A few senior managers left that company that fall to pursue other interests!

Onboard Revenue

Onboard revenue is key to the profitable operation of a ship and is thus a key element to the jobs of the hotel manager, the food and beverage director, the casino manager, and the cruise director. Look at it this way. If the marketing people have done their job, the ship is going to sail full. Everyone has already paid for their ticket. The only variable left that will determine the overall revenue (and, ultimately, the overall profitability) of a voyage is how much is spent on board. A number of factors determine how much money people will spend on board a ship, and successful operators understand that these are all key if they are to succeed in maximizing onboard profit. Believe it or not, one of the most important factor is the design of the ship. The single largest source of revenue on board most ships, especially in the Caribbean, is the sale of beverages. For some reason, drinking and vacationing go together in the minds of many people—at least those who enjoy cruising! Whether it's a piña colada by the pool, a rum punch in the disco, Cokes in the teen club, brandy in the show lounge, champagne at the caviar bar, or wine at dinner, money is spent every day by virtually every passenger on beverages. And because beverages are purchased duty free by the lines, the sale of beverages can be much more profitable than for hotels or restaurants ashore. So, one key to making money and satisfying guest needs on a cruise is simply to have a lot of beverages available in a lot of places and at all times. A second key is to make certain those places are not simply accessible but attractive and highly visible.

This is where ship design enters the picture. Good ship designs incorporate a lot of bars and serving stations. The idea is that you should be able to get a drink wherever and whenever you want it. Equally important, designers recognize that because the sale of drinks is as often an impulse buy as it is a planned purchase, bars must be situated in high-traffic areas. In a well-executed ship design, the most convenient way to go from your cabin to the dining room should take you past a lounge of some sort where you can stop for a cocktail before dinner or a drink afterwards. And because most ships sail in warm waters, you also need highly visible bars by the pool—or even in it! In fact, one can argue that there should be a bar everywhere! Some lines even station waiters near the library in case people want a drink while browsing. The key, of course, is to not make people feel that they are expected to buy a drink. We have heard passengers complain that on some ships you can't sit down anywhere "without someone trying to sell you a drink." Conversely, we've heard complaints that "there's no place around to get a drink." Remember, one of the main attractions of a cruise is that it is supposed to be pretty inclusive (and it is, when you consider the main components consisting of transportation, lodging, and food), and some passengers get turned off very quickly if they feel that an effort is being made to pry open their wallets or purses while on board. But the truth is, selling goes on all of the time all over the ship, as we will see, and it makes all the difference in the world to the bottom line.

In addition to beverages being readily available, it is equally important that there is an opportunity to consume them. Providing this on a cruise, where every hour is chock full of opportunities to do things from taking shore excursions to having a massage, is somewhat of an art. The artist, in this case, is the hotel manager, who, as we said earlier, orchestrates the vacation experience.

For example, let's take a close look at the first day of a seven-night cruise on the *Caribbean Princess* from Ft. Lauderdale to the Western Caribbean. Passengers for this cruise board the ship between 12:00 and 4:00 P.M. Sailing is at 5:00 P.M. They have arrived from all over the country. Some have traveled less then an hour from their Florida homes; others have been traveling all day from California or even Europe and South America. As soon as they have unpacked, they begin exploring this magnificent ship. Some are hungry and want to have lunch in the Horizon Court, where bar staff are readily available. Others immediately change into their swimsuits and start on their long-awaited suntan. It doesn't matter. The Outrigger and Blackbeard's pool bars open at noon and stay open until 10:00 P.M. and 8:00 P.M. respectively, while the Calypso Pool, home to "Movies Under the Stars," stays open until 2:00 A.M. The Lobby Bar opens at noon and remains open until 11:00 P.M. Crooner's Lounge, with a menu of fifty specialty martinis, stays open until 1:00 A.M.—around two hours after the last show is presented on the ship that evening. Then there is the Explorer's Lounge, which opens at 6:00 P.M. for the children's club registration, followed by a Welcome Aboard Dance party at 9:15. The Explorer's Lounge closes after the screening of an 11:15 movie. The intimate Churchill Lounge, a cigar and cognac bar, is open from 6:00 P.M. to midnight. The Sterling Steakhouse bar is also open from 6:00 P.M. to midnight. The Grand Casino opens thirty minutes after sailing, and although drinks are available there during gaming hours, there must be a place for winners to celebrate and losers to commiserate. There is the Princess trademark Wheelhouse Bar, which opens at 5:00 P.M. (for a before-dinner rendezvous) and stays open for easy listening and dancing music until 1:00 A.M. Club Fusion, a multifunction entertainment venue, opens from 7:15 to 9:15 P.M. for an introduction by the club's DJ and live music. Between 9:15 and 11:30, Club Fusion becomes the venue for a trivia challenge and bingo, followed by round one of *Princess Pop Star* (the Princess version of the hit TV reality show *American Idol*). From 11:30 until closing, Club Fusion hosts a "Dancing Through the Decades" dance party featuring a drink special called "the Pajama Slammer." Following a brief teen gathering, Skywalkers Nightclub opens at 10:00 P.M. for guests age eighteen and over to party into the early morning. The only time there are no bars open that first day is between 4:00 and 4:30 P.M., when everyone is required to attend a lifeboat drill. The lifeboat drill precedes the "Ja'maican Me Crazy Sailaway Party" at the Neptune's Reef Pool. There is, as you might expect, a "Ja'maican Me Crazy Rum Punch" drink special. In a souvenir glass, one of these babies can cost mucho dollars.

While the bars are the biggest source of onboard revenue, they are hardly the only source. When you board just about any cruise, the ship's photographer is at the gangplank to take a picture of the start of your vacation. He or she will photograph you at least two or three more times before you leave the ship. Everyone is photographed shaking hands with the captain at his reception when they're dressed to the hilt and thus look their best (often in a rented tuxedo, which is another source of onboard revenue). Then there's the picture taken of all the passengers at every dining room table. Coming down the gangplank is another photo opportunity—next to a prop such as a sign signifying where you are ("Look, Mom! This is us getting off the ship at Cozumel!"). When you buy the pictures in the photo gallery, which is usually posted in another prominent high-traffic area (outside the dining room where people line up before dinner is one popular venue), you'll pay somewhere between $7 and $20, depending on the size and the number of photos you purchase.

Assume a ship carrying 2,400 passengers sells only 2,400 photos, or one per person per trip. Using the $7 minimum figure, you can see that the revenue from those photos would be $16,800. If the ship is in service fifty weeks of the year doing two cruises a week (a three-day and a four-day), that's $1,680,000 in photos alone. On seven-day cruises, it is more likely passengers will buy more than one photo. In reality, these photos cost only a few cents to take and develop using the digital processing equipment on board. Many ships will also sell a video of your cruise vacation. If you sign up for one, they're able to ensure you will be one of the featured players. It's a popular item priced around $30 on most ships—sell another 200 video sales to every cruise, and it adds up!

In recent years, portrait photos have become an enormously popular item. Ships provide various professional backdrops that might range from fun-loving costumed Old West scenes to regal, elegant palaces. Folks love the convenience of having portraits sat for in only a few minutes on board versus the hours it takes to schedule the family portrait on land.

Then there's the casino. It's a myth that the casino is the biggest moneymaker on the ship. As we've already pointed out, on most ships the beverages do better. Typically, only about 30 percent of the passengers gamble at all—the rest watch. In truth, most people do not take a cruise to gamble. The casino is not open twenty-four hours a day—or at all, when the ship is in port—and thus gambling opportunities are limited. Rather, the casino is regarded as yet another diversion the ship offers along with shopping, partying, dining, sightseeing, and a host of other activities. For the most part, those who do gamble spend around $10 a day, though a few cruise lines offer high-roller programs that attract some of the big spenders (more about that later). From an operator's point of view, running a casino aboard a cruise line presents different problems than on land. For instance, if someone is suspected of cheating on land, they are simply asked to leave. But on a cruise ship, the suspect is a paying guest and must be handled in a different manner. Because table gaming is a first-time experience for many cruisers and some genuinely don't understand the rules, casinos on cruise ships tend to be more flexible and user-friendly than on land, where everything is black or white. If a passenger loses $5 because he didn't understand how to bet, some dealers are more apt to return it to them than they would be on land. Shipboard dealers, incidentally, usually gain their experience on shore; they are rarely trained on board. Their typical compensation, salary and tips, ranges from $1,500 to $3,000 per month, plus room, board, and medical expenses. They receive about ten weeks off each year.

For those who are put off by slot machines and blackjack, there are other gaming opportunities if they just want the thrill of betting on something. Carnival, for instance, runs bingo games with minimum jackpots of $600 and $700 on its three-day cruises to Nassau, horse racing, a daily lottery where participants can win as much as $50,000, and a Scratch and Match game where winning tickets are worth up to $1,000.

Shopping is another important source of on board revenue. Studies show that many people rank the quality of their vacation experience by the number and variety of shopping opportunities. The cruise lines have responded accordingly. Shops are not open in the ports of call because local governments insist visitors patronize local shops rather than shipboard shops. It's not difficult to understand why. One study of cruise passengers made by Bermuda showed the average cruise passenger spent $90 on shore while the ship was in port! But at sea, shops are big business, and their prices on items like liquor and perfume are competitive with those of the merchants of the ports that they visit. Onboard shopping has become much more sophisticated over the years. In addition to t-shirts, swimsuits, and the like, shipboard retailers can offer expensive watches, fine diamonds and jewelry, and Louis XIII cognac at $1,300 per bottle!

The cruise lines have learned, incidentally, that there's no need to give up all of the revenue their passengers spend in port. Most lines allow local merchants to promote their shops on board the ship. This is usually done by the cruise director in his or her port orientation talk, where guests are told about the tours that are available, where to eat and shop, and suggested good buys. Sometimes so-called super shoppers are employed to talk up the participating shops. Some lines show samples of participating shops' merchandise or stage fashion shows. Other lines include advertisers in a shopping video tour they show before the ship reaches port. Where local shops are promoted by the ships, a customer satisfaction guarantee by the line usually accompanies the merchandise. In any case, the cruise line charges a promotional fee to the shops that choose to participate in these promotions. A note of caution to cruisers: In many ports, stores that are not part of the ship's official program promote themselves by handing out flyers on the pier—often featuring "lucky cabin number" gifts. Supposedly passengers who occupy certain cabins and show up at these shops receive special prizes. Unfortunately, these are frequently not legitimate; unscrupulous merchants in some ports post numbers of cabins that don't exist or that they know to be unoccupied!

Another popular source of revenue is the beauty salon and spa, where passengers can get massages, mud baths, facials, hairstyling, and more. A vacation is a renewal experience, and what better way to renew yourself than to change your hairstyle, have a facial, and perhaps enjoy a massage or herbal wrap. As with land-based spas and resorts, you can easily spend $200 in half a day at sea in a modern spa, and the available time and convenience makes it an almost irresistible buy for many. Often the massage appointments for a seven-day cruise are fully subscribed by the second day out!

Shore excursions are one of the most popular parts of any cruise and can be extremely profitable to the line. Indeed, Why? Because the revenue produced by the shore excursions on some lines frequently exceeds the bar revenue. In Alaska, for example, cruises offer helicopter trips where you can land and walk on a glacier or fly into remote fishing lodges for the day for $240 or more per person. The profits on these items are enhanced when cruise lines own some of the infrastructure (such as lodges, hotels, buses, rail cars, and day boats) needed to offer the tours. Holland America and Princess are two notable examples of this. Not unreasonably, people are often fearful of exploring a new place on their own, especially if they do not speak the language. The success of shore excursions, however, has everything to do with the ports of call and the tours that local operators have been able to develop.

Alaska, on the other hand, is primarily a sightseeing destination where people go to see wildlife and nature's last frontier. These sights cannot be easily sampled by simply strolling around Skagway or Juneau. In Juneau, Princess, which calls its shore excursions "Adventures Ashore," offers a three-hour raft trip down the Mendenhall River (including some mild rapids and a stop for a salmon snack) for $112 ($75 for children ages six to twelve); a three-hour tour, including a fifty-minute floatplane ride to Taku Glacier Lodge, where passengers are offered a traditional alderwood fire salmon bake, including all the wine and beer you can drink for $249 ($199 for children); a two-hour helicopter glacier tour for $240; and a five-hour sports fishing expedition for king salmon for $199. There are also nature hikes ($79); a salmon bake ($35); and a chance to pan for gold ($65). In Ketchikan, you can take a tour of the area on a Harley-Davidson motorcycle for $265, and in Skagway there's a three-hour ride aboard the historic White Pass Scenic Railway $100 ($50 for children).

In just about all cases, tours are run by local operators, not by the ships. In many ports, one or two operators have a monopoly, so passengers get exactly the same tour no matter whose ship they arrive on. Some lines do what they can to customize their tours. Seabourn, for instance, never fills its buses more than half full so everyone gets a window seat, sends a staff member in every bus with a cooler of complimentary drinks, and includes a complimentary refreshment stop as well where feasible. Sometimes when local operators have virtual monopolies, their guides may speak little or poor English, others are noncommunicative, and many might insist on stopping for half an hour at bogus factory outlets where the operator pockets commissions on everything sold to the passenger. The cruise lines have a difficult time controlling this unless they're willing to pay extra or threaten to pull their lucrative business or even change ports of call. Jamaica, Italy, and China are notorious for these practices, but they can be found almost everywhere. Local governments can do a good deal through regulation to control these abuses. To their credit, some destinations, such as Bermuda, where the Department of Tourism has extraordinary power, have been able to do just that.

At sunset, for the ultimate tour, take a Seabourn Eastern Mediterranean cruise and book an "Exclusively Seabourn" experience such as an evening in ancient Ephesus (complimentary to Seabourn guests). When the great archeological site of Ephesus is closed to the general public, Seabourn guests are met at the gates by "Ephesians" in period costume, bearing torches and cornucopias of fruit and flowers. As dusk descends over the surrounding ruins, the guests—just 200 in all— are led down the ancient roadway of marble slabs by torchlight. The dancing shadows weave a sort of timeless spell over the guests. Their own footsteps echo the ringing of Roman legions' sandals, when they escorted Anthony and Cleopatra along these same stones long ago. As Seabourn's guests approach the Library of Celsus, the site's most impressive and romantic ruin, the façade is lit, and a string quartet, seated among the columns, strikes up a classical air. The Ephesian hosts silently direct the guests to candlelit tables dressed with linens, where they enjoy an interlude of cocktails and canapés under a canopy of stars. In this fantasy setting, listening to the strains of the music, they are no doubt imagining what life was like when this long-dead city was one of the most vigorous and exciting capitals of antiquity.

One perhaps surprising source of revenue that has become popular is art auctions. For some reason, the idea of buying Picasso lithographs, Norman Rockwell prints, or original pieces by well-known artists such as Britto and Tarkay, or sports memorabilia featuring big names like Muhammad Ali and Pete Rose, appeals to people. Art auctions, actually a form of entertainment with a fair degree of excitement, do very well. One vessel on a major contemporary line we know of sold $3.5 million worth of art on a European cruise. Another contemporary line sold $2.2 million on a Caribbean cruise (these were both billed as art connoisseurs' cruises featuring special art inventory. A typical cruise today can easily achieve $100,000 or more in art sales. Interestingly, what guests pay for art and sports memorabilia comes out of the family household budget, not the vacation budget. In other words, the art auction revenue is largely incremental to the pot of onboard revenue rather than a migration of spending from casino, shops, shore tours, etc.

Of course, many people can't tear themselves completely away from home, and they need to call the kids (if they didn't bring them along) or the office to see if they still have a job. There's money to be made in that too. In the old days, you had to go to the radio room to place or receive a call. Now you can call home instantly from the phone in your stateroom via satellite. The cost for this service can run as high as $10 a minute! And every ship these days has an Internet café where guests can log in and connect to anyone in the world.

We called this chapter "Pieces of Eight"—the traditional term for the gold doubloons the Spanish treasure ships carried from the New World back to Spain. Today's modern cruise lines acquire pieces of eight in more ways than most cruisers probably realize. As we hope we've illustrated in this chapter, different cruise lines have differing approaches to pricing, yield management, and onboard revenue opportunities. Successful lines can bring 10 to 20 percent or more of revenue to the bottom line. Why the huge range in performance? You may draw your own conclusions. Ours? It's management, no more, no less.

Booking Passage

9

A fresh look at today's travel agent

Of all forms of travel and tourism sold within the United States and Canada, cruising relies most heavily on travel agencies as its distribution channel. Exhibit 9.1 shows the percentage of sales through travel agents for a variety of travel components.

Cruising's heavy reliance on travel agents is historical. Steamship passage was highly regulated by the steamship lines themselves through organizations such as the International Passenger Steamship Association (IPSA) and the Pacific Cruise Conference (PCC). These organizations, under the auspices of the Federal Maritime Commission (FMC), set tariff rates for passage, set commission rates for travel agents, and, importantly, appointed travel agencies. Without these appointments, a travel agency could not book a cruise or earn a commission. These organizations disappeared in the late 1970s as the character of the steamship business completed its transformation from transportation to cruising. Their descendent, the Cruise Lines International Association (CLIA), is principally an industry marketing organization, not a regulating body.

From these early times, the industry took some small amount of direct business, but usually surreptitiously. Agents would become irate if they felt cruise lines were bypassing them and dealing directly with consumers, whom they considered their clients. Probably the biggest bypass program occurred in the 1960s and early 1970s within the short cruise market in South Florida. Back then, the superintendents of service of the large resort hotels could be "influenced" to steer guests to two-, three-, and four-night cruises as either a divertissement from a one-month or longer hotel stay (common in those days) or as a quick getaway if the weather was cold or rainy. However, as the number of travel agencies grew dramatically and the heyday of the Miami Beach resort hotel waned, this practice quietly disappeared. All the while the strong fear of agency backlash over bypass activities was exhibiting a strong, almost negative

263

EXHIBIT 9.1   **U.S.–Canada Reliance on Travel Agencies**

Travel Component	% Units sold by Travel Agents
Cruising	80–85%
Domestic air	60%
International air	90%
Amtrak	40%
Tours	50-60%
Hotels	12%
Rental cars	55-60%
Attractions	*

*less than 1%

influence on cruise operators. After all, the prominent South Florida travel agents had their roots in the greater New York area (just as their clients did; the predominant South Florida visitor of the time was from the New York area). These agents, like their New York brothers and sisters, were the most vocal and aggressive in the country. They were active in the American Society of Travel Agents (ASTA), then and now the dominant travel agency organization, and had ready access to the trade press. It was not uncommon to see an article in *Travel Weekly* or *Travel Agent* featuring agents berating a particular cruise line for selling a ticket directly and thus bypassing their member agencies. These articles invariably produced stammering apologies from a mortified, sweaty-palmed cruise line executive, which would strike fear in the hearts of cruise industry executives everywhere. "There but for the grace of God go I," was their universal reaction. As a result, cruise lines were determined to work virtually exclusively with travel agents, and they entered into a marriage that lasted over thirty years, until the mid- to late 1990s. For most of that period, of course, supply and demand were more or less in sync, and both industries enjoyed unrivaled growth. It was both inappropriate and unwise to express dissatisfaction with the travel agent distribution system!

But the ominous signs of discontent began to be expressed openly in 1995. In March of that year, at a Seatrade conference in Miami, the executives of three prominent cruise lines suggested that if the current distribution system—travel agents—couldn't "get the job done" (presumably by filling their ships), then these lines would look to alternative means. The first line to do so was Renaissance, which did about 40 percent of its business directly with the consumer. Ed Rudner, its president, preferred direct consumer contact because of the greater knowledge of his reservations personnel. Renaissance operated a fleet of eight 100-passenger vessels deployed all over the world and noted for their flexible itineraries. Few travel agents were prepared to deal with the intricate questions a Renaissance customer was likely to ask. In Rudner's view, the average agent simply didn't possess the geographical or product knowledge to sell his product effectively. In fact, when travel agents did get involved, Renaissance sales personnel frequently had to spend significant time undoing the damage of inaccurate or misleading information given to the customer by well-meaning but ill-informed agents. In such situations, a good argument can be made that when the customer can do business directly with the cruise line and not through a third party, direct sales are simply less costly and more efficient.

Subsequently, Renaissance embarked on an enormous building spree, replacing their eight small ships with eight 680-passenger vessels. This nearly sixfold increase in capacity put an enormous strain on the company's direct marketing and sales resources, which simply could not fill the ships. In a dramatic reversal, the firm implored travel agents to sell their cruises through a multimillion-dollar trade advertising campaign. Agents rebuffed them, and the company failed in the fall of 2001.

But the travel agency landscape was changing. The airline commission caps were followed by a series of commission cuts and then, finally, the elimination of airline commissions, apart from prenegotiated market share–driven deals. Predictably, the number of brick-and-mortar agencies began to decline as the lack of automatic airline commissions forced many to close their doors, as they could not cover their overhead. Still more locations were bought up and consolidated. Shared marketing and back-office services kept many of these rolled-up agencies competitive and even thriving. It was a case of the survival of the fittest; the travel people in business tended to fail, while the business people in travel succeeded.

Most of the agents themselves, however, stayed in the industry, typically shifting to one of two other models: home-based agent or outside agent of a brick-and-mortar agency. In 1995, CLIA membership was 22,722 agencies, of which it's estimated that 2,613 were home-based. In 2005, CLIA agency membership was 16,549, of which 8,275 were home-based—a dramatic shift in composition. Over this same period or longer, Joel Abels, the publisher of *Travel Trade* and the creator of the semiannual Cruise-a-Thon cruise conference, asked his audiences how many were home-based. From a smattering of home-based agents in the late 1990s, today roughly 80 to 85 percent of his audiences (frequently over 1,000 attendees per conference) indicated they are home-based.

Over the near term, this transformation did not bode well for the cruise lines. At the same time the industry was taking on double-digit capacity increases, their distribution was in a state of flux. Cruise lines had no choice but to open up direct distribution channels. The late 1990s saw another change in distribution: the Internet. Mega travel sites like Expedia and Travelocity were churning out huge numbers of airline, hotel, and rental car sales as a growing number of Internet-savvy consumers booked online whenever they chose to, 24/7. Remember, most brick-and-mortar agencies are daytime businesses; some are open on Saturdays, and only a very few on Sundays—the day the travel industry chooses to spend most of its consumer newspaper advertising dollars! As more homes accessed the Internet (77.5 million households in 2005, based on Jupiter Research), online agencies took a larger and larger share of travel sales. Agencies large and small rushed to set up their own websites—tens of thousands of websites. And therein lies a problem: How does one go about the process of standing out from the Internet crowd? There are several ways, but they are expensive. One is to build a strong brand, as Travelocity, Orbitz, and Expedia have done. Another is to pay marketing fees to Yahoo, Google, Ask.com, and other search engines so that when a consumer enters a key word like "cruise" or "Caribbean," the agency web address will be displayed in the top x names. How small the x is depends on the price bid for the spot at that point. A third way a website drives high traffic is the result of internal communication within an audience. A client base of an agency is solicited by email or direct mail to access the website for attractive travel deals. One of the keys to this strategy is to obtain the email addresses of as much of the client base as possible. Those agencies that do this successfully are able to replace expensive, sometimes difficult-to-time direct mail with cheap, instantaneous email campaigns.

When we wrote the first edition of this book in 1995, most cruise lines (Renaissance excepted) were taking direct business under duress. We believed back then that the vast majority of consumers found it more convenient and economical to use the services of a travel agent, at least when booking a cruise. The rise of the Internet and the decline of travel agency retail outlets forced the cruise industry to regroup. While we suspect most lines were quietly beginning to take more direct business, starting in 1998, only Carnival was openly doing so. Carnival's theory was that if direct business was necessarily a viable channel in the future, why not be open and honest about it? The challenge was how to explain to the agent community their worst nightmare was actually okay and not really a threat. A daunting task indeed!

The linchpin of Carnival's dramatic new strategy, as well as the rationale for the travel agency community to accept the strategy, was the result of a 1996 CLIA consumer study. This study focused on resort vacationers. When asked why they hadn't cruised or considered cruising, a majority of these folks indicated they booked their land vacations directly with the properties and did not have a relationship with a travel agent. Some indicated they had used an agent in the past but felt mistreated and would not use one again. Remember, these were consumers who otherwise fit the profile of a cruise vacationer—they were spending roughly the same amount of money and time vacationing at resorts. These consumers went on to say they perceived their lack of a travel agent relationship as a major barrier to purchasing a cruise. After all, virtually all cruise line advertising back then—TV, magazine, newspaper direct mail, etc.—said, "See your friendly travel agent," or words to that effect.

Alarmed at the severe beating the agency community was taking by the airlines at the time, convinced the airlines' endgame was disintermediation, with the result a further economically damaged distribution system, and facing planned capacity increases that would more than double the annual cruise sales needed to fill its fleet, Carnival took the plunge.

TV commercials were modified to say, "See any travel agent or 1-800-Carnival." Note the substitution of "any" for "your" in deference to the CLIA study. In other words, if you (the consumer) don't have a travel agent, no worries—*any* agency can make your Carnival reservation. The same modified calls to action were incorporated in print ads and brochures. For the first time, a major cruise line was openly giving consumers a choice about how to purchase its product.

The risks of this strategy were enormous. Agent backlash could take many forms: nasty letters to the editors, booing at industry events, or, worst of all, a stop-sell of the line's cruises. Given these risks, certain rules of engagement were imperative:

◆ Carnival did not offer the consumer a better price than a travel agent could.
◆ The reservationists were instructed to ask, at the beginning of the phone call, if the customer had an agent. If there was an agent, the reservationists went ahead and took the booking but transferred it to the agency, with the agency earning its full sales commission, just as if it had closed the sale itself.
◆ At the end of the booking process, the reservation agent again asked if the customer had an agency and transferred as above.
◆ Finally, the reservationists instructed the customers that they could transfer the booking to an agent at any time up until final payment.

Carnival chose to openly discuss these procedures in the trade press, cruise conferences, and during question-and-answer sessions (Q&A) with travel agents during shipboard inaugurals (which occurred at least annually). In the beginning, the topic was clearly emotional. At one memorable inaugural Q&A onboard the *Paradise* in 1998, with perhaps 800 agents in attendance, an agent challenged the veracity of Carnival's stated policy concerning transferring direct bookings to agencies and protecting full commissions. In response, one of the Carnival executives asked the agents if any of them had actually received a call from Carnival, transferring a direct booking. At least fifty hands were raised, which offered clear testimony that Carnival's rules of engagement were being followed. There was plenty of trade press in the room, so the story received wide coverage. Agents realized they were being treated fairly.

Carnival took the opportunity to make the point that, in reality, no one owns the customer. The fact that a customer used Agency X for his last cruise booking does not in any way obligate him to use the same agency for his next vacation. In fact, during the first few years of the direct initiative, Carnival transferred bookings to agencies about 16 percent of the time. Half of Carnival's business was first-time cruisers, which meant, as a minimum, that two of three clients who had used a travel agent to book the previous cruise had opted not to renew with that agency. This was certainly ample evidence that the agent did not own the customer! On the other hand, it would be unfair and hugely disruptive if a cruise supplier chose to undercut its agency distribution by offering the consumer better prices than an agent could. This was done, ultimately unsuccessfully, by Renaissance, as cited earlier. Other travel suppliers—car rental agencies, airlines, hotels—utilize this strategy, but their products tend to be commodities, they're not as dependent on travel agents as cruising, and they don't operate with a goal of utilizing 100 percent of capacity. A cruise is an experience rather than a commodity, and because only 18 percent of the public truly understands cruising, cruise lines must rely heavily on knowledgeable travel agents to explain the product and close the sale.

The challenge was to open a direct channel while maintaining a robust, motivated, and productive agency channel. Unlike the ill-fated Renaissance scheme, the goal wasn't to eliminate the agency channel and replace it with the direct channel but rather augment the agency channel with the addition of a direct channel.

An irony is that full-service travel agencies were selling ten land packages for every cruise they sold—yet 88 percent of hotel business and 40 to 50 percent of land tour business was direct! No one offered a viable explanation for this double standard.

In 1996, one-quarter of 1 percent of Carnival's business was direct; by 1999, it was 3 percent; by 2002, it was 12 percent; and by 2005, it was north of 15 percent. While this is nowhere near the levels of our land-based competitors, it still is meaningful. Assuming a 15 percent mix of direct business in 2005, the absolute number of Carnival direct passengers would have been 450,000. One could argue that some of these guests would have sailed anyway. On the other hand, based on the CLIA research cited above, we know that many vacationers prefer not to use a travel agent, so a considerable number of these direct consumers must be incremental. If we assume an arbitrary 50 percent incremental rate, that means 225,000 folks found their way to a Carnival cruise who would not have without a direct channel. If one assumes a 13 percent direct mix for the industry in 2005 and the same 50 percent incrementally, the result is 624,000 cruise vacationers, or 6.5 percent of the industry's total carrying capacity. Using our assumption that the industry generated 35 percent first-timers in 2005, then the direct channel accounted for about one out of every five first-time cruisers. These first-timers, as we know, create an annuity for the cruise industry. Research indicates that 80 percent will return again and again. Curiously, the agency channel will also be a beneficiary of this phenomenon, as some of these cruisers will be exposed to the special pricing some cruise lines give their preferred agencies as well as to the lower prices (through rebates) many agencies provide. Cruise passengers do have a tendency to compare prices.

The other challenge, and certainly the most critical one, is to maintain a robust agency channel. Exhibit 9.2 shows the growth of the cruise industry and the estimated channel share between 1995 and 2005. The table indicates that the agency channel was, in fact, robust and growing during this time frame despite the enormous upheavals it was experiencing. Because the channel was growing as a result of huge increments of added capacity, the cruise industry's direct initiatives quickly became a non-issue. There was plenty of business to go around.

EXHIBIT 9.2   **Sourcing of North American Passengers (000s)**

	1995	2005
Total Passengers Carried	4,223	9,672
%Direct*	5%	15%
%Travel Agency Sourced	95	85
Total Direct		
Total Travel Agency Sourced	4,012	8,221

Memo: agency growth 2005 versus 1995 = 105%
*Authors' Estimate

As an aside, the competitive reaction to Carnival's direct initiative was interesting, to say the least. The other lines were fully content to have Carnival front and center—and alone—on this issue. They appeared happy to have Carnival solely in the crosshairs of any agency backlash. Some lines tried to foment agent ire by bringing up the direct initiative in a disparaging way during travel agency sales calls. None-too-subtle comparisons were drawn between the Carnival initiative and the Renaissance debacle. Reports of these activities filtered back to Carnival as a result of most agents' innate sense of fair play: Agents generally don't appreciate it when a supplier knocks another during a sales call, when the "knockee" is not there to defend himself.

By monitoring competitors' help-wanted ads and other industry intelligence, Carnival noticed that other lines were quietly beginning to place resources against the direct channel. Beginning in 2000, Carnival challenged the other lines to come out of the closet and concede they were taking direct business. This process took several years, but finally, by 2004, all the major lines were openly pursuing direct channels. All were essentially employing the rules of engagement Carnival had been using. With this level playing field, there was little, if any, agency carping. Occasionally, an agent would complain in an Internet chat room that a line had undercut his price and "stolen" his customer. The vast majority of the time, a research of the booking records indicated this was not the case. Frequently it turned out the consumer misrepresented the cruise line price in an attempt to get an even better price from the agent.

In 2000, Carnival began an outbound telemarketing initiative. A staff of personal vacation planners (or PVPs, as they are known) work through leads generated by folks registering on the Carnival.com website or from consumers who had called the 800-Carnival direct line but who had not made a reservation.

PVPs are highly trained salespeople who receive the largest part of their compensation in the form of incentives for sales performance. This group is the antithesis of the order-taking model. They have to be proactive and make "dials" (outgoing phone calls) to build their book of business. These folks are trained and encouraged to have great personal relationships with their customers and to develop a deep understanding of the prospect's recipe for his or her vacation. They are supported by a sophisticated Customer Relationship Management (CRM) software system that facilitates keeping track of their customers.

Carnival officials give tours of "PVPland" when requested by travel agents, who invariably are impressed with the operation. There is no pride of authorship here; Carnival encourages agents to emulate the proven techniques employed by the PVPs. Not every PVP recruit has what it takes to be successful in this self-starting sales environment.

When that happens, there's a sort of natural selection, as marginal employees simply don't find the work sufficiently lucrative. This scenario is typical of car or real estate sales; if sellers don't produce, they quickly find another line of work.

Full-Service Agency

The full-service agency is still the most productive segment of the agency business. The average mix of business is shown in Exhibit 9.3. As you can see, with only 10 percent of sales revenue, selling cruises is far less important to the typical full-service agent than the agent is to the cruise industry. This is even more bizarre when you consider the mix of business and leisure travel shown in Exhibit 9.4.

This is the classic way of looking at an agency's business. Fully half the business is commercial or corporate in nature. A business account is signed by the agency and then serviced indefinitely or until the account is lost to bankruptcy or another agency, or the corporate client goes direct. The other half of the business is something called *leisure*. When pressed for an explanation of the term, most agents say, "You know, everything that's not commercial." While the logic is unassailable, it's nonetheless not terribly revealing. A more telling breakdown is shown in Exhibit 9.5.

In this breakout, while commercial business is unchanged, the leisure breakout is discarded altogether. The second-largest component is VFR business. Again, this is a service aspect of the business, just like the commercial business. It can't be sold or initiated by the agency. Rather, the agency passively waits for an order. If business is slow in August, let's say, the agency owner or manager can't call up the vice president of sales of

Exhibit 9.3 Average Agency Sales Mix

Component	% of Sales Revenue
Domestic Airlines	50%
International Airlines	10%
Rental Cars	7%
Hotels	11%
Tour Packages	8%
Cruises	105
Other	4%
Total	100%

EXHIBIT 9.4   **Average Full-Service Agency**

Component	% of Business Revenue
Commercial	50%
Leisure	50%
Total	100%

a corporate account and suggest he set up a sales meeting in some far-away place, with the agency handling all the travel arrangements. By the same token, the agency can't stimulate VFR business by suggesting that a client visit her mother-in-law in Minneapolis or his fraternity brother in Bismarck, North Dakota. Putting it bluntly, at least 80 percent of an average full-service agency's revenue is order taking. And while it's 80 percent of the revenue, it's a full 95 percent of its transactions due to both the low average cost for airline tickets, hotels, and rental cars and the high degree of canceled, rewritten, or double-booked commercial and VFR business.

The other 20 percent is retail vacation sales: tour packages, cruises, and Foreign Independent Tour (FIT) vacation arrangements. FIT business occurs when the agent bundles together travel components such as air, hotel, and rental car for a customized itinerary for the consumer. This portion of the business—5 percent of the total business on a transactions basis—at least can be created (sold) rather than simply taken as an order when someone walks in or calls. Why? Because these kinds of vacations, unlike visiting friends and relatives, are purely discretionary. Furthermore, the majority of prospects for a vacation have only a general notion of what they want to do or where they want to go. In a study by *Travel Weekly*, agents responded that 68 percent of their leisure clients

EXHIBIT 9.5   **Average Agency Location**

Component	% of Sales Volume
Commercial	50%
VFR (visiting friends and relatives)	30%
Vacation Sales	20%
Total	100%

asked their advice on hotels, 66 percent on package tours, and 56 percent on destinations! As discussed in the chapter on pricing, prospects have an even hazier concept of the cost of vacation alternatives. As a result, with the exception of an agency's ability to sign additional corporate business, a vacation sale is the one area of a full-service agency's business where the opportunity and the means exist to proactively generate new sales revenue.

That vacation sales account for only 5 percent of an agency's transactions should be disquieting, especially when you consider that most travel agents believe they are overworked and underpaid. A survey conducted in 2004 by *Travel Counselor* magazine (the official publication of the Institute of Certified Travel Agents) revealed that the average frontline agent was making only $27,320 per year, the average manager $38,230, and the average owner $41,710. We also know that most agents, when asked, say they are able to close only one retail vacation sale for every ten prospects that call on the telephone or walk in to inquire about a vacation. This low percentage of completed sales suggests the vast majority of the few successful encounters are, in fact, order-taking scenarios rather than the result of effective selling. But, when you think about it, this should be no surprise; after all, 95 percent of their business *is* order taking, isn't it?

The low closure rate also helps explain that 80 percent of the total vacation business bypasses travel agents entirely. That's because most of this business goes directly to hotels and resorts, as vacationers prefer to make their own reservations rather than suffer the frustration of dealing with ill-equipped travel agents.

Let's look at it another way. If nine vacation prospects leave the first agency they call on empty-handed, do they all immediately rush to a second agency? If they do, and it makes one sale, what about the unfulfilled eight? Do they go to a third agency, and then a fourth? At some point, frustrated that they can't get what they want, do they go directly to the supplier, or do they give up on the vacation altogether and spend the money on a new home theater, a dining room set, or jewelry? Do they trade in their car a year earlier than planned? After all, a vacation is a discretionary purchase, which from the point of view of travel sellers makes it a tougher industry to compete in than, say, the pharmaceutical business, where the product is not a matter of choice. Intuitively, then, some meaningful percentage of vacation sales, including (guess what?) cruise sales, are lost each year because too many travel agents don't know how or don't want to sell. They prefer to see themselves as professional travel counselors (note the name of their magazine), and counselors don't sell, they advise. Those who haven't yet reached the status of counselor in their own psyche (because they don't know enough) are simply order takers, ticket printers, or reservation clerks.

There is a certain irony here. You see, travel agents started in business in the nineteenth century to sell vacations. The first well-known travel agent was Thomas Cook. In the mid-1850s, Cook recognized that with the emergence of railroads and steamships there was a need for someone willing to make arrangements for people who wished to explore England and the Continent but were nervous about traveling on their own to foreign places. Soon Cook had established himself as a sales agent for these new and convenient forms of transportation, and in 1856 he offered his first Grand Tour of Europe. About the same time (1850), the American Express Company was formed in the United States. Originally formed with the purpose of shipping merchandise and money across America and then to Europe, the company soon grew to the point where it also offered travelers checks and dispensed travel information on foreign destinations. By 1920, there was a host of travel sellers in the United States and Great Britain. These agencies formulated elaborate FIT vacation itineraries, domestically and worldwide, and sold them to people in the community. Often a few couples or an even larger group would sign up. When this occurred, the agent would personally escort the group, acting as a tour guide. When Thomas Cook, who was a Baptist preacher, organized his very first trip in 1841, it was a railroad tour of 570 persons from Leicester to Loughborough, England, who he personally escorted to a temperance meeting!

With the new travel services, affluent local doctors, businesspeople, writers, and others with the means to travel had access to a world with which they were totally unfamiliar except through the writings of Marco Polo, Rudyard Kipling, Lord Byron, and Mark Twain, among others. Those were far less mobile times. People lived and died without traveling more than a few miles away from their birthplace. For the local jeweler, for example, to return to Kansas City and recite to his family, friends, neighbors, and business associates tales of personal experiences traveling along the Appian Way, where noble Romans had set out in chariots to conquer the world and early Christians had fled into the catacombs, visiting Montmartre in Paris and climbing the domed Basilica of Sacre-Coeur in the steps of Renoir and Toulouse-Lautrec, or traveling to Egypt and sitting in the moonlight staring at the Sphinx, with her great lion paws, this was heady stuff indeed, and conferred upon him a certain cachet. The local travel agent, who was himself a mysterious font of information, made all of this possible.

Horses, railroads, and steamships were the only forms of transportation until the automobile was introduced by the French in 1890, when Leon Serpollet, the inventor of the instantaneous steam generator, mounted one of his engines on a tricycle and drove it 295 miles from Paris to Lyon. At the same time, steam-powered road vehicles of various designs were being built in the United States. In Lansing, Michigan,

Ransom E. Olds built one of the earliest models in 1891, which he sold for $400 to a London patent medicine firm for use in its branch in Bombay, India.[1] It was Henry Ford who first realized that if an inexpensive car could be built, everyone would want one. In 1908, he introduced the Model T runabout—a 20-horsepower, 1,200-pound car—priced at $825. By 1916, using the assembly line to mass-produce cars, he was able to get the price down to $345. Cars completely changed the way people lived. Small, self-reliant agricultural communities lost many of their businesses and opened new ones that were dependent on tourists. Touring and sightseeing became increasingly popular as more Americans acquired cars. There were no places to stay, however, which naturally led to the growth of hotels and resorts.

The end of the World War I marked the beginning of commercial aviation on both sides of the Atlantic. The impetus was the experience gained in flying planes during the war and the number of trained pilots and mechanics available to exploit this new form of transportation. The air age got a tremendous boost when a young stunt flyer named Charles Lindbergh, whose act of standing on the top wing of a looping plane thrilled crowds all over the country, decided to compete for a prize of $25,000 offered to the first person to fly solo across the Atlantic Ocean. At 7:55 A.M. on 20 May 1927, Lindbergh took off from Roosevelt Field on Long Island, New York, and landed at Le Bourget in Paris thirty-three hours and thirty-nine minutes later. Lindbergh proved the airplane was a practical means of traveling long distances. As a result, investors who had been hesitant to put money into this new form of transportation lined up to back commercial aviation.

Also in 1927, a young World War I pilot, Juan Trippe, founded Pan American Airlines with a mail contract from the United States government to fly between Key West, Florida, and Havana, Cuba. The DC3, the first popular passenger airplane, was introduced in 1936. In 1958, Boeing introduced the 707, and the jet age was born. The plane went into service the following year on Pan Am's New York–Paris route. This new, fast transatlantic service was a huge stimulus to both the tourist and business travel markets and sounded the death knell of the steamship transportation business. In a strange twist of fate, the offspring of that very same steamship business helps sustain much of today's airline business. Carnival Cruise Lines alone buys over $120 million in airline tickets each year!

The phenomenal airline industry growth changed the nature of the travel agency business. When the first pure jets began operating in 1958, there were fewer than 4,500 agency locations in the United States. On 24

---

[1]James J. Flink, *The Automobile Age* (Cambridge, Mass.: MIT Press, 1992).

October 1978, when President Jimmy Carter signed into law the Airline Deregulation Act, there were 14,800 travel agency locations, an increase of 200 percent. In 1995, there were 32,100 full-service agencies. Today (2006) the number has shrunk to 22,043. Capping, cutting, and finally eliminating airline commissions took a dramatic toll.

Domestic airline passenger miles grew from 25 billion in 1958 to 391 billion in 1995, an increase of almost fifteen fold. At the same time, the airline industry shifted the bulk of its distribution from city ticket offices and direct phone reservations to travel agencies. In 1958, agents represented only about 20 percent of the domestic airline business; in 1995, the comparable figure was 82 percent. As a result of deregulation in 1978, airlines were free to change whatever they wanted—fares were no longer regulated. This led to a plethora of complex fares and complicated fare restrictions. It was simply cheaper for the airlines to have travel agents figure out the fare possibilities and explain it to the consumer than to do it themselves. The consumer viewed the travel agent more and more as his advocate in the battle to obtain the lowest possible fares, while the airlines were perceived, and rightly so, as wanting to maximize yields and thus trying to sell tickets at the highest possible fares.

While data on the second factor, the increased availability and accessibility of travel perks for travel agents, are largely anecdotal, it's clear to many industry observers (including both of us) that 75 percent reduced fare agent airline discounts (A.D. 75s), free or reduced rates for hotels, rental cars, tours, and cruises (even totally free familiarization trips) served as a huge magnet for folks to get into the travel agency business. It was an especially attractive career for people who already perceived themselves as having an abiding love of travel. In fact, love of travel and seeing new places is still cited most frequently as the primary reason for entering the travel agency business.

Airlines, hotels, tour operators, cruise lines, and other travel suppliers reason that if their properties had unused capacity (which they all did at some time or other), why not offer it to travel agents so they would become not only knowledgeable about the specific features and benefits of the product but also, perhaps, throw in a little beholding—wherein agents who had been hosted would make a special effort to steer business to the property to pay back for the gesture of generosity. Sales representatives of these travel suppliers hear this every day. "I can't sell product *x* if I haven't seen it," the agent explains as her reason for not having booked any business on product *x*. Sales representatives, hungry to grow their territory's business, succumb with great frequency to this siren song, hoping new business will materialize. After all, there is some logic to this. First-hand product knowledge gives the agent the comfort and assurance that a product is what it is, irrespective of the sometimes disingenuous prose of a sales brochure.

More often than not, agent experience makes no difference at all, especially given the order-taking mindset. Even worse are the few agents who are simply looking for a freebie—that's why they went in the business in the first place. We know, because both of us have encountered travel agents we have hosted on cruises and destination familiarization trips who separate themselves from the group to go shopping or sightseeing on their own and miss what it is we have invited them there to learn about. Nevertheless, human nature is fundamentally optimistic, especially among sales reps and sales executives of travel suppliers desperate to grow their businesses and fill idle capacity. There's also, of course, an unspoken competitive force at work here as well: If I can lure Mary Smith of Mary's Travel to vacation with my product, she won't have time to see what my competitor is offering.

Even though familiarization trips can be nice, still, the monetary compensation data gleaned from the survey of travel agents is somewhat discouraging to would-be and current agents. After all, who aspires to a career where the average pay is less than most college students receive in their first job? Nevertheless, it's not as bad as it may look at first glance. To begin with, no one aspires to be simply average. Motivated and skilled agents can and do bring home paychecks well above average. The top 5 percent of front-line agents earn more than $42,000, and some top the $100,000 level. In addition, there is always the perceived and real value of travel perks, which amount to nontaxable income for all practical purposes. These perks easily amount to $5,000, $10,000, or more of additional nonfinancial (and nontaxable) compensation per year, and thus it's not hard to understand why they are eagerly pursued!

Besides direct compensation, whether money or services, travel agents enjoy the additional benefit of seminars, trade shows, and the like. These can take the form of breakfasts, lunches, dinners, cocktail parties, weekend outings, and golf and other sporting events hosted by suppliers—you get the picture. In the larger metropolitan areas, agents can frequently have a difficult time deciding where to go because their options are so numerous. At a conservative value of just $50 per week, these additional, nontaxable "social and educational events" can amount to $2,600 per year. It's certainly true that travel agents in remote areas have far fewer opportunities of this nature, but agents have been known to drive two hours or more each way or even fly to attend a product seminar of one kind or another, and nearly all of them involve a meal. And the meals at some of these functions can be spectacular. We have attended British breakfasts with lavish portions of smoked salmon imported from Scotland, French luncheons (that took all afternoon) featuring a selection of the best wines in each region, and Italian dinners prepared by chefs flown in from Rome along with their ingredients! Often these are held at the best restaurants in town and sometimes in more exotic venues, like museums, after hours. They may be sponsored by airlines, tourism boards, cruise lines, or tour operators.

Suppliers, again, recognize the competitive nature of this process. If a Texas city's visitor and convention bureau trying to build its tourism business offers Tex-Mex tacos made with Velveeta cheese accompanied by Château Schmootz wine at an evening seminar, few, if any, agents will show up if on the same night the Swiss Tourist Bureau is serving fondue and the Bermuda Department is hosting a champagne and caviar reception featuring the Bermuda Regiment Marching Band followed by dinner and a drawing for a cruise to Bermuda. Moreover, if two suppliers offer dinners the same evening, the one that will draw the bigger attendance, everything else being equal, is the one with a track record of sit-down dinners versus stand-up buffets, or beef or veal versus mystery chicken. If both suppliers are known to offer comparable dinners, then other factors will determine which event will outdraw the other:

◆　Which venue (hotel, restaurant, or private club) has the best reputation or is the most exclusive.

◆　Which venue has the most central location, including commuting time from work.

◆　Which supplier will pick up parking costs (valet parking is a thoughtful touch).

◆　Which supplier gives away the most elaborate door prizes. These can range from a bottle of strange domestic champagne to a two-week cruise or two first-class airline tickets. One Caribbean country's tourist office gives a nice door prize to *everyone* in attendance! Needless to say, they draw consistently large audiences.

◆　Will there be entertainment? A Caribbean steel band is nice, but then, so is a Mexican mariachi band. "What, Aardvark airlines is featuring Neil Diamond? I'm in!"

◆　The personality of the supplier's sales representative. Will she or he be offended if I don't attend? Will that work against me the next time an elaborate familiarization trip comes up and the rep with a limited number of places is deciding who to invite? Is the rep gorgeous, handsome, single, well-off, affectionate? Would he recommend me for a position with the company?

◆　Finally, the tie-breaker question, among serious agents (and there are some), can actually come down to: "What are my chances of selling this product in my market?"

A few more points on this important topic: The supplier who offers Velveeta and bills it as a cocktail party will only fool the agents in a city one time. The next time, irrespective of how it's billed or what the invitation looks like, the number of attendees for the event can be hosted in a phone booth! The menu issue equally applies whether the meal is breakfast or lunch, not just dinner. A continental breakfast is a real yawn. Who wants to go anywhere for a cheese danish or toasted English muffin? Belgian waffles with strawberries or eggs benedict are much stronger draws. There are regional differences as well. Forget about serving coffee in Salt Lake City—the Mormons don't drink it. Don't offer anything less than a substantial breakfast in the Midwest—these folks have much healthier appetites than those on either coast. Bacon, eggs Benedict, sausage, and biscuits are mainstays, along with toast and danish. The notion of calories, fat grams, and any propaganda from the American Heart Association apparently have not reached the hinterlands—at least not when it comes to meals hosted by the travel and tourism industry.

A special perk for those lucky enough to be chosen is to be a member of the travel agent advisory board of a supplier. Not all suppliers have these, but those that do usually provide a sweet deal for the chosen few. Advisory boards meet quarterly or semiannually, generally over a two- or three-day period. A fine hotel, resort, or cruise ship makes an appropriate setting for the meeting. Accommodations are first class and totally complimentary, as are the round-trip airline tickets and transfers. All meals are on the house—and some suppliers even throw in the incidentals bill, which can include gift shop purchases! Along with a few days of wining and dining with the home office big shots and playing a few rounds of golf or sets of tennis thrown in for good measure, the serious business meeting is conducted. This usually starts with a presentation of an hour or two on how nifty the supplier has been in the past and will be even better, of course, in the future. Then the agents are urged to give their feedback and opinions on the supplier, competitors of the supplier, and any unusual market conditions or local occurrences. Travel agents approach this task in a variety of ways ranging from serious brown-nosing to the truth in such excruciating detail that the executives who invited them, cringing with embarrassment and with beads of perspiration on their brow, are wondering whose brilliant idea this advisory board was in the first place.

The fortunate agents, usually a dozen or two at the most, are typically selected for a two-year term to provide fresh input from the agent community. The objective of this input is questionable, of course. You cannot help but ask if the agents are so compromised by the process that they maintain any objectivity. Can a dozen or so randomly selected agents truly represent 250,000 agents' opinions? Probably not—it's not a legitimate sampling methodology by any stretch of the imagination. And, if a supplier truly wanted an opinion from travel agents, why not simply pick up the phone and call some? In reality, these boards allow the supplier to neutralize any turkeys in the agency community as well as spread the opulence by putting deserving agents on the gravy train. Be assured that the mere suggestion by a supplier's rep that an agent may be considered for the next advisory board opening will have that agent jumping through hoops—not only for two to four free boondoggles each year but for the prestige factor. Local market agent cocktail conversation is readily sprinkled with dropped lines such as: "Yes, Ethel and I just returned from Fantabulous Cruise Line's new ship launching in Monaco—Prince Albert was there—and then a few days in Paris at the George V. You do know I'm on their advisory board?"

A curious by-product of the advisory board process is the poor agent who has spent his term basking in the sun at Monte Carlo while tasting the Nouveau Beaujolais and is now off the board. A sort of postpartum depression sets in. Both the perks and the prestige have vanished. He is ordinary once again—just another lowly travel agent. Like Rodney Dangerfield, he gets no respect. Moreover, he no longer hobnobs with supplier biggies—the airline CEOs, the cruise line presidents, the tour operator owners. He finds he gets few calls, if any, from other advisory board agents. While not exactly ostracized, he may feel like a has-been. He has lost a big chunk of his identity. All is not lost, however. At this point of vulnerability, and with a little bit of luck, he can be easily revived by a competitive supplier who dangles a position on its advisory board. The word promptly goes out to the office staff. Forget about selling Abracadabra Cruises. They really weren't that good a product. Our new friends are Boondoggle Cruises, and we're going to push them as hard as we can. Ah, the charm of it all!

There can be no doubt that the domestic airline industry has molded and shaped full-service agencies. In order to open their doors, the owners must have received Airline Reporting Corporation (ARC) appointments. Without them, they cannot sell airline tickets. This involves negotiating through an elaborate set of requirements and procedures ranging from the employment of a manager with at least two years of ARC-appointed agency experience to a $20,000 bond/letter of credit and a safe. While most domestic airlines use e-tickets in lieu of ticket stock, a number of international carriers still use ticket stock. For those readers who aren't familiar with the system, the airlines view blank ticket stock as equivalent to real money. Once a name and a flight number are written on it, that ticket can be presented, and the owner is entitled to fly anywhere the ticket says. One first-class ticket to Europe is worth several thousand dollars. Now, when a travel agency collects those thousands of dollars, the airlines do not regard it as an ordinary account receivable. In other words, they don't wait to be notified that a ticket has been sold and then send out an invoice, hoping it will be paid promptly, like other businesses. They have a far more sophisticated system. An ARC-appointed agency has signed an agreement with ARC that requires them to submit weekly a list of tickets they have issued. ARC then deducts their commission from the total amount due and automatically withdraws from the agency's bank account the amount due to all of the airlines and distributes it to the carriers. Unlike other businesses, the agent has no float time so money from airline tickets that can be used to pay the rent or the electric bill. Nor do they have any time to earn interest on these funds, as they are paid out almost as soon as they are received. The airlines, of course, *do* get a float, as a ticket issued today may not be used for several weeks or even months. This is one more reason why it is so tough to make money in the agency business. It is also a reason why smart agents do not extend credit if they can help it. They have to pay for the ticket the same week it is issued, but a customer can easily take thirty days to pay them. With the advent of airline reservation automation in the mid-1970s, full-service agencies quickly invested in computerized reservations terminals (CRTs). With a computer on every desk, the agency even looked, let alone acted, like an airline reservations ticket office. Neophyte agents were schooled in Sabre, Apollo, Amadeus, or Worldspan—whichever airline system the agency utilized. This was and still is the primary training emphasis in a full-service agency—how to use that computer to reserve and issue airline tickets and boarding passes. Booking rental cars, hotels, tours and (sob!) cruises are all of secondary consideration.

How, then, does it happen that the agency distribution system—molded by the airlines almost in their likeness—has been able to support the cruise industry so admirably for twenty-five years—especially when cruise sales, like all other vacation purchases, seem like afterthoughts? There are several contributing factors.

First, as we have already made clear, the typical agent is primarily an order taker, second a counselor or advisor, and third, possibly a salesperson. When it comes to cruise sales, about 10,000 agency locations don't follow the norm. These are divided into three groups: vacation-oriented full-service agencies, cruise-only agencies, and home-based cruise and vacation agencies. The first, either for geographical reasons or, heaven forbid, because they like to make money, do a good job of selling vacations, including cruises. (When we're talking geography here, we mean the location of the agency.) Members of this group can be found in high-traffic urban locations, suburbs, or small towns folks simply *must* get away from—and have the money to do it. Midtown Manhattan, a suburban Chicago shopping mall, and Evansville, Indiana, are all examples. Then there are places like Leisure City, California, where everyone is retired and affluent and enjoys traveling. With the growth in homeport locations, agencies in places like Tampa, Jacksonville, Mobile, New Orleans, Houston, Galveston, San Diego, and Seattle have benefited from the huge opportunity afforded by having cruise ships sail right from their area.

Location isn't enough, usually, to ensure success. Agents must be inclined to sell vacations. They need front-of-the-house personalities, selling skills, and the desire to help people get in touch with their vacation needs. Trust us, while this seems reasonable and expected for someone in a front-line position in a retail store, it simply is not the norm in the travel agency business. Most agents don't know how to sell, as the data overwhelmingly demonstrate. Moreover, those agents who don't know how to sell have an almost universal apprehension of becoming a player in a selling scenario. More than anything they fear rejection, and as a result they are uncomfortable in any situation where they are likely to encounter it. Many, we think, would rather have their fingernails removed without the aid of anesthesia. To make matters worse, because of the reactive nature of order taking and the time needed to service commercial and VFR bookings, many of these agents view vacation prospects as unwanted intrusions. Carnival's mystery vacationer program had for many years sent back report after report from the field citing the all-too-common occurrence of agents either ignoring prospects or treating them less than civilly—as if the customer were somehow intruding on their workday. A prospect walks in, and agent Smith bends down to tie his loafers while agent Jones (with exceptional peripheral vision) subtly diverts her eyes into the gray-green glare of the CRT. Agent Black might look up with an annoyed "can't you see I'm busy?" look on his face. After all, this agent is busy reissuing a profitable $39 ticket to Las Vegas. As for the prospect? "Oh, he's just a shopper. He's really not interested in buying anything," they tell themselves. "He's just out to waste my time, and, after all, I *am* busy." And, of course, they *are* busy, but not necessarily making money for the agency. But then, does it matter? After all, these agents are typically paid on the basis of salary, with no thought to their contribution to the profit of the company. This concept is another distinguishing factor between the successful vacation sales agent and the average agent: The successful ones have a clear understanding that selling vacations is far more profitable than selling mere airline tickets. These agents don't just pay lip service to being in the travel agency business to make money; they are determined to, and do, make serious money by focusing on vacation sales and controlling their costs.

Probably the best example of this type of full-service agency is Liberty Travel, the sixth-largest travel agency in the United States. Privately owned, Liberty Travel comprises a chain of 200 agency locations in ten northeast states and Florida. The average Liberty agent is paid on a draw-against-commission basis; the manager, who also sells, works on a salary plus a percentage of the net operating profit of the store. Therefore, special attention is paid to directing business to the more profitable cruise lines and other preferred travel products that offer both higher levels of commission and high levels of customer satisfaction—the latter resulting in strong repeat business. Leisure travel accounts for 95 percent of Liberty's business. This strategy is enhanced with comprehensive sales training. Each Liberty seller undergoes a thorough sales training program before she ever deals with a customer.

The many other examples span a diverse collection of agencies. AAA Motor Club travel offices are a case in point. There are 1,003 locations scattered across the United States and Canada. While they all appear alike to consumers, they're actually split into about fifty separately run state and regional clubs with extraordinarily varying degrees of productivity. In fact, eight clubs account for 75 percent of AAA's total travel revenue.

In 1994, travel was elevated to the status of a core business within AAA, signaling to the clubs' CEOs that they needed to put as much emphasis on travel as they do on insurance, traveler's checks, and road service. In the last eleven years, the percentage of AAA members availing themselves of AAA travel has increased 82 percent, from 11 percent to 20 percent. At the same time, the average age of an AAA travel purchaser declined from fifty-five to fifty. There are over 49 million AAA members; the potential for further growth is awesome.

Finally, a host of individually owned and operated travel agencies successfully emphasize vacation sales. They may not be members of a consortium (a group of agencies that has joined together to maximize their buying power) or a marketing organization like American Express or Carlson Travel Network, but they all have a common focus on vacation sales.

Hundreds of business and marketing models have proven successful and productive in terms of selling cruises and other vacations. Here are a few examples:

◆ I.C.E. Gallery sells cruises to interval ownership customers by creating an exchange where owners swap out a week, let's say, of their annual resort ownership in exchange for a cruise.

◆ Cruise Events, a home-based agency, builds cruise groups around celebrities, using the Internet as an inexpensive communication vehicle. The agent has been able to successfully promote a wide range of groups built around folks like Jack Scalia, a star of the soap *All My Children,* and Dirk Benedict, star of the *A-Team.*

◆ Cruises Only, part of National Leisure Group (NLG), bills itself as the largest cruise retailer in the country. They have a heavy newspaper presence, taking advantage of their scale through sharp media purchasing and use of supplier co-op dollars. They promote both a price guarantee and a vacation guarantee as a means of instilling consumer confidence and as a way to differentiate themselves.

♦ The Vacations to Go model is built around a self-published travel magazine geared to senior citizens. In order to expand their reach, they've embraced the Internet, utilizing the search engines (Google, Yahoo) to drive folks to their site.

♦ Crown Adventures at Sea is a seven-day-a-week retail agency that dominates the greater New Orleans market. This agency values personal relationships with its clientele and has built much of its business through referrals of satisfied clients.

♦ SingleCruises.com focuses on the older (forty-plus) singles market. They arrange group cruises, making it comfortable for singles to travel together.

♦ Inspiration Cruises focuses on the Christian market. They promote popular religious music groups and inspirational speakers on dedicated full-ship charters.

♦ Straight A Tours and Four Seasons Tours concentrate on high school students. They provide escorted trips, endorsed by the high schools, and feature performing arts competitions such as band and dance.

Some full-service agencies go so far as to have a separate cruise-only division so they can focus resources on that business without the distraction of trying to run two businesses with one set of agents. The idea is that any business should focus on its core competency. More than one competency means more than one business. To try to combine them is a common mistake—and usually disastrous. Have you ever met a top car salesman who was also a top mechanic? We doubt it. Auto dealers understand this, and thus the service division is entirely separate from the sales division. They are treated as different businesses because they *are* different businesses. Customers have an entirely different set of expectations for sales than for service. Curiously, cruise-only divisions of full-service agencies are somewhat common, but vacation-only divisions are rare.

While CLIA doesn't have a breakout of cruise-only divisions of full-service agencies in its list of members, it does track standalone cruise-only agencies, as Exhibit 9.6 shows. Overall, CLIA membership has declined by 37 percent in the 1995–2005 time frame, reflecting the dramatic decline in ARC-appointed agencies due to the elimination of front-end agency airline commissions. The 160 percent increase in

Exhibit 9.6   CLIA Agency Membership

	1995		2005	
	Number	%	Number	%
Full Service	15,051	68%	5,627	34%
Cruise Only				
*Office	4,289	19%	3,476	16%
*Home	2,860	13%	7,447	50%
Total cruise only	7,149	32%	10,992	66%
Total locations	22,200	100%	16,544	100%

Source: CLIA agency membership roster

home-based agencies has been the one bright spot in this otherwise disturbing distribution picture. While there are no reliable research data on this subject (due to the bias of agency self-reporting), intuitively, cruise-only retail locations are the most productive cruise sellers, followed by full-service agencies and then home-based agencies, on a per location basis.

Bear in mind that while CLIA has the largest travel agency membership of any U.S. or Canadian travel business, about 19,300 agency locations are *not* members (about 54 percent of all locations). The safe presumption is that these agencies do little or no cruise business. This group includes dedicated corporate agencies, ethnic agencies (which focus on international marketing to and from their clients' home country), and agencies that are, in fact, suppliers (tour operators, cruise lines, etc., which have their own captive agencies).

In addition, a number of agencies do produce cruise sales, but their amount of cruise business is so low (random agent bookings) that the owner or manager can't justify CLIA membership (in 2006, the one-time sign-up fee was $90 and annual dues were $299 per location). Of course, a few owners enjoy their role as maverick and refuse to join CLIA just to be different. These are the folks who pride themselves on always being smarter than everyone else.

Imagine the simplicity of the cruise-only agency. No airline appointments, no expensive airline computer terminals and printers, no demanding corporate clients, no worrying about commission "restructuring" or whether an airline will decide to pull out of your market and thereby cut into your business. By not trying to be a jack-of-all-trades, these agencies focus on a few products—not the world. Ah, but there are drawbacks, as well. Everything is not peachy-keen. Consider, for example, how cruise-only agencies acquire their business. Sure, they advertise and promote and network like other agencies, but they have no opportunity, in their offices or via incoming phone inquiries, to convert land-based vacations prospects to cruising. After all, no one calls or strolls into a cruise-only agency to book Las Vegas or a Florida resort. Remember, full-service agencies sell ten land vacations for each cruise. The opportunity to spread the gospel to non-cruisers is simply lost to a cruise-only agency *unless* their agents proactively go out into the marketplace and approach consumers where they live or work. Missionaries do it all the time. So do Amway and Tupperware. It just takes a mindset, determination, and the discipline necessary to focus on that kind of fieldwork. Going door to door on foot helps, but so does direct mail, telemarketing, and the Internet!

We've devoted this chapter to what the travel agencies of today do and how they do it—some better than others. What is truly remarkable is the resilience of travel agents. At one time they were wooed and rewarded by the airlines, and their numbers grew dramatically. The bottom fell out beginning in 1995, when the same airlines began a steady strategy of disintermediation. Brick-and-mortar agencies closed their doors by the thousands, but many of the displaced agents embraced the home-base model as well as the Internet. This tumultuous period continues today, with suppliers constantly adapting to the ever-changing distribution models. Dominant Internet travel brands like Expedia, Travelocity, and Orbitz have also taken up part of the slack, as have more robust supplier direct channels.

The disruption in distribution most acutely affected the cruise lines because of their unique reliance on travel agents. But the disturbance has been relatively short term, a matter of a few years. At the end of the day, our best guess is that the changes are pretty well complete. The remaining ARC-appointed full-service agencies survive on the basis of back-end airline commissions as well as commissions on hotel, cruises, tours, and rental cars, plus service fees. Home-based agencies, without significant overhead, are multiplying like rabbits. Host agencies abound, creating demand for even non–travel agents to enter this still-somehow-romantic business.

Over fifty-five host agencies market nationally in support of home-based agencies. Some of the more interesting examples are shown in Exhibit 9.7.

As Exhibit 9.7 indicates, there is a wide divergence in host models, from very large member organizations to smaller, boutique (and generally more productive) models. By "productive" we mean those that generate high sales revenue per agent. America's Vacation Center, for example, conservatively did $500,000 per agent in 2005, while Global Travel averaged about $3,600 per agent.

EXHIBIT 9.7 **Data on Selected Host Agencies**

Organization	Number of Home-Based Agents	2005 Sales (000s)
Global Travel International	35,000	$125
Joystar, Inc.	3,700	100
Nexion, Inc.	1,900	160
Cruise Planners (franchise)	650	100
Travel Planners International	1,100+	57
Uniglobe Travel	300+	50
America's Vacation Center	200+	100+

As far as the big Internet players are concerned, there are a few schools of thought. One point of view is that their share of cruise business will explode in ten to fifteen years as the Gen Xers begin to replace the baby boomers in the sweet spot of the vacation purchase cycle. (In fact, an enterprising young entrepreneur has set up GenXCruise.com to focus on this emerging market.) Another viewpoint is that the future share growth of the online mega-agencies is dependent on their supplier relationships. Many vacation suppliers eagerly give these big players preferred pricing that average agencies cannot access. With this pricing philosophy, it's likely that their growth will continue, albeit at the expense of the little guy. Other suppliers take the opposite approach and offer their pricing on a channel-neutral basis. Their theory is that everyone should have access to the same pricing so that price drops out as a differentiator. Without price to talk about, the agent-prospect selling scenario turns to the merits of the product and the knowledge, selling skills, and service of the agent. This takes the discussion away from viewing the cruise vacation as a mere commodity, like an airline seat, hotel room, or rental car. Rather, the discussion focuses on the rich tapestry of the vacation experience—which is a much more positive reinforcement of the basic vacation purchase decision in the first place.

Some suppliers, such as Carnival, Marriott, and Sandals, take their pricing policy a step further. Not content to make sure there's no preferential pricing, these suppliers also forbid agents to advertise so-called unauthorized rates in public media. If the cruise price is $699, for example, an agent is not allowed to advertise in public media, "But at *x* agency, you'll pay only $649." The practice of promoting unauthorized prices derived from rebated commissions had tilted the playing field away from the 20,000-plus little guys who couldn't compete via rebates with the few dozen or so big players—who, because of lower advertised prices, saw their share of the business increase. As the big players grew larger, they in turn, reaped the benefits of even higher commissions, back-end overrides, and co-op advertising dollars—a case of the rich getting richer at the expense of both the balance of the distribution system and the suppliers themselves, who saw their acquisition costs (commissions and co-op advertising) climbing higher and higher.

Another aspect of this spiraling situation was occurring. While unauthorized prices were allowed to be promoted without restriction on the Internet, the supplier direct channel was also being disadvantaged because most suppliers had pledged not to undercut travel agents. The reality was that travel agents were, through rebating, undercutting suppliers. While no supplier can stop all forms of rebating, those that choose to could stop these unauthorized prices from being broadcast in public media, as the offending prices were always published within the context of the supplier's brand. The supplier controls the brand and hence can control the associated pricing if he so chooses. If an agent refuses to stop promoting unauthorized prices, the supplier can reduce the agency commission to 10 percent or eliminate commissions altogether by putting a stop-sell on the agency.

For many years, agencies were prohibited from promoting unauthorized rates in newspapers, radio, and television. In the travel lull after the millennium, many travel suppliers turned to the Internet to sell large amounts of unexpected last-minute space. Rather than have unused capacity, the suppliers tended to look the other way when, in an effort to kick-start demand, the then-emerging Internet players promoted rates much lower than those available elsewhere in the market. At that time, the Internet vacation travel space was much smaller than today, and suppliers felt they could offer lower prices in that medium without risking much dilution of their existing revenue. They were probably correct—and the Internet players certainly provided the extra demand needed to get suppliers out of their difficult situation. Unfortunately, the pattern was then established that the Internet was productive and a growing source of sales. Suppliers quickly became addicted to this new, robust channel, and the Internet space continued its dramatic growth with the results discussed above. Many smaller vacation suppliers continue to rely heavily on the Internet players to distribute their products through preferential pricing. That's their prerogative, and that's fine. Our view is that large, nationally branded suppliers should employ *all* channels of distribution equitably so *all* participants are motivated to sell the supplier's products because they know they have a fair chance at the business and won't be automatically undercut by a lower preferential price or a rebated price.

With all these available forms of distribution, which one makes sense today? The answer is that any of the models can be worthwhile as long as the business provides value to the folks who pay the rent: consumers and suppliers.

The most important question to answer is what can be done to improve the marketing and selling of cruises and other vacation products—and how to do it. In the next and last chapter, we describe our concept of an effective and profitable model. We've modestly called it Bob and Andy's Vacation Store.

BOB & ANDY'S VACATION STORE

10

Selling the sea—
the way we'd do it

Welcome to Bob and Andy's Vacation Store. It's not real—not yet, anyway. Creating it on paper, however, is a good way of illustrating how we believe travel agencies can and should operate to maximize their long-term profits instead of teetering on the edge of insolvency. Because we both live in the Miami area, we'll put our store on Main Highway in downtown Coconut Grove, one of the more affluent areas of the city. Because it's on the main drag, our store is located in an attractive retail environment with plenty of parking, good signage, and the high probability of walk-in traffic. We could just as easily have picked one of several strip malls or one of two shopping centers. The idea is to be seen and easily accessible by as many people as possible. Because today's shopper has a limited amount of time, we want to be in an area where people are walking around and shopping anyway, so they don't have to make a special trip to see us. That accounts for the popularity of shopping malls. We didn't pick one because the rents are high and the best locations go to the big chains. But there are lots of retail shops in downtown Coconut Grove as well as restaurants and movie theaters, which attract substantial traffic.

Our store windows are tastefully done with interesting displays, which we'll describe in a moment. They are not cluttered, and we have decided to forsake the forty-odd association and affiliation decals that are too frequently found stuck all over travel agency windows. Our interior is inviting. One side of our store is designed to evoke the feeling and ambience of a comfortable living room. We have a carpeted floor, a sofa and a loveseat, upholstered chairs, and two low coffee tables. On the other side, partially hidden by some planters with real plants, which we water daily (to give us a touch of class), are four workstations: desks, files, and a chair for each salesperson, with two additional chairs at each station for prospects. Note that we've called them *prospects*. We haven't lost sight of the fact that in our retail culture, an individual is a prospect to whom we expect to sell something when he walks through that door or calls on the phone or emails us, even if he has been our past client for many years.

291

The flat-screen computer terminal (optional) is mounted on a side return so as not to intrude on the prospect-seller scenario. Hotel research has shown that people often feel depersonalized when they see their arrangements being handled by computers—which is why many luxury hotels hide them from the sight of guests checking in. The desktops in our store also have a set of manila files representing current trips in process. These files most likely won't reflect the full set of current trip files our agents are working with but rather are for show, to indicate to our prospects that the salesperson is both productive (writing lots of business) and well organized. We're not being deceitful here; we just don't want our prospect to feel like he is the Lone Ranger out on the prairie by himself but among a large contingent of satisfied vacationers. The many folders silently speak of third-party endorsement.

There are absolutely no brochures on display in our office. Prospects cannot get their hands on them without the assistance of one of our counselors. We use the term *counselors;* however, we and our prospects know this is a retail store and the staff are really trained travel sales professionals. If they need personal counseling, there's a clinical psychologist down the street who charges $150 an hour. Our walls are decorated with a few colorful posters indicative of popular vacation spots such as Las Vegas, Mexico, Walt Disney World Resort, a cruise ship in the Caribbean, or scenes from Alaska and Europe. There's nothing unusual or exotic on display. We have left our yak teeth from Tibet and our kangaroo pouch from Australia at home. And that poster a tourist office sent us from Machu Picchu may be beautiful and serene, but as no one from our store has purchased a trip to that destination, why should we give up valuable space that could be used to showcase a popular destination or activity? We prefer posters featuring popular vacation *activities* rather than specific *destinations,* although they're tough to find. We know that generic sunbathing, tropical shopping, golfing, sailing, sightseeing, and fine dining scenes allow prospects to visualize what they'll be doing on vacation—and, more important, how they will feel about it. Our experience has taught us that too many prospects think they want specific destinations only because they think, or know from experience, their needs will be taken care of there. In reality, we know—because it is *our* business—that many different destinations and vacation products can fulfill their given list of needs. They may have never thought or heard of some of these possibilities, and we may be able to perform a genuine and valuable service by recommending one of these alternatives. We understand that prospects' needs are activity- and feeling-driven, so the proper visual emphasis in our store is on activities and feelings rather than on specific destinations.

Remember that two out of three folks who should be cruising haven't tried it yet. They fit the profile, and they have the time and money. As vacation specialists, we know from research that cruising is the superior vacation when it comes to guest satisfaction. The trick, as we've said (perhaps harped on) before, is consumer trial. By having our posters and other visuals focus on activities, we create the best possible scenario for prospects to open up to considering a cruise vacation. Our staff will take it from there.

To further make this point, our window displays—which we change every month or so, like our smart retail competitors do—are seasonal in nature and display activities that are hot sellers. In winter, we might feature a lounge chair on a sandy beach, complete with a tall drink and good book, just waiting for a lucky vacationer. Or we might show a pair of skis with poles, boots, and artificial snow. In the summer, perhaps we'll feature a small sailboat or canoe, or a compass and backpack. There would be binoculars, an Audubon guide to birds, and a camera as well. Perhaps we'll display a dining table for four, graciously set with fine china, silver, crystal, and a bucket with champagne. People do love to dine well on vacation, and the scene subtly reminds the spouse (who does most of the cooking) that he or she won't have to prepare the meal, set the table, and do the dishes. Aren't vacations wonderful?

Another window (if we have two) might contain a mannequin or two dressed in the latest fashion for golf or tennis. Perhaps we could display a deck of cards, dice, gambling chips, and a backgammon set. Prospects look at the window and fashion their own dream vacations in their mind's eye based solely on their individual tastes and desires. They quickly visualize themselves enjoying the activities they long to do—and will indeed have the time and opportunity to do when they take their vacation. This is good karma!

Where do all their neat props we put in our windows come from? You guessed it: For the most part (except for a few special items rented from a display company), they are on loan from cooperating stores in the area. Due credit is given to these firms with a tastefully discreet tent card placed in the front right corner of the display. As you might expect, we're active in the local business community, and because we all help each other, we're big on reciprocity. We encourage Connie's Sportswear, Joe's Camera Store, Tom's Runners Edge, and Millie's Bridal Boutique, as well as the movie theater, the Italian restaurant, and the bowling alley, to feature our props such as brochures, bag tags, and travel documents in their windows—giving our Vacation Store the same appropriate credit, of course.

Of course, we have a back office, and, like others, we have a refrigerator, coffee maker, and hot water for tea, but not just for us and our fellow counselors. No, we are actually prepared to, and always do, offer coffee or espresso, tea, mineral water (with or without bubbles), and a selection of soft drinks to our prospects. We want them to feel at home, to be comfortable, to feel looked after, and to know they are welcome guests. Trust us; the prospects who have been to regular travel agencies immediately discern—and appreciate—our warm, hospitable atmosphere. It's just good sense to put folks at ease when they're about to make an important discretionary purchase decision—spending not just their hard-earned money but their very valuable time on that oh-so-important vacation.

Our fellow counselors all have what we like to call front-of-the-house personalities. We all enjoy being with people and get a big kick out of helping them find terrific vacation products. We all are cognizant of being in the happiness-making business—and it shows. Each of us is a positive individual with a healthy level of self-esteem. We are good at what we do, and we know it. We're not cocky or arrogant; we simply have a deep sense of pride in our competency and enjoy doing a job as well as it can be done. We are fearless in a selling scenario because we realize both from our past successes and our mastery of selling skills that we'll likely be successful each time. Those few times when we're not successful don't crush us. Far from it! Unfazed, we learn from each failed encounter, which enriches our tapestry of experience. When we *are* successful, we don't view the experience just as a completed sale but rather as another satisfied client about to experience a terrific vacation—one *we* made possible. We know the odds are hugely in favor of the client being appreciative and grateful for the service we provided: putting him in the vacation picture that best suited his individual needs. We derive great satisfaction from knowing he'll return to us for all his vacation needs—and he'll tell his friends and associates. Why are we so sure? Because we made it easy for him! When he returns home after his cruise, he'll find a personally addressed envelope waiting for him from the counselor who made the sale. The letter trusts he had a good time (he will have, more than 95 percent of the time), thanks him for his business, and tells him what a pleasure it was to work with him. It goes on to ask that if he enjoyed working with us (of course he did!), would he kindly mail the enclosed stamped postcards (just two—so it seems easy enough) to friends and associates he believes would also enjoy the benefit of our vacation services? The postcard we have supplied features a color photo of our vacation store on the front and the handwritten notation:

> Dear_____,
>
> I just returned from a terrific vacation arranged by Sarah at the vacation store. She did a great job! When you're looking for a fabulous vacation, I recommend you call Sarah at 555-1111. Or just stop in and tell her I sent you.
> Regards,
> Harry

The enclosed letter to our client concludes by saying each lead will save him $25 on his next vacation—with us, of course!

Importantly, this seed was planted twice earlier. First, when the booking was made, Sarah asked if our prospect would like to travel with anyone else—perhaps another couple or a relative. It may not have occurred to the client until she brought it up. "Yes, now that you mention it, wouldn't it be great if the Dickinsons and the Vladimirs could join us?" Sarah just received two hot leads! Second, when she delivers the final documents (itinerary, e-tickets, cruise tickets, hotel vouchers, etc.), Sarah expressed once again her confidence that her client is about to embark on a great vacation, and she says ahead of time how much she enjoyed working with him and how she would appreciate it if he would tell his friends about her. "I'll take care of them personally," she tells him.

The Selling Scenario

Perhaps here it would be helpful if we gave the reader a look at the sales training we provide for our counselors. They may already be experienced travel agents, but we want them to understand *our* philosophy of doing business and to follow certain procedures we know will produce the kind of sales results we expect. So join us now at a sales training seminar on the subject of selling cruises, which Bob is leading:

> Good afternoon, everyone. Here at Bob and Andy's Vacation Store we offer a good range of vacation products. But we like to sell cruises because their high level of satisfaction guarantees us more satisfied customers then anything else we can offer. Having satisfied customers leads to referrals, which leads to new business. We also honestly believe cruising is the best value we can offer, and just about everyone who walks through that door is interested in value. Finally, because they're inclusive, we make more money and *you* make more money when we sell a cruise. Clearly, cruises are in both our customers' interest and our interest, and that's why we concentrate on selling them. However, the selling techniques you will learn today will allow you to sell any vacation—or anything else, for that matter.
>
> One more thing. In this session, I'm going to give you a script to follow almost word for word. We don't want you to take this the wrong way. We don't think you're stupid or can't figure out how to talk to customers. On the contrary, we wouldn't have hired you if we didn't think you were bright and articulate. But selling is a skill—one we're not born with. What

we want to do is not just tell you how to sell but also to show you how, and the best way to do that is to be specific. Once you understand the principles, of course you'll be much better off putting all of this material into your own words. We don't want you to sound like a robot or as if you're talking from a rehearsed script. So take what I tell you here today and put it in your own words so it sounds completely natural to you.

The first step in the selling process is to do what we call *qualifying the client.* In simple language, this step consists of establishing a relationship with this person who has just walked in the door or called on the phone and finding out what he's looking for—his needs and wants. The way to begin is by greeting the prospect properly. You might try, "Hi, welcome to the Vacation Store. You've come to the right place. My name is Bob. May I have your name please? May I have your address and your phone number?" The replies are written down on a prospect record sheet—legibly! If the prospect balks at providing the information, don't back down; take control. Ask, "Are you interested in having a great vacation?" This question invariably forces the prospect to say yes. After all, who would want anything less than a great vacation? "Well, we feature them at the Vacation Store. But, as you would suspect, we do so much business here that we simply don't deal with folks we don't know. I'm Bob. May I have your name please?"

A key to this process is the voiced question mark: The best way to accomplish this is with a pause. It's important to pause after asking a question. The pause forces the prospect to respond. If you don't pause long enough, you let the prospect off the hook so he doesn't feel compelled to reply. Five to ten seconds is usually more than enough time. If he still doesn't answer, simply say, "I'm sorry. Did you hear the question?" If he says he didn't, just repeat it and pause. If the prospect hangs up (if it's a telephone inquiry) or walks out, celebrate it! You've just flushed out someone who probably was shopping for the best rebate and not at all serious about giving you the business. At worst, you've wasted a minute or so of your time. Recognize that some people really don't want to buy or who are difficult clients because they enjoy controlling folks and running them ragged. Good riddance to bad rubbish! You don't have to deal with everyone, and you shouldn't want to. We don't expect you to. Be selective.

The next series of questions is the most important part of the qualifying step. How many in the party? Names and addresses? Who will be making the decision? If the prospect is not the only decision maker, simply ask when it would be convenient for all of us—the counselor and the decision makers—to get together? If he's reluctant to set a time, then it's probably best to stop the process at that point, except in unusual circumstances. You're wasting everyone's time if all the decision makers aren't present. It's important that everyone go through the selling process at the same time so no one feels psychologically disadvantaged or that his specific concerns or needs have not been addressed. For instance, you recommend to your prospect a cruise that departs from San Juan, Puerto Rico. He says fine, but when he takes the recommendation home his wife reminds him she wanted a cruise that leaves from Miami so they could visit her mother on the way back. Your prospect hates his mother-in-law and was trying to avoid this. This isn't your problem, but you will have spent half an hour selling a cruise he's not going to be able to buy.

Next you need to settle on dates. Ask questions like "When would you like to travel? For how long? You say you and your wife would like to go away for a week in March—would the week of the 20th be okay? No? You prefer the 13th? How does Sunday sound? Fine."

Having pinned down the dates, it's appropriate to inquire about activities. You need to know the dates first because if they want to go swimming, it would be a mistake to send them to Bermuda in March, for example; the water is still too cold. But if they're golfers, the weather there is gorgeous in March. So ask, "What are some of the things you and your wife would like to do on vacation?" Listen to the responses carefully and take careful notes. Probe. The prospect is giving you the recipe for their ideal vacation. Attempt to fill in the blanks, if there are any. "Does your wife enjoy shopping? What does she like to buy?" If the answer is antiques, a Caribbean cruise might not be as appropriate as a Mediterranean cruise would be. "Would you like to play some golf?" If he says yes, find out if they're serious golfers. Some destinations have much better golf courses then others. It can make a difference.

A good series of questions is "Where have you gone on previous vacations? For how long? Where did you stay?" This goes to the issue of budget without mentioning it directly. The truth is that most people will spend what they need to on vacation in order to buy what they want, if they can afford it. At this point, your prospect may have no real idea what her dream vacation will cost. Nor do you know whether she can afford it. A good clue is her past spending habits. If she went to

Hawaii last year, you'll know a lot by determining whether she stayed at the Days Out/Inn or the Halekulani in Honolulu, for instance. One tip: Don't make any assumptions based on dress, race, or accent. Your prospect may be worth several million dollars, but if he's been puttering around his garden all day or running errands, he may not look to you like someone who could afford a luxury cruise. If you don't get a clear answer from this question ("We rented a condo" could mean any price range, for example), ask about enjoyable dining experiences. "Yup, Denny's" is a fairly good clue, as is "We really enjoy Le Cirque in New York, and their range of older burgundies is quite marvelous."

At the Vacation Store, we keep things simple. We try to put prospects into one of three price bins: budget, mid-range, and top of the line. By asking the kind of questions I've suggested here, by listening and observing and taking notes, it's really quite easy to select among three different lifestyles.

As a thoroughly professional vacation specialist, you need still another piece of information before you are in a position to recommend a vacation your prospect will really enjoy. It's crucial if you want him to return—and you do, because a lot of our business is repeat business. You need to know what he doesn't like. "Is there anything you would prefer to avoid? What's the worst thing that ever happened to you on any of your vacations that you don't want to run into again? Any hassles?" These kinds of questions help jog the memory as well as help prospects be in touch with their vacation needs and priorities. Many prospects know they want to get away from the rat race, but they don't always realize how many ways there are to do that. They also may forget that while they may want to visit Germany and drive around visiting old castles, the traffic and speed on the Autobahn, along with signage in a strange language, could be nerve wracking for all but the most confident drivers. It is not an escape from the rat race—it's just a different kind of rat race! To the extent that a prospect consciously thinks about what things he wants to do and his priorities, you can recommend a vacation product that's a close fit. Obviously, the better the fit, the better the enjoyment.

Now step back and take a look at what's been happening here. During this entire qualifying step, you have been in total control of the situation. Your prospect did most of the talking and felt, therefore, that he was in control. Importantly, the situation was gratifying for the prospect because you appeared to be (and indeed you were) listening carefully and even taking notes! You were clearly interested in him, and that helps build a trusting relationship.

The second step is what we call *features and benefits*. You have just gleaned a vacation recipe from your prospect. Now is the time to play back your notes. "You said you and your wife wanted to get away from the cold winter and relax and get a tan. You want the possibilities of some nightlife, good food, and good service. You'd like to play some golf; she enjoys shopping for jewelry, perfumes, and souvenirs. If I can get you all those things in a casual, hassle-free environment for about the same price as your last vacation, how does that sound?" You've replayed the vacation recipe: the features the prospect is looking for. By doing so, you've established credibility with your prospect. He knows you know what his needs are. You are all on the same page of our sales training manual. If the prospect says it sounds good, you can move on to close the sale. If not, something is either missing or misunderstood. You then say, "I'm sorry, what did I leave out?" This question allows you to fill in or clarify the recipe. Then you recite the amended recipe to the prospect, ending with the same question: "How does that sound?" If you have the right recipe now, he'll say yes. If you don't, he'll say no until you ask further probing questions, like "What did I leave out [of your vacation recipe]?" until, finally, all the recipe needs are out on the table. The moment he says, "Yes, it sounds good," you are ready to close the sale. But there's another piece to this step that goes a long way to mitigating buyer's remorse. Buyer's remorse is that sickening, queasy, unsettling feeling we all sometimes get when we make what we perceive to be a rash or impetuous purchase decision. This feeling can take all the fun out of the purchase—perhaps even the vacation! You alleviate these symptoms by supplementing the required features you've already identified with extra benefits the vacation you have in mind offers that haven't yet been discussed. So, a good strategy is to ask, "What if, at the same time, I could also give you a vacation that offers twenty-four-hour room service, free? You mentioned you enjoyed dancing. How about the choice of four different bands and orchestras and a state-of-the-art disco? You said your wife liked shopping. How about duty-free shopping, where she can get terrific bargains? How about being able to watch continuous movies in your own room for free? You didn't mention it, but what if you had the option of enjoying casino gambling along with everything else?"

In other words, if your prospect was ready to buy based on features one through eight (which matched his stated vacation needs), chances are he'll be even more eager to purchase after he understands all the extra benefits your recommendation has to offer (features nine through fifteen). He is now ready to purchase, content in the knowledge that both you and he have been in touch with his and his wife's vacation needs; you both understand what they are; and you have the product which will deliver them.

What makes this step work so effectively for us is that our office sells about fifteen products—that's all. Therefore, we expect each of our travel counselors to be thoroughly conversant with each of those fifteen travel suppliers and the features and benefits of their products. We've sampled the products and not only know them but also what kinds of people enjoy them. Without sufficient product knowledge, how do we have any hope of matching the product to the vacation recipe?

That's why we're here today. Vicki Freed, senior vice president of Carnival, points out: "The truth of the matter is that product knowledge rarely gets used if you don't have proper sales training." She's right, and we're giving you the training now. It is also our policy to give you the opportunity to obtain more product knowledge. The way we do that is to give you five paid days off in addition to your regular vacation each year for educational purposes to learn about our suppliers. Not only do we give you the time but also we pay your expenses for familiarization and inspection trips you may be invited to attend—providing of course, they are for one of our preferred suppliers. Additionally, we expect you to attend travel industry conferences, trade shows, supplier seminars, and destination and product specialist courses like those offered by CLIA. We know from experience that salespeople with great product knowledge are simply more effective and, therefore, more productive.

You're very likely to encounter a prospect who asks for the product of a different supplier. What we'd like you to say is, "I'm sorry, we don't handle that product," and smile. You can expect two possible responses—either "Oh, why not?" or "Well, what *do* you sell?" To the first, we reply, "Because we've had such terrific success with this [generally similar] product." Nine times out of ten the prospect will be satisfied and inquire about the product we do sell. If it is that tenth time, we go on to explain that we only sell the vacation products we can recommend with confidence. All retail stores carry only brands of merchandise they're sure their customers will like.

Sak's Fifth Avenue and Macy's don't carry every brand of suit or dress made. Their buyers select the ones they consider best. That's why their customers are loyal to them. We do the same thing. If they ask what we do sell, we reply with the name of one of our preferred suppliers. We do hedge our bet a little and supplement our product lineup with an additional thirty or so suppliers of exotic destinations for our market, such as African safaris, South Pacific resorts, and East Indian sightseeing tours. Two brochures of each of these suppliers are kept in alphabetical order in a tub file. We make no pretense of being conversant with them. They are there just in case. Additionally, two of us are available, schedule permitting, to prepare FIT (an industry term originally standing for "foreign independent tour" but today meaning individual customized itineraries) itineraries at our regular consulting rate of $90 an hour. Frankly, the rate is too low to make the return we desire but, fortunately, it's high enough to discourage all but the most earnest clients.

At this point, you go to the phone and *close the sale,* which is the third step. "I've got just the vacation for you two. You'll be very happy with what I've selected. But, as you may expect, this vacation is popular, so before we do anything else, let's check availability." This introduces the concept of scarcity—the suggestion that this great vacation dream may evaporate if there's no space. Upon hearing this, our prospect is eager to learn if the space is available. The desire for the product (which is still unknown to the prospective buyer) just intensified.

Because you've determined which of the three budget bins the prospects are in during the qualifying phase, you can be specific about the accommodations you are requesting. When you call the supplier's reservations department or use your PC or CRT (computer reservation terminal) to make an automated booking, you have all the information you need, written down, at your fingertips. You don't have to bother the prospect (who is now busy fantasizing about the upcoming vacation or concerned about its availability) with mundane issues like name, address, and so forth. After making the booking, you say to the prospect, "You're in luck! They have the availability. You will need just $500 to secure this reservation. Will you be using a credit card or a check?" As a matter of policy, our counselors are forbidden to give their prospects a reservation option. If prospects can't pay then, we encourage them to do so quickly in the hopes that we can still secure the same space. We never offer to hold anything. This sense of urgency helps close the sale—that is, to get the money. Of course, we do take an option on the space if we can, but that's between us and the supplier. We don't give options to prospects not to be deceitful but because it allows us to give better service to all of our clients. Suppliers love dealing with us because our cancellation rate is many times lower than regular agencies, which indiscriminately give out options on suppliers' space on the off chance someone might book. This is a benefit that ultimately accrues to our customers and thereby differentiates us from our competitors. Because we go out of our way to develop this kind of supportive relationship with our suppliers, when we really need a favor for one of our clients, we can often get it when others can't.

A second reason for the no-option policy is our knowledge that the absence of an option forces the moment of truth: whether or not the prospect will decide to purchase our recommendation by putting down a deposit. As explained in chapter 9, this is a powerful tool for our store, as it virtually eliminates shopping for a lower price elsewhere.

By this point, please notice that if we've done our job well, the prospect is prepared to purchase the vacation without knowing where he is going! When you get down to vacation needs, destination is frequently not all that important. Sure, if one's primary vacation need is specific sightseeing opportunities like Paris or London, the destination is critical. No matter what, if someone wants to visit Paris on his vacation, no other destination or vacation option can substitute. But, on the other hand, the vast majority of vacationers do not have such a specific sightseeing objective. Therefore, their vacation needs can be met with a host of vacation options.

Naturally, you'll tell the prospect what you're recommending when you ask for the deposit. Let's just say, as fate would have it, that your recommendation is a one-week Caribbean cruise. (Say hallelujah, because that's what Bob and Andy like to sell!) If you've taken step one and qualified properly, and you know you've identified and matched features and benefits, which is the second step, then chances are very good, at least fifty-fifty, that you'll successfully close the sale, which is the third step. However, you might run into an obstacle—some objection you'll need to overcome. Doing this requires an optional fourth step.

Notice that this fourth step *is* optional. There's likely to be no resistance at all to your recommendation, because, after all, it *did* meet the vacation needs of the prospect, which you covered in step two. Furthermore, step four can only occur *after* trying to close the sale. In other words, the sales process itself is not disrupted in any way between the prospect and the seller. This too is great karma! Also, if there is an objection to a cruise, it can only be motion discomfiture, a term we prefer to *seasickness*. The other potential objections to cruising that frequently pop up in consumer surveys—cost, boredom, regimentation, and confinement—simply should not apply in our sales scenario if you have properly taken the second step of matching features and benefits. Cost issues have also been resolved in advance, as you have selected your recommendation on the basis of what it'll cost in relation to the prospect's last vacation (the three buckets). Remember, too, most folks have a very fuzzy notion of the cost of a vacation (refer to chapter 8).

Because cost, boredom, confinement, and regimentation are all non-issues because the features and benefits step assured the prospects that all their activity and other needs would be met in a hassle-free environment, what's left to object to when selling a cruise? The only remaining potential bugaboo is mal de mer. In the event this objection is raised, the first thing to do is get in step with the prospect. Empathize with him—don't argue. It's poor psychology to be contentious with someone you wish to spend potentially several thousand dollars in your store. Say something like, "I certainly can understand how you might be concerned about seasickness." Note it's not a "problem" but merely a "concern." "I had [be sure to use the past tense] the same concern until I took my first cruise. Then I discovered that the ship was so large and the ride was so smooth that I couldn't figure out how all those palm trees were moving past the picture windows. Finally, I realized they weren't moving—we were!" At this point, you are, of course, making direct eye contact (if the prospect is in front of you) and speaking confidently as you continue. "Don't take my word for it. As you can well imagine, many folks we've done business with have had the same concern you and I have had. [You're still talking in the past tense.] They've been so delighted with their cruises and so pleased they didn't let their concern stop them from trying this terrific vacation that they've willingly offered to answer questions from any of our clients who might have this same concern. May I give you their names and phone numbers so you can give them a call?" Again, you have a confident approach, and your direct eye contact allows you to look for telltale signs that his reluctance is melting away. Now here's the clincher we've used successfully a number of times: "I'll tell you what. Don't take my or anybody else's word for it. I want you both to truly enjoy this vacation. So I'm going to give you an insurance policy. [Pause here for a moment to let this sink in.] When you pick up your documents, I'm going to give you a set of Sea-bands. These are elastic wrist bracelets that employ the principle of acupressure. People swear by them, and there are no side effects. So you don't need to be concerned any more. Now, will you be depositing by credit card or check?"

This approach, in our experience, works about 80 percent of the time. It's not perfect—nothing in this world is—but it's pretty darned effective. Occasionally, we've encountered prospects who say, "A cruise is out of the question. I'll get seasick." Rather than trying to end the conversation and throw in the towel, the door-opening response is, "If I can show you a way to have this great vacation and not have to be concerned about seasickness, how would you feel about that?" Usually, they'll relent and be open to considering it. Then you go into your pitch. If they're not open, then sell them a tour or another vacation package offered by one of our other preferred travel suppliers.

Notice, please, that this three- or four-step sales process never involves more than one vacation option. Presenting two or more options is a cop-out. To the prospect, it sounds like you are not confident or competent enough to select the ideal vacation. You're asking *them* to select from two or more, even though *you're* supposed to be the expert! We subscribe to the K.I.S.S. theory of selling: Keep it simple, salesperson! Folks want and appreciate one recommendation. To present two or more creates confusion, takes more time, and sets up the risk that the wrong choice (or no choice) will be made. No one wants to make the wrong choice, especially concerning one's vacation. Furthermore, if the prospect has to make the choice, what's the point of coming to you in the first place?

I have another suggestion for you. I've covered a lot of ground in this seminar. For a more thorough treatment of these selling steps, our counselors, and ourselves, frequently watch the videos on how to sell their products made by our most important travel suppliers. One of the ones I like best, as you can imagine, is the sixty-minute video "Bob Live—On Winning Selling Techniques," which Carnival Cruise Lines sells for $15. They offer a money-back guarantee if you're not satisfied. So far as I know, no one's asked for his money back yet!

I also have a confession to make to you. For thirteen years, until 1986, I went around the country telling thousands and thousands of travel agents at breakfast, lunch, and dinner seminars and speeches to suggest cruises when prospects inquired about *any* vacation. I used to tell them that no travel agent was ever killed or maimed for doing this. I was dead wrong. I was suggesting that agents begin the selling the process with the product. Prescription without diagnosis is malpractice! The sales techniques you're learning today starts with the prospect, not the product. This is the only intelligent approach to successful selling. Master these four steps, and you'll derive tremendous satisfaction because, by putting them into practice, you'll be able to allow folks to be in touch with their needs and then provide them with the means to fulfill them. This process is the essence of sound communication—asking and listening to the other person's response—and conflict resolution. The benefits of this to our personal lives, besides our careers, should be obvious to all!"

Keeping Score

At the Vacation Store, Bob, Andy, and all of the agents keep close track of our sales prospects and sales. Each uses a sales contact sheet (Exhibit 10.1). This allows us to see how we're progressing and how we compare to the others in the office, both in terms of the number of prospects and the closure rate. This year, our top counselor is closing about 80 percent of the time, and our rookie (six months in the business) is closing about 40 percent.

To make sure all of us have an equal chance at prospects, we use the "up" system. Commonly used in men's suit departments and auto showrooms, among other selling situations, the "up" system rotates the prospects through the sales force. Among the five agents, I'll get the first, sixth, eleventh, etc., prospect as long as I'm available. If I'm already with someone, or out of the office, I'm out of the rotation until I'm available.

Now you may ask what happens if a client I've been working with needs servicing while I'm not available? What's the motivation for another counselor to pitch in and help? The answer is the golden rule. My coworkers are eager to look after my clients because they're smart enough to realize there will be times they'll be out of the office and their clients will need servicing. In addition, we're very much a customer-focused organization. When a customer walks in, he wants immediate service, and we are committed to giving it to him. If he indicates he wants to wait for his usual counselor, that's fine, but then it's his choice, not ours.

On the wall in the back office, we have a series of bar charts that show week-to-date, month-to-date, and year-to-date sales for each of us. This visual reminder is highly motivational! To keep things focused, we don't count revenue; rather, we count cabins. A three- to five-day cruise counts as one-half a cabin or trip, a seven- to nine-day cruise as one cabin or trip, ten to fourteen days as two cabins or two trips, etc. This eliminates

EXHIBIT 10.1   **Contact Sheet**

Sales Person: _____

Day: _____

Week Of: _____

Prospect Name, Address, Phone # and Email	Phone/ Walk-In	#In Party	Referred By	Disposition	Next Steps	Why no Sale?	Follow-Up

the question of how many individuals are in the cabin or on the land vacation and desensitizes us to the quixotic cruise pricing so prevalent today. If Sally sold a cabin for $1,000 and later the cruise line offered a special two-passengers-for-the-price-of-one promotion, Sally still gets credit for the entire cabin, not half the revenue. Now, we know some travel agents will say our system doesn't recognize our counselors for selling up—that is, convincing the prospect to buy something more expensive. They're absolutely right! It recognizes them for selling—period! Our theory is that selling up is a myth. We sell what the prospect needs and can afford. We classify folks in three budget categories. Agents who sell up didn't really go through that discipline. They assume everyone is looking for the cheapest price to begin with. Selling up, in reality, is merely putting the prospects in one of the other two categories they should have been in from the beginning! So we don't encourage it or reward it.

The productivity bar graphs are a constant visual reminder of who is doing well and who is not. The pressure to perform as well as one's peers is quite strong. Folks tend to spur themselves on to hustle and catch up to those with higher sales activity. At least at the subconscious level, the laggards are thinking about what they need to do to close the gap. Silently, but effectively, the chart exhorts folks to do their best. A typical counselor may see it a dozen or more times a day. Trust us, it works!

We have weekly and monthly contests to recognize the counselor who sold the most cabins during the period. Of course, we have a counselor of the year as well. We reward these achievements with monthly dinners, quarterly familiarization trips, and, once a year, a suite on a preferred supplier. These rewards are over and above our normal compensation and fam policy. Our goal is to motivate through the powerful tool of recognition. The visual reminder is seen by all of us. It gently but firmly allows us to stay focused on our individual (and therefore collective) goals. Unlike many others, we record a sale on the day the deposit is received (normally, the day the sale is made), *not* the day of final payment or the day the cruise sails or returns. This is because we choose to emphasize closing the sale and GTM (getting the money). Any of these other events may occur months later, too far away from the sale itself to effectively reinforce the positive sales behavior we want. Our competitors sometimes ask us how we can control things if someone subsequently cancels and the sale unravels. The answer is simple: We reverse the booking in the week it cancels.

Our counselors are each compensated differently because each had a different salary history. Sarah, our rookie, with no prior salary history, was hired on a draw against commissions; she's paid $500 a week as a draw. That's $26,000 per year for a sharp twenty-year-old with no prior agency experience. Her commission breakdown is simplicity itself. Here's how we figure it:

Commission per Cabin

Length of cruise	Commission
2–5 days	$40
6–9 days	$100
10–14 days	40%*
15–20 days	40%*
21+ days	40%*

*of the agency commission

We figure she's on track to sell 400 cabins this year for an expected earned income of about $40,000. As with the sales contests, she and all of the counselors receive full commission credit with the deposit, *not* final payment. This is not too generous; it's simply smart business. It recognizes successful behavior quickly and simply. Again, if there is a cancellation (only 5 percent of the time, on average), then the commission income is reversed in the week of cancellation. Every one of us knows how this works, understands the system, and has signed off on it. When the rare cancellation occurs, there are no surprises or recriminations. Rather than cry the one time a sale is reversed, we celebrate the nineteen times we're being compensated many months in advance of final payment.

Our most senior counselor, Sally, has been a travel agent for fifteen years. She's used to a steady paycheck and is, frankly, set in her ways. She has no desire to take any risk on the downside, compensationwise. We respect her position, of course, but still want to reward her for enhanced productivity. Accordingly, we do not lower her salary. Rather, we provide her with a lower level of incentive that kicks in after her performance funds her base salary (and benefits). Her base is $30,000, and we calculate our benefit package off an additional value of $6,000 annually. Therefore, she must sell a sufficient number of cruises each month to fund $3,000 a month. The numbers look like this:

The Vacation Store Average Commission

Average Revenue/Cabin	$2,000
Average Commission Rate	16%
Average Commission Income/Booking	$320

If Sally sells 400 cabins a year, she'll generate $128,000 of revenue for the Vacation Store. Our guideline is that compensation (salary plus fringe benefits) should equal 40 percent of commission revenue:

$$\$128,000 \text{ commission revenue} \times 40\% \text{ salary and fringe benefit contribution} = \$51,200$$

Per booking, the contribution to salary/fringe works out like this:

$$320 \times 40\% = \$128 \text{ contribution to salary/fringe}$$

For Sally to fund $3,000 compensation per month, she needs to sell twenty-four cabins per month, or 288 each year. Accordingly, our incentive begins with the twenty-fifth cabin Sally sells each month. Her incentive is 50 percent less than Sarah's per booking for each booking beyond twenty-four:

Commission per Cabin

Length of cruise	Commission
2–5 days	$20
6–9 days	$50
10–14 days	20%*
15–20 days	20%*
21+ days	20%*

*of the agency commission

The reason the incentive is less is that Sarah is willing to take downside risk and Sally is not. If we have a slow month (August is usually troublesome), Sarah may not earn her draw, reducing our labor cost. Sally's base compensation is fixed. There's an important stipulation: The base sales quota of twenty-four cabins rolls each month. In other words, if Sally sold eighteen cabins in January, she has to sell thirty in February before she qualifies for the incentive. If she sells twenty-eight cabins in February, then she'd have to sell twenty-six cabins in March before the incentive goes into effect. This methodology assures our Vacation Store will not inadvertently overpay Sally for uneven sales activity. It also discourages Sally from unfairly loading one month's sales activity.

So, if Sally sells 400 cabins a year, the same as Sarah, her compensation is as follows:

$$24 \text{ cabins} \times 12 \text{ months} = 288 \text{ cabins} = \text{base quota}$$
$$400 \text{ cabins} - 288 \text{ quota} = 112 \text{ incentive cabins}$$
$$\text{average incentive: } \$50/\text{cabin}$$
$$\text{total incentive } \$50 \times 112 \text{ cabins} = \$5,600$$

Sally's total salary and incentive earnings are $30,000 salary plus $5,600 incentive = $35,600.

Sally earns only 11 percent less than Sarah for the same number of cabins sold. With each additional cabin, however, Sarah earns 100 percent more than Sally.

Which leads us to Jack. In the business ten years, Jack is a bit of a gambler, but not completely. He was willing to cut his monthly salary of $2,500 (the same as Sally's) in half in exchange for a richer incentive. With not-quite-Solomonic precision, we partially split the difference and created an incentive that was 90 percent of Sarah's that kicked in at the thirteenth booking. Jack responded and sold $1,000,000 worth of cabins. At an average rate of $2,000 a cabin, that amounted to 500 cabins a year.

His compensation is as follows:

Base cabins 12 months × 12 cabins/month = 144
Incentive cabins (500 − 144 = 356)
Incentive: 356 cabins × $90 cabin = $32,040

Jack's total compensation is $15,000 salary plus $32,040 incentive = $47,000. Had he sold 400 cabins, he would have earned $38,040—more than Sally but less than Sarah for the same amount of business sold. Because he was willing to take a salary cut, he receives 80 percent more incentive than Sally (90 percent versus 50).

So here's how our compensation sorts out:

The Vacation Store–Annual Results

Employee	Booking	Base Salary	Incentive	Total
Sarah	400	$0	$40,000	$40,000
Sally	400	30,000	5,600	35,600
Jack	500	15,000	32,040	47,040
Andy*	600	0	60,000	60,000
Bob*	600	0	60,000	60,000
Clerk	0	18,600**	4,400***	23,000
Total	2,500	$63,600	$202,040	$265,640

  *Our productivity is blended so that Andy, who is also our main rainmaker (sales and marketing director), doesn't feel too bad.

  **A clerk magnifies our usefulness.

  ***The clerk gets a year-end incentive based on the overall profitability of the Vacation Store. And it is meaningful: almost 25 percent of his base pay.

You might be thinking, "Whoa! How can a six-person agency afford to pay so well?" The answer is the fundamental productivity of the agency: five counselors are averaging $1,000,000 in sales each, over twice the norm of the so-called leisure travel agent. Let's look at the overall Vacation Store profit and loss statement for the year:

Vacation Store P & L

Revenue: Gross Cruise Revenue $5,000,000

Cabins Sold	2,500
Average Commission Rate	16%
Gross Commission Revenue	$800,000
Year-End override incentives	$25,000
(1 point retroactive on 50% of the business)	
Total Revenue	$825,000

Costs: Compensation

Salaries	$63,600
Incentives	$202,040
Total Compensation	$265,640
Fringe Benefits	$53,000
Rent (1,500 sq ft. @ $60/foot)	$90,000
Utilities	$24,000
Marketing Budget ($56/cabin × 2,500 cabins)	$140,000*
R&D (seminars/fams @ $5,000/counselor)	$25,000
Travel and Entertainment	$25,000
Postage, Accounting, Misc @ $2,000/month	$24,000
Clients gifts, champagne, lunches, limos, etc.**	
at $30 per cabin	$75,000
Total Cost	$731,640

Profits

	$93,360
Profit reinvestment	$13,360
Profit distribution to owners	$80,000***

*We target to negotiate an average of $15/passenger or $30/cabin as marketing co-op money from our six preferred cruise line suppliers. That gives us additional marketing funds of $30 × 2,500 = $75,000, for a total marketing budget of $215,000.

**The value depends on the length of the cruise as well as how easy the client is to deal with. Let's face it; some clients exact a charge against psychic income! In those instances, we scale back or eliminate client gifts.

***This gives Andy and Bob total annual income of $100,000 each.

This profit and loss statement represents a fat marketing budget. As a result, we'd expect the $215,000 to generate sufficient traffic to support the sale of at least 3,000 cabins in the next year. This raises an interesting question: Can the five of us sell an average of 600 cabins apiece without being run ragged? That amounts to almost three bookings per day per counselor. The answer is probably yes, with an average sale and service time of two hours per booking. Don't forget, we have a clerk to help us. But even if we added an additional counselor on full incentive, like Sarah, and he sold the additional cabins himself, the additional profit to the Vacation Store is still significant:

Incremental Revenue

500 cabins @ $2,000/cash	$1,000,000
Commission @ 16%	$160,000
Override Bonus @ 1% on 50% of overall business	$5,000
Total incremental revenue	$165,000

Incremental Costs

Compensation 500 cabins @ $100/cabin	$50,000
Fringe @ 20%	$10,000
Client gifts @ $30/cabin	$15,000
R&D (seminars, fams etc.)	$5,000
Travel and Entertainment	$5,000
Postage/accounting/misc.	$5,000
Total incremental costs	$90,000
Incremental profit	$75,000

If we generated the incremental businesses ourselves by adding another clerk instead of another counselor, we'd make even more profit for the Vacation Store, while each employee would also make proportionately more than in prior years. Candidly, the average cruise-only agency did not grow its sales proportionately to the growth of the cruise industry in the 1995–2005 period, which saw dramatic capacity increases. We believe the biggest single reason for this was the typical agency's inability to take the steps necessary to manage growth, including the critical component of adding staff.

In all the calculations, we assumed that 100 percent of the actual vacation products sold were cruises. You may suspect that we are unduly biased. (Who? Us?) We did this to assist cruise-only agencies by using unit cost and revenue data pertinent to their operations. In actuality, there are over 9,000 cruise-only agencies (including home-based), but, at the moment, there are only a few hundred vacation stores.

To adjust the data to include land-based vacation packages, use the following average package price and commission data. You'll quickly understand why we want to sell every cruise we can!

Average Unit Sale Data (per booking)

	Land Package	Cruise
Revenue	$1,000	$2,000
Blended Commission Rate	13%	16%
Average Commission/Booking	$130	$320

As you can see, the unit commission revenue for a land vacation is less than half that of a cruise vacation. Accordingly, incentive payouts have to be scaled back disproportionately to ensure the land vacation sale contributes an adequate contribution to overhead. Using Sarah's full incentive as a reference, here's how we would compensate a land vacation:

Length of Stay	Land	Cruise
2–5 days	$5	$40
6–9 days	$10	$100
10–14 days	20%	40%*
15–20 days	20%	40%*
20+ days	20%	40%*

*of the agency's commission

The land incentives of the other folks are prorated from Sarah (who was on 100 percent incentive) in the same way as the cruise incentives detailed above.

Importantly, incentives—cruise or land—are paid on sales of preferred suppliers products only, of which we have the following in our store:

Vacation Store Preferred Suppliers

Cruise:	1	Mass Market
	2	Premium
	4	Niche (Luxury specialty, Hawaii, Riverboat, Exploration)
	1	Luxury
Total Cruise Lines	8	
Tour Operator:	1	Hawaii, West Coast
	2	Major Airline Captive (including Las Vegas, Orlando, and other domestic U.S., Europe, South America)
	1	Caribbean
	1	Mexico
	1	Pacific Rim
	1	Canada
	1	Africa
	2	European (budget and escorted)
Total Tour Operators	10	
Grand Total	18	

We do have brochures available on thirty-four other products because they either have some brand recognition, as a safety net in case of lack of availability (much rarer in practice than perception), or because some few folks in our market have asked for the off-the-beaten-path destinations they prefer, such as India and the Galapagos.

We don't pay incentives on these thirty-four products because:

◆ There's not enough volume to earn override commissions (override commissions fund most, if not all, of the incentives).

◆ We want to stay focused selling a few products—so we can know them better and direct prospects to them to drive up commission revenue. All our preferred suppliers give us the opportunity to increase the percentage of commission we can earn if we improve our sales volume with them to stipulated levels.

◆ We want to reinforce the appropriate behavior—which is selling preferred suppliers, not order-taking obscure products.

Oh yes, beyond the fifty-two products, incentives are a non-issue. There is no sale. We just simply tell folks, "Sorry, we don't handle it." Anyhow, the request for other products, as we have pointed out, is very, very rare.

Marketing Efforts—Advertising

As you might suspect, we don't just wait for the business to come to us. We advertise our Vacation Store, using co-op supplier dollars with the brand positioning slogan "Greater Miami's Best Vacation Store." We like preemptive positioning! Our Yellow Pages ad catches the eye—it was designed *after* we looked at what the regular agencies were doing. Andy writes a gratis travel column for the local paper and a three-minute travel advisory for one of our radio stations in exchange for plugging the Vacation Store with publicity at the end of the column. This gives us free exposure in each Sunday's travel section and on the air while positioning Andy and our other counselors as travel experts.

Reciprocity

We do business with a good variety of folks: accountants, lawyers, insurance agents, building managers and owners, electricians, print shop, local Fed-Ex office, restaurants, deli coffee service, florist, etc. Because we do business with them, we let them all know that we expect them to do business with us—and tell their friends about us, too! And we do the same: We send them additional business based on our referrals, and we make certain we get credit for their new business. This creates a sort of obligation, if you will, that reinforces our relationships and motivates our vendors to help us even more. To aid in the process, we've created a one-panel envelope stuffer promotional piece, in color, that speaks to the advantages of using the Vacation Store. It says, in part:

Bob and Andy's Vacation Store: Who Needs Us?

If you're a person who doesn't know how important a good vacation can be, you don't need us.

If you don't believe a vacation can provide some of the most exciting and memorable experiences in your lifetime, you don't need us.

If you don't care whether you end up with an average vacation at an average price, you don't need us.

But if you don't fall into any of those three classifications, then you're our kind of client—someone who can't stand mediocrity in travel or anything else. Someone who takes a vacation not because you have money to spend but because you have dreams to be filled. Someone who demands a really terrific vacation and a good value at the same time.

That's what Bob and Andy's Vacation Store provides: travel consultants who listen to you to make sure you get what you want.

Trained professionals who know what they're talking about and provide superior service and sound advice.

Courteous folks who will be pleased to assist you by phone or in person.

Find out for yourself why everyone calls us "Greater Miami's Best Vacation Store."

Our brochure has a photo Bob and Andy and our staff to personalize the business. The bottom quarter of the piece is our business card, which can be cut off and appropriately filed by the prospect.

Networking

We've inventoried all the organizations each of the six of us belongs to as well as those of our close friends and relatives with whom we have some influence. In our community, that process gave us a list of forty-two organizations, including churches, synagogues, garden clubs, Rotary, Kiwanis, the Jaycees, a bowling league, Toastmasters, and three local PTAs. One of us has been designated as the lead salesperson for each group lead—responsible for creating as much exposure and group and individual business as possible.

Our company belongs to the local chapter of the Executive Association. This organization solely exists to promote reciprocity business and business leads among 100 noncompeting member companies. Not only is the business good but also the social opportunities have allowed us to become personal friends with a lot of nice people.

The Mix of Business

Our 2,500 sales units each year represent about 2,100 sets of buyers. We strive to have 40 percent of these be new customers each year. This is the only way we know to truly grow our business and afford ourselves the continuing luxury of *not* dealing with everyone. With a robust base of business, we can continue to choose who we deal with. Also, as with any community, Coconut Grove has a certain amount of annual turnover, and, while it's true that we can and do service clientele who live elsewhere, we believe it makes good sense to keep generating first-time customers to the Vacation Store. Why 40 percent? Due to our high focus (by choice) on the cruise industry, we believe it makes good sense to mirror the industry's stated—if perhaps optimistic—first-timer sales experience. To do any less would inevitably mean that, over time, our store would lose share—our sales would become less important to our suppliers, our profits would be lower than they should be, and we would not be taking full advantage of the industry's growth and attendant advertising, public relations, and goodwill.

Therefore, using our customer contact sheets, we record and track new and repeat customer statistics. What we've found, over time, is that our sales counselors find new customers in inverse proportion to their salaries. The hungrier counselor is less likely to rest on his or her laurels of repeat business and is more aggressive in finding new business.

Business Promotions

We scouted the local beauty parlors and determined which was the best for our purposes. We found Madge's, an established salon with a middle-income to upscale clientele, including a number of trendsetter types. We approached the owner and offered her a free cruise for two for each fifteen cabins sold from leads through her shop. We stock and maintain a brochure holder next to the beauty parlor's magazine table, promoting our favorite cruise line. The brochure has a sticker that invites prospects to bring it in when they're ready to book for a free cabin upgrade. This allows us to track Madge's progress. The cost? At a maximum, 6.25 percent of sales (39 percent of our store commission) as a commission to Madge, who, in effect, is acting as an outside agent for us with practically no overhead. Now that she's returned from her first cruise (and juiced), she's talking about putting a group together! There is also a popular deli in a strip shopping center a mile away from us, and we're doing the same thing with a brochure rack strategically placed by the cash register. The gregarious owner touts our cruises to those of his clientele who he feels would enjoy them—and who wouldn't?

Every few weeks, we have a drawing for a free lunch for two at a popular restaurant several miles from our store. We buy the lunch—at the restaurant, of course. In exchange, we receive all the business cards submitted for the drawing—leads we never would have had otherwise. The patrons of the restaurant are exposed to our name, phone number, address, and our slogan as "Greater Miami's Best Vacation Store." The restaurant owner appreciates both the business and that he's offering his clientele a chance to win something for nothing. We'll change the promotion when the number of new leads dwindles. Then we'll experiment with $50 and $100 discount coupons with a limited (two-week) redemption window. This will be timed to coincide with a slow booking period. Again, the restaurateur is motivated to offer his clientele an exclusive deal. And it *will* be exclusive to him for at least a few weeks on either side of the promotion window.

We always participate in the local annual bridal fair but continue the promotion year-round by utilizing a joint effort flyer promotion that includes the top florist, photographer, limousine company, bridal store, and tux rental firm in the area. The flyer extols the virtues of each of us and touts the years of experience we have working together to assure fabulous weddings—and honeymoons (that's where we come in)! These flyers are prominently displayed at each of the participating firms. Great exposure at practically no cost, and great leads. Also, there's a sort of seal of approval aspect of all this; after all, the Vacation Store is being associated with some of the best stores in town!

Because we don't display brochures in our store, we have plenty of wall space. In addition to attractive vacation posters and a beautiful world map (so we can show people exactly where they'll be visiting), our eyecatcher is a photo display of happy, smiling clients, captioned with their names, having fun on their (mostly cruise) vacations. This is a subtle but effective third-party endorsement both for our store and for our terrific vacations. We give our customers a ten-dollar bill when we present their travel documents, asking them to kindly buy an extra photo of themselves from the ship's photographer for us to display. They are invariably flattered and frequently comply with two or three photos! In addition to posters of gleaming white ships in exotic locales, vacation prospects in our store see friends and neighbors—real people—enjoying themselves. To a first-time cruiser, this makes the cruise experience more tangible and accessible. The photos silently transmit the message, "They're having fun, they chose to cruise, so can I." We have a separate section of the display for groups. These photos are captioned with the names and residential areas of each individual and the group name and sailing date. All photos mention the ship and itinerary (Alaska, Lower Caribbean, Bahamas, etc.). They are rotated seasonally to emphasize products that are likely to be booked at the time. For example, family travel photos are prominent in the first half of the year, Alaska travel in the fall and winter, Caribbean year-round. At all times, however, we try to show the diversity of our clientele to increase the chances of having all prospects relate to the photos.

⚓ Customer Relationship Management (CRM)

The key to our CRM is old-fashioned follow-up. We make it a matter of policy to call our clients within three business days of their return from a trip. From our travel agent research, we can report with confidence that less than one travel agent out of five takes advantage of this opportunity. The vast majority never call a client upon his return for fear the trip was problematic. Does this fear have any basis in reality? Of course not! Given cruising's high guest satisfaction, 95 percent of the time problems aren't an issue. In the 5 percent instances, the client will either call the agent or simply never use the agency again. Either way, even in the worst case, it's better to proactively call and deal with the problem, as there's a good chance the customer can be satisfied and saved. Remember, we focus on a few preferred suppliers and give them meaningful business. When something does go wrong, these suppliers are eager to fix the situation or offer some appropriate form of restitution, both because they want to salvage their hard-earned customer and to mollify one of their top agencies.

Our experience shows that calling and interacting with clients when the wonderful memories of the trip are fresh in their minds is an ideal situation. The interaction subtly reminds them that we, the vacation counselors, made their happy memories and great experiences happen.

In the call, we ask them to tell us what they particularly liked or disliked. We're showing interest and adding to our file of information to help in qualifying for their future vacations. We ask them when they'd like to start planning their next vacation. Surprisingly, about a third begin this process right away. Would they if we hadn't called? Would they have gone elsewhere? Of course, we use the call as an opportunity to ask for referral business and remind them of our appreciation for that business.

Have you ever had a doctor call you at home to follow up on the treatment of an illness and ask how you are doing? Or an auto repair shop call to see if your car is now running to your satisfaction? If it's ever happened to you—you had to be impressed. Chances are you told a number of people about your remarkable experience. Well, we safely assume that positive scenario repeats itself daily with our customers. Think of the magnitude of this: We make about ten of these calls a day, on average. That's ten opportunities to touch our clients and provide them with truly remarkable service. They are *very* likely to talk about our service to others!

Web Presence

Naturally, we have a website. It seems that every agency that can spell the word has one. In our case, we actually have two sites: one for consumers and an intranet site for agents. (More about that later.)

Our consumer site is primarily for information purposes. It's a way for consumers to access our business around the clock. We feature photos of our Vacation Store team members and brief descriptions of each. There's a section of what the Vacation Store is all about: fulfilling dreams by providing great vacations tailored to the needs of the customer. We stress our expertise and buying power, which implies value. We stress our Vacation Guarantee, which says we stand behind our product. We promise to make things right, should they go wrong (excepting air transportation and weather-related issues). This is an easy promise to make, as it applies only to our preferred vacation partners. If something does go wrong (a ship mechanical problem, flooded cabin, etc.), our suppliers are going to do the right thing and offer appropriate consideration to all affected guests. Why? It's the right thing to do, and failure to do the right thing is terribly costly. In today's instant media world, the last thing a supplier wants is the negative publicity (TV, newspaper, Internet) of dozens or hundreds or even thousands of guests claiming maltreatment by the cruise line. Of course, even equitable compensation doesn't guarantee that someone won't seek his fifteen seconds of fame and ham it up before the TV cameras. Media are undeniably focused on the negative side of any story. On many occasions we've witnessed reporters triaging debarking guests, looking for the one in thirty who is grumpy and ignoring the twenty-nine who are satisfied. We guess the rationale is that everybody is supposed to be satisfied, so it's "news" when someone is not. On the positive side, why not treat those who have stepped up and purchased your product as special folks? Suppliers should have no qualms about trying to retain customers, which is invariably a cheaper strategy than finding new ones. A good customer is an annuity both for our suppliers and the Vacation Store. Our guarantee has cost us practically nothing out of our pockets, but it's been a great differentiator for our company. It's prominently featured on our home page.

We have a click-to-call feature that invites prospects to have a counselor call or email to begin a dialog. While we have our preferred suppliers' booking engines on our site, in truth, we get only about 2 percent of our business booking through automation. We like it that way! Our reason for being is to make a personal difference in the selection of vacation travel. We are not selling commodities. Our personal expertise and service is how we add value to customers. If it were up to us, we'd have no automated booking capability. But we recognize that some folks prefer that channel (mostly Gen Xers), so we have to satisfy them.

Our personal interaction with the prospect assures that we're giving him what he needs, not just what he wants. Automation can't easily make this distinction. Over many years of selling seminars, we've witnessed thousands of agents who just took orders, gave the prospects what they wanted, and felt the ire and resentment of unhappy returning vacationers who blamed them for doing so! You see, from the customer point of view, after the fact of a bad experience, the agent should have known better and not simply have taken the order but rather taken the time to qualify. The customer would not use the term *qualifying*, but the gist is the same: "Give me what I need, not what I think I want." This is perhaps the biggest reason why more consumers don't use travel agents. Our guarantee assures customers that we are different—and that we must be good!

Host Agency

A few years back, we set up a separate host agency operation. We watched the growing trend of home-based travel agencies and saw a need. It was easy for us, as it gave us the opportunity to accommodate employees who had moved out of South Florida for various reasons. Why walk away from a productive trained employee? A few ads in travel industry publications such as *Travel Weekly* and *Travel Trade* have allowed us to grow to a network of forty home-based agencies around the country. Most of these are part-time individuals with varying degrees of productivity.

Why do they use us? We provide them with our preferred supplier relationships, our back office accounting systems, and a web presence.

We view these agents as independent contractors (ICs). Because they are associated with our brand, we conduct background checks on each and provide errors and omissions insurance. We compensate them based on a 10 percent commission on our preferred suppliers only. Four of our home-based agents are so productive that they pay us a flat fee of $200 per month and retain all the base commission (14–16 percent). We manage and populate home pages for each of the forty ICs at a cost to them of $69 per month. The information on their websites mirrors the Vacation Store itself, so it is always up to date. A typical home page may be "Vicki's Vacation Store" or "Dan's Vacation Store." "Vacation Store" is always part of the name.

Every three weeks, at 2:00 on Friday afternoon, one of our preferred suppliers is featured in a webcast. The format consists of a product update, any new marketing initiative, and an open forum among all the participants. When the ICs log in to our intranet site each day, they must indicate they've read the product and market update that Andy provides in order to gain access. This helps assure that everyone is fully up to speed on new developments.

Because we have a manageable number of home-based agents, we provide our preferred suppliers with their contact information, and the suppliers deal with them directly with respect to sending documents and emailing. While we realize that a number of host agencies don't operate this way for fear that suppliers would bypass us and poach the production home-based agencies, we measure the risk of losing someone against the added cost in dollars and time incurred by serving as an unnecessary intermediary.

Through our preferred suppliers, we offer email blast opportunities, templates created by the marketing whizzes of those suppliers proven to make sales happen. The home-based agents personalize and distribute them through their email database. Carnival offers another neat feature called Carnival Connections—a sort of e-vite meets Google meets Cruise Critic. There's a search feature geared to ships, itineraries, date of sailing, and duration. After the product is secured, agents create invitations for group leaders, family reunions, girls' getaways, birthdays, celebrations, and so on through an easy-to-follow planner. These invites are sent to the specific distribution, who can then create a closed chat room with all the other participants. Agents can now promote groups electronically, without the hassle or expense of flyers, mailers, postage, etc. This new technology creates community and a sharpened sense of anticipation and excitement before the cruise. Without a doubt, other travel suppliers will emulate this program, benefiting both agents and their customers.

Sales Representatives

We see very few sales reps, mainly because we deal with so few suppliers. This saves time for us and for the reps of the products we don't sell. They appreciate our honesty, which enables them to use their time where they can possibly be more productive. When we do initiate an appointment with a sales rep for one of our twenty preferred suppliers, we have specific objectives that we review with the rep by telephone, *ahead* of the meeting. We want to give the rep every opportunity to know what we are looking to accomplish at the meeting so he or she can prepare whatever answers may be needed or obtain approvals from the home office. In other words, we don't use the meeting itself to ask the questions but to obtain the answers! This process applies to a scheduled sales call where we're looking to the supplier to help us sell more of their product. Then we have an annual goal-setting and co-op budget request meeting—held each September or October, and a subsequent meeting, if necessary—to discuss a midcourse correction on the year's plan—say, in April, after reviewing the first-quarter sales activity, or a meeting to discuss a new project, unanticipated in the previous budget process.

Sometimes the reps will call us to set up a meeting. When that happens, we use the same technique. What is the purpose of the meeting? Is there anything we should prepare in advance to ensure that the meeting successfully achieves your objective(s)? How long do you think the meeting should last? This allows both of us to schedule our time appropriately. Sometimes these meetings are unnecessary. The rep might say she'll be in the area next week and would like to give our staff a product update. We'll ask on the phone, "What's new?" Frequently, not too much! The rep is either just making a courtesy call or trying to hit a sales call quota. Moreover, reps like to spend time in their star agencies—those that embrace their product to the virtual exclusion of direct competitors. On those visits, they feel at home, supported, and unthreatened. Cold calls and sales calls where the agents are order takers with no control over their business represent over 95 percent of all sales reps' accounts. On these calls, sales reps either feel threatened (their fear of rejection) or disheartened (encountering agents who need to get a life—who need to get in control of their business and make a difference) or both! After days or weeks of being in this sort of hostile environment, a safe harbor, an oasis, looks pretty good. But, from our prospective, if a call is unnecessary and we are pretty busy with prospects, we will take control and politely but firmly decline the appointment. We like our reps, but we're not their nursemaids. After all, we *do* have a business to run!

The Home Office

We make it a point to personally know key people in the home offices of our preferred suppliers. The more important the supplier is to our business, the more people in the home office we want to know and the better we want to know them. Even more important, we want them to know us and our agency very, very well. Some of these suppliers may do business with 20,000 or 30,000 agencies. We don't want to be lost in the crowd. We want to stand out and be recognized as practically a dealership for the company's products.

We want our extraordinary sales performance to be recognized, appreciated, and rewarded. On a per location basis, we strive to be one of the top twenty outlets for at least five of our suppliers, and certainly among the top one hundred for the fifteen others. When favors are needed, we want to hear, "You bet!" When fams and inaugural cruise cabins are being passed out, we want them—and with appropriate accommodations that match our performance.

We want to know what makes their senior management tick, how they think, what's made them and their companies successful. We want to pick their brains! What's new? What's hot? What are other successful agencies and vacation stores doing in other parts of the country? What are their suggestions to improve sales for us? From experience, we know we will be treated better when these executives know us. Let's face it: Our Vacation Store's success is riding on the successful relationship we have with a few key suppliers (five suppliers account for 75 percent of our business). Our company is our people; their companies are really all about their people as well. The truly successful companies know, appreciate, and build successful person-to-person relationships. It's a two-way street. Imagine how flattered we are when a senior executive of a major cruise line or tour operator calls us and thanks us for the business or asks our advice—and actually listens to what we have to say. Imagine how we feel when he recognizes us in a sea of agents at a conference, or when he invites us to sit with him at his table on a ship or at an agent's function? All of this is psychic income: gratifying, special, and never taken for granted. We make friends with these folks where chemistry allows and treat them as friends. Some, unfortunately, are either too stuck up or arrogant to notice us. It seems beneath some travel executives to waste their time with lowly travel agents. Others seem to have the personalities of dead cod!

Throughout the home office, in each and every department, there's usually a key employee or two who really makes things happen—beats or bypasses the system, perhaps, but gets things done! These people are invaluable, whether in reservations, air/sea, groups, accounting, guest relations, marketing, or sales. We discover many of them by accident, encountering them through the years when the occasional problems arise and they are able to solve them. When we stumble on them, we write down their names, get the correct spelling of their names and titles, and write thank-you notes to their bosses. All concerned appreciate the acknowledgment of superior service. It motivates our suppliers to go the extra mile again and reinforces the Vacation Store as a caring, thoughtful marketing partner. These people are immediately added to our key employee list that we maintain for each supplier. This list is distributed to our entire office staff, properly filed, and regularly consulted when needed.

When the opportunity presents itself, we make it a point to visit our suppliers' home offices. This allows many employees we have known only by telephone to meet us (and vice versa) and put faces to the voices they've been hearing over the years. When the spirit moves us, we create and present a plaque to a deserving company or department.

Well, there you have it: what makes the Vacation Store tick. All of us truly enjoy what we do—providing terrific vacations for appreciative customers. We are well compensated and have the opportunity to expand our business and earn greater incomes. We are optimistic concerning the future of our company, as we expect the vacation business to be a growth industry for many years to come. Moreover, we recognize that 80 percent of all vacations are booked directly by customers with suppliers. There is an enormous opportunity here to garner increased business because we *know* (not just believe) we can provide prospects with better vacations than they are likely to discover on their own—and at no additional expense to them.

As cruising continues to enjoy the highest satisfaction ratings of any vacation alternative, our strategy of focusing on cruises is right on target. In our view, cruising will continue to be the largest growth sector of the vacation business. Capturing only 3 percent of today's North American vacationers, cruising has the clear prospect of growing threefold or more in our lifetimes.

When we wrote the first edition of this book in 1995, we were confident that the industry, while navigating choppy waters at the time, would quickly navigate to calmer seas. We were encouraged by the trend to retire older vessels; the enormous capacity additions coming on line (we had visibility at the time only through 1999); and the fact that the industry was approaching critical mass: a sufficient number of past passengers and new cruisers each year to help fuel a chain reaction of new demand. With fleet expansion, we reasoned that large, well-financed cruise lines had the possibility of becoming truly branded—household words—that would help create top-of-mind awareness to what was still an obscure industry.

We pointed out the challenges at the time:

◆ A surplus of underfinanced, poorly positioned or nonpositioned me-too cruise lines that will assuredly fall by the wayside.

◆ The reality that the cumulative effect of individual lines' market share strategies inhibits the market expansion of the industry.

◆ A tendency of many lines to overpromise the cruise experience—especially when lower-than-anticipated yields (remember the pyramid) inevitably put pressure on cost and result in product underdelivery.

This prophecy generated nothing but good news for the industry. Twenty-three cruise lines went out of business, including the entire bottom-feeder stratum of the cruise pyramid. This left a cleaner, easier-to-understand, less cluttered cruise market. We are happy to report that market share strategies have largely given way to market expansion strategies as cruise lines today extol their virtues against the larger vacation market rather than in direct competition with other lines. As shown in chapter 6, the lines have done (we think) a credible job of positioning their brands and targeting various segments of the market. Moreover, the scale resulting from consolidation of the surviving brands as well as from their organic growth has allowed the lines to significantly enhance product quality both in terms of the hardware (fantastic ships undreamed of eleven years ago) and the software (food, service, activities, and entertainment).

Parenthetically, it's beyond serendipitous that the cruise industry expanded capacity and added new innovations to its products. Remember, land-based competition wasn't standing still either; Orlando doubled its hotel room capacity and added many new features to the Walt Disney World Resort and Universal Studios. Las Vegas? Wow! Completely reengineered and expanded, with a seemingly never-ending array of new, larger, glitzier hotels, resorts, and time-share properties. There's a whole spate of tony, boutique hotels now available in New York, San Francisco, Chicago, and Miami, among other cities. Hotel chains and resorts are constantly upgrading, refining, and refurbishing their properties to keep pace with the ever-changing needs and tastes of the traveling public.

But, while much has changed in this intervening decade, one thing remains constant. Our conclusion ten years ago is just as appropriate today—and tomorrow:

> At the end of the day, the customer, the marketplace, will determine the composition of the cruise industry—its size and scope—its winners and losers. We believe there's an inherent fairness about all this. Cruise lines and other leisure travel providers exist solely to provide for customers' vacation needs. Only the buyers, not the sellers, should decide who does it right—and who missed the boat. That's the way it should be, and we expect to have fun watching it all play out!

Appendix
CLIA Member Cruise Lines

American Cruise Lines
741 Boston Post Road, Suite 200
Guilford, CT 06437
Phone: (203) 453-6800
www.americancruiselines.com

Carnival Cruise Lines
3655 NW 87th Avenue
Miami, FL 33178
Phone: (305) 599-2600
www.carnival.com

Celebrity Cruises, Inc.
1050 Caribbean Way
Miami, FL 33132
Phone: (305) 539-6000
www.celebrity.com

Costa Cruises
200 South Park Road, Suite 200
Hollywood, FL 33021-8541
Phone: (954) 266-5600
www.costacruises.com

Crystal Cruises
2049 Century Park East, Ste 1400
Los Angeles, CA 90067
Phone: (310) 785-9300
www.crystalcruises.com

Cunard Line
24303 Town Center Drive, Suite 200
Valencia, CA 91355-0908
Phone: (661) 753-1000
www.cunard.com

Disney Cruise Line
P.O. Box 10020
Lake Buena Vista, FL 32830
Phone: (407) 566-3500
www.disneycruise.com

Holland America Line
300 Elliott Avenue West
Seattle, WA 98119
Phone: (206) 281-3535
www.hollandamerica.com

MSC Cruises
6750 North Andrews Avenue
Fort Lauderdale, FL 33309
Phone: (954) 772-6262
www.msccruises.com

Norwegian Coastal Voyage, Inc.
405 Park Avenue, Suite 904
New York, NY 10022
Phone: (212) 319-1300
www.norwegiancoastalvoyage.us

Norwegian Cruise Line
7665 Corporate Center Drive
Miami, FL 33126-1201
Phone: (305) 436-4000
www.ncl.com

Oceania Cruises, Inc.
8300 NW 33rd Street, Suite 308
Miami, FL 33312
Phone: (305) 514-2300
www.oceaniacruises.com

Orient Lines
7665 Corporate Center Drive
Miami, FL 33126-1201
Phone: (305) 436-4000
www.orientlines.com

Princess Cruises
24305 Town Center Drive
Santa Clarita, CA 91355
Phone: (661) 753-0000
www.princess.com

Regent Seven Seas Cruises
1000 Corporate Drive, Suite 500
Fort Lauderdale, FL 33334
Phone: (954) 776-6123
www.TheRegentExperience.com

Royal Caribbean International
1050 Caribbean Way
Miami, FL 33132
Phone: (305) 539-6000
www.royalcaribbean.com

Seabourn Cruise Line
6100 Blue Lagoon Drive, Suite 400
Miami, FL 33126
Phone: (305) 463-3000
www.seabourn.com

Silversea Cruises, Ltd.
110 E. Broward Boulevard
Fort Lauderdale, FL 33301
Phone: (954) 522-4477
www.silversea.com

Windstar Cruises
300 Elliott Avenue West
Seattle, WA 98119
Phone: (206) 281-3535
www.windstarcruises.com

INDEX